Lecture Notes in Computer Science 12785

More information about this subseries at http://www.springer.com/series/7409

Panayiotis Zaphiris · Andri Ioannou (Eds.)

Learning and Collaboration Technologies

Games and Virtual Environments for Learning

8th International Conference, LCT 2021
Held as Part of the 23rd HCI International Conference, HCII 2021
Virtual Event, July 24–29, 2021
Proceedings, Part II

 Springer

Editors
Panayiotis Zaphiris (iD)
Department of Multimedia and Graphic Arts
Cyprus University of Technology
Lemesos, Cyprus

Andri Ioannou (iD)
Research Center on Interactive Media,
Smart Systems and Emerging
Technologies (CYENS)
Cyprus University of Technology
Limassol, Cyprus

ISSN 0302-9743   ISSN 1611-3349 (electronic)
Lecture Notes in Computer Science
ISBN 978-3-030-77942-9   ISBN 978-3-030-77943-6 (eBook)
https://doi.org/10.1007/978-3-030-77943-6

LNCS Sublibrary: SL3 – Information Systems and Applications, incl. Internet/Web, and HCI

This Springer imprint is published by the registered company Springer Nature Switzerland AG
The registered company address is: Gewerbestrasse 11, 6330 Cham, Switzerland

Foreword

Human-Computer Interaction (HCI) is acquiring an ever-increasing scientific and industrial importance, and having more impact on people's everyday life, as an ever-growing number of human activities are progressively moving from the physical to the digital world. This process, which has been ongoing for some time now, has been dramatically accelerated by the COVID-19 pandemic. The HCI International (HCII) conference series, held yearly, aims to respond to the compelling need to advance the exchange of knowledge and research and development efforts on the human aspects of design and use of computing systems.

The 23rd International Conference on Human-Computer Interaction, HCI International 2021 (HCII 2021), was planned to be held at the Washington Hilton Hotel, Washington DC, USA, during July 24–29, 2021. Due to the COVID-19 pandemic and with everyone's health and safety in mind, HCII 2021 was organized and run as a virtual conference. It incorporated the 21 thematic areas and affiliated conferences listed on the following page.

A total of 5222 individuals from academia, research institutes, industry, and governmental agencies from 81 countries submitted contributions, and 1276 papers and 241 posters were included in the proceedings to appear just before the start of the conference. The contributions thoroughly cover the entire field of HCI, addressing major advances in knowledge and effective use of computers in a variety of application areas. These papers provide academics, researchers, engineers, scientists, practitioners, and students with state-of-the-art information on the most recent advances in HCI. The volumes constituting the set of proceedings to appear before the start of the conference are listed in the following pages.

The HCI International (HCII) conference also offers the option of 'Late Breaking Work' which applies both for papers and posters, and the corresponding volume(s) of the proceedings will appear after the conference. Full papers will be included in the 'HCII 2021 - Late Breaking Papers' volumes of the proceedings to be published in the Springer LNCS series, while 'Poster Extended Abstracts' will be included as short research papers in the 'HCII 2021 - Late Breaking Posters' volumes to be published in the Springer CCIS series.

The present volume contains papers submitted and presented in the context of the 8th International Conference on Learning and Collaboration Technologies (LCT 2021), an affiliated conference to HCII 2021. I would like to thank the Co-chairs, Panayiotis Zaphiris and Andri Ioannou, for their invaluable contribution to its organization and the preparation of the proceedings, as well as the members of the Program Board for their contributions and support. This year, the LCT affiliated conference has focused on topics related to the design and development of learning technologies, the use of technologies such as games and gamification, chatbots, AR, VR, and robots in learning, and learning, teaching and collaboration experiences, with particular focus on the issue of online versus in class learning brought about by the pandemic.

I would also like to thank the Program Board Chairs and the members of the Program Boards of all thematic areas and affiliated conferences for their contribution towards the highest scientific quality and overall success of the HCI International 2021 conference.

This conference would not have been possible without the continuous and unwavering support and advice of Gavriel Salvendy, founder, General Chair Emeritus, and Scientific Advisor. For his outstanding efforts, I would like to express my appreciation to Abbas Moallem, Communications Chair and Editor of HCI International News.

July 2021   Constantine Stephanidis

HCI International 2021 Thematic Areas
and Affiliated Conferences

Thematic Areas

- HCI: Human-Computer Interaction
- HIMI: Human Interface and the Management of Information

Affiliated Conferences

- EPCE: 18th International Conference on Engineering Psychology and Cognitive Ergonomics
- UAHCI: 15th International Conference on Universal Access in Human-Computer Interaction
- VAMR: 13th International Conference on Virtual, Augmented and Mixed Reality
- CCD: 13th International Conference on Cross-Cultural Design
- SCSM: 13th International Conference on Social Computing and Social Media
- AC: 15th International Conference on Augmented Cognition
- DHM: 12th International Conference on Digital Human Modeling and Applications in Health, Safety, Ergonomics and Risk Management
- DUXU: 10th International Conference on Design, User Experience, and Usability
- DAPI: 9th International Conference on Distributed, Ambient and Pervasive Interactions
- HCIBGO: 8th International Conference on HCI in Business, Government and Organizations
- LCT: 8th International Conference on Learning and Collaboration Technologies
- ITAP: 7th International Conference on Human Aspects of IT for the Aged Population
- HCI-CPT: 3rd International Conference on HCI for Cybersecurity, Privacy and Trust
- HCI-Games: 3rd International Conference on HCI in Games
- MobiTAS: 3rd International Conference on HCI in Mobility, Transport and Automotive Systems
- AIS: 3rd International Conference on Adaptive Instructional Systems
- C&C: 9th International Conference on Culture and Computing
- MOBILE: 2nd International Conference on Design, Operation and Evaluation of Mobile Communications
- AI-HCI: 2nd International Conference on Artificial Intelligence in HCI

List of Conference Proceedings Volumes Appearing Before the Conference

1. LNCS 12762, Human-Computer Interaction: Theory, Methods and Tools (Part I), edited by Masaaki Kurosu
2. LNCS 12763, Human-Computer Interaction: Interaction Techniques and Novel Applications (Part II), edited by Masaaki Kurosu
3. LNCS 12764, Human-Computer Interaction: Design and User Experience Case Studies (Part III), edited by Masaaki Kurosu
4. LNCS 12765, Human Interface and the Management of Information: Information Presentation and Visualization (Part I), edited by Sakae Yamamoto and Hirohiko Mori
5. LNCS 12766, Human Interface and the Management of Information: Information-rich and Intelligent Environments (Part II), edited by Sakae Yamamoto and Hirohiko Mori
6. LNAI 12767, Engineering Psychology and Cognitive Ergonomics, edited by Don Harris and Wen-Chin Li
7. LNCS 12768, Universal Access in Human-Computer Interaction: Design Methods and User Experience (Part I), edited by Margherita Antona and Constantine Stephanidis
8. LNCS 12769, Universal Access in Human-Computer Interaction: Access to Media, Learning and Assistive Environments (Part II), edited by Margherita Antona and Constantine Stephanidis
9. LNCS 12770, Virtual, Augmented and Mixed Reality, edited by Jessie Y. C. Chen and Gino Fragomeni
10. LNCS 12771, Cross-Cultural Design: Experience and Product Design Across Cultures (Part I), edited by P. L. Patrick Rau
11. LNCS 12772, Cross-Cultural Design: Applications in Arts, Learning, Well-being, and Social Development (Part II), edited by P. L. Patrick Rau
12. LNCS 12773, Cross-Cultural Design: Applications in Cultural Heritage, Tourism, Autonomous Vehicles, and Intelligent Agents (Part III), edited by P. L. Patrick Rau
13. LNCS 12774, Social Computing and Social Media: Experience Design and Social Network Analysis (Part I), edited by Gabriele Meiselwitz
14. LNCS 12775, Social Computing and Social Media: Applications in Marketing, Learning, and Health (Part II), edited by Gabriele Meiselwitz
15. LNAI 12776, Augmented Cognition, edited by Dylan D. Schmorrow and Cali M. Fidopiastis
16. LNCS 12777, Digital Human Modeling and Applications in Health, Safety, Ergonomics and Risk Management: Human Body, Motion and Behavior (Part I), edited by Vincent G. Duffy
17. LNCS 12778, Digital Human Modeling and Applications in Health, Safety, Ergonomics and Risk Management: AI, Product and Service (Part II), edited by Vincent G. Duffy

38. CCIS 1420, HCI International 2021 Posters - Part II, edited by Constantine Stephanidis, Margherita Antona, and Stavroula Ntoa
39. CCIS 1421, HCI International 2021 Posters - Part III, edited by Constantine Stephanidis, Margherita Antona, and Stavroula Ntoa

http://2021.hci.international/proceedings

8th International Conference on Learning and Collaboration Technologies (LCT 2021)

Program Board Chairs: **Panayiotis Zaphiris,** *Cyprus University of Technology, Cyprus,* **and Andri Ioannou**, *Cyprus University of Technology and CYENS, Cyprus*

- Ruthi Aladjem, Israel
- Kaushal Kumar Bhagat, India
- Fisnik Dalipi, Sweden
- Camille Dickson-Deane, Australia
- David Fonseca, Spain
- Francisco J. García-Peñalvo, Spain
- Yiannis Georgiou, Cyprus
- Tomaž Klobučar, Slovenia
- Birgy Lorenz, Estonia
- Alejandra Martínez-Monés, Spain
- Nicholas H. Müller, Germany
- Antigoni Parmaxi, Cyprus

The full list with the Program Board Chairs and the members of the Program Boards of all thematic areas and affiliated conferences is available online at:

http://www.hci.international/board-members-2021.php

HCI International 2022

The 24th International Conference on Human-Computer Interaction, HCI International 2022, will be held jointly with the affiliated conferences at the Gothia Towers Hotel and Swedish Exhibition & Congress Centre, Gothenburg, Sweden, June 26 – July 1, 2022. It will cover a broad spectrum of themes related to Human-Computer Interaction, including theoretical issues, methods, tools, processes, and case studies in HCI design, as well as novel interaction techniques, interfaces, and applications. The proceedings will be published by Springer. More information will be available on the conference website: http://2022.hci.international/:

General Chair
Prof. Constantine Stephanidis
University of Crete and ICS-FORTH
Heraklion, Crete, Greece
Email: general_chair@hcii2022.org

http://2022.hci.international/

Contents – Part II

Chatbots in Learning

AR, VR and Robots in Learning

Contents – Part I

Learning, Teaching and Collaboration Experiences

On-line vs. in Class Learning in Pandemic Times

Games and Gamification in Learning

Quiz Tools in Algorithms Courses: Applying Educational Gamification Design Principles and Encouraging Students' Interaction

Carmen Scorsatto Brezolin[1,2(✉)], Larissa de Quadros[1],
and Milene Selbach Silveira[2]

[1] Instituto Federal Sul Riograndense Campus Passo Fundo, Passo Fundo, RS, Brazil
carmembrezolin@ifsul.edu.br
[2] Pontifícia Universidade Católica do Rio Grande do Sul, Porto Alegre, RS, Brazil
carmen.brezolin@edu.pucrs.br, milene.silveira@pucrs.br

Abstract. One of the main obstacles faced by students initiating their academic life in the courses of the computing field is the difficulty to comprehend the concepts related to the construction of algorithms. To promote interaction of students with these concepts, their peers and with the teacher, one of the methodological resources used is gamification. To investigate the potential use of this resource, specifically in relation to quiz tools and their contributions to the teaching and learning process in this scenario, the following methodological steps were taken: (a) analysis of gamified quiz tools in relation to principles of educational gamification design; (b) selection of one of the analyzed tools; (c) use of the selected tool in class; and (d) discussion about its potential and questions related to the design of this kind of tool for use in this context. For the analysis of the potential use of gamification and the chosen tool, a practice of exploratory nature was made, in a classroom environment with a total of 31 students, in the first semester of a course of Computer Science. Highlighting only the question of potential use in the scenario in question, gamification motivated the class and constituted challenges for both the professor and the students, insofar as establishing flexibility, creativity and partnership among professor and students.

Keywords: Gamification · Gamified tool · Construction of algorithms

1 Introduction

One of the main obstacles faced by students in the courses of the Computing field initiating their academic lives are the disciplines of Algorithms, because it is the moment they are presented to the principles of logic of computer programming. Numerous students present difficulties in understanding the abstract concepts and the rules involved in the construction of algorithms. These disciplines tend

© Springer Nature Switzerland AG 2021
P. Zaphiris and A. Ioannou (Eds.): HCII 2021, LNCS 12785, pp. 3–16, 2021.
https://doi.org/10.1007/978-3-030-77943-6_1

to create trauma in novice students, generating high dropout rates in the first years of the courses [9].

For Muller [11], some of the main difficulties that the students of Computer Science encounter with the resolution of algorithmic problem-solving involve little ability of analogical reasoning. This competence, for the author, may demand a relatively large quantity of cognitive processing and problem abstraction.

The abstraction is part of higher mental processes (thinking, language, volitional behavior) that develop from social processes, which are mediated through tools and signs. A tool is something that can be used to perform/execute a task, a sign is the meaning of something. Consequently, it is understood that mediation, tool and sign are connected: for one of them to occur it is taken into consideration the other and it is in the mediation that internalization (that is the internal reconstruction of the external operation) [10] happens. The author, supported by Vygotsky, highlights that society builds the tools and the signs system, which modify throughout life, and that social interaction is fundamental for the cognitive and linguistic development of any individual.

To promote the interaction of the students with the contents of a discipline, with their peers and with the professor, one of the resources that has been researched is gamification. Deterding et al. [3] proposes a definition of gamification "as the use of game design elements in non-game contexts". To investigate the potential use of this resource, specifically in relation to quiz tools and their contributions to the teaching and learning process in this scenario, the following methodological steps were taken: (a) analysis of gamified quiz tools in relation to the educational gamification design principles (based on the work of Dicheva et al. [4]); (b) selection of one of the analyzed tools that did not require a great effort from the professor in its customization and use and, at the same time, allowed to explore matters related to the use of gamification as well as their potential use in the described scenario; (c) use of the selected tool in class; and (d) discussion about its potential use and questions related to the design of this kind of tool to use in this context.

The activities proposed with the use of the tool in a classroom were applied to a class from a Computer Science course, in the discipline of Logic and Algorithms, and the description of this application as well as the analysis of the results obtained are discussed in this article.

The article is organized as follows: Sect. 2 presents some concepts related to gamification and the principles of gamification design used; Sect. 3 deals with the analysis of gamified tools (Duolingo, Socrative and Kahoot!); Sect. 4 shows the chosen tool (Kahoot!), the profile of the participants, the application of the gamified tool and the results found; Sect. 5 brings related work; Sect. 6 establishes a brief discussion and lastly, Sect. 7 presents the final considerations of the paper.

2   Gamification in Education

Gamification is the use of game resources for non-game applications, preferably when in these resources the rules incentivize the users to explore and learn through the use of feedback mechanisms [15]. The idea to use elements of game design in non-game contexts to motivate, to increase the activity and retention of the user gained traction in interaction design and digital marketing. This idea has generated copious applications, that offer reward and reputation systems with points, badges, levels and leaderboards [3]. For Dichev and Dicheva [5], with the growing popularity and the success of its application, gamification has been used in educational contexts as an approach to increase the motivation and engagement of the students.

In this scenario of application of gamification in educational contexts, Dicheva et al. [4] have identified educational gamification design principles that are listed on Table 1.

Table 1. Educational gamification design principles [4].

Design principles	Description
Goals	specific, clear, moderately difficult, immediate goals
Challenges and quests	clear, concrete, actionable learning tasks with increased complexity
Customization/personalized	personalized experiences, adaptive difficulty challenges that are perfectly tailored to the player's skill level, increasing the difficulty as the player's skill expands
Feedback	immediate feedback or shorten feedback cycles immediate rewards instead of vague long-term benefits
Visible status	reputation, social credibility and recognition
Unlocking content	access
Freedom of choice	multiple routes to success, allowing students choose their own sub-goals within the larger task
Freedom to fail	low risk from submission, multiple attempts;
Storytelling/New identities	and/or roles
Onboarding	the process of orienting new users to a system
Time restriction	
Social engagement	Competition and cooperation/loops

The authors have highlighted that the most used gamification design principles in educational contexts are: **Visible status, Social engagement, Freedom of choice, Freedom to fail** and **Feedback**. They have reported that the examples of application of the **Visible status** principle seek to maintain people engaged and encourage friendly competition among users, since their reputation increases as they answer questions and receive points for their answers. It has also been stressed that the **Social engagement** includes individual or team competitions, cooperation and interactions with other students. Concerning the **Freedom of choice**, they have observed the possibility of the students choosing what kind of challenges and/or activities they could complete, the possibility of choice of deadline, the attribution of personalization and voting on the extent of grades deduction as penalties for absences or non-completion of the tasks. The **Freedom to fail** principle does not presume penalties for unsatisfactory performance of the tasks and normally allows the student to review, answer again and re-submit the tasks and the **Feedback** should be immediate or with shortened cycles [4].

Raymer [15] has also indicated some game mechanisms that can make learning more attractive, for instance: establishing goals and objectives; providing frequent feedback; measuring progress, character updating; rewarding effort (not only success); reward schedules and providing peer motivation. These mechanisms are close to the educational gamification design principles highlighted by Dicheva et al. [4]

3   Analysis of Gamified Tools

As examples of apps based on the concepts of gamification used in educational contexts [2,13], we have Duolingo, Socrative and Kahoot!:

• **Duolingo**[1]: a free app for language learning that allows the users, during the learning process, to follow their progress through a ranking and medals. Besides that, to instigate the use of the app, the user can race against the clock, level up and personalize the app.

•**Socrative**[2]: it is a questionnaire platform where teachers can create content related to the discipline in various ways, for example: true or false, multiple choice or open questions. The teacher can follow in real time the progress of the students in the activity, analysing the chosen alternative and the speed of answering with the possibility to comment results simultaneously with the class.

•**Kahoot!**[3]: it is a system (and a free app) that allows quiz creation to revise contents, reinforce the knowledge, recapitulate the learning. Its functioning is simple, the questions appear on a shared screen and the players answer on their own devices or computers. To instigate the students to play, after each question is presented a ranking and at the end of the game there is a final ranking.

After an initial study of these tools, they were analysed according to the educational gamification design principles listed on Table 1. Table 2 presents a synthesis of this analysis, which is discussed subsequently.

It can be observed on Table 2 that with **Duolingo** it is possible to work with the principle of **Freedom of choice**, that the Socrative and Kahoot! tools do not allow it, at least not in an accessible manner. This resource gives the student

---

[1] https://pt.duolingo.com/.
[2] https://socrative.com/.
[3] https://kahoot.com.

Table 2. Gamified tool X principles

Design principles	Duolingo	Socrative	Kahoot!
Goals	X	X	X
Challenges and quests	X	X	X
Customization/personalized		X	X
Feedback Visible status	X	X	X
Visible status			X
Unlocking content	X		
Freedom of choice	X		
Freedom to fail	X	X	X
Storytelling/New identities			
Onboarding	X	X	X
Time restriction			X
Social engagement			X

the protagonism of choosing when and which activity to perform. However, the app is designed for language learning, thus restricting its application with other contents.

Socrative, in turn, allows **Customization**, being a platform where teachers can create quizzes with contents related to their disciplines in different formats (multiple choice, true/false or short answer). It also enables the **Freedom to fail** principle, allowing the student to repeat an activity (quiz) as many times as necessary. Nevertheless, as with Duolingo, these activities are executed in an individual setting, hindering the **Social engagement** and the **Visible status** principles.

From the analysed tools, **Kahoot!** stood out for allowing – in an easy way, from the perspective of the professor - quiz creation to review or reinforce subjects, meaning that the tool allows **Customization**, being possible to personalize the activity with any content. It is possible to promote **Visible status** and **Social engagement/competition**, instigating the students through rankings (option presented on each question and at the end of the activity). And it is also possible, for each question, to restrict the time to answer, as per the **Time restriction** principle. Kahoot! also favors the **Freedom to fail** principle, because at the moment of configuring the quiz, the tool has two options: Teach (play a live game together with learners over video or in class) and Assign (a challenge game to learners who play it at their own pace).

For those reasons, Kahoot! was selected to continue the research, as it will be detailed in the next section.

4   Exploring Kahoot!

Kahoot! was selected for classroom use, being a tool based on gamification concepts, that allows the teacher to create their own quizzes, in accord with the necessities of the group, being able to support the revision and the retention of subjects previously worked in the classroom in a fun way. The following subsections present the detailing of the profile of the participants, the use of the tool and the analysis of the results.

4.1   Profile of Participants

The participants of the research belonged to a class of Computer Science that was subdivided in two groups at the beginning of the term by choice of the professors who teach it: **T1**, with 18 students, formed by the ones who had previous knowledge of logic and algorithms (repeaters or who had already studied in other institutions) and **T2**, with 23 students without any previous knowledge of logic and algorithms. The same division of groups was used for analysis of the gamified tool: the group that had knowledge in the field (**T1**) did not use the tool and the group that had no knowledge (**T2**) used it.

Considering, then, just group **T2**, the first practical step of this research was the application of a questionnaire in the last week of March 2019. As the classes started in February, there were seven weeks of lessons, in order to obtain information about the learning difficulties, through the perspective of the students. The questionnaire had three questions. The first sought to assess the level of difficulty (1 being none or almost none and 5 - great difficulty), the second wanted to identify why they believed to have difficulties in the discipline and the third questioned what could be done to overcome them.

It can be observed that the majority of the students (from **T2**) recognized to have some difficulty, 16 students answered the questionnaire among the 23 of the group: 3 students reported to have no difficulties, 5 students reported to have moderate difficulty, 2 students (12.5%) reported to have considerable difficulty and 1 student reported to have great difficulty, as illustrated in Fig. 1.

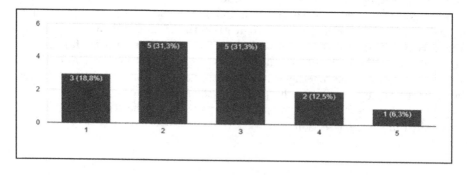

Fig. 1. Chart of the scale of difficulty in the discipline.

It was also asked to the students why they believed to have difficulties in the discipline and what could be done to overcome them. Concerning the difficulties, the students said they exist due to: lack of a more efficient method of teaching, difficulties in the programming language in relation to the language syntax, not having worked with the computational thinking in high school and that they got used to using "built-in formulas".

In relation to how these difficulties can be diminished, it stood out: divide the groups, use other forms or methods to exercise logic, "take it slow" with the contents to understand how everything works.

In short, based on the applied questionnaire it can be observed that the students consider that difficulties do exist and they believe that these issues arise for a lack of studies, lack of teaching methods and the baggage they carry until they start their higher education. In their opinion, the difficulties would be decreased by studying more, with different methods of teaching and inserting the disciplines in elementary school.

4.2 Gamified Tool Application

The tool was used in 3 classes, one activity per class, after break time. The first Kahoot! activity was built with content from the discipline in a gradual manner with a complete revision for an evaluation test. The conception of each activity was done with the contents previously studied in the classroom, in a personalized way, in accord to the reality of the group, as illustrated in the example of Fig. 2, and, in the most part, was composed of questions that demanded attention and concentration from the students, with an average of 12 questions per activity.

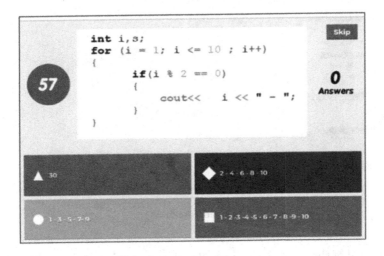

Fig. 2. Kahoot! exercise.

The example illustrated on Fig. 2 dealt with a question related to the use of repetition loops, in which the students should interpret and select the option that this code would present on the screen. During the application, it was possible to observe that, in general, the group interacted substantially, became restless when they had a correct or wrong answer and also made various comments about the questions. An important factor is that the tool allows for a pause between each question of the game. And this resource was copiously used by the professor, because when there was a high number of mistakes in a given question, the professor stopped, opened the question again and gave an explanation about the possible results. The interaction was decidedly meaningful, because a good part of the students discussed with their peers the reason why the answer was correct or not.

As a result of each class with the use of Kahoot!, the ranking of the days was saved and those scores were inserted on the app Student – Ranking. Besides the Kahoot! scores, it were also inserted the scores of the activities made available at the Moodle platform and the students could check the class ranking. The Student – Ranking was developed by one of the authors, with the objective to provide higher motivation for the students; this app shows the activities done and the score received and generates a ranking of the top 10. The app allowed the professor to register activities, register students and add a score for the activities to each student. The student could visualize their finalized activities with a score, the group ranking and their individual ranking as seen in Fig. 3.

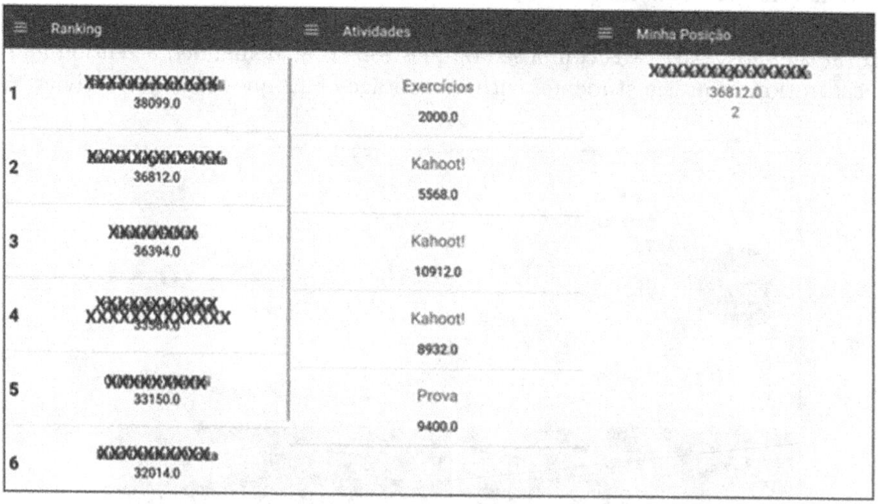

Fig. 3. Student ranking.

At the end of the three classes and after the application of the evaluation test of the discipline, the app was updated with the grades from the tests and the activities. To finalize the application of this research with the students, medals were given to the top 3 students according to the ranking of the app. Thus, it was observed that the students, given the generation of a class ranking, showed more motivation in doing the proposed activities in the classroom, besides that, the majority of them appreciated to be in the higher positions and competing.

4.3 Result Analysis

After the use of Kahoot!, it was applied a new questionnaire to the students to learn their opinion referring to this tool and the app Student - Ranking. The questionnaire was printed and handed to the students to answer on the day of the final test. As soon as the student handed back the test, they received the questionnaire. Out of the 23 students of **T2**, 20 answered the questionnaire. As for the use of Kahoot! during the classes, the response of the students was certainly positive: they highlighted that the tool really helped in the retention and clarification of the contents and questions; that it was "very cool" and fun to use and that it was interesting, because it made the class more dynamic and stimulated quick thinking.

As for Kahoot! helping with the learning of the discipline in some way, it was possible to observe that 19 out of 20 students who answered the questionnaire considered that yes, it helped, stressing that it helped to focus on the resolution of the exercises, influenced the competitivity and made it possible to revise the subject in a simple and fun manner. Only 1 student answered that it helped to an extent, but felt bothered with the competitive situation.

The answers presented by the students fits with the systematic mapping done by Dicheva et al. [4] where they have drawn a conclusion that the majority of authors of reviewed articles shared the opinion that gamification has the potential to improve learning if well designed and used correctly. The authors have affirmed that more substantial empirical researches are necessary to investigate the motivating effects of the use of unique game elements in specific educational contexts and for specific types of students.

Referring to the question about the use of the Student – Ranking app, the students answered that it was important to follow the performance of the group; because that incentivized them to always be the best. Therefore, it was possible to observe that to a certain degree the app stimulated the students to do not only the Kahoot! activities, but also the activities proposed by the professor to get a higher score and reach the top positions.

In relation to the educational gamification design principles previously mentioned [4], the following is stressed:

- **Goals/Challenges and quests:** the activities created were presented with clear, concrete learning objectives, with complexity increasing in a gradual manner. Despite the tool giving the necessary support for the questions to be shown in a clear way, the instructions were created by the professor, who also controlled the complexity of the questions presented in a gradual manner.

- **Customization:** the tool allowed customization, which was done by the professor, with activities created with subjects from the discipline, in a personalized manner, in accord with the reality and the group.

- **Onboarding:** the Kahoot! activities were constructed with beginner students in mind, with the intention of helping them to progress and integrate.

Using the "Teach" option of the tool, it was possible to have the quiz live in class, promoting a higher integration, which is important to keep students engaged.

- **Feedback:** during the use of Kahoot!, the Feedback is immediate. This option is already configured by the tool, showing the information of the answer being correct or incorrect. However, more details about the questions or whenever they generated more questions, the professor stopped, opened the question again and a new explanation was done about the possible results.
- **Social Engagement:** after each activity done with Kahoot!, it was observed that the interaction was highly significant, the students were discussing with their peers the reasons why an answer was correct or not. Another available resource in this tool, related to this principle are the teams; it is possible to configure it so that the students play as a team, having an extra time to discuss the answers before giving them on the tool.
- **Freedom to fail**: while configuring how to play on Kahoot! with the option "Assign", it is possible that the students play whenever they want and at their own pace.
- **Time restriction:** for each question created on Kahoot!, it was stipulated a maximum amount of time for the selection of the answer. For the first three, 60 s were set and for the remainder it was reduced to 30 s. It was observed that the time restriction challenged and motivated the students to compete and to answer the proposed activities.
- **Visible Status:** after each answered question, the student could visualize their score, as well as their position in relation to the other participants of that round (this resource is already built-in in the tool). After each class with the use of Kahoot!, the score rankings were inserted in the Student – Ranking app. The scores referring to the activities made available in the Moodle platform of the discipline were also inserted, thus enabling each student to visualize the group ranking and their individual ranking, taking into account all the activities of the disciplines, as illustrated on Fig. 3.

5   Related Work

Previous experiments have shown that gamification can improve the learning results, make the classes more attractive and dynamic, increase the engagement and the motivation of the students and refine learning.

For Bullon et al. [2], gamification on the teaching of Engineering as a tool to boost the comprehension of mathematics concepts has instigated the students to answer, has helped them to develop the associated abilities and competences, has generated reflection moments, has motivated learning and has facilitated teamwork.

Lima et al. [7], in turn, have developed the Methodology of the 7Cs (Comprehension, Creation, Contemplation, Compatibility, Correction, Construction e Contribution) with the objective of minimizing the difficulties faced by the undergraduate students in courses of the Computing field in the process of learning and the comprehension of basic contents of the discipline of Algorithms.

They have used **Kahoot!** to apply the Methodology in the Contemplation, Compatibility and Correction dimensions. According to the authors, the use of this tool has shown new possibilities to apply the proposed methodology to make the classes more dynamic and attractive, not losing its value as a learning proposal [7].

A different study, by Pereira, Santos e Suárez [14], has verified if the leaderboards can stimulate the exercises practice and the learning of Discrete Mathematics. The authors have made a controlled experiment with two sample groups (one with a gamified scenario and a non-gamified one) in order to measure/distinguish the performance in relation to the numbers of questions answered, as well as the quantity of correct answers between the groups. For the gamified scenario, the Kahoot! tool has been used and there has been a significant statistical difference between the groups only in the quantity of correct answers, demonstrating that the leaderboards can encourage specific behaviors due to the competition during the question resolution process and consequently, in learning. Still, in the execution process, the authors stressed that it was possible to observe how motivated the students felt for participating in the experiment, because in the proportion that they answered the questions, they also competed among themselves because of the time that the system provides for each answer. In the non-gamified scenario, they have observed that the traditional paper-and-pencil method was adopted and the students answered in a remarkably calm manner [14].

Specifically in relation to problem resolution, Niemivirta [12] has examined the performance of students with different behavior patterns to achieve the objectives, in a complex problem solving task under different instructional conditions. Contrary to the point of view that the support of the performance goals, specially in a determined context (for instance in a competitive situation), could promote engagement and motivation for the tasks, the condition of ego involvement has resulted in a highly negative pattern of self-handicaps in students that emphasized the performance goals. The results have shown how the students with different orientation patterns related to goals experienced the task situations in different ways, even when no differences were found in their real performance. In the authors opinion, the differences in the group level varied even more due to the instructional condition [12].

Hakulinen and Auvinen [6] analysed badges in a Data Structures and Algorithms course from the perspective of Goal Orientation Theory. The authors have added badges in an online learning environment used in a Data Structure and Algorithms course and examined the answers of the students with different profiles and analysed how the students who were more motivated by the badges differed from others in terms of orientation and behavior to achieve the goals. The authors have discovered that the students more motivated by the badges had mastery-intrinsic, mastery-extrinsic and performance approach orientation significantly higher and less orientation to quit. They have also discovered that all the students already had a good performance before the introduction of badges e that, not all high performing students were motivated by the badges. They have detected that the same gamification mechanism can be a motivator to some students while not appreciated by others [6].

For Buckley and Doyle [1], gamification has affected the students with different kinds of motivation in different ways. Their results have demonstrated that it is particularly effective for students who are intrinsically motivated, mainly by a motivation to know or related to stimulation. The effect on students who are extrinsically motivated seems to have been limited to the students who are motivated by identification. In general, the results have suggested that gamified learning interventions have a greater impact over students who are intrinsically motivated. For the authors, this result is not an argument against gamification, but rather, considered a good practice to encompass a variety of learning interventions designed to engage a variety of learning types, and crucially, guarantee that no-one is deprived.

6   Discussion

Having the research analysed in relation to the research done by other authors [1,2,6,7,12,14] and taking into account that a teaching and learning environment is being dealt with, the student who stressed that using Kahoot! helped him "to an extent" can't be ignored.

As Hakulinen and Auvinen [6] have indicated, the same mechanism of gamification can be motivating to some students while not appreciated by others. Niemivirta [12], in turn, affirms that contrary to the point of view that a competitive situation could promote engagement and task motivation, this can also result in a negative pattern in students who emphasize performance goals. Therefore, it is highlighted that in all gamified activities, the major concern is always focused on using intrinsic stimulation, promoting the cooperation, fun and enjoyment in the classroom, much more than with extrinsic stimulation as scores, levels and ranking. These serve as support to the agreement of rules associated with gamification used and to challenge the students to execute the tasks proposed in the discipline. This concern was also marked by Dicheva et al. [4] who have emphasized that finding and sharing new ways to apply gamification to learning contexts that are not limited to extrinsic rewards as achievements and medals and that are more significant for the students is crucial to increase the application of this emerging technology in education.

7   Conclusion

It is observed that the insertion of technological tools based on the concept of gamification in the classroom is well-received by the students, as an extra resource to help them in the teaching and learning process, since it makes the classes more dynamic, fun and competitive. This scenario is constituted of challenges to both the professor and the students, insofar as establishing flexibility, creativity and partnership among professor and students.

In terms of design, the attempt to use the lessons learnt with games to make the interfaces more pleasant is an old topic in the field of Human-Computer Interaction (HCI) [8]. Considering, in this context, the analysis of the gamification design principles of Dicheva et al. [4] it was possible to notice an array of possibilities that the design of these tools offer for the use in an educational context.

While evaluating this array of possibilities, it is stressed how much the design of tools influenced the viability of activities that the professor can create. However, even if some of these principles are not directly configurable via the tool, their knowledge can help the professor to think how to favor them, via applied teaching methodology or even relating them with other tools. One example was the developed app, Student – Ranking, that possibilitated each student to follow their own performance or the one from the group, gamifying other classroom activities that were not developed with Kahoot!. The combination of both allowed the exploration of different resources related to gamification and their impact in this scenario.

It is intended, in future research, to make new activities using the Kahoot!, with the possibility to work in teams, to observe and not expose the students that are not comfortable with the competition situation. Moreover, it is indicated the necessity to analyse how the design of these tools could intrinsically stimulate the users and what other possibilities they could present, to better favor the interaction.

References

1. Buckley, P., Doyle, E.: Gamification and student motivation. Interact. Learn. Environ. **24**, 1162–1175 (2017). https://doi.org/10.1080/10494820.2014.964263
2. Bullón, J.J., Encinas, A.H., Sánchez, M.J.S., Martínez, V.G.: Analysis of student feedback when using gamification tools in Math subjects. In: IEEE Global Engineering Education Conference, EDUCON 2018, pp. 1818–1823 (2018)
3. Deterding, S., Dixon, D., Khaled, R., Nacke, L.: From game design elements to gamefulness: defining gamification. In: Proceedings of the 15th International Academic MindTrek Conference: Envisioning Future Media Environments (MindTrek 2011), New York, pp. 9–15 (2011). https://doi.org/10.1145/2181037.2181040
4. Dicheva, D., Dichev, C., Agre, A., Angelova, A.: Gamification in education: a systematic mapping study. J. Educ. Techno. Soc. **18**, 75–88 (2015). http://www.jstor.org/stable/jeductechsoci.18.3.75
5. Dichev, C., Dicheva, D.: Gamification in education: gamifying education: what is known, what is believed and what remains uncertain: a critical review. In: International Journal of Educational Technology in Higher Education, vol. 14 (2017). https://doi.org/10.1186/s41239-017-0042-5
6. Hakulinen, L., Auvinen, T.: The effect of gamification on students with different achievement goal orientations. In: IEEE International Conference on Teaching and Learning in Computing and Engineering, Kuching, pp. 9–16 (2014). https://doi.org/10.1109/LaTiCE.2014.10

7. Lima, Á., Diniz, M., Eliasquevici, M.: Metodologia 7Cs: Uma Nova Proposta de Aprendizagem para a Disciplina de Algoritmos. In: Anais do XXVII Workshop sobre Educação em Computação. SBC, pp. 429–443 (2019). https://doi.org/10.5753/wei.2019.6648

8. Malone, T.W.: Heuristics for designing enjoyable user interfaces: lessons from computer games. In: Proceedings of the 1982 Conference on Human Factors in Computing Systems (CHI 1982), pp. 63–68. Association for Computing Machinery, NY (1982). https://doi.org/10.1145/800049.801756

9. Medina, M., Ferting, C.: Algoritmos e programação: teoria e prática. Editora Novatec, São Paulo (2006)

10. Moreira, M.A.: Teorias de aprendizagem. Editora pedagógica e universitária, São Paulo (1999)

11. Muller, O.: Pattern oriented instruction and the enhancement of analogical reasoning. In: Proceedings of the First International Workshop on Computing Education Research (ICER 2005), pp. 57–67. Association for Computing Machinery, New York (2005). https://doi.org/10.1145/1089786.1089792

12. Niemivirta, M.: Motivation and performance in context: the influence of goal orientations and instructional setting on situational appraisals and task performance. Psychologia **45**, 250–270 (2002)

13. Pantoja da Silva, A., Pereira, L.M.: Gamificação: como jogos e tecnologias podem ajudar no ensino de idiomas. Estudo de caso: uma escola pública do Estado do Amapá. In: Estação Científica, UNIFAP 2018, vol. 8, pp. 111–120 (2018)

14. Pereira, I.B., Santos, J., Suárez, P.: Análise de uma aplicação gamificada para o aprendizado de Matemática Discreta. In: Simpósio Brasileiro de Informática na Educação. SBIE, pp. 636–643 (2019). https://doi.org/10.5753/cbie.sbie.2019.636

15. Raymer, R.: Gamification: using game mechanics to enhance eLearning. ELearn, 1–9 (2011) https://doi.org/10.1145/2025356.2031772

FLCARA: Frog Life Cycle Augmented Reality Game-Based Learning Application

Malek El Kouzi[1]([✉]) and Victoria McArthur[2]

[1] School of Information Technology, Carleton University, Ottawa, ON, Canada
MalekElKouzi@cmail.carleton.ca
[2] School of Journalism and Communication, Carleton University, Ottawa, ON, Canada
VictoriaMcArthur@cunet.carleton.ca

Abstract. The increased ubiquity of technology in everyday life, as well as the value placed on technology skills, has resulted in increased use of technology in the classroom. STEM education has become a focal point in modern K-12 classrooms, with educators seeking ways to create technology-rich learning spaces. We propose that pedagogical design around Augmented Reality (AR) technology can be used to provide students with novel learning opportunities that take advantage of tangible printed materials and mobile technology that is readily available at home. As a learning resource, augmented reality (AR) has shown its versatility at all levels of education (C. H. Chen et al., 2015, T. Bratitsis et al., 2017, A. M. Amaia et al., 2016). In this paper, we present FLCARA; the Frog Life Cycle Augmented Reality Application, which presents the frog life cycle stages to students as a complete three-dimensional model placed in front of them. Using printed cards representing the various stages of the frog's life cycle, the students organize the cards to reflect the correct order of the cycle and then use the application to check if the order is correct. The application's design can be mapped easily onto other subjects, providing teachers with additional pedagogical tools to utilize in the classroom. The results of our initial study on the usability of the application are quite promising and reflect positively on this application's usability for the intended educational purpose. Overall, 90% of our participants agree that the application is effective; they were satisfied with the application's educational content (mean $= 4.56$, st dev $= 0.76$).

Keywords: Augmented reality · Educational application · Science · STEM

1 Introduction

Educators have a difficult task to prepare learners to become a productive part of the workforce in an ever-changing digital world. This global phenomenon has resulted in contemporary teaching being tangential to learners. Although technology can help resolve this conundrum, educators must have an understanding of how technology can be integrated into the curriculum to support learning outcomes for learners. Teachers harbour certain concerns, the most prominent being the displacement of the role of teachers in the classroom by technology. However, this concern is unfounded as the teacher's role

© Springer Nature Switzerland AG 2021
P. Zaphiris and A. Ioannou (Eds.): HCII 2021, LNCS 12785, pp. 17–30, 2021.
https://doi.org/10.1007/978-3-030-77943-6_2

has progressed to facilitating technology use in the learning process and giving students a basis for how they can strategically use the technology. There is consensus amongst educators around the globe that the integration of technology in the learning process is vital in contemporary society (Gallou and Abraham 2018). Therefore, educators must create a learning environment where every learner can learn to use technology effectively. This involves integrating technology into the curriculum, which inadvertently helps educators develop their teaching skills. This development is attained by revamping the class environment with technology-based learning that supports learners who have been familiarized with technology in the digital age. The right of learners to access the most advanced pedagogical practices is tied to their success in an ever-changing job market.

As a learning resource, augmented reality (AR) has shown its versatility at all levels of the educational field and is a relevant step towards a technology-based learning environment primarily due to the features that differentiate it from other learning resources (Petrov and Atanasova 2020). The ability to interact with AR pedagogical technologies provides the student with a different perspective from which to scrutinize information and ideas. Furthermore, it allows teachers to incorporate a variety of materials and utilize different formats, such as URLs, videos and text (Cabero and García 2016). More importantly, the peripherals required for AR use, such as smartphones, are sometimes readily available to learners as they have become commonplace (Yáñez-Luna and Arias-Oliva 2018), although we acknowledge that such access is depending on socio-economic status.

This ubiquity is vital as we look towards the literature of technology in educational fields. AR, as an emerging technology, has been swiftly adopted and incorporated into educational areas not only due to the diverse possibilities it offers (Johnson et al. 2016, Villalustre and Moral 2017, Bacca et al. 2014) but also due to the accessibility of smartphones/ tablets. The characteristic of AR having supporting peripherals that are already in conventional use bodes well for its continued use in the educational sphere (Cano and Sevillano-García 2018). Educators have an opportunity to help students develop 21st-century skills by introducing AR in the classroom. Prior research suggests that there is sufficient evidence to support the implementation of AR-based technologies in education to encourage interest in a variety of subjects and provide a holistic learning experience to learners by linking outcomes in the virtual and physical world (El Kouzi, Malek et al., 2019).

Forbes described AR as one of the dominant technological advances that could bring about a shift in the educational landscape over the next ten years (Forbes 2019). The characteristic of AR is its capablity of augmenting real world items with digital assets makes it stand out among other technologies. Furthermore, the scrutiny and consumption of media in real-time in AR using accessible technologies such as smartphones places it in a promising position to bring about a paradigm shift in the use of technology in education (AASA 2014). From the perspective of educational technology or EdTech, AR can offer a more personalized educational experience due to the embracing of audio-visual elements in its use and because it engages the kinetic senses of the user. This can pique the interest of learners and give them greater enthusiasm for the learning experience. Moreover, AR offers a memorable experience to learners as it is a relatively novel technology that can bring about an emotive undertaking for learners.

2 Literature Review

Consensus on how technology should be used in education is moving towards creating learning experiences that promote better learning outcomes and improve accessibility to all students, rather than the previously held reservations on whether technology should be used at all (AASA 2014).

This requires that educational content be designed in a way that improving learning outcomes becomes a priority. Research by Park et al. (Park et al. 2015) indicates that learning outcomes can be enhanced when interactive or illustrative teaching tools and methods are used under low working memory conditions such as narration. Their findings further posit that due to the cognitive processes, selecting and organizing information into logical models can be supported by these illustrative tools and methods if implemented correctly. This has been established through fresh developments in learning sciences, which has given a new understanding of how technology can reshape and vitalize learning experiences (Bransford et al. 2000).

Implementing technology use in education has offered learners and educators the prospect of accessing resources and expert knowledge unbound by geographical limitations. It also allows communities to become educational hubs as they can still access resources related to a variety of subjects through virtual connectivity, almost matching the in-person school experience (Office of Educational Technology 2016).

Furthermore, developments in computing technology have created new avenues for cooperation on a global scale while allowing for the creation of self-adaptive systems that facilitate real-time academic appraisal. These developments could make the learning process more user-centric, allowing students to have a curriculum based on their strengths and limitations (Zhu and Tang 2017).

When evaluating AR learning applications in the classroom, developers and educators must be aware that initial findings may be subject to novelty effects, especially when considering the level of exposure in particular age groups. Young children are exposed to 3D interactive graphics through games, but their lack of exposure to newer technology such as augmented reality can take away interest from the subject matter. This novelty effect brings about curiosity in the technology itself rather than effectively delivering educational content through AR. Such considerations should be made when attempting to integrate AR in education (Seo et al. 2006).

Given that most technologies introduced in education have their benefits and drawbacks, research highlights that AR is not exempt from this phenomenon. A literature review on the positive and negative outcomes of AR in education by Radu (2012) highlighted that AR provided a more holistic understanding of content requiring spatial awareness such as geometrical objects, astrometry, geometrical profiling and in understanding how words can be symbolically associated with other phrases. On the other hand, the negative learning outcomes were evident in need for greater scrutiny and deliberation, which, at lower and intermediary levels of education, can be challenging. This might result in some students not concentrating fully on the content and adversely affect team-related contributions.

Over time, research has provided evidence that virtual environments and related games can have positive social outcomes such as improvements in compassion, emotional control and social consciousness (Chen et al. 2015; Li et al. 2017). Virtual environments can also improve individual learner outcomes such as problem-solving, improved collaborative instincts, and abatement in behavioural issues and suspensions from school (Hanna et al. 2014).

Comparisons to traditional learning content are essential to examining the net benefit of AR use. Diaz et al. examined these comparisons, pitting static content against dynamic AR content. Their discovery was that 90% of students surveyed indicated that comprehension of new topics was made easier with AR content, and 80% favoured interactive animations to understand new learning concepts (Diaz et al., 2015).

Hands-on aspects of STEM notwithstanding, learning these subjects from texts can be daunting for learners. Research highlights that activities outside of the usual syllabus can incentivize students to take more interest (Fortus and Vedder-Weiss 2014) UNESCO recommend that providing a context of how science can be used outside the classroom can help motivate learners. By highlighting the impact of science-based application in society, AR in education can enhance the real-world use of science (Fensham 2008). AR has the potential to overlay relevant information in these very same texts, pre-senting animated simulations and interactive digital content that engages users while being situated in the context of curriculum-approved texts.

Dunleavy and Dede assessed 14 AR-based games and interactive applications related to science. They discovered that AR provides the best outcomes when used in extracurricular activities that entail in-depth examination, immersion and investigation. Smart devices and AR-based devices offer a platform where complex scientific concepts can be explicated through simulations and combinations of real and virtual object assessment (Dunleavy and Dede 2014).

In-class projects promote positive learning outcomes through developing relevant skills needed in the modern-day in areas such as ingenuity, cooperation and leadership if suitably implemented. Furthermore, critical thinking skills can be developed through project-based activities. Digital games give learners an opportunity to vary their choices, use their judgment and respond to outcomes in a nurturing environment (Reardon 2015).

Freitas and Campos assessed how AR could be used in 2nd-grade level subjects such as transportation means, animal classifications and similarities in semantics, as used by Kerawalla. The design of these scenarios and how they are to be evaluated were also considered in their assessment. The results showed that AR could help sustain significant levels of motivation in 2nd-grade learners while also providing positive outcomes for underperforming students by improving their learning experiences (Freitas and Campos 2008).

Based on the review of literature, there is enough evidence to support the implementation of AR-based technologies in education can be useful in encouraging interest in a variety of subjects and providing a holistic learning experience to learners by linking outcomes in the virtual and physical world. This linkage allows for a better understanding of abstract concepts and topics that make their real-world application more relevant for learners.

This work builds on preceding theory and research to an additional perspective of how AR technology in an educational context can be used predominantly by approaching AR as a supportive tool for teachers and examining the impact on learners' academic achievement, usability/satisfaction and motivation.

3   Motivation

In our review of the literature presenting STEM-based AR applications, we noted a lack of augmented reality applications as an emergent technology which are developed for classroom science text books specifically for the Animals Life Cycle. Our first stage was to create and application which addresses the Frog Life Cycle dedicated to primary school students. the Frog life cycle for primary school students. To this end, we developed FLCARA to improve the student's memorizing this lesson through an interactive AR application. In this study, we present a preliminary usability analysis of this application using heuristics presented in the PREMEGA framework (Shoukry 2015). FLCARA encourages a self-driven approach to learning by introducing textbook material as an immersive, 3D model that can be uncovered by discovering the parts of their school textbooks using our application.

The FLCARA application takes the frog life cycle stages out of a two-dimensional textbook and presents it to students as a complete three-dimensional model placed in front of them. Using the application, which runs on a smartphone or tablet, students can develop a visual understanding of each stage by tilting, rotating, and panning the camera around the 3D virtual content. Not only the application presents 3D virtual content (EL Kouzi et al. 2019) also it poses students with interactive buttons that allow them to check if they have placed the markers in the correct stage place. This is a novel application for several reasons:

- To the best of our knowledge, this is the first Augmented Reality application to visualize the frog life cycle. It enables students to look at each stage and memories the correct sequence.
- This application is easy to use. And the activity which the users will be doing is fun.
- The markers of this application are intentionally made simple so that the participants will
- expect what to see as AR above each figure.
- The presence of the button allows participants to test for unlimited trials if they have placed the stages correctly without worrying about failing or being judge by other students.

4   The Application

The development tools that have been used for this application are Unity editor 2019.3.14f1 and Vuforia Software Development Kit (SDK) for Android. The Android SDK is also required for compilation. The Unity engine supports the development of applications for PC, Android, and IOS using the Unity graphics engine. Vuforia is an Augmented Reality SDK for mobile devices that uses computer vision to recognize markers, allowing developers to link virtual content (e.g., pictures, movies, 3D models, audio files, etc.) to real-world objects. The Vuforia SDK is available for Android Studio, XCode, and Unity, which was selected for this application.

The application was developed to recognize specific markers to display the 3D model on top of it. The 3D model consists of five stages of the frog life cycle. The users should put the stages correctly organized in the life cycle diagram, as in Fig. 1. Then they check if they have put them correctly by pressing the "check" button. After that, the student will be informed if they have put it in the right order or not by a text appearing on the screen. In case they have placed them incorrectly, they will be able to change their order until they are ordered correctly.

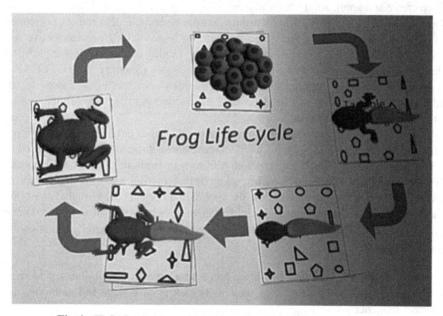

Fig. 1. FLCARA markers placed in correct order in life cycle diagram

5   Bloom's Digital Taxonomy

In 1956, educational psychologist Benjamin Bloom developed a taxonomy of learning objectives, as a composition to recognize the learning procedure. He had divided his taxonomy into three psychological domains:

- Cognitive: processing information
- Affective: attitudes and feelings
- Psychomotor: physical skills.

His taxonomy advanced from Lower Order Thinking Skills (LOTS) to Higher Order Thinking Skills (HOTS). Later, Lorin Anderson and David Karathwohl revisited his

Taxonomy. They have used verbs instead of nouns, and they reorganized the order of categories. After that, Andrew Churches extended Anderson and Karathwohl's categories and developed it to become a digital environment (Churches 2010). We used Bloom's Digital Taxonomy to facilitate learning. Below how does the AR application follow this taxonomy:

1. Remembering: First, the students will view the 3D frog life cycle models above each marker. They will be able to match the name written on the marker with the figure above it. So the student will be able to visualize this stage.
2. Understanding: the students will be able to identify the 3D figure by looking at their physical parts from all sides. Also, they can compare the stages of the life cycle with each other.
3. Applying: In this stage, the students will display the markers in the empty life cycle picture. So, they will construct the life cycle and present it properly. The students will take their knowledge and understanding of different situations.
4. Analyzing: In this stage, the students will think critically and explore the best way to order the markers in the correct structure by organizing them correctly.
5. Evaluating: After placing the markers in their places, the students will press the check button to evaluate their work. They can judge by themselves if their work is correct by testing it. This will let them find effective solutions to the puzzle and justify conclusions while drawing on their knowledge and understanding.
6. Creating: After building the cycle and combining the markers in their correct place, the students will be able to view the elements which are put together to form a coherent or functional whole.

6 Methodology

The purpose of this project is to design a complementary learning application through the use of AR technology. This application will facilitate the mapping of interactive content into instructor-selected textbooks to support the curriculum. The incentive behind the development of this educational AR application is to provide an exhibition of the demonstrable benefits of AR integration in learning beyond novelty effects. This is in addition to the improvement in learner comprehension of complex STEM topics. In this paper, the usability of the application will be tested in the use case of a unit in a Biology course, with the corresponding study presented. Usability issues can significantly affect the effectiveness of this AR application, according to prior results in some studies (Akçayır et al. 2017; Radu et al. 2016). Hence the importance of assessing the application's initial usability in a learning setting. Future studies will help understand anecdotal usability issues for a target user group and evaluate the prospect of using the application in a real learning setting.

In this evaluation, we resolved to use the Pre-MEGA framework designed by Shoukry et al. (2015). The rationalization for selecting this framework is based on its provisions for detailed heuristics that facilitate the assessment of mobile-based pedagogical technologies targeted towards children. Despite some heuristics related to game mechanics and user-generated avatars being inapplicable in this paper, the framework addresses issues of usability, ease and functionality of interaction, and pedagogical content design. Addressing these issues provided a basis from which we could design our usability questionnaire.

6.1 Participants

Eighteen adults had participated in this study. The participants were between 18 and 45 years old. Although this group does not represent the target age group of the application, it is not uncommon in HCI to use low-risk populations to first evaluate the usability of an application before moving on to studies involving the target group (e.g., minors). Participants were recruited using convenience sampling and by advertising the study on the Carleton Research Participants Facebook page. They were told that they might withdraw at any time they wish. After they submit the questionnaire, they may not be able to cancel their participation since the data will be saved anonymously, so no name or code number was saved with the questionnaire. The participants had read the consent form and agreed to participate in the study. The consent form was sent by email to those who agreed to participate in the study.

6.2 Procedure

The participants who read the consent and accepted it had received an email containing the link for the application on Google Play Store and a pdf attachment with the required markers to print at home (markers are used by the application to interact with the AR experience), and a link to an online questionnaire. They installed the application on their devices. Then they've printed the two markers, M1 (Fig. 2) & M2 (Fig. 3).

Fig. 2. FLCARA square markers M1.

The marker M1 contains 5 square markers; each marker has the name of the frog life cycle stage. They looked from the device at that M1. The augmented reality figures appeared floating above the five markers found on M1. After that, the participants cut and removed the markers from M1 and place them on M2. They looked through their devices and checked if they have placed them correctly by pressing on the "check" button. If they set it incorrectly, they would get "incorrect, try again" else, they get "correct." After placing the markers in the correct places, the participants had to answer the provided questionnaire.

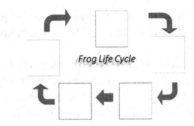

Fig. 3. FLCARA empty life cycle diagram M2

7 Results

7.1 Results from the Questionnaire

67% of the participants were ones in the age range $40 - 40 +$ and 33% were in the age range 18–28 years old. When asked how comfortable they are when using a mobile device on a daily basis, 83% said that they are very comfortable, and only 17% were neutral. 61% of the participants describe their overall experience after using the application as "very good," while 39% described it as "good." When asked if they used augmented reality before, 56% said yes, and 44% didn't use it before. Only 33% of the participants have used an AR application before playing this App.

7.2 Heuristic Evaluation

Next, mobilizing heuristics from the PreMEGA framework (Shoukry et al. 2015), we evaluated participant feedback on the usability of our application.

Efficiency:

- The application started quickly.
- The application enables independent use after first use.
- The application consistently responses to user actions.
- The application has clear, fun actions to reach educational goals.

Effectiveness:

- The application makes connections to learning content.
- The application is supportive rather than distractive.
- The application show figures based on real-life experiences.
- The application uses a theme meaningful to children.
- Augmented Reality is a good tool to be used for educational games.

Satisfaction:

- I felt satisfied with the educational content found in this AR application.
- It was easy to understand the differences and similarities between the two cells in this application.

- The elements of the application the interface was easy to identify.
- I felt comfortable to hold the device and press the virtual button.

Efficiency. We used the heuristics of the PreMEGA Framework to evaluate the efficiency of the application design. Heuristics were presented as positive statements on usability using a 5-point Likert scale where high values indicate agreement with the heuristic. Efficiency here refers to the overall responsiveness of the application (e.g., content loading time, response to user inputs, etc.). System efficiency relates not only to the computational power of the device running the application but also coding choices that can impact system responsiveness and lag. Overall, FLCARA scored very well on efficiency heuristics. Participants indicated that the application started quickly (mean = 4.6, st dev = 0.90). Regarding User Interface (UI) design and ease of use, participants indicated that the application design enables independent use after first use (mean = 4.83, st dev = 0.50). When asked about the consistency response to the user actions of the application, participants noticed that the application response well to user actions (mean = 4.83, st dev = 0.37). Overall, participants indicated that the educational goals of the application were clear (mean = 4.67, st dev = 0.58). Participant feedback on the efficiency of the design was consistently high. We assert that these preliminary results reflect positively on the usability of this application for the intended educational purpose.

Effectiveness. Where efficiency heuristics are linked to general usability, effectiveness heuristics assess the ease of use of the application regarding the interactivity of educational content. We asked participants to reflect on whether the application makes a strong connection to learning content. participant feedback on this heuristic was positive (mean = 4.72, st dev = 0.45). Most of the participants found the application supportive of learning goals rather than distractive (mean = 4.61, st dev = 0.76). The participants also evaluated the content delivery and presentation of the interactive 3D AR models as appropriate to the subject matter (mean = 4.94, st dev = 0.23). Participants also indicated that the application design seems meaningful for the target age group (mean = 4.94, st dev = 0.23). The application will be considered effective if it has a high degree of success in increasing the learner's interest in the subject matter and if it provides a fun and engaging way to interact with educational content. Overall, 90% of our participants agree that the application is effective, which does reflect positively on the usability of this application for the intended educational purpose. we were further interested in learning whether or not our participants felt as though AR would be a useful pedagogical tool – beyond the initial novelty effect. Although the duration of the study does not allow us to accurately assess novelty effects, we note here that participants agreed that AR is a good tool to support traditional classroom teaching (mean = 4.94, st dev = 0.23).

Satisfaction. The final set of questions was used to assess the features that were unique to this application. specifically, we were interested in whether or not the educational content of the application was easy to understand, if the differences between the cell types were presented effectively, and how participants felt about the interactive content and virtual buttons. Overall, participants agreed that they were satisfied with the educational content of the application (mean = 4.56, st dev = 0.76). The participants also agreed that it was easy to understand the differences and similarities between the two types of cells presented in this application. None of the participants disagreed about the easiness of it. The results were (mean = 4.89, st dev = 0.31). The participants also noted that the elements of the application interface were easy to identify (mean = 4.89, st dev = 0.31). This application required the user to hold the device and point it to the marker; then, the user has to press on the virtual button found on the marker (paper). Although participants indicated that they were comfortable viewing and interacting with the virtual button for the duration of the study (mean = 4.83, st dev = 0.37), some participants indicated some fatigue in performing this type of interaction over extended periods of time, which could introduce problems in-classroom use, where students would likely be using the application more frequently and for longer periods of time. Overall, the results of our initial study on the usability of the application are quite promising. User feedback was overall quite high, and the design of the application seemed to spark our participants' interest in learning more about the subject matter. Using these results going forward, we plan to modify the application to take some of the usability concerns into account before launching a longitudinal study in our local schools. also, we hypothesize that the design of FLCARA can be mapped easily onto other applications in science topics, especially when there is a certain sequence that should be organized in a specific way.

7.3 Participants Subjective Feedback

Assessment determines the learning and appropriate assessment practices are used to stimulate required knowledge. The purpose of the assessment is to help the students gain a better understanding of what it is they are learning, improving the efficiency of what the student can absorb (Anderson 2007). Some of the participants were glad to share with us some of their comments after using the application. Following are some of their feedback:

- "AR can plays a constructive roles in helping students grasp complex concepts and make it attainable not only for above average student but also for the majority of student who may have difficulty realizing these concepts otherwise."
- "I would highly recommend the use or AR in classroom since it is simple fun and has a great potential to simplify and attract the attention of future generations."
- "Due to different types of student's learning abilities I think this is type of learning could help support and improve the process of learning."
- "AR would enable the students to link abstract concepts to real life contexts and this is very beneficial since our kids are becoming more and more visual learners."
- "This applications is like a self study because the kids can know the correct answer after the picture appears."
- "It is really easy to use this application. Some kids don't like to read books and listen to the teacher so this is a very good alternative to normal boring learning."
- "With such applications the students will learn while enjoying technology."

8 Conclusion and Future Work

Prior research indicates the effectiveness of AR in improving the impetus to learn in classroom situations. In this project, the authors demonstrated an educational application called FLCARA with the intention of promoting STEM-related subjects in a classroom setting. The initial evaluation presented in this paper addressed a specific unit in biology, with future evaluations providing an exploration of how heuristic sets can be generated for purposes of educational AR. The application was designed to take advantage of 2D content present in textbooks and overlay interactive 3D content over them, providing students with supplementary pedagogical tools for scientific practice. The application uses the Frog Life Cycle topic, providing visual contexts that improve comprehension. Participant feedback from using the application was largely positive, which gives us further guidance on how to approach the next phase of development and evaluation. The research study corroborates the author's assumption that the AR application supports individual student learning, and the underlying technology enhances enthusiasm in STEM-related subjects. It is the opinion of the authors that AR technology use will burgeon as an educational tool.

One of the drawbacks of this study was it used adult learners as usability testers of the application. Although it is customary practice to do so in preliminary usability studies, there is a possibility that the outcomes obtained in this study may slightly differ from the outcomes using the target population as subjects. To overcome this, future work will include usability studies from the target age group and comparisons will be drawn to pinpoint differences in some aspects of usability, such as cognitive differences. This will be done before longitudinal studies on the learning effects of AR are conducted. The results of the participant questionnaire provided assurances that future work on educational AR applications in STEM learning can be productive. This research will also be applied in future work where the authors will examine the other areas of STEM-based learning using a similar methodology. Teachers and students in Grade Two classes will be a vital part of this stage as they will provide a better understanding of the application from a real-world, classroom perspective. With this in mind, the authors theorize that a co-design approach to AR pedagogical tools will be beneficial to researchers in surmounting the design challenges and novelty effects that limit progress in this area.

References

Akçayır, M., Okçe Akçayır, G.: Advantages and challenges associated with augmented reality for education: a systematic review of the literature (2017). https://doi.org/10.1016/j.edurev.2016.11.002

American Association of School Administrators (AASA): Consortium for School Networking, and National School Boards Association. Leading the digital leap (2014). https://www.cosn.org/about/news/aasa-cosn-and-nsba-team-%E2%80%98lead-digital-leap%E2%80%99. Accessed: July 10, 2020

Anderson, T.R.: Bridging the educational research-teaching practice gap: the power of assessment. Biochem. Mol. Biol. Educ. **35**(6), 471–477 (2007)

Bacca, J.; Baldiris, S.; Fabregat, R.; Graf, S.; Kinshuk, G.: Augmented Reality Trends in Education: A Systematic. Review of Research and Applications. Educ. Technol. Soc. **17**, 133–149 (2014)

Bransford, J., Brown, A., Cocking, R.: How People Learn: Brain, Mind, Experience, and School. Commission on Behavioral and Social Sciences and Education: National Research Council, 133. Retrieved from how-people-learn-brain-mind-experience-and-school-expanded-edition (2000)

Cabero, J., García, F.: Realidad Aumentada. Tecnología Para La Formación; Síntesis: Madrid, Spain (2016)

Cano, E.V., Sevillano-García, M.L.: Ubiquitous Educational Use of Mobile Digital Devices. A General and Comparative Study in Spanish and Latin America Higher Education. J. New Approaches Educ. Res. **7**,105–115 (2018)

Churches, A.: Bloom's digital taxonomy (2010)

Diaz, C., Hincapié, M., Moreno, G.: How the Type of Content in Educative Augmented Reality Application Affects the Learning Experience. Procedia Comput. Sci. **75**, 205– 212 (2015)

Dunleavy, M., Dede, C.: Augmented Reality Teaching and Learning. In: Spector, J.M., Merrill, M.D., Elen, J., Bishop, M.J. (eds.) Handbook of Research on Educational Communications and Technology, pp. 735–745. Springer, New York (2014)

Fensham, P.J.: Science Education Policy-making: Eleven emerging issues (UNESCO) (2008). http://goo.gl/0erjiV

Forbes: "How Is Augmented Reality Being Used In Education?" (2019). Accessed May 2020

Fortus, D., Vedder-Weiss, D.: Measuring students' continuing motivation for science learning. J. Res. Sci. Teach. **51**(4), 497–522 (2014). https://doi.org/10.1002/tea.21136

Hanna, N., Richards, D., Jacobson, M. J.: Academic performance in a 3D virtual learning environment: different learning types vs. different class types. In Pacific Rim Knowledge Acquisition Workshop (pp. 1–15). Springer, Cham, December 2014

Li, J., van der Spek, E., Hu, J., Feijs, L.: See Me Roar. Abstr. Publ. Annu. Symp. Comput. Interact. Play - CHI Play '17 Ext. Abstr., no. October, pp. 345–351 (2017)

Johnson, L., Adams, S., Cummins, M., Estrada, V., Freeman, A., Hall, C.: NMCHorizon Report: 2016Higher Education Edition; The New Media Consortium: Austin, TX, USA, 2016. http://blog.educalab.es/intef/wp-content/uploads/sites/4/2016/03/Resumen_Horizon_Universidad_2016_INTEF_mayo_2016.pdf

Seo, J., Kim, N., Kim, G.J.: Designing interactions for augmented reality based educational contents. Lect. Notes Comput. Sci. **3942**, 1188–1197 (2006)

Office of Educational Technology, United States of America, 2016, Section 1: Engaging and Empowering Learning Through Technology. https://tech.ed.gov/netp/learning/, Accessed 16 July 2020

Park, B., Flowerday, T., Brünken, R.: Cognitive and affective effects of seductive details in multimedia learning. Comput. Hum. Behav., 267–278 (2015). https://doi.org/10.1016/j.chb.2014.10.061

Petrov, P.D., Atanasova, T.V.: The Effect of Augmented Reality on Students' Learning Performance in Stem Education. Information **11**(4), 209 (2020)

Freitas, R., Campos, P.: SMART: a System of Augmented Reality for Teaching 2nd grade students. In: Proc.of BCS-HCI '08, vol. 2, pp. 27–30 (2008)

Radu, I., MacIntyre, B., Lourenco, S.: Children's crosshair and finger interactions in handheld Augmented Reality: Relationships between usability and child development. In: Proceedings of The 15th International Conference on Interaction Design and Children, pp. 288–298. ACM (2016)

Reardon, C.: More than toys—Gamer affirmative therapy. Social Work Today, 15(3), 10 (2015). http://www.socialworktoday.com/archive/051815p10.shtml.

Radu: Why should my students use AR? A comparative review of the educational impacts of augmented-reality. ISMAR 2012 - 11th IEEE Int. Symp. Mix. Augment. Real. 2012, Sci. Technol. Pap., pp. 313–314 (2012)

Sotiriou, M., CH Tong, V., Standen, A.: Shaping Higher Education with Students–ways to connect Research and Teaching, p. 346. UCL Press (2018)

Shoukry, L., Sturm, C., Galal-Edeen, G.H.: Pre-MEGa: A Proposed Framework for the Design and Evaluation of Preschoolers' Mobile Educational Games. In: Sobh, T., Elleithy, K. (eds.)

Innovations and Advances in Computing, Informatics, Systems Sciences, Networking and Engineering. LNEE, vol. 313, pp. 385–390. Springer, Cham (2015). https://doi.org/10.1007/978-3-319-06773-5_52

Villalustre, L.; Del Moral, M.E. Expeirencias Interactivas Con Realidad Aumentada En Las Aulas; Octaedro: Barcelona, Spain (2017)

Yáñez-Luna, J.C., Arias-Oliva, M.: M-learning: ttechnological acceptance of mobile devices in online learning. Tecnol. Cienc. Educ. **10**, 13–34 (2018)

Zhu, Q., Tang, Y.: Design of an augmented reality teaching system for FPGA experimental instruction. In: 2017 IEEE 6th International Conference on Teaching Assessment and Learning for Engineering (TALE), pp. 35–38 (2017). ISSN 2470–6698

3C Institute: Serious games (2015). https://www.3cisd.com/what-we-do/serious-games. Accessed 3 July 2020

"Let There Be Light": Evaluating a Serious Game Using Image Schemas for Teaching Preschool Children Scientific Concept and Developing Their Creativity

Zhuolin Gu, Wenyuan Ling, Bo Liu[✉], and Zhao Liu

Shanghai Jiao Tong University, Shanghai 200240, China
{Lingwenyuan,bibobox,hotlz}@sjtu.edu.cn

Abstract. More and more digital scientific apps appear in children family education due to their attraction, but they are difficult to help children deepen the understanding of abstract scientific concepts. Herein, in order to further help children learn light science, we evaluated a serious game which is based on the image schema theory. The game uses the interactive strategy of analogy to bridge the gap between children's intuitive cognition and scientific explanation, and integrates the gamification to achieve the training goal. The degree of children's concept understanding was compared by the pre-test and post-test results of 15 children. The results show that children can more accurately understand basic optical concepts and actively create their own light stories.

Keywords: Science concept · Image schemas · Constructionism · Serious game · Preschool children · Light · Creativity

1 Introduction

The informal Science Education, as a way to influence the formation of children's scientific literacy, is being widely paid much attention by scholars [1]. According to the survey results, more than half of preschool children have watched videos, played games or listened to stories through mobile phones or tablets [2]. With the increasing maturity of digital user interface, children's education apps are accepted by more and more families, thus the market prospect of these apps is very promising [3].

However, at present, although the popular science education apps for children have certain educational functions, they are still only an additional role with games. The original design idea is also based on leisure and entertainment to attract children's attention rather than the goal of helping children form certain scientific concepts, therefore, it is difficult to help children deepen their understanding of abstract scientific concepts [4].

Aiming at the problem that children don't have a deep understanding of scientific concepts, this paper designs an interactive way to bridge the differences gap between children's intuitive cognition and scientific explanation on the basis of image schema theory. Combining the research results of game-based learning with the game strategy

© Springer Nature Switzerland AG 2021
P. Zaphiris and A. Ioannou (Eds.): HCII 2021, LNCS 12785, pp. 31–46, 2021.
https://doi.org/10.1007/978-3-030-77943-6_3

of integrating learning objectives into life events, this paper designs a tablet based game model to balance education and entertainment. Games enable children to understand abstract scientific knowledge more clearly. Moreover, this paper aims at the scientific concept of optics to help children understand and learn the physical properties of light and its role in life, and improve their scientific literacy.

This paper reviews the research status from three aspects, including the formation of children's scientific concepts, the application of image schema in children's education and the existing research results of game learning. On this basis, a game prototype based on tablet computer is designed as a case study. Then, the results before and after the test were compared to measure children's understanding of the concept of light.

2 Background

As an independent individual, children have their own unique life world and the ability to understand and explain things around them. Before receiving formal education, they have already formed a personalized primary understanding. Constructivist learning theory holds that children construct new knowledge on the basis of their original experience and knowledge.

Preschool children tend to use daily life experience to explain natural phenomena, which is often contrary to hierarchical and systematic scientific concepts. Ponser and George J. proposed that the formation of children's scientific concept is a process of conceptual change [5]. In this process, children first find that the daily concept is insufficient, then understand the new scientific concept model, and finally integrate the scientific concept with life experience to explain the problems they encounter.

The teaching strategies of conceptual transformation can be divided into two categories [6]: contradiction and assimilation. The former is the teaching strategy based on cognitive conflict and conflict resolution, which holds that the core of learning is learners' active participation in the reorganization of knowledge. The teaching process needs to create a certain situation causing cognitive conflict, so as to start the autonomous exploration. The latter is based on the learner's original ideas, providing support for new ways of thinking expands the primitive ideas to new areas by using metaphor and analogy.

Preschool children lack enough critical thinking ability, and need to be properly guided. Therefore, this study mainly focuses on assimilation strategy to promote conceptual change.

3 Related Studies

3.1 Image Schema

Image schema is an abstract structure prior to concept and language. It comes from daily physical experience [7] and is based on sensory perception and interactive experience. When people need to learn new knowledge from old knowledge, they will subconsciously use it as a cognitive structure [8] (Table1).

Table 1. Overview of typical image schemas

Group	Examples
Space	LOCATION, UP-DOWN, FRONT-BACK, LEFT-RIGHT, NEAR-FAR, VERTICALITY, CENTER-PERIPHERY, STRAIGHT, CONTACT
Force	COMPULSION, BLOCKAGE, RESISTANCE, DIVERSION, COUNTERFORCE
Containment	CONTAINER, IN-OUT, SURFACE, CONTENT, FULL-EMPTY
Locomotion	MOMENTUM, PATH
Balance	AXIS, BALANCE, POINT BALANCE, EQUILIBRIUM
Identity	MATCHING, SUPERIMPOSITION
Multiplicity	MERGING, COLLECTION, SPLITTING, LINKAGE, COUNT-MASS
Existence	REMOVAL, CYCLE, OBJECT, AGENT, PROCESS

The basic image schema mainly includes the description of space and power. For example, they can form more conceptual categories through the expansion and transformation of combination, metaphor, metonymy and other mechanisms, which are beneficial to form the ability of abstract thinking and reasoning.

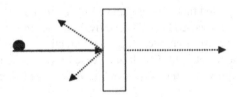

Fig. 1. The Blockage image schema

For instance, children can understand the phenomenon that light can't pass through the box because they recognize the image schema of blockage (see Fig. 1), as the box blocks the light. However, blockage cannot explain that light can pass through the glass, so in order to help children understand the transmission principle of light, other schemas are needed to help complete the cognitive structure.

Image schema can also be identified from drawing and activities. In previous studies, researchers found that children's level of psychological participation increased when the apps contained a symbolic system that was consistent with the image schema of children and science [9, 10]. Local teachers use the narrative picture book named Winterwatch, which describes the story of how cold controls a small town, as popular science teaching materials. The book establishes a link between the scientific model and the real world by merging the characteristics of cold and heat and the influence of natural forces on people, and adding them to the role shaping and story events. The research results indicate that the book can greatly improve the cognition of thermodynamics knowledge for children [11]. Charalampos Kyfonidis has produced interactive device [12], diabetes popular science game, which connects diabetes knowledge with tangible objects. Preschool children can interact with the characters in the game through a toy with RFID tags and a pen with insulin detection, helping children intuitively understand "what is insulin", "nutritional content of food", "which foods are healthy". The research results are considered to be attractive and effective.

This study combines learning content with life phenomenon by designing an interactive way of image schema in line with the scientific concept, so as to help children learn new concepts in the way of assimilation.

3.2 Learning Through Play

In previous studies, researchers have explored that game based learning and practice in science education may promote rote learning of facts, but it is not possible to promote deeper conceptual understanding [13]. Exploration and discovery without any guidance or scaffolding may not provide sufficient support for learning. To promote effective learning in a flexible environment, children can support the exploration, questioning and exploration of scaffolding when they work towards clear learning goals [14].

Kathy Hirsh Pasek [2] analyzed the problems of excessive entertainment and lack of education in preschool children's education app, and pointed out when children actively interact with learning materials, keep their mental concentration, and carry out social sharing, they will learn better by providing clear learning goals and the game content related to life.

Some scholars suggested that adding game elements to the teaching of the concept of light can keep children focused [15]. This study combines the formation of scientific concepts with games, and uses rich interaction and attractive stories to guide children to actively explore the nature of light. Children's sense of science and learning initiative can be cultivated or improved in the play, which is vivid, interesting, and attractive.

4 Method

Children have a lot of experience about light. Optical phenomenon is the most frequently occurring and directly perceived one in daily life and activities. The previous research, investigation of 6-year-old children's understanding of light and shadow, has shown that children understand light by stages. It is found that most children are able to realized that people could see the object when light irradiates it. Children's understanding of generation, direction and size of shadow is vague. Children can observe the basic light phenomenon in daily life, however, it is difficult to fully comprehend the scientific explanation behind it. The research explored the children's understanding of light from three aspects including the generation, propagation and function of light by asking children 9 questions (see Table 2).

4.1 Procedure

The pre-test was designated according to the POE (predict-observe-explain) strategy, which allows immediate observations and demonstrations and is widely used in science

Table 2. Questionnaire for Pre-Test

Topic 1: Generation of light
Q1. There are some animals can give out light
Q2. The Moon and the sun can give out light by themselves
Topic 2: Propagation of light
Q3. Light hitting a mirror keeps going
Q4. Sunlight has different colors
Q5. A magnifier can enlarge an object
Q6. You can block light to make shadows in dark
Topic 3: Function of light
Q7. We need light to see
Q8. The sunlight has temperature
Q9. Plants need light to grow

class [16]. First, children need to determine what the answer to the questionnaire is and explain the cause independently. Second, experimenters demonstrate related physical phenomena on children by simple props and materials. Finally, children are demanded to amend or add their explanation to take account of the observation. As Events that surprise create conditions where children may be ready to start reexamining their personal theories according to Constructivist theories of learning.

15 pre-school kids, 8 boys and 8 girls, with an average age of 5 years and 4 months, were participated in the research that is made in a child classroom one by one. Two experimenters encouraged children to spoken out their ideas and record them. In addition to dictation, children were required to draw their opinions on paper. After the experiment that each child has half an hour of it is end, the experimenter would give the children snacks as a reward.

4.2 Results

The result has shown that children have a basic knowledge of light, but they can't explain the generation and propagation of light by words logically.

There are 10 children who correctly answered the question about what luminous source is. It is difficult to distinguish the different between the self-luminous body like the sun and the reflection (It doesn't give out light except reflected light.). Most children acquiesced the idea that light propagates through a straight line. There are 10 children who correctly answered the question, in addition, other children can correctly describe the reflection path of light in the demonstration. At last, they also admitted the same idea. 8 children of them were able to predict the correct direction of light after reflecting. 4 children of them thought that the size of the object they seen is related to the thickness of lens. 8 children of them understood that light can work on plants growth. There is one child mentioned the concept of "refraction", however, they don't explain details of it. It may be a term they learned from popular science articles after school.

The participant's understanding model of the concept of light will be known through their explanations and sketches of the question. The image schema identified from the understanding model could be used to build similar game interaction methods. For example, question number 5, children prefer to explain how light propagates by using the pattern of the object movement. When the participant P3 found that the laser pointer irradiating the lens would leave a spot of light then change its direction, he described that light hits the lens, then light is cut into halves and keep going. Table 3 records the image schema picked-up from the answers of the participant P3.

Table 3. The image model identified from the participant's P3 explains of Q5.

Image Schema	Notation
PATH	Extracted from "walk forward line and turn on line" of children's sketches
BLOCKAGE	Extracted from the word "block", it implies that the lens is an obstacle that light can penetrate
PART-WHOLE	Extracted from the word "be cut into halves", it implies light can be cut into different parts

There are some image schemas that often shown in children's explains including PATH, BLOCKAGE and SCALE. Shown as Table 4, image schemas accorded with science explains were extracted, game contents explained the image schemas were designed, through analyzing the children's answers and sketches to all questions. In order to building a relationship between the science explanations and the familiar knowledge of children.

Table 4. Image schemas and corresponding game designs identified from science explanation.

Image Schemas	Annotations	Interaction	Game Design
CENTER-PERIPHERY	Light source shines	Drag the light source into the game screen, the light spreads out from the center	Different light sources can be created to activate scenes
SCALE	The brightness of light will attenuate	Different light sources have different illumination ranges	Changing the position of light can find objects in the darkness

(continued)

Table 4. (*continued*)

Image Schemas	Annotations	Interaction	Game Design
PATH	Light travels in a straight line	The illuminated area of the flashlight can be controlled by marking	Adjusting the direction of the light can find objects in the dark
BLOCKAGE	Light goes through some things and refraction	Irradiating different objects, light changes direction	Moving the lens can change the direction of light, looking for objects in the darkness
PART-WHOLE	The sun light with different colors	Shade can be gotten by combination	Harmonizing different colors of light can create a new color
ENABLEMENT	Plants need light to grow	Putting light to plants then plants growth	Long time light irradiation can get fruits ripe
ATTRACTION	All animals like light	Putting light to animals, animals flee or gather	Light can affect animal behaviors to look for objects

5   Game Design

This essay assessed a serious tablet-based game that allows preschool kids, from 4 to 6 years old, to explore the concept of light and show their own light and shadow works. Through pretesting 15 children's the understanding and science explanations of light, several image schemas were picked up and game symbol system was designed.

The game system was composed of scenes, elements and targets. Targets and voice guidance will set a clear learning goal. Children need to think, add the proper props to the scene, use the nature of light to find all goals to fulfill them. There are three levels in the game system, corresponding to the generation, propagation and function of light.

At the first level, children touch different sources of light to observe how light is generated. At the second and the third level, children explore how light is propagated by adjusting the irradiation angle and color of light (Fig. 2). At the last level, children explore how light works on the animals and plants by adding any source of light and non-luminous to the scene or interacting with virtual objects in the scene. Children can also record the screen, share the mysteries they find in the scene to create and share themselves meaningful light and shadows works (Fig. 3).

At the first level, the scene is set in the darkness, player need to add source of light and other elements. Different sources, the sun, flashlights, firewood, jellyfish, and other micro animals, have corresponding lighting scale. For example, the sun can light the entire scene while the flashlight light only one area which is a metaphor of scale.

Fig. 2. Level 1 (left) and Level 2 (right). To the left: light sources. To the right: light reflection

Fig. 3. Level 3 (left) and Level 4 (right). To the left: RGB color. To the right: light (Color figure online)

At the fourth level, the scene is set in the nature, where small animals and plants are influenced by light. At last, because children need to learn repeatedly to gain knowledge, the game encourages children to explore over one time, the corresponding rewards will be triggered. Children can record and share the mysteries they found in the nature scene.

6 Evaluation

6.1 Participants

We invited 15 children who had participated in the previous test to participate in the JL assessment process and a delayed post-test, with a one-week interval between the two experiments. By comparing the results of the pre-test, post-test, and delayed post-test, the impact of the prototype design on the conceptual change and the playability of the game were measured. All children participated in the study with the consent of their parents and their own wishes and everyone reported having used smartphones or tablets. One teacher and two researchers participated in the experiment.

6.2 Procedure

The experiment was conducted in a children's training classroom, comfortable environment allows children to feel natural and safe. Each child in the company of a teacher and a researcher was asked to play the prototype, JL for no more than 30 min. At the end of the interaction, the participant needs to do the POE test again and use the 5-point Smiley Face Likert Scales to answer several questions concerning to game playability. One week later, child participants were asked to complete the delayed post-test in the same classroom. In the interactive experiment, researchers encouraged children to continue their interaction of the game when they were distracted, and inspired children to think about why different interactive processes were triggered, and recorded the children's behavioral characteristics.

In order to avoid interferences, considering that child participants could had remembered the answers, questionnaires used in the three tests were distinct to one another, but the scientific concept of each question was based on the same. After all experiments were over, we interviewed the teacher, and the interview was transcribed into text data.

6.3 Measurements

In this study, the degree of change in children's concepts was measured by using a diagnostic test that included the following questions. Child participants may be able to answer the right questions but do not understand the reasons, so for each question, the researcher both recorded whether the child answered correctly and gave the correct explanation. This paper used the Two-Tier test [17] classifying different situations: Initial, Scientific and Synthetic. The Initial category is used for correct answer and correct reason (Table 5). The Scientific category is used to correct answer and wrong reason. Synthetic category is used for wrong answer and wrong reason or wrong answer and correct reason. In addition, the researchers added up the total scores of each child for all topics, and the scores were then divided by the total score to get the child's overall understanding.

Table 5. Two-tier test

Criteria		Score
Initial	Correct answer + Correct reason	3
Scientific	Correct answer + Wrong reason	2
Synthetic	Wrong answer + Correct reason	1
Synthetic	Wrong answer + Wrong reason	0

We used two projects (see Fig. 4) from Fun Toolkit [18] to measure children's engagement. The Again-Again table asks the children whether or not they would do the activity again and Fun sorter gathers children's opinions about specific features.

Finally, child participants' works created for social sharing in the game were saved to measure their creativity. The evaluation method is adapted from the Torrance Creative

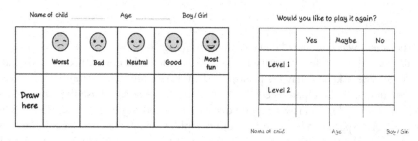

Fig. 4. Picture of Fun sorter (left) and the Again -again (right)

Thinking Test (TTCT) [19]. The fluency of drawing refers to how many drawings are completed within the specified time; the originality of drawing is judged based on the unusual level of the drawing; The abstractness of drawing is to evaluate the description of the drawing, and comprehensively explore the comprehensive and organizational capabilities.

6.4 Findings

Conceptual Change. As shown in Table 6, before using the prototype, many participants' answers belonged to "FF" (Synthetic). But after using the prototype, the number of students belonging to the "TT" (Initial) and "TF" (Scientific) categories has been increased. These reactions were also maintained in the delayed post-test. A paired sample t-test (see Fig. 5) shown that there were statistical differences between the mean scores on the 9-item diagnostic test from pre-test to post-test ($t = -8.393$, df $= 8$, $p < 0.001$) and delayed post-test ($t = -6.737$, df $= 8$, $p < 0.001$). This indicates that children can answer questions more correctly and predict experimental results. However, children may get the correct answer by guessing. When the researcher shows them the results of the experiment, they did not understand it. In fact, the proportion of people who can really achieve the theoretical level of understanding was not high (Q3: 20%, Q7: 20%, Q8: 7%).

During the evaluation process, the researchers found that some children need to be reminded to notice the required goals in the level and the props that can be used in the interface. Otherwise, they will not verify the game play through active thinking and experimental comparison. Will not practice gameplay and light cognition. This means that researchers need to focus on showing children clear goals and the connection between play and life in future design practices.

Children showed different levels of comprehension of light concepts on different topics (See Fig. 6). For T1, the source of light, the level of understanding of children after the test was significantly higher than the level before the test. For the transmission of light T2, child participants' understanding level after the test was slightly higher than the level before the test compared with the post test, but the understanding level of the post-test was slightly lower than delayed post-test in two items (Q3,Q6). For T3, the function of light, the degree of improvement in understanding was moderate. This may be because the role of light source and light is closely related to children's daily life,

Table 6. Percentage of participants' responses for two-tier test for categories of understanding

Categories		Pre-test	Post-test	Delayed test
Q1	T-T	14	67	73
	T-F	27	20	7
	F-T	7	–	–
	F-F	52	13	20
Q2	T-T	20	53	40
	T-F	7	20	33
	F-T	–	7	–
	F-F	73	20	27
Q3	T-T	7	20	20
	T-F	27	39	47
	F-T	20	14	14
	F-F	47	27	27
Q4	T-T	20	33	33
	T-F	33	40	27
	F-T	20	27	33
	F-F	27	–	7
Q5	T-T	47	60	53
	T-F	14	40	33
	F-T	20	–	14
	F-F	19	–	–
Q6	T-T	14	40	47
	T-F	33	39	32
	F-T	20	14	14
	F-F	33	7	7
Q7	T-T	7	20	20
	T-F	26	53	67
	F-T	14	7	–
	F-F	53	20	13
Q8	T-T	7	14	7
	T-F	27	59	46
	F-T	46	20	33
	F-F	20	7	14
Q9	T-T	27	53	53
	T-F	27	33	33
	F-T	13	–	7
	F-F	33	14	7

while the refraction and reflection of light are rarely observed, so children can understand T1 and T3 quickly in later tests. Through communication with children, the researchers learned that after the game prototype showed children the form of light transmission, the

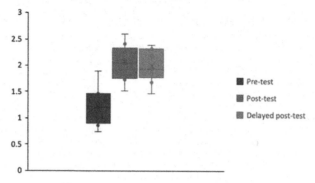

Fig. 5. The mean scores in the POE tests

children would consciously observe the light phenomenon in life, so their understanding ability was slightly improved in the delayed later test. In addition, as the optical concepts related to linear propagation, reflection, and refraction are becoming more and more abstract, it is more difficult for children to understand, and some participants confused the difference between these.

This result showed that game training has a positive effect on establishing a relative scientific understanding of optical concepts. A relatively scientific understanding means that children abandon their original ideas and use simple scientific ideas to try to explain the phenomenon. Through repeated learning, preschoolers can master some scientific concepts, but they are unlikely to accurately describe accurate and complete scientific theoretical models. For example, it was difficult for children to understand light as a kind of energy.

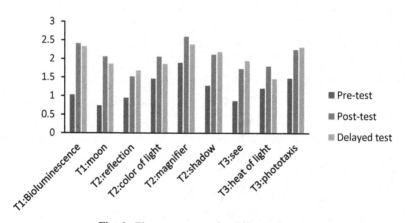

Fig. 6. The mean scores for different themes

Table 7 shows that the difference between each test score was statistically significant, and there was a statistically significant difference between the test scores ($p < 0.05$). However, multiple comparisons (based on the Tukey post-test [20]) showed that although there were statistically significant differences in test scores ($p < 0.05$) between the pre-test and post-test scores and between the pre-test and the delayed test No significant difference was observed between the post score and the delayed test score ($p < 0.05$). This indicated that the game prototype developed in this research can help students retain their own ideas in long-term memory [21].

Table 7. Multiple comparisons of the test scores (Tukey post-hoc test)

Tukey HSD		Mean difference (I-J)	Std. error	Sig
(I) Test	(J) Test			
Pre-test	Post-test	−.84889[a]	.16094	0.000
	Delayed post-test	−.79111[a]	.16094	0.000
Post-test	Pre-test	.84889[a]	.16094	0.000
	Delayed post-test	.05778	.16094	0.932
Delayed post-test	Pre-test	.79111[a]	.16094	0.000
	Post-test	−.05778	.16094	0.932

[a] Correlation is significant at the 0.05 level (2-tailed)

Participants' ideas could change differently depending upon the context through the POE task. For instance, the color that sun light includes depends upon whether a person is present or not, or whether it is night or day, concerning to some participants.

Table 8. Correlations between children's understanding level and indicators of engagement.

	Fun sorter	Again and again
Post-test	.717*	.646**
Delayed post-test	.609	.549*

[a] Correlation is significant at the 0.05 level (2-tailed).
[b] Correlation is significant at the 0.01 level (2-tailed).

Engagement. Participants showed a strong interest in the game at the beginning of the test, and they would actively explore the interactive elements in the interface. When encountering difficulties in the game, they showed doubts and lack of concentration, and would take the initiative to communicate with the researchers, and when they successfully passed the level, they will express their love for the game.

The statistical results showed the correlation between the engagement index and the score of comprehension of light. As shown in Table 8, there was a significant positive correlation between the degree to which children were liked by different levels (Fun sorter) and the level score (after testing: $r = 0.717$, $p < 0.05$; after delay testing: $r = 0.609$, $p > 0.05$), negatively correlated with the number of correct answers. There was a significant positive correlation between children's love for games and children's total score (after test: $r = 0.646$, $p < 0.01$; after delayed test: $r = 0.547$, $p < 0.05$).

This proves the positive impact of learning through play on conceptual changes. By using the game prototype, children can roughly understand the phenomenon of light and form a simple scientific concept of what light is. Game experience is also crucial for children to learn very abstract scientific concepts in school education. In communicating with children, we found that children's understanding of light comes to a large extent from the portrayal of light in cartoons and books. For example, the red sun makes children think that light is red. The artistic expression of visual elements may have misunderstood children. In future design practices, researchers will also pay attention to avoiding such situations.

Creativity. Qualitative observations show that in general, students were excited about recording short stories in games. When they were told that their creations could be shared with their parents and friends, they behaved more actively in finding interactive elements in the game and giving them own understanding.

Participants who performed well in the POE test reported that they like to make short stories on tablets, search for "light" codes, and watch animations of animals and plants. A participant named his story "Colorful lambs". In the recorded video, he obtained three colors of light by adjusting the color and light, and used them to awaken the lamb in the dark. However, child participants with average performance were more interested in the animation effects and operations (such as sliding) in the game, and were not interested in recording the screen, but simply triggering the elements in the game. In addition, two child participants asked to play the former levels to get a better understanding of the game, which indicated that the recorded video can enhance children's motivation.

6.5 Interview Results

After all the tests were over, researchers discussed with the teacher present. The teacher said that JL has turned the learning process of abstract scientific concepts into a lively and interesting one. Children could understand the nature of light unconsciously while playing, which helps preschool children understand and accept a certain science or feature.

In addition, interactive games require children to participate in person, so it is also a kind of scientific inquiry. Some children seldom thought about the reasons behind common optical phenomena before, but in order to pass the game levels, children's desire for knowledge and strong curiosity were stimulated. It helped to promote the conceptual transformation of children and the enlightenment of scientific thinking. Additionally, science game that combines image schemas should be combined with more teaching strategies, such as tangible teaching toys.

7   Conclusion

This study designed a serious game prototype based on tablet to allow children aged 4–6 to understand some optical laws, and conducted experiments in a teaching environment. By extracting image patterns that exist in both preschool concepts and scientific concepts of children, researchers design corresponding game interaction forms and multimodal feedback, combining science education with games, so that children can more easily understand abstract scientific models.

Qualitative and quantitative examples suggest that (i) Clear learning goals and inter-action from image schemas seem to help understand basic abstract concepts; (ii) Children who show higher levels of engagement tend to have a higher score; (iii) Records for shar-ing enhances children's learning motivation. We present our research results, children's interaction and creation, and provide inspiration for designers and developers of science education games.

Possible limitations in our work include revised scales and insufficient attention to assessing the creativity of participants' works. In the future, we will iterate existing prototypes and integrate other game design paradigms, such as social connections. By doing this, we seek an understanding of the design space of serious science education games and how it can reduce the difficulty of understanding children's concepts.

References

1. Hui, Z.: How educational activities promote the formation of children's scientific concepts: a case study based on the theme of "Meeting·Light." Natural Sci. Museum Res. **1S**, 131–136 (2019)
2. Hirsh-Pasek, K., Zosh, J.M., Golinkoff, R.M., Gray, J.H., Robb, M.B., Kaufman, J.: Putting education in "educational" apps: lessons from the science of learning. Psychol. Sci. Public Interest **16**(1), 3–34 (2015)
3. McEwen, R.N., Dubé, A.K.: Engaging or distracting: children's tablet computer use in education. J. Educ. Technol. Soc. **18**(4), 9–23 (2015)
4. Jirout, J., Zimmerman, C.: Development of science process skills in the early childhood years. In: Trundle, K.C., Saçkes, M. (eds.) Research in Early Childhood Science Education, pp. 143–165. Springer, Dordrecht (2015). https://doi.org/10.1007/978-94-017-9505-0_7
5. Posner, G.J., Strike, K.A., Hewson, P.W., Gertzog, W.A.: Accommodation of a scientific conception: toward a theory of conceptual change. Sci. Educ. **66**(2), 211–227 (1982)
6. Scott, P.H., Asoko, H., Driver, R.H.: Teaching for conceptual change: a review of strategies. Research in physics learning: Theoretical issues and empirical studies, pp. 310–329 (1992)
7. Lakoff, G.: Image metaphors. Metaphor. Symb. **2**(3), 219–222 (1987)
8. Liu, L., Li, M.: The progress and frontiers of the theory of image schema. J. Harbin Inst. Technol. (Social Science Edition) **04**, 110–117 (2008)
9. Hurtienne, J., Israel, J.H.: Image schemas and their metaphorical extensions: intuitive patterns for tangible interaction. Paper presented at the Proceedings of the 1st international conference on Tangible and embedded interaction, Baton Rouge, Louisiana (2007)
10. Xiao, Y., Jiang, C.: Conceptual change in preschool science education: evaluating a serious game designed with image schemas for teaching sound concept. In: Fang, X. (ed.) HCII 2020. LNCS, vol. 12211, pp. 503–520. Springer, Cham (2020). https://doi.org/10.1007/978-3-030-50164-8_37

11. Fuchs, H.U.: A direct entropic approach to uniform and spatially continuous dynamical models of thermoelectric devices. Energy Harvesting Syst. **1**(3–4), 253–265 (2014)
12. Kyfonidis, C., Lennon, M.: Making diabetes education interactive: tangible educational toys for children with type-1 diabetes. In: Proceedings of the 2019 CHI Conference on Human Factors in Computing Systems, pp 1–12 (2019)
13. Baker, E.L., et al.: Problems with the Use of Student Test Scores to Evaluate Teachers. EPI Briefing Paper# 278. Economic Policy Institute (2010)
14. L J. Learning science and children's situational learning: teaching design for happy and efficient classrooms. Educ. Res. **34**(11), 81–91 (2013)
15. Lu, P., Lu, H.: Analysis of the status quo of children's cognition of the concept of light and shadow and teaching suggestions. J. Shaanxi Preschool Teach. College **36**(02), 60–65 (2020)
16. Coştu, B., Ayas, A., Niaz, M.: Investigating the effectiveness of a POE-based teaching activity on students' understanding of condensation. Instr. Sci. **40**(1), 47–67 (2012)
17. Bayrak, B.K.: Using two-tier test to identify primary students' conceptual understanding and alternative conceptions in acid base. Online Submission **3**(2), 19–26 (2013)
18. Read, J.C., MacFarlane, S.: Using the fun toolkit and other survey methods to gather opinions in child computer interaction. In: Proceedings of the 2006 Conference on Interaction Design and Children, pp. 81–88 (2006)
19. Almeida, L.S., Prieto, L.P., Ferrando, M., Oliveira, E., Ferrándiz, C.: Torrance test of creative thinking: the question of its construct validity. Thinking Skills Creativity **3**(1), 53–58 (2008)
20. Coştu, B., Ayas, A., Niaz, M., Ünal, S., Çalik, M.: Facilitating conceptual change in students' understanding of boiling concept. J. Sci. Educ. Technol. **16**(6), 524–536 (2007)
21. Wehmeyer, M.L., Palmer, S.B.: Adult outcomes for students with cognitive disabilities three-years after high school: The impact of self-determination. Education and training in developmental disabilities, pp. 131–144 (2003)

Transforming Classic Learning Games with the Use of AR: The Case of the Word Hangman Game

Ilias Logothetis, George Papadourakis, Iraklis Katsaris, Konstantinos Katsios, and Nikolas Vidakis(✉)

Department of Electrical and Computer Engineering, Hellenic Mediterranean University, Heraklion, Crete, Greece
mtp166@edu.hmu.gr, {papadour,katsarisir,nv}@hmu.gr

Abstract. Augmented Reality in combination with playful learning is used to enhance students' engagement in blended learning environments. This paper presents an AR game with hand tracking & hand interaction that transforms the classic Hangman word game. The thematic word areas of the game are recycling and Covid 19, two areas that are of great interest today.

The game offers alternative interaction through a 3D hand model and 3D objects/letters. The player moves the 3D letters to complete words and collect paper cards with the words' image. These paper cards are then placed, in any order, by the student to create a picture story and a virtual maquette with AR objects is generated. This maquette allows player to create different picture-stories by shuffling the order of found words' paper cards. A field study has been contacted with two groups of students, one group used classic learning techniques and the other group used our AR game. Preliminary results of the study show that all students improved their language skills but only the group with the AR game evolve into being more active, involved, participative and engaged in the educational process and developed their creativity skills.

Keywords: AR game-based learning · NUI · Gamification · Blended learning · Creativity development

1 Introduction

Technological advancements in software and hardware and specifically the major improvements of the performance of smart devices have diversified our everyday life. One of the areas in which these technological changes are gradually becoming apparent is that of education. Augmented Reality (AR) is expected to diversify teaching in the coming years as AR applications blend physical and virtual worlds through a touch screen, a camera, or a head-mounted device [1]. AR technology is compatible and can be used in conjunction with the Game Based Learning (GBL) methods to boost educational processes. It can also help students both in the cognitive part and in gaining motivation for learning, but also in developing basic 21st century skills [2, 3].

© Springer Nature Switzerland AG 2021
P. Zaphiris and A. Ioannou (Eds.): HCII 2021, LNCS 12785, pp. 47–64, 2021.
https://doi.org/10.1007/978-3-030-77943-6_4

Traditional teaching methods do not make much use of new technologies with the result that students often lose interest in education due to the way they learn. While in their daily lives, students are accustomed to function and interact within environments with multiple stimuli, the traditional school remains a place with limited options [4]. The change to a new model is imperative to make learning more creative and interactive by introducing new visual forms of learning [5].

Through play students can develop their thinking and concentration [6] around a topic via a fun and entertaining way of achieving specific learning goals [7]. Students' engagement helps to achieve multiple goals outside of learning, such as in-depth understanding of the topic and greater awareness of the topic [8].

Augmented reality allows information and 3D virtual objects to be displayed on top of real-world objects. Furthermore, AR offers the ability on such objects and information to be processed in real-time [9, 10]. As smart mobile devices become more powerful (computationally) they can support augmented reality applications and thus make AR reachable to more people.

In addition, software libraries and frameworks such as ARCore and ARToolkit have helped the software development community to have effortless access to AR technology and include it in their applications. Research about the interaction in such environments with bare hands are also evolving along with the improvements on the hand tracking field of study making possible, for mobile devices, to run such algorithms [11].

1.1 Game Based Learning

The educational community is shifting the goals, that had been set in previous decades, related to the acquisition of knowledge and the traditional model of teaching to a new approach. One of the main goals of this new approach is the utilization of knowledge but also the development of a pleasant environment for enhanced creativity in the classroom [4]. Discussion, research, and experimentation can help students activate their interest and make learning more interactive.

GBL creates a framework where students have additional motivation compared to the traditional teaching method. Their participation because of games is greater, while the willingness they show towards the lesson in general increases [2]. According to Fotaris et al. [12] learning using digital games in education reported significant improvements in subject understanding, diligence, and motivation. In this way the game becomes an educational tool to achieve the goals set by the teacher. In addition, as Sitzmann states [13], through play, students' performance can be improved and relationships between them can be strengthened.

According to Prensky [14] an educational game is designed not only to develop players' skills but also to maintain and apply this object in the real world. Thus, it is important to connect education with everyday life as in this way it will be possible to develop students' metacognitive skills and their awareness of important issues.

1.2 Augmented Reality in Education

AR is a relatively new technology that combines the physical with the virtual world through the addition and integration of virtual information [15]. In terms of education, it is important to connect the two worlds namely the physical and the virtual as opposed to VR where the user is completely immersed in a virtual environment [16]. The use of AR enables students to diversify and enrich the physical world through new technology and the use of smart devices rather than completely replace it [9]. The additional information, images and objects provided help students to effectively understand abstract concepts, thus helping to improve knowledge and learning [17, 18].

Mobile AR is considered one of the most up-to-date technologies in education for the coming years as it is easily accessible due to the high penetration of smart devices [19]. The reasons are that it is an inexpensive technology, easy to apply in the classroom and safe. With AR, students can simultaneously interact with both the real and virtual worlds in real time [20]. This turns AR into an exciting entertainment and learning tool for kids. In addition, the new features it offers help to develop their imagination and creativity [21] and at the same time helps to connect the game with learning.

AR can be used as a learning tool in the hands of the teacher to activate students' interest and gain their attention, so that they can focus more on the lesson. According to Oranç and Küntay [22], through AR applications, students delve deeper with this technology. In addition, they believe that to be effective there must be utilization of the knowledge and skills that students acquire in their daily lives. According to Hirsh [23], the principles that should guide the use of AR in education are essential: (a) to encourage students to be actively involved in the process, (b) to include additional material, (c) to provide important new experiences with which they can relate, and (d) to offer an environment of socialization and cooperation.

Moreover, the combination of AR with game-based learning (ARGBL) has gained momentum in the field of education as it creates a playful and enriching learning experience [24]. Utilization of this technology leads to the creation of new interactive visual learning environments [5] that allow new approaches to teaching and learning experience in various disciplines.

2 Background Work

Game Based Learning is an approach that is constantly gaining ground in the field of education and teaching due to the opportunity it gives students to learn through enjoyable and creative activities. The field of literature & language is no exception since this is one of the most frequent courses in the typical school curricula. Through the electronic or non-electronic games students can develop their vocabulary [50] both in their mother tongue and in the second foreign language [51-53].

2.1 Alternative Educational Tools for Literature and Language Education

The field of literature & language as mentioned is one of the most important in education. The pedagogical teaching methods used are many and range from traditional to modern and innovative. From creative writing and the use of everyday objects to the use of technology with computers, smart devices, applications, games, VR and AR, educational robotics.

Creative writing is a method that utilizes various techniques to spark students' imagination and help them create their own texts using language in a different way [49]. However, in addition to the classical methods, the use of technology is a new way to encourage students to improve their language and vocabulary skills [28]. Mobile games [54, 55] are increasingly being used in classrooms, presenting positive results in the areas of knowledge and skills [26, 29]. In fact, studies have shown that mobile games are an effective tool for both high school and younger ages as students developed their knowledge in repeating/reviewing, using multiple modalities and means, and having control over their own learning [30].

According to Hwang, W. et al. [31] game-based learning activities can significantly improve students' speaking skills if they work in combination with a mobile game-based learning system. The WhatsApp Social Networking Tool (WSNT) seems to work for older ages [25] as it helps students learn English interactively and collaboratively. Furthermore, Ghazisaedy [27] argues that educational robotics can help in learning English as a foreign language as the new way of learning helped them to develop additional motivation and to learn more effectively in the long run.

In their research, Cai, S. et al. [17], on 38 students of the eighth grade of an AR and motion-sensing learning technology that teaches magnetic fields in a junior high school physics course observed the effects of using natural interaction on students can improve students' learning attitude and learning outcome.

2.2   AR in Literature and Language Education

A significant number of AR applications, related to education, have use cases from language & literature education as shown by Parmaxi's et.al. [41] systematic review of 54 studies regarding language learning between the years 2014–2019. According the review, most AR studies dealt with vocabulary (23.9%), reading (12.7%), speaking (9.9%) writing (8.5%) or generic language skills (9.9%). However, the authors point out that no special connection was found with learning theories during the application of AR. This gap can be filled through the creation of applications in collaboration with stakeholders in the educational community.

AR-related language applications and research have shown positive results in terms of vocabulary and spelling development [4], improving student motivation and increasing memory. Similar results appeared in a study on the improvement of vocabulary and grammatical structures [42]. Also, positive results were found regarding the learning of English as a second foreign language through the application of AR [43] in relation to the traditional teaching methods.

The use of AR seems to help students significantly in the complex and demanding field of language as they seem to achieve higher performance, to retrieve knowledge from memory more easily [44], and also to improve their narrative ability, the size of their stories as well as their creativity and imagination [45]. Another important fact is that in most researches it seems that, at the same time with the cognitive objects increases the motivation, social collaboration, and interest of the students for the lesson [38, 46].

Collectively, we have researched more than 30 studies and the conclusions can be summarized to: (a) naturalistic approaches applied to AR technology help to foster positive attitudes towards AR, (b) AR facilitate collaboration and (c) AR-related language applications enhance the users' social collaboration, personal development and skills.

2.3 Hand Interaction with AR

Research on hand interaction with the use of AR suggests that one should use the hands like when interacting with the musical instrument called Theremin. In this way the errors are minimized when hands block or confuse. A gesture-based interaction has been developed which includes functionalities as menu selection, object manipulation and more [33]. A method for realistic grasp is proposed that uses predefined rules for the movements of the hands as a physics simulation would be computationally heavy. The system checks if an object is considered grabbed and if two or more points of the hand are interacting with the object from opposite sides [34]. A similar method to the above is proposed but with the use of a glove that will provide haptic feedback as well [35]. A system to control the tv functionality is developed using Convolutional neural networks and Convolutional pose machines for hand recognition [36]. Another system for interaction with 3D objects in museum is proposed using the Leap Motion device for the hand recognition [37]. Using the Leap Motion device, researchers developed an application for learning geometry, that students can draw 2D and 3D shapes of geometrical shapes on top of a marker [32].

Objectives

The purpose of our study is to raise awareness and develop students' vocabulary and creativity on the topics of recycling and Covid 19. The research utilized the approach of game-based learning and AR hand interaction technology. Our goals were for students to:

- Develop their vocabulary around the topics of recycling and Covid 19.
- Utilize AR hand interacting technology to become more active in class (motivation).
- Develop concentration, engagement, and enjoyment using an AR game.
- Develop their creativity by making a story of their own based on the objects they found.
- Be aware of recycling and Covid issues 19.

3 Field Study Methodology

Our field study was carried out at the Elementary School of Plakia, Crete, Greece, in October 2020. While further expansion of the research was originally planned, the field study was stopped due to the mandatory quarantine in respect with covid-19. The research sample was homogeneous in language and consisted of 36 students (16 boys, 20 girls). The age of the students was 10 years old. The requirements regarding information, consent, confidentiality and use of data were met carefully, both orally and in writing, by informing school staff, students, and parents about the purposes of the study and their right to deny their participation. The students were divided into two groups based on their classroom.

We also obtained the approval of the Primary School Directorate to conduct this study in schools in its area. Then, in respect to the protocol of the institutional review committee, we contacted the school principals to describe the study and ask for permission to meet with primary school teachers, to explain the study and determine their interest in participating.

The study was conducted in two levels, the first concerned the teachers and the viewpoint they had about the lesson and the second had to do with the students. In this way, the aim is for the study to capture a more comprehensive opinion of the process and how to use an AR game in the learning practice. For the teachers, the semi-structured interview [47] was used as a tool while for the students, the observation method [48] was used. The interviews were conducted shortly after the end of the process, so that the conclusions and thoughts of the teachers are fresh.

4 Our AR Hangman Game

In this section of our paper we present a game that we have implemented in Unity3D Game Engine using (AR foundation and ARCore) a custom tool built to facilitate the process of game development that requires interaction with physical hands in augmented reality environments.

4.1 Constructing the Game

The design of our application is separated in two main modules (see Fig. 1), the first module, namely the hand tracking module is a service that is implemented for hand recognition and tracking and the second module, namely the Unity toolset, constitutes the functionality and representation of the hand in the game. The separation in two different modules allows for higher frame rates of the game as the device running the game is relieved from the hand recognition process.

The main components of our application, in a high architectural level, are presented in Fig. 1 while Fig. 2 shows the usage of these components described in a workflow diagram of a common usage scenario created with our application.

The Unity toolset provide basic components such as a socket client for the communication with the hand tracking service and an image capture method that is required to send a stream of images on the service. The rest components concern the game creation and interaction process. These components are a virtual hand, hand actions, gestures, selectors, and raycasters (see Fig. 1 right part & see Fig. 2(a)).

To better use the hand points, we have separated them on their corresponding fingers, so when there is a need to retrieve specific hand points, they can be accessed by calling the involved fingers. Predefined gestures also exist that can be used as is without the need of accessing the finger classes or the hand points. To add on this and make it even easier and simpler to use a gesture type enumerated value is assigned to each gesture that is implemented and a gesture manager class has been created. Through the gesture manager class all gestures can be accessed by using the interrelated gesture type name.

The HandAction class (see Fig. 2(a)), is responsible for defining the behavior of the virtual hand when interaction occurs with another virtual object in the application. Such actions involve the movement of a virtual object. This class exists mostly to cover additional behaviors or different implementations of already existing behaviors.

Selection Interfaces (see Fig. 2(a)) include Ray cast provider that is a component that describes the type of a ray caster to be used. This ray caster is used on the selector classes that their responsibility is to check if the hand is about to interact with a virtual object or not. Finally, in this category of components the selection action classes are also included, which are used to visually inform that a virtual object is about to or interacting with the hand.

The hand is represented virtually within the visualHand class which is wrapped in the actionHand class. In the actionHand class further information about the hand is given such as the method to detect possible interactions.

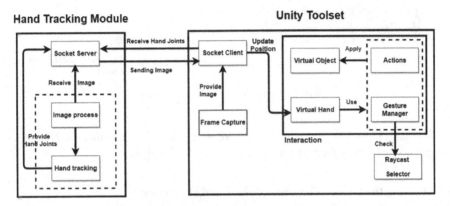

Fig. 1. Architecture diagram

The service which connects the Image process module and Socket Server (see Fig. 1), is responsible for receiving a stream of images from the device and processing the image to a form that is compatible with the hand recognition algorithm. The hand recognition algorithm can be changed easily as the rest of the service is not bound to a specific algorithm. This allows each developer to use their desired algorithms. For this project we use a modified version of for the handtracking [39].

The game was implemented following the Unity toolset flow Diagram (see while Fig. 2(b)). When the game starts it initializes a connection to the service and the virtual hand. After the connection is established it starts to update the position of the virtual hand to the corresponding position of the real hand on the screen. Each frame we check if a "grab" gesture is detected that is defined by the ray cast hits of the thumb and one more finger at least to a virtual object. If the gesture is detected, then a "performAction" method is fired that starts to move the grabbed object with the hand. To place the grabbed object to the user desired position, the application calculates the distance between the target position and the grabbed objects' relative position. To help the player to put the object easier we have set a "wider" area for the desired position.

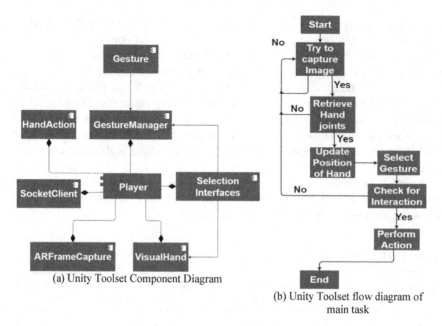

(a) Unity Toolset Component Diagram

(b) Unity Toolset flow diagram of
main task

Fig. 2. Component and flow diagrams

The game has taken advantage of ARCore augmented images to link the 2D images that get acquired from the first part to their respective 3D objects.

4.2 Playing the Game: The Case of the Word Hangman

The game aims to (a) raise students' awareness about recycling and Covid 19, (b) enable students to develop their vocabulary in relation to the thematic areas and (c) develop creativity skills by making their own virtual picture stories and telling their own stories as stated previously at Sect. 2 where the objectives of our work were defined.

The game involves two main tasks, the first task is to support language learning and the second is about enhancing creativity. In specific, the first task is based on the classic word game of hangman and its goal is for the student to complete five words correctly to progress to the second task of the game which is to present a short story involving the previously completed five words.

The first task of the game has 5 levels, each of increasing difficulty. Each level contains a word that the student needs to fill and a set of letters that represents possible matches to the word's letters that needs to be completed. Additionally, to make it more challenging the student has five "lives" for each word. The given word is presented with the first letter on spot and the rest letters are presented by empty dashes. The student must grab a letter from the given set and place it on an empty dash. On a correct move the letter will be fit on top of the dash and stay there until the word is complete. On a wrong move the letter will change color as an indication of a wrong placement and after that it will disappear, and one player life will be lost.

For each level a pool of words has been created (see Table 1) for an indicative selection of words per game level. The selection of the word on each level is done randomly by the game. As levels advance the number of letters per word increases making it harder for the student to complete the word.

Each time a word is completed the student receives a card representing this word, then the game continues to the next level where the student must find a new word. The game completes when the student wins all levels or when the student ends the game earlier.

For every word the student has 5 wrong guesses. To help the student guess, if two wrong guesses are made, a picture representing the word is shown as help. If the student cannot find the word and loses all the guesses, then a "retry level" option is presented offering a restart of the level again with a new random word. When this option is selected the letters to choose from will be more straight forward as extra help to the student.

This help is given to the student as motivation and encouragement to not give up or have an unpleasant experience. The goal of the game is for the student to complete all the levels without skipping any. Also, it is important to increase students' confidence and thus not lose interest on the game and complete all levels. The completion of the levels is also important for the next part of the game as it allows students to build on the imagination and storytelling when more words are involved.

Table 1. Sample words per game level.

Level 1	Level 2	Level 3	Level 4	Level 5
Words concerning recycling				
Soda can	Waste	Cardboard	Efficiency	Greenhouse compost
Metal	Rubber	Paper bag	Glasshouse	Conservatory
Glass	Bucket	Waste bin	Garbage truck	Regenerate
Oil	Plastic	Trash bag	Disposable	Biowaste
Bin	Plant	Recycle	Ecosystem	Biodegradation
Words concerning Covid-19				
Flu	Medical mask	Hygiene	Quarantine	Social distancing
Virus	Vaccine	Anosmia	Dispenser	Stethoscope
Soap	Gloves	Pandemic	Epidemic	Asymptomatic
Nurse	Hospital	Sanitation	Infection	Contagiousness

As stated, before a word pool has been created for the needs of the game and an indicative set of words is presented on the above table. The difficulty of each level is based on the number of letters in each word. As the levels progress the student has not only more compound words to find but also has to think and understand better the thematic areas of the game.

In respect with the game-flow, players first choose the thematic area and then the game begins by presenting as many dashes as necessary for the word of the first level.

Players use their hand to grasp and move letters that appear on the screen (Fig. 3(a and b)). For each incorrect letter placement, the player loses one live. Player lives are denoted with red hart images.

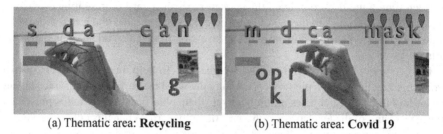

(a) Thematic area: **Recycling**   (b) Thematic area: **Covid 19**

Fig. 3. Virtual Hand Moving Letters

When all letters are placed in the correct position a 2D object representing the word is displayed (Fig. 4). Consequently, in the classroom the teacher gives the student a paper-card corresponding to the word completed in the AR game (Fig. 5). In this way the game materializes Blended learning as students play in both virtual and real worlds.

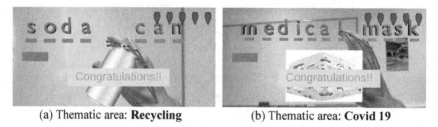

(a) Thematic area: **Recycling**   (b) Thematic area: **Covid 19**

Fig. 4. Completed word and 2D word object

Through storytelling students have the opportunity to develop both their vocabulary and their imagination. They are able to consider new ideas and express them in words.

Once the last game level has been reached and the students have collected all their paper cards, representing the artefacts that describe the words found, they can place them on their desk in any order they want and create their picture story (Fig. 6). Once the paper-cards are in the desired sequence, students can place the mobile device that they use to play the game, e.g. a smart phone or a tablet, on top of the paper-cards to generate the 3D virtual objects (Fig. 6). The story can be presented to and shared with their classmates.

As explained at the Field study Methodology section above our students have been seperated into two groups according to their classroom. The students of the first classroom had at their disposal the teaching tools they use in their daily student life such as the blackboard and the projector. These students played the traditional hangman game and were then asked to write a story related to these words using as many as they could.

Fig. 5. Paper-card icons

(a) Thematic area: **Recycling**   (b) Thematic area: **Covid 19**

Fig. 6. AR based story

The students of the second classroom were given smartphones with the application. During the use of the application they were given additional image paper cards after the successful completion of a word to place them anywhere in the room they wanted. Respectively, these students were asked to create a story. At the end of the process there was a general awareness of students about the issues of recycling and Covid 19.

5 Discussion - Research Outcomes - Results

Research has shown that using GBL in conjunction with AR can help elementary school students develop their vocabulary, become more active in class, and become more aware of important areas such as the areas recycling and Covid 19 that were investigated in our research. Both teachers and students converged in this direction and support the above statement. The table below (Table 2) shows the questions by topic and some typical answers of teachers.

5.1 Field Study Results' Analysis

The following results emerged through participatory observation and interviews with teachers. The students had a great interest and participation in the exploitation of the AR game. It piqued their interest as a new and different teaching tool through which they can learn by playing. At the same time, the teachers were positive with the use of this

Table 2. Questions & typical answers by topic.

Interdisciplinary unified curriculum framework	Questions	Typical answers
Vocabulary - learning tool interdisciplinary learning	Did they develop their vocabulary around the two topics? And how?	"The students learned some new words and understood them through play." "Through the game they began to use in their written word the words they learned"
	Has the spelling improved?	"I saw a slight improvement in their spelling." "Some weak students have significantly improved their spelling on the words in the game"
	How did playing with QR codes help them?	"Almost all students were excited about the game and would like it to be repeated"
Game based learning - alternative motivational training tool	Motivation	"Almost all students wanted to win the game to get the cards with the QR codes"
	Concentration	"While playing the game, the students were completely focused on the screens of their smartphones"
	Engagement	"I saw students with reduced participation be interested and play an important role in all activities"
	Enjoyment	"Rarely do all students rejoice and enjoy the lesson as with the use of the AR game"
Connection with society awareness	Have you noticed any changes in their behavior regarding the issue of recycling?	"I have noticed that most students are now more actively involved in recycling, either inside or outside the school" "They are much more careful about where they put garbage, and they have a lot of ideas for improving recycling in their school and in their area"

(continued)

Table 2. (*continued*)

Interdisciplinary unified curriculum framework	Questions	Typical answers
	Did you notice any changes in their behavior regarding Covid 19?	"The students understood the actions that are necessary to protect themselves and the means at their disposal." "Now they use the sanitary ware for Covid 19 with great comfort and ease"

technology as a teaching tool. They believe that with game involvement teaching goals can be achieved as a result of a pleasant experience. More specifically, the results per thematic unit were the following:

In the field of vocabulary, no significant differences were observed between the two classes. Both in the class that the hangman game was played in the traditional way and in the second class, students developed their vocabulary and their ability to spell. The difference observed between the two classes has to do with the way the students behave. In the first case the students had a similar behavior in relation to the daily lessons. However, in the second case, they considered that they were participating in a game and not that they were taking part in a school lesson.

Significant differences were observed in the part where they used the cards with the QR codes and created their own stories. Students who attended the lesson in the traditional way did not have many ideas as opposed to those who used AR game technology. The students became more active from the moment the teacher announced that they would receive a card when they found a word and seemed to be more enthusiastic. They liked to place the cards with the QR codes in different parts of the classroom, "decorating" it with their own style. In this way they started to have more ideas and to think differently about the stories that the teacher asked them to make. The collaboration between the students increased and they started discussing and proposing thoughts and ideas to each other.

In terms of awareness, in both cases an increase was observed with a slight difference in the part using the AR game. Students in both classes learned about the possibilities offered by recycling and how they can protect themselves and those around them from Covid 19. After the end of the lesson, most of them started coming up with ideas for ways that could improve the spirit of recycling both inside and outside the school. This showed that through various activities within the school, students can become more aware and acquire new habits in their daily lives. In addition, their activities helped them gain a better knowledge and argument to propose changes in the local community. An example is that the students suggested a meeting with the local mayor to raise their concerns and suggest ideas about the recycling framework. This showed that there was a connection between the school and the local community. About Covid 19 the activities helped the students to better understand the dangers and to change some of their daily habits. In addition, they learned to use disinfectants properly and to be vigilant so as not to be exposed to the virus.

5.2 Conclusions

The use of new technologies can help significantly in the learning process if the tools used to fulfill the goals are set by teachers. Using Augmented Reality games as an educational tool can help students in a variety of ways. Students become more active throughout the lesson and are more focused for longer. This helps them to gain more benefits from the course than traditional teaching. In addition, the new way of learning and the different stimuli help them to develop their thinking and their creativity. This was evident in the present study as the stories they created had great diversity, strong signs of imagination and new ideas that these students had not used in the past. This had showed that it is not only the application that matters but the general educational approach that can highlight the potential of technology and is in line with Juhee's findings in paper "Problem-based gaming via an augmented reality mobile game and a printed game in foreign language education" [40].

Using our AR game and the activities that followed, the students got to know better and in depth the areas of recycling and Covid 19. The AR game did not make much difference in terms of improving spelling, but students were more motivated for the lesson and were more positive in continuing until the game was over. Finally, addressing these two important issues of daily life helped students become more aware of recycling and Covid 19, take initiatives and develop active social action.

6 Future Work

The research was carried out during the first semester in only two classes. According to our original schedule, the goal was to expand to more students so that they could get safer and clearer results regarding the relationship between an AR game and the classic learning process. However, the field study was stopped due to the mandatory quarantine that last three months and up to this day. The goal for the future is to continue and add new modules to our AR game that can provide additional information such as the xAPI library which can create data for learning analytics. Through XAPI, the AR game will be able to note players' actions in more detail, as well as the points that made it difficult or aroused their interest to a greater extent. Another point that can be explored in the future is the connection of AR games with the STEM teaching method. In other words, students should combine their ideas with virtual models and then apply them in practice.

References

1. Radu, I.: Augmented reality in education: a meta-review and cross-media analysis. Pers. Ubiquit. Comput. **18**(6), 1533–1543 (2014). https://doi.org/10.1007/s00779-013-0747-y
2. Hamari, J., Shernoff, D.J., Rowe, E., Coller, B., Asbell-Clarke, J., Edwards, T.: Challenging games help students learn: an empirical study on engagement, flow and immersion in game-based learning. Comput. Hum. Behav. **54**, 170–179 (2016)

3. Riemer, V., Schrader, C.: Learning with quizzes, simulations, and adventures: students' attitudes, perceptions and intentions to learn with different types of serious games. Comput. Educ. **88**, 160–168 (2015). https://doi.org/10.1016/j.compedu.2015.05.003

4. Mahayuddin, Z., Saif, A.F.M.: Augmented reality based AR alphabets towards improved learning process in primary education system. JCR **7**(19), 514–521 (2020)

5. Huang, T.C., Chen, C.C., Chou, Y.W.: Animating eco-education: to see, feel, and discover in an augmented reality-based experiential learning environment. Comput. Educ. **96**, 72–82 (2016). https://doi.org/10.1016/j.compedu.2016.02.008

6. Schechter, R., Macaruso, P., Kazakoff, E.R., Brooke, E.: Exploration of a blended learning approach to reading instruction for low SES students in early elementary grades. Comput. Sch. **32**(3–4), 183–200 (2015). https://doi.org/10.1080/07380569.2015.1100652

7. Alarcia, D.T., Barco, D.I.: Videojuegos y aprendizaje de la Historia: la saga Assasin's Creed. Contextos Educativos. Revista de Educación **17**, 145 (2014). https://doi.org/10.18172/con.2598

8. Chu, H.-C., Hung, C.-M.: Effects of the digital game-development approach on elementary school students' learning motivation, problem solving, and learning achievement. Int. J. Distance Educ. Technol., 472–487 (2015). https://doi.org/10.4018/978-1-4666-8200-9.ch023

9. Milgram, P., Kishino, F.: A taxonomy of mixed reality visual displays. IEICE Trans. Inf. Syst. **E77-D**, 1321–1329 (1994)

10. Ronald, T.A.: A survey of augmented reality. Presense **6**(4), 355–385 (1997)

11. Gouidis, F., Panteleris, P., Oikonomidis, I., Argyros, A.: Accurate hand keypoint localization on mobile devices. In: Proceedings of the 16th International Conference on Machine Vision and Applications (MVA) (2019). https://doi.org/10.23919/MVA.2019.8758059

12. Fotaris, P., Mastoras, T., Leinfellner, R., Rosunally, Y.: Climbing up the leaderboard; an empirical study of applying gamification techniques to a computer programming class. Electr. J. E-learn. **14**(2), 94–110 (2016)

13. Sitzmann, T.: A meta-analytic examination of the instruction effectiveness of computer-based simulation games. Pers. Psychol. **64**, 489–528 (2011)

14. Prensky, M.: Digital Game-Based Learning. McGraw-Hill, New York (2007). https://doi.org/10.1145/950566.950567

15. Enyedy, N., Danish, J. A., Delacruz, G., Kumar, M.: Learning physics through play in an augmented reality environment. Int. J. Comput. Support. Collab. Learn. **7**(3) (2012). https://doi.org/10.1007/s11412-012-9150-3

16. Bacca, J., Baldiris, S., Fabregat, R., Graf, S., Kinshuk: Augmented reality trends in education: a systematic review of research and applications. Educ. Technol. Soc. **17**(4), 133–149 (2014).

17. Cai, S., Chiang, F.K., Sun, Y., Lin, C., Lee, J.J.: Applications of augmented reality-based natural interactive learning in magnetic field instruction. Interact. Learn. Environ. **25**(6), 778–791 (2017). https://doi.org/10.1080/10494820.2016.1181094

18. Laine, T.H., Nygren, E., Dirin, A., Suk, H.J.: Science spots AR: a platform for science learning games with augmented reality. Educ. Technol. Res. Dev. **64**, 507–531 (2016)

19. Alakärppä, I.; Jaakkola, E.; Väyrynen, J.; Häkkilä, J.: Using nature elements in mobile AR for education with children. In: Proceedings of the 19th International Conference on Human-Computer Interaction with Mobile Devices and Services, Vienna, Austria, 4–7 September (2017)

20. Hockly, N.: Augmented reality. ELT J. **73**(3), 328–334 (2019)

21. Shabalina, O., Malliarakis, C., Tomos, F., Mozelius, P.: Game-based learning for learning to program: from learning through play to learning through game development. In: Pivec, M., Gründler, J. (eds.) Proceedings of the European Conference on Games Based Learning, vol. 11, pp. 571–576. Academic Conferences and Publishing International Limited, Reading, UK (2017)

22. Oranç, C., Küntay, A.C.: Learning from the real and the virtual worlds: Educational use of augmented reality in early childhood. Int. J. Child-Comput. Interact. **21**, 104–111 (2019). https://doi.org/10.1016/j.ijcci.2019.06.002

23. Hirsh-Pasek, K., Zosh, J.M., Golinkoff, R.M., Gray, J.H., Robb, M.B., Kaufman, J.: Putting education in educational apps: lessons from the science of learning. Psychol. Sci. Public Interest. **16**, 3–34 (2015). https://doi.org/10.1177/1529100615569721

24. Tobar-Muñoz, H., Baldiris, S., Fabregat, R.: Augmented reality game-based learning: enriching students' experience during reading comprehension activities. J. Educ. Comput. Res. **55**(7), 901–936 (2017)

25. Mwakapina, W., Mhandeni, J.S., Nyinondi, O.: WhatsApp mobile tool in second language learning: opportunities, potentials and challenges in higher education settings in Tanzania. Int. J. English Lang. Educ. **4**(2), 70 (2016). https://doi.org/10.5296/ijele.v4i2.9711

26. Önal, N., Çevik, K.K., Şenol, V., Önal, N.: The effect of SOS Table learning environment on mobile learning tools acceptance, motivation and mobile learning attitude in English language learning. Interact. Learn. Environ., 1–14. https://doi.org/10.1080/10494820.2019.1690529

27. Alemi, M., Meghdari, A., Ghazisaedy, M.: The impact of social robotics on L2 learners' anxiety and attitude in English vocabulary acquisition. Int. J. Soc. Robot. **7**(4), 523–535 (2015). https://doi.org/10.1007/s12369-015-0286-y

28. Gilakjani, A.P., Branch, L., Branch, L.: A review of the literature on the integration of technology into the learning and teaching of English language skills. Int. J. English Linguist. **7**(5), 95–106 (2017). https://doi.org/10.5539/ijel.v7n5p95

29. Berns, A., Isla-Montes, J.-L., Palomo-Duarte, M., Dodero, J.-M.: Motivation, students' needs and learning outcomes: a hybrid game-based app for enhanced language learning. Springerplus **5**(1), 1305 (2016). https://doi.org/10.1186/s40064-016-2971-1

30. Butler, Y.G.: The use of computer games as foreign language learning tasks for digital natives. System **54**, 91–102 (2015). https://doi.org/10.1016/j.system.2014.10.010

31. Hwang, W.-Y., Shih, T.K., Ma, Z.-H., Shadiev, R., Chen, S.-Y.: Evaluating listening and speaking skills in a mobile game-based learning environment with situational contexts. Comput. Assist. Lang. Learn. **29**(4), 639–657 (2016). https://doi.org/10.1080/09588221.2015.1016438

32. Le, H.Q., Kim, J.I.: An augmented reality application with hand gestures for learning 3D geometry. In: 2017 IEEE International Conference on Big Data and Smart Computing, BigComp, pp. 34–41 (2017). https://doi.org/10.1109/BIGCOMP.2017.7881712

33. Cui, C., Sourin, A.: Mid-air interaction with optical tracking for 3D modeling. Comput. Graph. **74**, 1–11 (2018). https://doi.org/10.1016/j.cag.2018.04.004

34. Kim, J.S., Park, J.M.: Direct and realistic handover of a virtual object. In: IEEE International Conference on Intelligent Robots and Systems, vol. 2016, pp. 994–999 (2016). https://doi.org/10.1109/IROS.2016.7759170

35. Liu, H., et al.: High-fidelity grasping in virtual reality using a glove-based system. In: Proceedings of the IEEE Conference on Robotics and Automation, vol. 2019, pp. 5180–5186 (2019). https://doi.org/10.1109/ICRA.2019.8794230

36. Wu, Y., Wang, C.M.: Applying hand gesture recognition and joint tracking to a TV controller using CNN and Convolutional Pose Machine. In: Proceedings of the International Conference on Pattern Recognition, vol. 2018, pp. 3086–3091 (2018). https://doi.org/10.1109/ICPR.2018.8546209

37. Kyriakou, P., Hermon, S.: Can i touch this? Using natural interaction in a museum augmented reality system. Digit. Appl. Archaeol. Cult. Herit. **12**, 1–9 (2019). https://doi.org/10.1016/j.daach.2018.e00088

38. Sdravopoulou, K., Castillo, J.J.G., González, J.M.M.: Naturalistic approaches applied to AR technology: an evaluation. Educ. Inf. Technol. **26**(1), 683–697 (2020). https://doi.org/10.1007/s10639-020-10283-4

39. Victor, D.: HandTrack: a library for prototyping real-time hand tracking interfaces using convolutional neural networks, GitHub Repos. (2017). https://github.com/victordibia/handtr acking/tree/master/docs/handtrack.pdf

40. Juhee, L.: Problem-based gaming via an augmented reality mobile game and a printed game in foreign language education. Educ. Inf. Technol. (2020).https://doi.org/10.1007/s10639-020-10391-1

41. Parmaxi, A., Demetriou, A.A.: Augmented reality in language learning: a state-of-the-art review of 2014–2019. J. Comput. Assist. Learn. **36**(6), 861–875 (2020). https://doi.org/10.1111/jcal.12486

42. Martinez, A.A., Benito, J.R.L., Gonzalez, E.A., Ajuria, E.B.: An experience of the application of augmented reality to learn English in infant education. In: 2017 International Symposium on Computers in Education, SIIE 2017, vol. 2018, pp. 1–6 (2017). https://doi.org/10.1109/SIIE.2017.8259645

43. Dalim, C.S.C., Piumsomboon, T., Dey, A., Billinghurst, M., Sunar, S.: TeachAR: an interactive augmented reality tool for teaching basic English to non-native children. In: Adjunct Proceedings of the 2016 IEEE International Symposium on Mixed and Augmented Reality, ISMAR-Adjunct 2016, pp. 344–345 (2017). https://doi.org/10.1109/ISMAR-Adjunct.2016.0113

44. Solak, E., Cakır, R.: Investigating the role of augmented reality technology in the language classroom . Croatian J. Educ. **18**(4), 1067–1085 (2017). https://doi.org/10.15516/cje.v18i4.1729

45. Yilmaz, R.M., Goktas, Y.: Using augmented reality technology in storytelling activities: examining elementary students' narrative skill and creativity. Virtual Reality **21**(2), 75–89 (2016). https://doi.org/10.1007/s10055-016-0300-1

46. Tobar-Muñoz, H., Baldiris, S., Fabregat, R.: Augmented reality game-based learning: enriching students' experience during reading comprehension activities. J. Educ. Comput. Res. **55**(7), 901–936 (2017). https://doi.org/10.1177/0735633116689789

47. Bartholomew, K., Henderson, A.J.Z., Marcia, J.E.: Coding semi-structured interviews in social psychological research. In: Reis, H., Judd, C.M. (eds.) Handbook of Research Methods in Social and Personality Psychology, pp. 286–312. Cambridge University Press, Cambridge (2000)

48. Lapassade, G.: L'observation participante. In: Hess, R., Gabriele, W. (eds.) L'observation participante. Paris. ECONOMICA, Anthropos (2006)

49. Hall, G.: Recent developments in uses of literature in language teaching. In: Teranishi, M., Saito, Y., Wales, K. (eds.) Literature and Language Learning in the EFL Classroom, pp. 13–25. Palgrave Macmillan, London (2015). https://doi.org/10.1057/9781137443663_2

50. Calvo-Ferrer, J.R.: Educational games as stand-alone learning tools and their motivational effect on L2 vocabulary acquisition and perceived learning gains. Br. J. Edu. Technol. **48**(2), 264–278 (2017)

51. Ragatz, C. M.: Playing vocabulary games and learning academic language with gifted elementary students (Doctoral dissertation). Retrieved from ProQuest Dissertations & Theses Global. (Order No. 3689691) (2015)

52. Taheri, M.: The effect of using language games on vocabulary retention of Iranian elementary EFL learners. J. Lang. Teach. Res. **5**(3), 544–549 (2014). https://doi.org/10.4304/jltr.5.3.544-549

53. Casañ-Pitarch, R.: Gamifying content and language integrated learning with serious video-games. J. Lang. Educ. **3**(3), 107–114 (2017)

54. Vidakis, N., Barianos, A.K., Trampas, A.M., Papadakis, S., Kalogiannakis, M., Vassilakis, K.: Generating education in-game data: the case of an ancient theatre serious game. In: Proceedings of the 11th International Conference on Computer Supported Education, CSEDU 2019, vol. 1, pp. 36–43 (2019)
55. Vidakis, N., Syntychakis, E., Kalafatis, K., Christinaki, E., Triantafyllidis, G.: Ludic educational game creation tool: teaching schoolers road safety. In: Antona, M., Stephanidis, C. (eds.) UAHCI 2015. LNCS, vol. 9177, pp. 565–576. Springer, Cham (2015). https://doi.org/10.1007/978-3-319-20684-4_55

Educational Video Game Design for Teaching and Learning Musical Harmony

Daniela Medel[1]([envelope]) and Jaime Sánchez[2]

[1] Universidad de Las Artes, Ciencias, y Comunicaciones (UNIACC), Santiago, Chile
daniela.medel@uniacc.edu
[2] Universidad de Chile (UChile), Santiago, Chile
jsanchez@dcc.uchile.cl

Abstract. Video games are used as tools for the educational process in various areas of knowledge, including language, mathematics, history, and many others. However, its use for teaching and learning musical harmony is limited.

This research aims to propose the design of a prototype of a video game for teaching and learning musical harmony. For this, the study is based on the social constructivist theory of learning, promoting a greater connection with intrinsic motivation and collaborative learning to achieve the learning contents. To attain this goal, a Research and Development (R&D) methodology was implemented. This methodology is divided into two parts: (1) Research until reaching a product, which, in this case, is a design prototype; (2) product evaluation and improvement for implementation.

First, we proposed a design prototype based on research and design principles, and then, we evaluated the design usability. This evaluation reviews the interfaces and how the user interacts with the game.

We applied various usability methods taking into consideration aspects of interface, playability, and education. We also redesigned the original prototype and improved it based on the evaluations' results to accomplish the final design prototype. In summary, we designed a video game prototype for teaching musical harmony based on the social constructivist theory of education and fully validated it by using diverse usability testing methods.

Keywords: Musical harmony · Music education · Technology in education · Serious video games · Video games in music education · Social constructivism · Intrinsic motivation · Usability · Evaluation of games

1 Introduction

The musical language is a fundamental part of the study of music. This set of organized elements allows us to understand what we hear, read, and play to interpret, create and communicate through this art. However, its study is not trivial since it comprises multiple parameters (rhythms, melodic gestures, pitches, attacks, intensities, speeds), and, specifically in the area of harmony, interval, and chord logics, which can become a barrier incomprehensible to students with low motivation.

© Springer Nature Switzerland AG 2021
P. Zaphiris and A. Ioannou (Eds.): HCII 2021, LNCS 12785, pp. 65–83, 2021.
https://doi.org/10.1007/978-3-030-77943-6_5

Then the question arises. What is it that makes something motivating or entertaining to learn?

Ultimately this is the key to the commitment that a person has to an activity. The flow generated by an activity motivates someone to carry it out despite having difficult and tedious challenges. Flow is that "zone" in which one is completely focused on a specific activity. When experiencing flow in any activity, which can be a game, a physical activity, or even a religious experience, the person is fully aware and concentrated on the acts or challenges of the activity itself, not on their problems or the outside world. The existence of flow is what makes people do the activity again [3].

How can we bring this concept to the design of a pedagogical tool so that it captivates the student as well as educates him/her?

To answer this question, we will work with one of the immersive agents par excellence: the video game. As an educational tool, the video game can be an important contribution to the individual's intrinsic motivation as it is "deeply engaging, visually dynamic, rapidly paced, effective tools for exposing students to knowledge" [6] (p. 2). Video games deal with a playful tension between pleasure and desire that can generate a powerful intrinsic motivation source [4].

2   Theoretical Framework

When integrating technologies in education, the fundamental thing we should consider is that they have to be used harmoniously and functionally to the learning goals since technologies are not an end by themselves, but a learning tool that must go in subordination to an educational purpose. The focus must always be centered on the educational objective and use information and communication technologies (ICT) in an "invisible" way [18].

The use of ICT enhances learning in groups of students, mentioning as advantages such as the development of transversal competencies, the increase of student participation, the interaction between students, improvements in learning and motivation, among others [8].

As we mentioned earlier, the use of ICT is not an end in itself and have also be accompanied by a theory of knowledge. Social constructivism affirms that knowledge cannot be transferred intact from the teacher's brain to that of the student, but is the student who interprets and decodes, with their own previous experiences, what is transmitted by the teacher [2]. Deep down, the teacher can teach something and can be as many interpretations of what is taught as there are students in the class. In this sense, the teacher should be a facilitator and provider of tools for constructing meanings since it is essential for the student to understand how they learn and not just what they learn.

Sánchez [18] emphasizes the idea of experiencing knowledge through the senses and, in an active way, being able to make sense of the world from one's own experiences, beliefs, mental structures, or ideas that one has to interpret objects and events. He proposes that to address the use of ICT in education, one have do it from a constructivist perspective instead of the objectivist one that sees the student as someone who has to "absorb" content that the teacher transfers.

This learning theory also emphasizes the importance of interacting with other knowledgeable individuals, stating that it would otherwise be impossible to make sense of symbol systems and learn to use them. A child does not learn to speak by interacting only with other children, and they must interact with adults who use language to develop these skills [13].

Learning with video games is among the multiple possibilities that technologies offer us in education, and they can be used as autonomous learning tools inside and outside the classroom, evidencing excellent results.

It is important to emphasize that games can be effective learning environments, not because they are "fun", but because they are immersive, require the player to make frequent and important decisions, and have clear objectives, in addition to developing social skills [17]. Video games specifically promote cognitive skills such as attention, executive functions, and visuospatial skills and incorporate good pedagogical practices: a system of progressive practices with increasing levels of difficulty, positive reinforcement, and systems of progress, achievements, and rewards.

To take advantage of the benefits that the educational video game can give us, such as cognitive development, memory, language, perception, problem-solving, and planning, among others [10], it must comply, in general, with some basic requirements [4]:

1. Knowledge must be within interactions and not as static information.
2. Players should be provided with ways to confront and evaluate the rules, experiencing meaningful feedback to their inputs.
3. Eliminate barriers that prevent the use of the game. Evaluate and calibrate the usability of the game.
4. The design must provide players with alternatives and space that allows for daring, creativity, and exploration - critical aspects of fun and learning.
5. Games should promote communication to collaborate, negotiate, draw, and compete. Players can discuss game-related issues during play, fostering game strategy and broader socialization, possibly continuing the game afterward.

In his book The Design of Everyday Things [16], Donald Norman talks about the principles that a good interface design of an application must fulfill, such as: Visibility. Important parts must be visible and convey the right message. Affordances. They are the properties that determine how an element/object/tool/technology can be used. When affordances are exploited, the user knows what to do just by looking - so no image, label, or instruction is required. Mental Model. The conceptions and models we have of our environment and ourselves. Conceptual Model. Mental model applied to objects. A good conceptual model allows us to predict the effects of our actions on objects. Mapping. The relationship of controls with their functions. Feedback. Feedback on actions that the user has carried out (or is being carried out) and what results have been achieved, showing the effect of an action.

Now that mobile devices exist everywhere, we can access information in a new format. While we can apply the same design principles, websites must have a mobile format or a downloadable application made especially for that format, taking into account the limitations of the devices themselves, such as screen size or storage capacity. This transforms the user's context, and their needs completely change. When considering an application to be viewed from a mobile device, the processing capacity, small screens, screens with different resolutions, and the data entry method should be considered [5].

For example, buttons should be bigger to be pressed with your fingers, animations should not be too heavy, and images should look good in small dimensions.

3 Methodology

Two aspects are essential in creating an educational video game: the pedagogical aspect and the game's design. From the pedagogical point of view, we considered learning theory, content design, and learning strategy. In the game's design, we considered design principles and aspects of a game that allows fun and immersion [11]. The research method used for this project is Research and Development (R&D). This type of research in education is based on the results of an investigation being used to design new products, which are then evaluated and refined to reach the required quality standard [9]. It can be divided into two parts:

- Research until creating a product: The product we reached in this part was the prototype of the video game's design.
- Evaluation and improvements of the product for its implementation: The product we reached in this second part was an improved video game design prototype based on the usability evaluations carried out.

4 Prototype

4.1 End-User and Context

The context where this application could be used can be both in musical language classes, with a teacher's guidance, or in any other place. The advantage of making an application for mobile devices is how easy the user can access it from anywhere. The multiple levels of difficulty allow for a wide range of player types, from beginners to connoisseurs to experts, which perhaps would motivate the study in beginning students. Three users were defined: *Amateurs*, those with no formal music studies. They are those who practice an instrument as a hobby. *Students*, learners of some instrument, composition or musical education for professional purposes. *Professionals*, musicians dedicated to the interpretation, composition, or teaching of music.

Users must be over 15 years of age, with normal hearing and basic mobile device handling.

4.2 Type of Game

Since music is a language, and since every language has rules, the idea of creating a Scrabble-like crossword game came up. The American code, which uses letters of the alphabet to refer to notes, is a much more universal language, and this is why we have chosen this code. In the American code, the letter A is la, B is si, C is do, D is re, E is mi, F is fa, and G is sol. With the letters, different chords can be built within a key, taking advantage of the notes that these chords have in common. Considering tonal harmony rules, we can navigate through different tonalities through tension chords (dominants) that lead us to different rests (tonic). Thus, crossword puzzles with chords can be constructed by occupying the letters that correspond to scale notes within the tonality. The game has different levels of difficulty that we defined according to the following:

By achievements. As the player improves, s/he can unlock stages or rewards within the game.

By option. Once a stage has been passed, the player can replay it to improve their skills and achieve higher goals.

By other players. Depending on the player's skills (s) being played with, the game can be made more or less challenging.

The game's objective is to obtain the game's highest score and move up on the different categories. To achieve this, the player must build chords with the given tiles and the ones on the board and use the best harmony strategies to build chords within a tonal context, taking advantage of reward boxes.

It is important to emphasize how fundamental it is for meeting the criteria for a successful design of an educational video game, the fact that this is an online multiplayer video game. Interaction with other players is essential within the conception of social constructivism proposed in this project. For this reason, it is essential to play with other people and not just with artificial intelligence. The importance of doing it online is the ability to play from anywhere and at any time and play several games at the same time without the need to do it synchronously.

We defined the name *ToneCluster* for the video game. Cluster is a term used in music to refer to an agglomeration of notes. As the same term is used in other disciplines, we decided to add the word Tone to give it the particularity of music.

4.3 Visual Design

Although mobile devices have many advantages, the screen's size limitation requires that the user interfaces have a design according to space and comply well with the proposed functionalities.

The interface is intended to be as straightforward as possible, and the intention was not to put excessive information within them. We designed large and clear buttons that make it easy to identify the possibilities of the application. We based most icons on successful and popular icons, and we expected them to be user-friendly. The application includes a chat that allows commenting on questions or thoughts with other users, so the group's collaboration is essential.

There is constant feedback during the game to account for what is happening and what will happen. The user knows who is playing and is notified when it is his/her turn (see Fig. 1).

Home. On this interface, we find all the functions of the application. We can enter the User and Messages page at the top. Then we can go to the active games and continue playing with other players' pending games and, in an attractive button, start a new game. The application has six buttons with independent icons to enter the Piano, the Circle of Fifths, Harmonic Functions, Rules, Friends, and Settings.

User. Here we can see the achievements and the level at which the user is in the game.

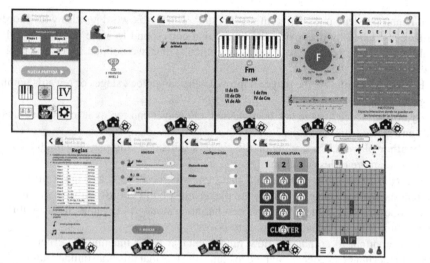

Fig. 1. Home, User, Messages, Piano, Circle of Fifths, Harmonic Functions, Rules, Friends, Settings, Stages, and Game interfaces.

Messages. On this interface, we can see the messages or invitations left by other players.
Piano. Here an interactive piano is displayed where we can build intervals and chords of all kinds. It also indicates what function this chord fulfills in different keys.
Circle of Fifths. On this interface, we will find the circle of fifths where you can explore the different major and minor keys, and learn about the different scales' alterations.
Harmonic Functions. On this interface, we can choose any key and indicate what the functions of that key are in major and minor mode.
Rules. Here are the general rules of the game.
Friends. Here we can see our friends and add friends from Facebook or Google. Also, players can be found within the same application and added as friends to play with them. In this interface, we can chat and see if we are connected to play.
Settings. Here we can make basic game settings.
Stages. To unlock a stage of the game, we must win the previous stage at least once.
Game. After choosing friends and the level at which we will play, we get to the game itself. Here the board and different functions are displayed to help in the performance of the game.

5   Measured Usability Attributes

We subjected the prototype to usability tests that revealed possible improvements in the video game's interaction and interface. As it is a video game design project, some aspects cannot yet be measured concerning pedagogical results. However, we have evaluated three important aspects to assess the prototype and propose an informed video game design: interface, playability, and education [1].

We evaluated five aspects of interfaces and eight aspects of education and playability.
Interfaces - Nielsen interface attributes [14].

Learning. The user quickly learns the interface.

Efficiency. The interface is efficient in its use.

Memorability. The interface is easy to remember.

Error. The interface has a low error rate.

Satisfaction. The interface is pleasant to use.

Education and gameplay: EGameFlow attributes [7].

Concentration. Games must require concentration, and the player must be able to concentrate on the game.

Challenges. Games must be challenging enough and match the skill level of the player.

Autonomy. Players must have a sense of control over their actions in the game.

Purpose clarity. Games must provide the player with clear goals at the right times.

Feedback. Players should get the right feedback at the right times.

Immersion. Players should experience deep but effortless participation in the game.

Social interaction. Games should support and create opportunities for social interaction.

Enhance knowledge. The game promotes and enhances the player's learning.

6 Methods and Usability Instruments

As we are in a COVID-19 pandemic emergency, usability evaluations have not been possible in presence, and, therefore, we prepared online questionnaires through Google forms and meetings through the Zoom platform. We built an interactive prototype and a video with the interactions and possibilities that the application would have in a mobile device context. We invited some users to play with a cardboard prototype in order to respond to the playability aspects. Finally, we summoned a focus group to close the usability tests. We carried out the evaluations in the following order:

6.1 Icon Usability

This method is of icon intuitiveness [15]. Different icons are shown to the user and asked what s/he thinks it represents. The answers give an account of the degree to which the chosen graph is similar to the represented concept. This method is suitable for evaluation since it allows obtaining a background regarding the efficiency and memorability of the use of icons and anticipating a low rate of errors in their development.

It was essential to implement this open questionnaire first, as users did not have to know what function the icons had. In this way, we collected intuitive responses to icons.

An open questionnaire with six icons (see Fig. 2) was sent with the questions "What do you suggest this button can do?" and "Name three concepts to describe the image."

Eight users carried out this evaluation: 4 amateurs, 3 professionals, and 1 student. We made a cloud of concepts to analyze these results and observed the trend and convergence.

Icon 1: Friends button. It takes the user to the interface where the user's friends are. Overall this icon was well understood and resulted in a meaningful cloud of concepts. Concepts such as multiplayer, friends, sharing, connecting, and people were repeated,

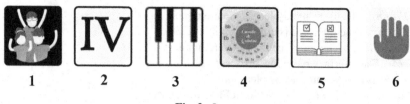

Fig. 2. Icons

suggesting that it is a reasonably intuitive icon. There are no concepts that are far from what the icon intended to represent.

Icon 2: Functions button. It takes the user to explore the functions in different keys. This icon presented problems as it is not intuitive for those unfamiliar with the concept of harmonic functions in music. Those users in the fan group did not understand the purpose of this button. On the other hand, those who did know about harmonic functions did not know what this button could do. While they are familiar with the concept of musical grades, many said four, fourth grade, subdominant.

Icon 3: Piano button. It takes the user to the interface that has an interactive piano. This icon was one of the most intuitive. There were no concepts far from the idea of a piano, and the idea of a virtual piano or keyboard appeared quite a bit in the concept cloud.

Icon 4: Circle of Fifths button. It takes the user to a place for interaction with the circle of fifths. This icon presented problems in the amateurs' group since it is a concept widely used in music theory. Among amateurs, the concept of "roulette" appeared. However, among students and professionals, the concept was fully understood and very intuitive.

Icon 5: Rules button. It takes the user to the general rules of the game. This is another icon that presented problems since none of the answers pointed to what we expected. Concepts like "correct", "questionnaire" and "evaluation" were quite common.

Icon 6: Question button. This icon is used to ask another player for explanations for a move made. According to the evaluation responses, this icon is quite intuitive. Being a red hand, our mental model immediately tells us "stop", "error", "attention", concepts that were repeated a lot in the concepts used to describe this image. It works by being a button that stops a process, or, in this case, the game's progress.

As a summary, the result of this evaluation revealed that icons 1, 3, and 6 were very intuitive. However, icons 2 and 5 should be corrected as they do not symbolize what we expected. Icon 4 was only identified by the student and professionals since it is a concept handled in music.

6.2 End-User Questionnaire

This method consists of the end-users completing a questionnaire after interacting with the application and/or the game. Since it is an evaluation during the design process, to carry out this questionnaire, we sent a prototype with interactions recorded on video, demonstrating how the application works and a prototype with limited but interactive functions. We invited some users to play in a cardboard prototype to account for aspects of gameplay and education. However, complications derived from the health emergency caused by the COVID-19 pandemic forced us to take an alternative by creating an online game with the Gamestructor online program.

This method is suitable to measure preliminary aspects of the video game development that account for the usability of the interface, playability, and educational possibilities and visualize them in comparative tables or graphs.

To demonstrate usability aspects of the video game interfaces and, in turn, learning and playability, we used two questionnaires:

Videogame Usability Questionnaire. Elaborated by Jaime Sánchez (updated version, 2020) [19]. This questionnaire assesses the usability aspects of videogame interfaces. As it was an evaluation during the videogame design process, the statement "Interfaces load quickly" was eliminated since this statement does not make sense in evaluating a prototype. Twenty-three users carried out this evaluation: 7 amateurs, 8 professionals, and 8 students. For the analysis of this questionnaire, bar graphs were made as a complete set and separating the different users. Also, we reviewed the comment of each user to reveal possible improvements to the prototype.

Fig. 3. Answers to question "How would you qualify the current game?"

The assertions evaluated in the questionnaire were mainly between the ranges "Strongly agree" and "Agree", which gives an impression of a positive response to the video game in general. This is reinforced by the graphic in Fig. 3, where the video game is very well accepted, where 22 out of 23 users rated it between "excellent" and "good". When we see the graphics of the type of user, we realize that the video game's appreciation is more significant among students. In turn, each group's comments also revealed that the most interested in the game were students, who found it entertaining and useful to learn. Those with the least interest were amateurs, as they found it challenging to learn. However, it was also well received by these end-users. The professionals had a favorable opinion, especially from the educational field. The color of the game was somewhat criticized.

EGameFlow. We specifically used a test constructed by Fu et al. [7], called EGame-Flow, to evaluate educational video games based on the attributes raised by Sweetser and Wyeth [21]. This questionnaire's aspects are Concentration, Clear objectives, Feedback, Challenges, Autonomy, Immersion, Social interaction, and Enhance knowledge. After

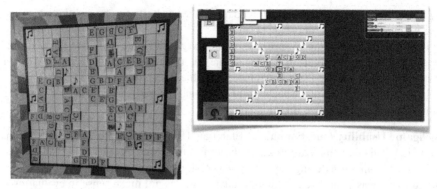

Fig. 4. Cardboard prototype and online game prototype made with Gamestructor.

playing the game in person or online through the Gamestructor platform (see Fig. 4), the users carried out this questionnaire. Nine users carried out this evaluation: 4 professionals, 2 students and 3 amateurs. We made graphs to analyze the results and show the different scores for each user's assertions. We separated them into attributes.

- Concentration: The average evaluation of this attribute was 6.7 out of 7.0. This accounts for a high concentration on the part of the players with the video game.
- Clarity of Objective: The average evaluation of this attribute was 6.6. In general, the objectives seem to be well planned.
- Feedback: The average evaluation of this attribute was 6.5. There are feedback events during the game to account for the player's progress, although there are discrepancies among users in terms of task and event notifications.
- Challenges: The average evaluation of this attribute was 5.9. The challenge levels are adequate. However, more support is needed from the game to solve them.
- Autonomy: The average evaluation of this attribute was 6.1. Some users report a feeling of lack of control and impact on the game. However, the steps to follow for the development of the game are understood.
- Immersion: The average evaluation of this attribute was 5.8. The player manages to have a feeling of immersion in the game. However, there is a low level of emotional or visceral involvement in the game in some players.
- Social interaction: The average evaluation of this attribute was 5.8. The evaluation shows a lack of support for learning communities inside and outside the game. Players are not very cooperative with other players.
- Knowledge improvement: The average evaluation of this attribute was 6.9. This shows that the video game meets the proposed educational objectives and enhances the knowledge of whoever plays it.

6.3 Prototype Evaluation

This method consists of presenting the user with different interfaces to collect their impressions and comments. This method is suitable for this evaluation since it allows obtaining information from users directly and shows possible improvements in the prototype interface.

Seven interfaces (see Fig. 1) were sent to the users with the instruction "Would you change something about this interface?" We applied this open questionnaire after the end-user questionnaire since here users already know the functions of the different buttons and interfaces before making comments about possible improvements to the prototype.

The results of the open questionnaire were the following:

Interface 1: Home. The main criticism of this interface was the color palette used. However, it is intuitive and works well.

Interface 2: Stages. Criticism of the color palette appears again. However, it works and is simple and straightforward.

Interface 3: User. More achievement statistics are needed. However, it works well and is transparent.

Interface 4: Piano. A good idea came up from the comments by suggesting the keyboard's horizontality, making it difficult to manipulate a small keyboard with the fingers.

Interface 5: Friends. This interface was quite liked.

Interface 6: Circle of Fifths. The main problem is the size of the objects. However, it stands out that it is simple and clear.

Interface 7: Game. Criticism of the color palette arises again. In general, the users did not like the layout of the board.

6.4 Heuristic Evaluation Questionnaire

This method consists of the evaluation of the application by experts in human-computer interaction. Since it is an evaluation during the design process, to carry out this questionnaire, we sent the same video and prototype as those sent to the users who took the End User Questionnaire. This method is suitable for obtaining an expert point of view in the area of usability.

The Heuristic Evaluation of the Usability of Videogames Questionnaire was prepared by Jaime Sánchez (updated version, 2020) [20]. As it is an evaluation during the design process, the option "Does not apply" was added to the evaluation to give the evaluator the possibility of not answering certain statements that do not make sense within the prototype evaluation. We evaluated 13 heuristics:

- Video game status visibility
- Relationship between the video game and the real world
- Player control and freedom
- Consistency and standards
- Error prevention
- Recognize instead of remembering
- Flexibility and efficiency of use
- Aesthetics and minimalist design
- Recognition, diagnosis, and recovery of errors

- Help and documentation
- Treatment of content
- Speed and media
- Interactivity

We obtained the heuristic evaluation of two experts in usability and human-computer interaction. The answers were not so far apart from each other, showing elements to improve. The lowest rated heuristics were "Error prevention", "Error recognition, diagnosis, and recovery", and "Help and documentation". The best evaluated were "Recognize instead of remembering", "Interactivity", "Video game visibility", and "Player control and freedom".

We received opinions from the evaluators highlighting positive aspects of the application interfaces and things to improve.

Things to improve:

- Indicate in the interface of a game the stage that is being played at that moment.
- Check the "share" button on the game board interface since it can suggest a page change by being on the left side.
- Review the feedback screen at the top since it looks like a button.

Positive things:

- The button to play a new game stands out from the rest.
- Top bar with standard elements such as user, notifications, and button to go back.
- Important shortcuts at the bottom (friends, the home page, and settings) with easy to understand icons.
- In the "friends" interface, the green circles are highlighted to indicate users' connection in the application.
- One can clearly see which person is playing in the game.
- There is quite a bit of feedback when interacting with buttons.

6.5 Focus Group

This method is a relatively informal technique to attend to the user's needs and feelings and can be done before, during, or after making a design. This method is suitable since concepts can be discussed and problems identified more freely. They produce data at three levels of analysis:

- Data at the individual analysis level.
- Degree of consensus within the group, collecting data at the level of group analysis.
- Specific exchanges that take place between individuals, which could generate new ideas or hypotheses that the researcher can explore later.

We made this evaluation to close the usability tests and address three significant issues: Interface, education, and fun. We organized an online focus group through the Zoom platform with seven users: 2 professionals, 3 amateurs, and 2 students. Following the previous evaluations, we developed six guiding questions for the focus group:

- Is it an entertaining video game? Why?
- In what contexts do you think the video game application could be used?
- What educational elements do you think are enhanced with the use of this tool?
- Is there something that you find unnecessary in the design of the video game or application?
- Is there something that you think is fundamental in the design of the video game or the application?
- What is your opinion of the artificial intelligence of the game?

In general, the acceptance of the video game is high, and there are good expectations from users for the development of the application for mobile devices. Users find it an entertaining and immersive game. It allows concentration and abstraction from the environment, and it is quite challenging and competitive. It is easy to learn but challenging to master.

Users believe that the use of the application can take place in a classroom and leisure context. It could be given as a playful space or, even, as a pause within a class. It allows access to knowledge from other ways. It allows generating breaks in the development of the music theory class and thus capturing the student's interest in the study of harmony.

Regarding the pedagogical aspects, it allows a speed in the understanding and practice of harmony. It helps to take learning out of context and position it in a playful space. It helps with adequate vocabulary in music and with connection to the practical world. By working on theoretical elements in a virtual environment, it is easier to take it to the real world since the language is the same. The idea of holding tournaments, or creating evaluations based on the game, came up.

Regarding the use of artificial intelligence, it was suggested to allow the player to decide whether to maintain it. Artificial intelligence allows you to play and learn autonomously, but you could deactivate it and access another level of challenges when playing with other people. For example, a score could be earned for correcting another player.

A concern in the group's conversation was how tiring it was if the game was too long. It was suggested to lower the number of chips in the most difficult stages or incorporate clauses to finish the game earlier. It would be nice if the player could choose his/her type of game. For example, speed game, long game and short game. The user could also add the variable time as another level of challenge.

7 Analysis of the Results

In this project, we applied usability methods, using evaluation instruments with end-users, during the videogame design process of ToneCluster. We detected strengths and weaknesses in different aspects according to the attributes mentioned in Sect. 5.

Learning. According to the evaluations, it is not difficult to learn, and the interfaces are quite intuitive. However, there are discrepancies between fans and the rest of the users since it is more difficult for them as they have less basic knowledge of music.

Efficiency. The interfaces are efficient when used. The buttons make sense within the interface, and there are intuitive ways to get to places. However, by themselves, some icons do not produce meaning for all types of users. There is a discrepancy between fans and the rest of the users as they have less basic theoretical knowledge, making some icons less obvious.

Memorability. The interfaces are easy to remember, and the user can return to the previous interface easily and intuitively.

Error. Although the way to get to the interfaces is intuitive, the ways to solve errors in the interaction were not evident in the prototype. There is no help within the application.

Satisfaction. The interfaces are pleasant to the user and help to have a good experience during the game. However, the colors used were quite criticized and require a review for the video game's final design.

Concentration. The user manages to maintain concentration during the game and is not distracted from the tasks s/he should concentrate on. The workload seems adequate, although we have to review the game's duration in the more difficult stages and find ways to finish the game in a better way.

Clarity of the objective. The game has clear and adequately presented objectives that allow the smooth development of the same. However, it is suggested that at the beginning of each game, the specific characteristics of the level are remembered, and more feedback be given in each play.

Challenges. The result indicates that the game offers different challenges presented at an appropriate pace. However, it seems to contain little help from the game itself in achieving these challenges.

Autonomy. The player feels a sense of control and impact over the game. His/her actions influence the video game's outcome and they know what the next step is to advance in the game. It is suggested to incorporate more achievement indicators to account for the user's progress within the application.

Feedback. Feedback is adequate and gives information on the success or failure of the players' moves. It is suggested to give the player more clarity in the point count.

Immersion. Players achieve a good level of involvement in the game, evidenced by an altered sense of time and a disregard for everyday worries during the game.

Social interaction. The video game requires other players' participation for their progress, which makes the game support learning within interactions. It is suggested to limit the use of artificial intelligence and have the option to eliminate it to promote interaction with other players.

Enhance knowledge. Players demonstrate that knowledge is used during the game, and it is necessary to know more and more to improve in-game performance. The video game promotes the search for knowledge outside the game.

It is important to mention the acceptance that the video game had, especially among students, who saw it as a fun way to learn difficult subjects. All types of end-users had fun playing on the prototypes, creating a fluid, dynamic and educational game that was useful.

8 Redesign

Based on the results of the usability evaluations, we proposed an improvement of the initial prototype. We kept the initial minimalistic idea but made a redesign of the colors of the application. We used the Marshall amplifier as a palette and model. Also, a question mark was added in the upper right corner to indicate help. We reduced the number of application buttons and added a bottom navigation bar. We redesigned icons and incorporated sound elements for feedback. We added short instructions to specific interfaces to guide the user, and incorporated mechanisms to learn the game mostly through interactions and not by written rules.

Home. In this interface, we find all the functions of the application. We can enter the User and Help page at the top. Then we can go to the active games and continue playing with other players' pending games and, in an attractive button, start a new game. The application has two independent application buttons to enter the Piano, and the Circle of Fifths. We can go back to Home in the navigation bar, see Friends, Settings, and User's page. The User icon is placed inside a circle to generate a similarity with social network applications (conceptual model already incorporated in our mental model) (Fig. 5).

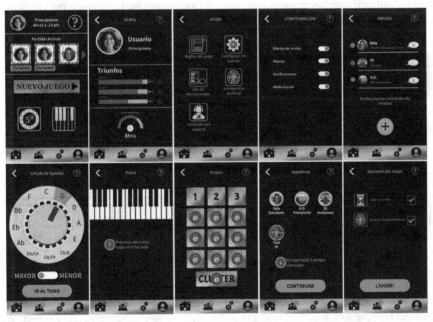

Fig. 5. Home, User Profile, Help, Settings, Friends, Circle of Fifths, Piano, Stages, Choose Player, and Game Options interfaces.

User Profile. We added achievement indicators by stage and an indicator of the time it takes the user to play his/her turn. Achievement levels are incorporated: Beginner, Student, Professional, Expert, Master.

Help. This interface is incorporated to help in the knowledge and use of: Game Rules, Account Configuration, Use of Tools (Circle of Fifths and Piano), Artificial Intelligence, and Contact with Support in case of errors. We redesigned and added the "Rules" interface (first prototype) into the "Help" interface in the application.

Settings. Added the ability to put the game in dark mode.

Friends. We eliminated the "Messages" interface and added its function to the "Friends" interface.

Circle of Fifths. We added the use of a knob type Marshall amplifier and a switch to indicate whether it is a major or a minor mode. We added the possibility of listening to the scale, the notes, and the chord. We eliminated the "Functions" icon and added this function to the "Circle of Fifths" tool.

Piano. We added a small text box to indicate what the user should do. We added the "Help" icon and the possibility to put the keyboard in landscape mode to improve finger interactivity.

Stages. We changed the colors to the application design's gold characteristic, and the lock icon was improved.

Choose Players. We added the option to play only with artificial intelligence "Cuai". The level of it can be graduated (Beginner, Student, Professional, Expert, Master).

Game Options. We added this interface before the start of the game to define game type options. Artificial intelligence can be removed from the game to increase the challenge level, and the temporary variable is added as a challenge level.

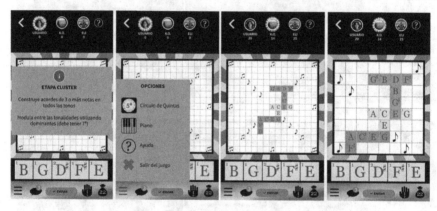

Fig. 6. Game interface.

Game. We added a message at the beginning to indicate basic rules of the stage. We added the board zoom function, and a chat, to allow communication in any context. We incorporated the tools ("Circle of Fifths" and "Piano") into the options in the lower left corner of the bottom bar. A redesign of the board's colors and images is done. We added different colors into the different keys in the more challenging levels. The number of chips is reduced in the later stages to reduce game time. A player can add points by objecting to a play by another player (Fig. 6).

9   Conclusions

This main purpose of this study was to propose a video game design prototype for teaching and learning musical harmony. As a result of the interface design and interaction process and a diverse methodological process for evaluating the usability of the interfaces and the designed interaction, a video game design prototype for teaching and learning musical harmony is presented here, ready to be implemented and used on a mobile device.

We added elements into the design that support the social constructivist theory, promoting students' autonomy in searching for knowledge and interaction with peers to support learning. This is evidenced by the different levels of achievement and stages that the player must overcome to advance within the game. We placed particular emphasis on the levels of challenges and the promotion of curiosity according to what was proposed by Malone [12] concerning intrinsic motivation and the design of educational video games. On the other hand, we evaluated interface design attributes, the achievement of educational objectives and fun, and interaction, which allowed us to account for the tool's effectiveness and essential improvements in it.

The design of an educational video game is a task that requires the attention of multiple edges. It is important to take care of educational, fun, and design elements. This makes permanent interaction with end-users essential to give shape and foundation to the needs that are expected to be covered with the development of the tool. Also, usability evaluations in the design process are crucial to enhance the tool's appropriate development and incorporate end-users' opinions into the design. A user-centered design can avoid errors in interaction and help in the achievement of educational objectives.

Due to the health emergency context due to pandemic of COVID-19, usability evaluations have been tricky, especially those that have an ideal requirement of presence. In remote meetings, body communication is lost, and it is a less familiar communication space for many, adding to this the connectivity issues. However, it was possible to collect the necessary evidence of the end-users' perceptions and specifically improve the video game design. The use of online questionnaires was a facilitator to receive, in an expeditious and orderly manner, closed surveys and user opinions.

In general, the video game design meets the proposed educational objectives and is widely accepted by end-users. Interesting contributions were collected regarding the uses that this technological tool could be given within the classroom and the possible educational benefits it could have in the long term. Therefore, it can be said that the development of this tool will be a contribution to the teaching and learning of musical harmony, enhancing and supporting knowledge from the most basic to the most complex levels.

10   Future Work

The future of ToneCluster now is the programming and implementation of the video game to make it available to the public on mobile devices. This will require an impact evaluation once the video game is developed to see the attainment of the educational objectives and review and improve any errors in the interfaces and the interaction with the application.

It will be interesting to see how the application is finally used in the classroom and what educational objectives are achieved in the short and long term.

Acknowledgements. This work was supported by Fomento de la Investigación UNIACC, DIP 02ART-2020, Chile. Also supported by CONICYT's Basal Funds for Centers of Excellence, Project FB0003, Chile.

References

1. Al Fatta, H., Maksom, Z., Zakaria, M.H.: Systematic literature review on usability evaluation model of educational games: playability, pedagogy, and mobility aspects 1. J. Theor. Appl. Inf. Technol. **31**(14), 4677–4689 (2018)
2. Anderson, T., Dron, J.: Three generations of distance education pedagogy. Int. Rev. Res. Open Distrib. Learn. **12**(3), 80 (2011). https://doi.org/10.19173/irrodl.v12i3.890
3. Csikszentmihalyi, M.: Play and intrinsic rewards. J. Hum. Psychol. **15**(3), 41–63 (1975)
4. Denis, G., Jouvelot, P.: Motivation-driven educational game design: applying best practices to music education, pp. 462–465 (2005)
5. Enriquez, J.G., Casas, S.I.: Usabilidaden aplicaciones móviles. Informes Científicos - Técnicos UNPA **5**(2), 25–47 (2013)
6. Fu, F.-L., Yu, S.-C.: Three layered thinking model for designing web-based educational games. In: Li, F., Zhao, J., Shih, T.K., Lau, R., Li, Q., McLeod, D. (eds.) ICWL 2008. LNCS, vol. 5145, pp. 265–274. Springer, Heidelberg (2008). https://doi.org/10.1007/978-3-540-85033-5_26
7. Fu, F.-L., Su, R.-C., Yu, S.-C.: EGameFlow: a scale to measure learner' enjoyment of e-learning games. Comput. Educ. **52**, 101–112 (2009)
8. García-Valcárcel, A., Basilotta, V., López, C.: Las TIC en el aprendizaje colaborativo en el aula de Primaria y Secundaria. Comunicar **42**, 65–74 (2014)
9. Gall, M., Borg, W., Gall, J.: Educational research: an introduction Br. J. Educ. Stud. **32**, 274 (2003)
10. Hong, J.-C., Liu, M.-C.: A study on thinking strategy between experts and novices of computer games. Comput. Hum. Behav. **19**, 245–258 (2003)
11. Ibrahim, R., Jaafar, A.: Educational games (EG) design framework: combination of game design, pedagogy and content modeling (2009)
12. Malone, T.: Toward a theory of intrinsically motivating instruction. Cogn. Sci. **5**, 333–369 (1981)
13. McComas, W.F.: Social constructivism. In: McComas, W.F. (ed.) The Language of Science Education, pp. 99–99. SensePublishers, Rotterdam (2014). https://doi.org/10.1007/978-94-6209-497-0_89
14. Nielsen, J.: Usability Engineering. Morgan Kaufmann, Londres (1994)
15. Nielsen, J.: Designing and maintaining a highly usable site. In: 5th International World Wide Web Conference, Tutorial Notes, Paris, France (1996)
16. Norman, D.: The Design of Everyday Things (2002)
17. Oblinger, D.: Simulations, Games, and Learning. EDUCAUSE Learning Initiative. Boulder, Colorado (2006)
18. Sánchez, J.: Bases Constructivistas para la Integración de TICs. Revista Enfoques Educacionales. **6**, 75–89 (2004)
19. Sánchez, J.: Cuestionario de Usuario Final "Evaluación de Usabilidad de Videojuegos". Departamento de Ciencias de la Computación. Universidad de Chile (2020)

20. Sánchez, J.: Cuestionario de UsuarioExperto "Evaluación de Usabilidad Heurística de Videojuegos". Departamento de Ciencias de la Computación, Universidad de Chile (2020)
21. Sweetser, P., Wyeth, P.: GameFlow: a model for evaluating player enjoyment in games. Comput. Entertain. **3**(3), 3 (2005). https://doi.org/10.1145/1077246.1077253

A Video Game-Like Approach to Supporting Novices in Learning Programming

Ami Sakakibara and Hiroshi Hosobe[✉]

Faculty of Computer and Information Sciences, Hosei University, Tokyo, Japan
hosobe@acm.org

Abstract. In the education of introductory programming, people often adopt block-based visual programming languages such as Scratch and Blockly that allow programmers to construct programs by placing visual blocks. A previous study showed that a block-based language was more effective than a text-based language in introductory programming education. However, even with such block-based languages, it is still necessary for novices to learn programming in traditional ways, for example, by hearing lectures, reading textbooks, or watching tutorial videos. In this paper, we propose a video game-like approach to supporting novices in learning programming. We introduce two concepts into a block-based programming system: one is a staging mechanism that allows novices to gradually obtain more complex means of programming; the other is an assistant chatbot that helps novices to gain knowledge of programming. We implemented the system by applying our approach to turtle graphics. We present results of the experiment that we conducted to evaluate our approach.

Keywords: Block-based visual programming · Programming learning · Gamification

1 Introduction

Programming education is being actively conducted throughout the world to increase students interested in computer science and to acquire excellent human resources for the information technology industry. In the education of introductory programming, people often adopt block-based visual programming languages such as Scratch [7,10] and Blockly [9] that allow programmers to construct programs by placing visual blocks. A previous study showed that a block-based language was more effective than a text-based language in introductory programming education [12]. However, even with such block-based languages, it is still necessary for novices to learn programming in traditional ways, for example, by hearing lectures, reading textbooks, or watching tutorial videos.

In this paper, we propose a video game-like approach to supporting novices in learning programming. We introduce two concepts into a block-based programming system: one is a staging mechanism that allows novices to gradually

© Springer Nature Switzerland AG 2021
P. Zaphiris and A. Ioannou (Eds.): HCII 2021, LNCS 12785, pp. 84–93, 2021.
https://doi.org/10.1007/978-3-030-77943-6_6

obtain more complex means of programming; the other is an assistant chatbot that helps novices to gain knowledge of programming. We implemented the system by applying our approach to turtle graphics [1]. We present results of the experiment that we conducted to evaluate our approach.

The rest of this paper is organized as follows. Section 2 describes previous work related to our approach. Section 3 proposes our approach, and Sect. 4 gives its implementation. Section 5 presents results of the experiment, and Sect. 6 discusses the approach. Finally, Sect. 7 provides conclusions and future work.

2 Related Work

One of the most related work was done by Arawjo et al. [2]. They proposed a progression design of a visual programming system that could be seen as being similar to our staging mechanism. However, they adopted functional programming, which is very different from block-based programming that is often used for introductory programming education.

Game-like approaches have been adopted also in the visual programming community. Bauer et al. [3] developed a block-based programming game called Dragon Architect to directly teach computational thinking strategies. Malizia et al. [6] developed a game-based system called TAPASPlay to foster computational thinking skills, focusing on playfulness and collaboration. Taylor et al. [11] developed a toolkit called IntelliBlox to enable learners to create block-based programs in immersive game-based learning environments. Lytle et al. [5] developed a game called Resource Rush to allow users to learn programming in open-ended game environments.

Fujimoto et al. [4] discussed research trends in game-based learning and open education. Open education refers to practice that eliminates barriers from education and increases educational opportunities. They recognized these two areas as becoming increasingly popular in the next few years.

Mineuchi et al. [8] developed a chatbot-based tool to allow students to easily perform preparation and review of their lessons by using a communication tool called LINE. They claimed that it would enable the students to increase opportunities for learning, to prepare without fear of failure, and to organize their thoughts.

3 Proposed Approach

We propose an approach to supporting novices in learning programming. The characteristic of our approach is that it allows novice users to enjoy learning programming as if they play introductory parts of video games. For this purpose, we particularly introduce the following two concepts into a block-based visual programming system.

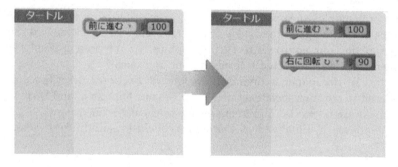

Fig. 1. Staging mechanism that gradually increases the available types of blocks as the user achieves goals for stages.

Staging Mechanism: The system initially limits the types of visual blocks that the user can employ to construct a program, and it gradually increases the available types of blocks as the user achieves goals for stages (Fig. 1).

Assistant Chatbot: The system provides a chatbot that assists the user in learning programming by him/herself. As a help function, it explains in detail how to use blocks, and also it communicates with the user by making simple conversations.

Figure 2 shows the initial screen of our visual programming system. It allows the user to construct a block-based visual program for turtle graphics on part (a) of the screen, and presents the resulting graphics on part (b). On part (c) of the screen, it shows the points that correspond to the current stage. On part (d), it presents available blocks for the current stage. The user can call a chatbot by pressing button (e), which opens window (f) and makes the chatbot talk to the user.

3.1 Staging Mechanism

The staging mechanism increases the available types of blocks when the user achieves a given goal. It currently presents the following four stages:

Stage 1: Draw a straight line.
Stage 2: Draw a polygon.
Stage 3: Draw a geometric shape with a "repeat" block.
Stage 4: Draw free shapes.

Each stage is associated with a goal. For example, the goal for stage 1 is "Draw a straight line." The current stage is indicated by the points shown on the screen (at (c) in Fig. 2). When the user achieves a goal, 100 points are added. The user can ask the chatbot about goals and points.

At stage 1, only one block "move forward or backward" is available. When the user achieves the goal by using and executing ore or more blocks, points and a new block are added. When the system reads blocks to execute the program,

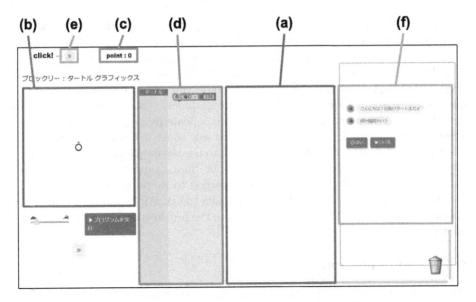

Fig. 2. Initial screen of our visual programming system.

it judges whether the goal has been achieved. If the goal has been achieved, it adds 100 points and reloads a page for stage 2 with an additional block.

At stage 2, two blocks including a new block "turn right or left" are available. At stage 3, a block "repeat" further becomes available. At stage 4, many types of blocks become available and can be freely combined.

3.2 Assistant Chatbot

Basically, the user communicates with the chatbot by selecting a message that is sent to the chatbot.

Help Function. The user can ask the chatbot about various things such as how to use a block and how to effectively apply a block, by selecting "Help" from the menu that pops up when the user right-clicks a block. For example, when a block "move forward" is selected, a figure is presented to show that it draws a straight line, other related blocks also are given, and examples that can be drawn by combining other blocks are shown. Instead of immediately teaching the answer, it aims at enhancing the user's ability to think about how to achieve the goal.

Conversation Function. Unlike the help function that can be asked about specific blocks, the conversation function answers more general questions such as a question about the user interface. The conversation function of the chatbot is triggered when the button (e) in Fig. 2 is pressed. It particularly aims at resolving questions of novice users who do not know what to do initially.

The conversation function always begins by asking whether there is any question. If there is no question, it finishes the conversation. Otherwise, it presents several choices to the user to identify what is the actual question. The first questions are about four things, i.e., "turtle graphics," "how to use," "points," and "blocks." After one of them is selected, it repeatedly presents more detailed questions. For example, if the user wants to ask about a block and selects the question about blocks, the users is prompted to use the help function. As another example, if the user selects the question about "how to use," it shows a screenshot of the user interface with numbers attached to its parts, which allows the user to select a part about which the user wants to ask. After reading the answer about the selected part, the user can return to the previous question to ask about another part.

4   Implementation

We implemented the system as a Web application by using Blockly [9] and its turtle graphics application. We used a JavaScript framework called BotUI to implement the assistant chatbot. The chatbot can be called by using a right-click pop-up menu as well as by pressing the button (e) in Fig. 2.

The staging mechanism was implemented as reloading the page, which adds points and new blocks. Right after the reloading, the system displays a dialog box to inform that points have been added and new blocks have been introduced. When beginning stage 4, it additionally opens a pop-up window that informs that the final stage has been reached.

5   Experiment

We conducted an experiment to evaluate our approach. The purpose of the experiment was to examine whether the system based on our approach could improve its users' motivations for learning programming as well as whether it could reduce differences among the skills of the users caused by their past experiences in programming.

5.1   Participants

We recruited five participants (all male and 14.3 year old on average), three of whom had no experience in programming. In the following, we refer to them as participants A to E. Participants B and D had previous experiences in programming.

5.2   Procedure

We asked the participants to use our system. We measured the times that they spent to complete stages, and conducted questionnaires before and after the experiment.

Time Measurement. To examine the influence of the past experiences of the participants in programming, we measured the times that they spent to complete each of the first three stages. For this purpose, we took them on video during the experiment. A camera was placed diagonally to the rear of each participant to make his hands and the computer screen visible to the camera.

Questionnaires. To examine the changes of the motivations of the participants for learning programming, we conducted questionnaires with the five-level Likert scale before and after the experiment. Both pre- and post-questionnaires included the following questions:

- Do you think that you are good at programming?
- Do you think that you enjoy programming if you learn programming in the future?
- Do you think that programming is difficult if you learn programming in the future?
- Do you positively want to learn programming in the future?

The post-questionnaire additionally included the following questions about our system:

- Did you use the chatbot?
- Was the chatbot easy to understand?
- Did you have a sense of achievement when you reached a goal?

The post-questionnaire also collected free descriptions of what difficulties the participants faced while using the system.

5.3 Results

We report the results of the experiment below.

Time Measurement. Table 1 shows the times that the participants spent to complete stages 1, 2, and 3. Table 2 shows how many times they used the chatbots. The conversation function of the chatbot can answer the following questions: what is turtle graphics (indicated as "TG" in the table); I do not know how to use this user interface (indicated as "Interface" and with the numbers shown in Fig. 3); I want to know about points (indicated as "Point"); I want to know about blocks (indicated as "Block"). Also, the help function of the chatbot can answer the following questions: how to move forward or backward (indicated as "Move" in the table); how to turn right or left (indicated as "Turn"); how to repeat (indicated as "Repeat").

The times of the participants A, B, C, and E show that stage 2 took longer than stage 1. By contrast, participant D spent a longer time at stage 1. This was probably because when the program should be executed was not explicitly explained. It was observed that participant D pressed the execute button before

Table 1. Times that the participants spent to complete stages.

Participant	Stage 1	Stage 2	Stage 3	Total
A	0:01:19	0:16:27	0:02:34	0:20:20
B	0:01:31	0:06:16	0:04:22	0:12:09
C	0:05:39	0:34:18	0:06:59	0:46:56
D	0:13:20	0:00:52	0:04:00	0;18:12
E	0:02:57	0:22:56	0:40:57	1:06:50
Average	0:04:57	0:16:10	0:11:46	0:32:53

Table 2. Numbers of the uses of the chatbots by the participants.

Participant	Conversation										Help		
	TG	Interface							Point	Block	Move	Turn	Repeat
		1	2	3	4	5	6	7&8					
A			2	1				1		1			
B	1			1	1			1		3		1	
C	2		4	3	1	1	1	2					
D	1		2	1				2			1		
E		1	4	1			1	1			1		
Total	4	1	12	7	2	1	2	7	0	4	2	1	0

placing blocks in the workspace and did not press the execute button long after placing blocks. Also, participant D had a previous experience in programming, and did not spend particularly long times at stages 2 and 3.

Participants A, B, and C spent shorter times at stage 3 than at stage 2. This was probably because the goal for stage 3 was not very different from the goal for stage 2. By contrast, participants D and E spent longer times at stage 3 than at stage 2. This was probably because they initially thought that a repeat block could contain only one block. We prepared a help function about a repeat block that explains that it could contain one or more blocks. However, no participants used this help function as shown in Table 2.

Questionnaires. Table 3 shows the results of the questionnaires. The five-level Likert scale consists of the following: "strongly agree" as 5, "agree" as 4, "undecided" as 3, "disagree" as 2, and "strongly disagree" as 1. We performed a paired t-test between the scores of the pre- and the post-questionnaire. The results show that there were no significant differences concerning the four questions described in Subsect. 5.2. This means that our system did not bring sufficient psychological influences.

The questions about our system in the post-questionnaire showed the following. All the participants used the chatbot. Four participants strongly agreed to

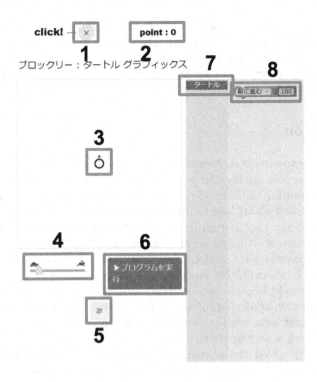

Fig. 3. User interfaces about which the chatbot can be asked.

the question "Was the chatbot easy to understand?" and the other one agreed to it. Four participants agreed to the question "Did you have a sense of achievement when you reached a goal?"

In the post-questionnaire, participants A to E provided the following free descriptions of difficulties in using the system:

Table 3. Results of the questionnaires before and after the experiment.

Participant	Good at programming		Enjoy programming		Programming is difficult		Want to learn programming	
	Before	After	Before	After	Before	After	Before	After
A	3	4	4	5	4	4	5	5
B	3	4	4	5	3	2	3	5
C	2	2	4	3	3	5	3	2
D	4	4	4	5	4	4	3	3
E	2	1	5	4	4	5	5	4
Mean	2.8	3.0	4.2	4.4	3.6	4.0	3.8	3.8
Variance	0.7	2.0	0.2	0.8	0.3	1.5	1.2	1.7

A. I did not know what I should do before the chatbot taught me about it.
B. I spent a little long time in repeating blocks.
C. I did not understand the goal "geometric shape" for stage 3.
D. It was hard to draw a polygon by combining various blocks in stage 3.
E. It was difficult to draw a polygon.

6   Discussion

Although the experimental results did not statistically show psychological influences, differences among the participants' reactions and spent times were observed. A cause for the large differences among the novice participants was that the explanation about how to use a repeat block was insufficient. Although we had included the explanation in the help function, no participants used it during the experiment. It might seem plausible that the help function should be moved to the conversation function because the conversation function was relatively more used. However, this would largely increase choices when the number of block types would become large. Since there were participants who did not use the help function at all, the right-click pop-up menu is considered to be inappropriate. It might have been possible to trigger the help function by placing a block about which a user wants to know.

Our system enabled the participants to achieve the goals by themselves, which suggests that we were able to develop a programming system for novice programmers. However, our system is still not sufficient for improving computational thinking because it does not sufficiently support the participants in correctly using repeat blocks.

7   Conclusions and Future Work

We proposed a video game-like approach to supporting novices in learning programming. We introduced a staging mechanism and an assistant chatbot into a block-based programming system. The experiment that we conducted suggested the usefulness of the staging mechanism and the conversation function of the chatbot. However, it showed that the help function of the chatbot was not useful. This problem could be solved by simplifying the interface for triggering the help function. The experiment also suggested the necessity of a function for supporting users in understanding repeat blocks.

Acknowledgment. This work was partly supported by JSPS KAKENHI Grant Number JP17H01726.

References

1. Abelson, H., Goodman, N., Rudolph, L.: LOGO Manual. AI Memo 313, AI Lab., MIT (1974)

2. Arawjo, I., Wang, C.-Y., Myers, A.C., Andersen, E., Guimbretière, F.: Teaching programming with gamified semantics. In: Proceedings of the ACM CHI, pp. 4911–4923 (2017)
3. Bauer, A., Butler, E., Popović, Z.: Dragon architect: open design problems for guided learning in a creative computational thinking sandbox game. In: Proceedings of the International Conference on the Foundations of Digital Games (FDG), vol. 26, pp. 1–6. ACM (2017)
4. Fujimoto, T., Shigeta, K., Fukuyama, Y.: The research trends in game-based learning and open education. Educ. Technol. Res. **39**(1), 15–23 (2016)
5. Lytle, N., Echavarria, J., Sosa, J., Price, T.W.: Resource rush: towards an open-ended programming game. In: Proceedings of the Workshop on Blocks and Beyond, pp. 91–93. IEEE (2019)
6. Malizia, A., Turchi, T., Bell, D., Fogli, D., Danesi, F.: Fostering computational thinking through collaborative game-based learning. Multimed. Tools Appl. **78**, 13649–13673 (2019)
7. Maloney, J., Resnick, M., Rusk, N., Silverman, B., Eastmond, E.: The Scratch programming language and environment. ACM Trans. Comput. Educ. **10**(4), 16:1–16:15 (2010)
8. Mineuchi, A., Matsuba, R., Toda, M., Suzuki, K.: Design of an educational supporting tool for encouragement of learning with a chat bot. In: Proceedings of the Annual Meeting of the Academic Exchange for Information Environment and Strategy, vol. TF2-5, pp. 1–6 (2017). (in Japanese)
9. Pasternak, E., Fenichel, R., Marshall, A.N.: Tips for creating a block language with Blockly. In: Proceedings of the Workshop on Blocks and Beyond, pp. 21–24. IEEE (2017)
10. Resnick, M., et al.: Scratch: programming for all. Comm. ACM **52**(11), 60–67 (2009)
11. Taylor, S.: IntelliBlox: a toolkit for integrating block-based programming into game-based learning environments. In: Proceedings of the Workshop on Blocks and Beyond, pp. 55–58. IEEE (2019)
12. Weintrop, D., Wilensky, U.: Comparing block-based and text-based programming in high school computer science classrooms. ACM Trans. Comput. Educ. **18**(1), 3:1–3:25 (2017)

Completeness and Collaboration in the Early Design Phase of Learning Games: Do Ideation Cards Provide Scaffolding?

Rabail Tahir[✉] and Alf Inge Wang

Norwegian University of Science and Technology (NTNU), Trondheim, Norway
{rabail.tahir,alf.inge.wang}@ntnu.no

Abstract. Game-based learning (GBL) has proliferated rapidly in recent years, with both industry and academic research communities calling for collaborative work practices in the educational game design process that need to address all the key GBL aspects and create a shared understanding among team members. Design cards have the potential to improve idea generation and communication between stakeholders. However, potential scaffolding for completeness (focusing on all key GBL dimensions) and collaboration (working together to produce something) in learning game design are not explored. Therefore, in this paper, we investigate how this design approach can scaffold for collaboration and completeness in the early phase of the learning game design process using a card-based GBL ideation toolkit in design workshops. Seven teams were analyzed using design artifacts and video recordings of the workshop session. The results are encouraging in terms of the applicability of ideation cards in the GBL design process to scaffold completeness and collaboration.

Keywords: Game-based learning design · Learning games · Collaboration · Completeness · Early design process · Ideation

1 Introduction

Game-based learning (GBL) is a multidimensional phenomenon depending on several aspects (e.g., users, learning, game factors, usability, environment, and affective reactions) for it to be effective [1, 2]. There is no single way to design a learning game. Not many specific methods scaffold for incorporating all the vital elements of an educational game considering different experts' involvement in its development, making it a different task [1, 3]. Researchers have pointed out that complex design products need to be understood from multiple aspects [4]. Therefore, an essential requirement for a learning game design process is to focus on all the critical dimensions of GBL [5]. We refer to this as "completeness" in GBL design. Additionally, there is a need to achieve an adequate balance between these key elements (i.e., different aspects such as learning factors, game factors, technical factors, and user experience related factors) in the learning game to keep learning integral but still providing an enjoyable user experience for learner engagement [5, 6].

© Springer Nature Switzerland AG 2021
P. Zaphiris and A. Ioannou (Eds.): HCII 2021, LNCS 12785, pp. 94–114, 2021.
https://doi.org/10.1007/978-3-030-77943-6_7

The design process of learning games is complex involving several professionals from different domains working together for a common end product [7]. Therefore, team collaboration is a critical factor in determining and maintaining effectiveness in design [8]. Researchers have highlighted that team members (i.e., experts in particular domains, e.g., designers and educators) often face difficulties in sharing knowledge in a multidisciplinary setting. Each has a different area of expertise, ways to communicate, operating procedures, and use different idea representation approaches [4]. Therefore, communication between them is not very simple to manage [1]. Researchers argue that it is important for a design team to communicate and negotiate with each other to make decisions by entering compromises [9]. Industry and research communities both require collaborative work practices in the design process [9]. "Collaboration" stresses knowledge co-creation through a common design process, and peer collaboration stimulates cognitive engagement and motivation [10].

Researchers have already used design games to understand design as a social activity or for staging collaborative design efforts involving many stakeholders [9]. Playful tools and design games have been used to structure the design dialogues between stakeholders and are suggested to support and enhance collaborative ideation and concept design. The focus on play downplays the power relations and factors hindering idea generation [11]. Some researchers have used ideation cards for designing exertion games [12] and tangible games [13]. They found them useful for idea generation, articulation, offering guidance, expanding participants' horizons, focusing on the aim, formative evaluation, and providing common vocabulary. However, how completeness and collaborative process for GBL design are facilitated through ideation cards is not explored.

According to Markopoulos et al. [14], the use of novel methods in the early design phase can help adopt a broader perspective, and Lucero et al. [15] advocates that the general characteristics of design cards make them an effective tool for collaborative design practice. In this paper, we hypothesize a card-based tool as a scaffolding for collaboration and completeness in the ideation process of learning game design. We chose to focus on these elements for two reasons. *First*, considering the nature of learning game design, these are vital for GBL design practice. *Second*, they can also be used as means for learning about the GBL design process as a collaborative design activity engaging various stakeholders. Our research objective is to investigate ideation cards as scaffolding for completeness and collaboration in the early phase of the learning game design process. For this purpose, the LEAGUÊ ideation toolkit (see Sect. 2.4) was used as the intervention in this study. Our analysis describes how collaboration and completeness are facilitated by using the card-based tool in the ideation process of learning game design. The contribution of the paper is twofold: 1) it demonstrates the usefulness of ideation cards in the GBL design process (specifically in terms of completeness and collaboration), and 2) it reflects on factors and design decisions in the employed card deck/activities that advance the key outcomes: completeness and collaboration.

2   Related Work

This section presents relevant research studies that explored or demonstrated the importance of collaboration and completeness in the GBL design process, the use of innovative approaches to aid the design process, and card-based methods in various domains. Moreover, we underline efforts in the GBL domain to acknowledge areas where future research may take shape.

2.1 Collaboration and Completeness in the Design Process

Several researchers focus on "completeness" in GBL design, i.e., addressing all the essential elements of a learning game in the design process [1, 5, 16]. De Lope et al. proposed a five-stage methodology (in which the story plays a key role) suitable for designing learning games focusing on five key elements [5]. The study focused on the design phase, which structures the game with these five essential elements and proposes modeling tasks resulting in design artifacts such as diagrams or descriptive documents that can facilitate communication between design team members. Similarly, Silva [1] also presented a methodology divided into steps to support educational games' design process to be more all-encompassing. It identifies the steps required to define the learning mechanisms in an educational game starting from the topic choice and ending with the user experience. Another study by Kellner et al. [16] presented guidelines for developing adventure learning games (based on existing guidelines and frameworks) that help evoke all key aspects in the design. However, these studies are limited in scope, focusing on specific game types or lack thorough validation to provide evidence to support completeness in the design process based on generated game designs. Flexibility and the ability to work in a broader perspective are recognized as key skills required for the 4th generation industrial revolution. They should also be addressed in the field of educational game design [17]. The collaborative design emphasizes that all people are creative, and if provided with appropriate tools and settings, can effectively contribute to the design [18]. Da Costa et al. [19] described a co-design process based on a user-centered design approach in defining the concepts of a civic educational game. They relied on including the institution and users in the initial phase of the design process to provide an effective learning game. However, the results are limited in scope and showed that experience with only 4 or 5 children was productive. Tran and Biddle [7] presented an ethnographic study focusing on the studio team's day-to-day collaboration for development practices in a small company working in the domain of serious game development. Their finding emphasizes that social and technical factors influence collaboration in the development process of serious games. They found that co-location and a positive social environment facilitate the participation of different professionals in game development. The study reports on collaboration occurring within the game development team (consisting of six members) in a real context and not using any method or tool for scaffolding the team collaboration efforts. The team members had experience working together for at least six months to two years, which might have influenced collaboration. Marne et al. [20] aimed to create a language with a design pattern library based on their six facet approach that should enable the team of designers and teachers to brainstorm and communicate their ideas and work together for holistic coherence. This study's results are limited in scope to indicate support for collaboration, as initial results were with single designers (either teacher or game designer working alone). Some researchers [18] followed an event-driven design process for co-design. In this process, the collaboration with team members is enabled through co-design events consisting of a predesigned structure, tasks, and facilitation resulting in a co-constructed understanding concerning potential designs, experiences, and context.

2.2 Use of Innovative Approaches to Aid the Design Process

Hannula and Irrmann [11] studied a design game to plan a service co-design project using video recording of interaction between an inter-organizational group of participants playing the game. The case selected for the study consisted of six players. Four out of six were from the platform provider organization, while two other players had no prior experience of the case before. The results highlight the ability of design games to scaffold for co-creation and interaction in the early phase of service co-design projects. Kayali et al. [21] used a mixed-method approach to develop informatics and society learning games with the collaboration of high school students, university students, and researchers. They employed playing research and game analysis (which require students to learn about games by playing them reflectively) to prepare students for educational game design tasks. In these tasks, they use explorative design and design thinking methods to create the game. The research advocates the possible success of playful participation (without explicitly stating the encouraging aspects) for GBL design. However, complete results are not presented, and the project was still at the early stage. Schmoelz [22] investigated playful activities in the classroom for enabling co-creativity. The classroom activity design involved students playing the C2L storytelling card game called 4Scribes to explore different ways to deal with problems and find solutions. He used qualitative data collection methods for analysis, including narrative-Socratic dialogues, gameplay videography, and field notes. The results support the use of playful classroom activities to facilitate co-creative reframing, co-creating a shared story, expressing emotions, and engaging in dialogue.

2.3 Use of Card-Based Tools in Various Domains

Card-based tools have been used in various domains to facilitate user participation and creativity [23]. According to [24], the process most supported by creativity support tools (such as design cards) is ideation or idea generation. Roy and Warren [23] analyzed 155 card-based tools, with most aiming to aid human-centered design, creative thinking, or domain specific-methods. According to the review, some scientific trials indicated the usefulness of these tools to help designers generate innovative ideas. Feedback showed that cards could provide relevant information in handy form and support the design process. However, more testing and independent trials are required to confirm their effectiveness. Bekker et al. [25] presented a card-based design tool that describes the five perspectives on play. Only two of the five lenses were evaluated, which showed promising results such as applicability for a variety of users. The cards proved inspirational for the design process (such as brainstorming and other design activities) and useful in analyzing the initial concepts, structuring information, and reflecting on design decisions. Similarly, Chasanidou [26] also presented a design tool named DEMO to design for motivation and found the use of artifacts such as cards and the structured processes as effective practices for the early phase of the design stage. Sintoris et al. [27] used a card-based gamification approach in two engineering courses to teach ideation.

They examined the produced design ideas and students' opinions regarding the tool and the design process. The students showed a positive response. However, there was a contradiction between students' responses and results of the workshops, as not many innovative ideas were produced, and there were issues with the feasibility of some cards.

Pernin et al. [28] employed the tangible version of the ScenLRPG method (built on visual formalism) based on a board game to design GBL systems specific for vocational training context. They investigated the use of game mechanisms to promote GBL designers' creativity and cooperation and the effectiveness of board game-based design tool. Some researchers, such as Mueller et al. [12] and Deng et al. [13], used card-based tools to support the design process of creating exertion games and tangible learning games, respectively. They got positive results from the participants' survey. However, they have not investigated if these tools facilitate completeness and collaboration in the design process from the generated game ideas and team interactions.

From the previous work, we find evidence for the importance of completeness and collaboration in the design process of learning games and the use of card-based tools to aid the design process by supporting initial idea generation, structuring information, reflecting on design decisions, offering guidance, introducing different perspectives, help in focus shift, and evaluation. However, not much work has been done exploring using a card-based approach to scaffold for collaboration and completeness, particularly in the GBL design process and investigating the contributing factors. Most of the existing card-based design tools were specific for a game genre or type, e.g., [12, 13, 28]. Therefore, they could not be used for our study as they did not incorporate the key GBL concepts, which are essential to investigate support for completeness. However, a particular tool focusing on GBL design is the LEAGUÊ ideation toolkit [29] used in this study. The motivation for using this card-based tool has been the particular focus of the toolkit on key GBL concepts.

3 Material and Methods

This section presents the research questions and approach, the LEAGUÊ card-based ideation toolkit for GBL design, research context, participants and procedure, and data collection and analysis methods.

3.1 Research Questions and Research Approach

The research goal of the user study presented in this article was to investigate how ideation cards facilitate completeness and collaboration in the learning game design process. We organized workshops as the research approach for the user study [30]. We conducted three design workshops using the LEAGUÊ ideation toolkit as the intervention to investigate card-based ideation tools as scaffolding for completeness and collaboration in the ideation phase of the learning game design process. The produced design artifacts and video recordings from the design workshop sessions were the primary data sources [31, 32]. We achieved our objective by focusing on the following two research questions:

- RQ1: Does the card-based toolkit support teams address all GBL key dimensions when ideating learning game design?

- RQ2: Which factors contribute to collaboration among team members when using the card-based tool to ideate learning game design?

3.2 LEAGUÊ Ideation Toolkit

The LEAGUÊ toolkit [29], containing four card decks, a board with a playbook, five design activities with ideation sheets, and a log sheet, is used for this study to ideate learning game design in a workshop format (see Fig. 1). It focuses on the multidimensionality of GBL design and offers cards concentrating on six key GBL dimensions (each detailing specific concepts). These six dimensions are *learning*, *game factors*, *affective reactions*, *usability*, *user*, and *environment* that need to be considered in any learning game design to be effective.

The toolkit contains the following different cards: *Primary* (28 cards), presenting 28 GBL design concepts (categorized in six GBL dimensions) in the form of a question or task, *trigger* (113 cards), providing hints and example ideas for GBL design concepts, *custom* (28 cards), blank cards to come up with own design ideas or custom solutions and lastly, seven *reflection* cards providing critical lenses or evaluation criteria to reflect on generated design ideas and further refine them.

Primary cards are the main deck of cards presenting 28 GBL concepts (the building block of learning game design) grouped in categories emphasizing the six key GBL dimensions (using color-coding). Out of these 28 primary cards (GBL concepts), there are five cards for the dimension "learning", three cards focusing the dimension "environment", five cards of "affective reactions", seven cards for "game factors", four cards for "usability" and, four cards for the dimension "user". The playing team successively selects the primary cards through collaborative discussion to ideate their learning game design using trigger or custom cards. Therefore, these cards are useful for investigating scaffolding for completeness (achieving multidimensional focus) in the ideation phase of learning game design.

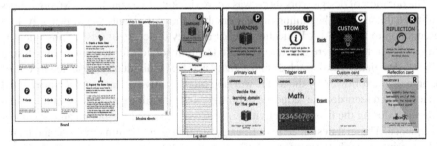

Fig. 1. The LEAGUÊ toolkit items (on the left) and four card types (on the right)

The *playbook* of the LEAGUÊ toolkit introduces five design activities for ideating learning game design in a team of four to six participants using cards, ideation sheets, and a log sheet. Each design activity has a separate ideation sheet used to produce the required design outcome of that activity. The design activities are played in sequence and are as follows: 1) *Idea generation*: coming up with an initial concept of a learning game using provided primary, trigger, and custom cards. 2) *Idea development*: expanding the initial idea from the first activity and developing it further into a more detailed and concrete one using provided primary, trigger, and custom cards. 3) *Idea refinement*: improving or refining the developed ideas by reflecting on the design choices and identifying the limitations and questionable decisions using the reflection cards to think about the trade-offs between different GBL aspects that can negatively affect the design of the learning game. 4) *Idea illustration*: planning the game's overall flow (illustrating how a user will play the game from start to exit) using a flow diagram, screen prototypes, or user scenarios. 5) *Idea documentation*: recording the final state of learning game design idea by producing a short version of a game design document (a format is provided to fill in the final idea details).

3.3 Research Context, Participants, and Procedure

The learning game design workshops (using LEAGUÊ toolkit) were organized in three different contexts: as a research study, in a doctoral summer school, and a graduate "Game development" course. In total, 34 people (ages 25–40) including, 16 master students and 18 researchers (Ph.D./postdoc), participated in the workshops that formed seven teams (each with 4–6 members). Two teams had 4 participants each, four teams had 5 participants, and one team had 6 participants. There were 13 females and 21 males. The primary subject of study was computer science for all participants except two researchers from electrical engineering. Most participants (24 out of 34) had no background in learning game design, 3 had little experience, and 7 had moderate experience. The participants with no to moderate experience were selected to fully explore the support for completeness provided by the card-based toolkit and not influenced by their experience and knowledge, ensuring data validity. The participants were selected through opportunity sampling, and none of the participants had previously used the LEAGUÊ toolkit. The participants were informed about the study's research objective, asked to sign a consent form, and were informed that their participation was voluntary.

The duration of design workshops was approximately two hours, and two organizers facilitated them. At the beginning of the workshop, the participants were given a 10-min introduction to the LEAGUÊ ideation toolkit and key concepts of GBL. Subsequently, participants in teams were asked to start the ideation session for learning game design with five design activities. Each design activity was first individually presented by one of the organizers, followed by the teams working on that activity. One team member acted as a logger and recorded the sequence of primary and reflection cards used by the team in a log sheet during the first three activities. All activities were time-bound and organized in sequence. The first design activity (idea generation) was 10 min duration, and teams had six primary cards (focusing six GBL dimensions) to solve using trigger or custom cards. After that, all teams summarized their initial ideas in a minute. The second activity (idea development) was 30 min in which teams had 22 primary cards (categorized in six GBL dimensions) to solve using trigger or custom cards, followed by teams presenting their developed ideas in a minute. The third design activity (idea refinement) was 10 min, and teams had seven reflection cards to refine their ideas. Subsequently, each team in a minute reported the refinements they made in their design idea. The fourth (idea illustration) and fifth activity (idea documentation) were run in parallel (20 min duration in total). Finally, after completing all design activities, there were group presentations in which each team summarized the idea of their learning game design. The ideation and log sheets of teams were collected, and the play sessions of teams were also video recorded. Figure 2 presents one of the teams using the toolkit during the workshop and their ideation sheets and log sheet.

3.4 Data Collection and Analysis

Previous work shows that participants' subjective opinion is not enough to evaluate design cards [27]. Therefore, for this study, we used the *toolkit artifacts* (ideation sheets and log sheets), along with *video recording* for collecting data to investigate the ideation process with the card-based toolkit (see Fig. 2). For data analysis, we used descriptive statistics and the grounded theory approach [33]. The study focused on two main aspects: *completeness* and *collaboration* in the ideation process. Below we detail the data collection and analysis process for these aspects.

Fig. 2. GBL design workshop session (left side); teams' ideation and log sheets (right side)

Completeness (focus on all key GBL dimensions to ideate learning game design): means that a team must focus on and incorporate at least one or more concepts for each of the six GBL dimensions (categories) in their learning game design during the ideation process. For this study, the "completeness" is examined by investigating six key GBL dimensions (learning, game factors, affective reactions, usability, user, and environment) in the learning game design ideas produced by the teams. Although it is not essential to use all the 28 GBL concepts for ideating a learning game to achieve completeness as different concepts might be more or less relevant for different types of learning games, this thinking is in line with [34]. Nonetheless, it is crucial to cater to all high-level dimensions (looking at the game from multiple angles achieving multidimensional focus) in every learning game design to be effective, focusing on the concepts/factors deemed important for that specific game.

The toolkit artifacts were used to capture teams' design decisions to investigate "completeness" in their learning game design ideas. The team's log sheet details the order of primary cards (GBL concepts) they used in the ideation process. Each team's ideation sheets provide insights into the total GBL dimensions (out of six) covered in each activity. We used descriptive statistics to analyze the data for completeness.

Collaboration is explored by recording and analyzing the instances of interaction, discussion, and communication between team members facilitated by the card-based tool. The video recording of the play sessions (using a single fixed-point video camera next to the table, as shown in Fig. 2) provided the data for team dynamics during the learning game design's ideation process. Here, we were interested in investigating the ability of the card-based toolkit to scaffold collaboration. We used video-based micro ethnography [11], a qualitative research method, to gather information and understand how collaboration occurred in the teams using the toolkit and the main contributing factors that initiated it. Many researchers have applied ethnography to study speech and moment-to-moment gestures in contexts such as workplaces, virtual environments, or classrooms [35, 36]. Our analysis focused on investigating the design dialogues between team members to ideate learning game design throughout the video data. One case (team) was selected for video analysis in the context of this study to focus on detailed analysis and moment-to-moment interaction. The selection was based on random sampling. We used video analysis software V-Note Pro for analyzing the data for collaboration. The complete video recording for the selected case was 1 h and 44 min in length and included the team's ideation session (consisting of design activities, debriefing, and the focus group after the workshop closing). The video analysis was guided by the process presented by Heath et al. [37]. The analysis consisted of three rounds: in the *first round*, we watched the whole video and created a content log; in the *second round*, we identified the events of interest in the data corpus; and in the *third round* of analysis, we selected the segments for detailed speech act level analysis. We selected five segments related to the five design activities for detailed analysis because these segments were most active concerning collaboration and relevant to illustrate how the tool affected the team's collaborative design process. Next, a grounded theory approach by Gioia et al. [33] is followed to model, analyze and interpret the qualitative data collected through video analysis and present it as a data structure. We coded the events and actions using the V-Note Pro tool. Events are the episodes in the video recording referring to different activities. The selected segments were coded using data-driven categories that resulted in actions. The actions are the collaborative acts (instances of collaboration) undertaken by the players within the activities. The result of the analysis is presented in the next section.

4 Results

This section presents the design workshops' results regarding the card-based ideation tool's effectiveness to scaffold for completeness and collaboration in the early phase of the learning games design process. The LEAGUÊ ideation toolkit was used as the intervention in this study to analyze the scaffolding provided by the ideation cards. The results are compiled from the ideation session of seven teams using the toolkit through five design activities to ideate the educational game design.

4.1 Research Question 1: Completeness (GBL Dimensions Covered)

This section reports the use of primary cards (28 GBL concepts grouped in six categories) and total categories (six key GBL dimensions) covered by each team in different design activities and, overall, in produced game ideas. The used primary cards detail the GBL concepts focused on by each team.

Most to Least Used GBL Concepts. Figure 3. shows the classification of primary cards with regard to team usage. The figure highlights three categories: most used cards (that were used by more than 70% of teams), moderately used cards (used by nearly half of the teams), and less used cards (used by less than 30% of teams).

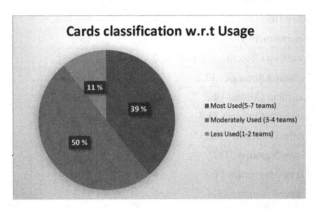

Fig. 3. Classification of primary cards (GBL concepts) according to team usage

The results from Table 1 show that learning domain, game genre, user, and learning objectives are the GBL aspects that were addressed by all seven teams, i.e., 100% usage. Following these aspects were environment, reaction, usability, gameplay, motivation, learner profile, and technical aspect considered by more than 60% of teams. The least important aspects, according to usage, were satisfaction, cognitive needs, and psychological needs, which were used by only 1 or 2 teams. It is also evident from these aspects' nature as they require much deeper focus and analysis, which is hard to realize within 30 min duration of the activity. Interestingly, all primary cards were used at least by one team, indicating that all GBL concepts were useful for ideation. However, it is also important to note that not even a single team used all primary cards. It does not necessarily mean that all GBL concepts are not important or required but more possibly that different concepts are more important for different types of games. Also, the time restrictions explain why not all cards were used.

Total GBL Concepts Used. Figure 4 presents the percentage of primary cards used by each team. Primary cards are 28 different GBL concepts (grouped in six categories focusing on GBL dimensions). There are six primary cards in the first activity and twenty-two in the second, with six categories (dimensions) offered in both activities. Four teams (57%) used all six primary cards in the first activity, meaning they focused on all six categories (key GBL dimensions).

The minimum number of cards used in activity 1 to generate a learning game idea was three (out of six) cards used by "team 1". However, this did not affect the overall "completeness" of this team, as shown in Fig. 5. In the second activity, none of the

Table 1. Team usage for individual GBL concepts

Primary cards (GBL concepts)	No of teams	Team usage (%)
Learning domain-DL	7	100%
Game genre-DG	7	100%
Reaction-DA	5	71%
Usability-DU	5	71%
User-DÊ	7	100%
Environment-DE	6	86%
Learning Objectives-FL1	7	100%
Learning Strategies-FL2	4	57%
Learning Content-FL3	3	43%
Learning Outcome-FL4	4	57%
Game Definition -FG1	4	57%
Game Narrative -FG2	4	57%
Game Mechanics-FG3	4	57%
Game Resources-FG4	4	57%
Game Aesthetics-FG5	4	57%
Game Play-FG6	5	71%
Enjoyment-FA1	3	43%
Engagement-FA2	3	43%
Motivation-FA3	5	71%
Flow-FA4	4	57%
Interface-FU1	4	57%
Learnability-FU2	3	43%
Satisfaction-FU3	2	29%
Learner Profile-FÊ1	5	71%
Cognitive Needs-FÊ2	2	29%
Psychological Needs-FÊ3	1	14%
Technical Aspects -FE1	5	71%
Context-FE2	4	57%

teams used all 22 cards. The maximum number of cards was used by "team 3" (16 cards), meaning they addressed 16 GBL concepts (out of 22) in the second activity. The minimum number of cards was used by "team 4" (only six cards). Similarly, the teams' total cards also vary, "team 3" and "team 7" used 21 cards (maximum in total), and "team 4" used only 12 cards (minimum in total).

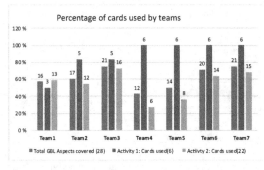

Fig. 4. Percentage of primary cards used by teams

GBL Dimensions Covered. Figure 5 (left) shows the percentage of key GBL dimensions (out of six) addressed by teams in each design activity and overall, in their produced game idea. It is interesting to note that overall, the teams addressed all six GBL dimensions in their produced game idea, which shows that the employed toolkit was useful in scaffolding for "completeness" in the GBL design process. However, it is important to note that they were not fully covered (teams used not all primary cards/GBL concepts within a category/dimension). We further analyzed the percentage of each category/GBL dimension covered by the seven teams, presented in Fig. 5 (right).

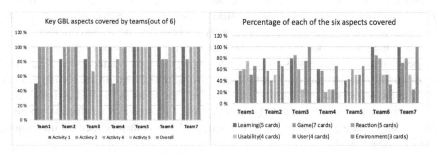

Fig. 5. GBL dimensions covered (left); percentage of each GBL dimension covered (right)

We also investigated for any common pattern (order of primary card usage) that most teams followed in developing their learning game design idea. These patterns could be useful to guide the process to other novice GBL designers. As primary cards are different GBL concepts used for building learning game design, a successful pattern could guide the GBL community regarding the best practice to tackle multiple GBL aspects for efficiency and effectiveness in the learning game design practice.

As explained before, the 28 primary cards are divided into the first two design activities: six in the first activity and twenty-two in the second activity. Therefore, to identify any pattern, we calculated the mode of "order of use of each card" for the seven teams for activities 1 and 2. Figure 6 highlights the pattern (concerning the order of primary card usage) in activity 1 (left) and activity 2 (right).

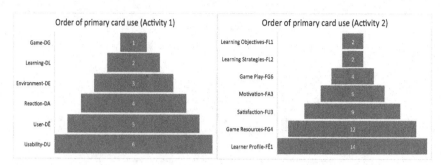

Fig. 6. Pattern in activity 1 (left); pattern in activity 2 (right)

The typical pattern identified in activity 1, "idea generation", as shown in Fig. 6 (left), was: First, the primary card "game" was used, then "learning", followed by the "environment" of the game. Further, the teams typically used the "reaction" card to address the affective-cognitive reaction the learning game intends to generate, followed by target "users", and lastly, the "usability" aspect. For the second activity, "idea development", the set of data values for only seven primary cards (out of 22) had a mode. These cards' order is presented in Fig. 6 (right), where the remaining cards had no mode value. One reason for this is the small sample size (only seven teams), and the percentage of usage for these cards was low; therefore, no frequent number was identified. Thus, we assume that it is possible to identify a clear pattern if the study is repeated with more teams (large sample size). From the identified order of use, we can see that "learning objectives" and "learning strategies" are mostly addressed at the second number (out of 22). It also means that once the vital GBL dimensions are addressed in the first activity in a specified order, most teams focus on addressing concepts related to the "learning" dimension followed by "game". Therefore, the teams' initial focus in the second activity is also on factors related to "learning" and "game", the same as the first activity. After that, "motivation" is addressed mostly in sixth place, followed by "satisfaction" in ninth place. Finally, "game resources" and "learner profile" was mostly focused on number 12 and 14, respectively.

The Produced Learning Game Design Ideas. The learning game designs ideated by the seven teams are presented below to exemplify the multidimensional focus in each idea.

Team 1 (NTNU runners!): All students at NTNU university with assignments learn to work as a team to achieve a common objective that is deadline extension by running away. The NTNU campus has sensors that are linked to GPS location used in the web game. The students work as a team and define mass escaping strategies, and the goal is not to get caught by the professors. The players use different avatars and colors for professors and students. Each student team has to use the same color of t-shirt and cannot leave the NTNU campus. The environment changes depending on the difficulty level of the assignment using 3D-videos. If the team succeeds in escaping from the professor, they get a deadline extension for that specific assignment, which gives them a sense of achievement and stress relief.

Team 2 (Math-ur-mind!): A puzzle-based mobile game for kids aged 8–12 years to understand math concepts through drill and practice using great graphics. The game can be played anywhere to develop math competencies and improve processing speed by solving exciting tasks in an interactive and fun way providing immediate feedback on actions for satisfaction.

Team 3 (Save the planet!): An outdoor tablet game for the elderly to change attitude and behavior regarding global warming and shopping behavior because they are not well informed about climate change. The game has vibration keys with easy navigation and audio features. Different interesting tasks (e.g., earn points by picking up the trash to clean the planet, shoot the plastic bags to free the planet) with constructive feedback allow the elderly to learn about recycling and mass production. The game provides fun facts on how to recycle and avoid global warming.

Team 4 (Swing or Die/ My swinging 20's (or Die)): An augmented reality game for the elderly with mobility issues to learn how to dance. The players get to dance with their idols. They have to learn to dance correctly according to the indicated move patterns shown by colored areas. The game uses an AR headset and motion tracking to indicate player to step in the right boxes at the right time to compete in dancing with some famous idols. The game uses a 3D environment with old-school aesthetics. Players can choose between different levels with various dancing patterns, locations, and dance types, along with increasing difficulty. If the player loses the competition, they will die.

Team 5 (PROGBOT): A cross-platform game for school children grades 5–7 to learn programming and related concepts. The player guides the robot through the levels by using simple symbolic programming as the main mechanic. The game has different levels on a world map, and players complete each level to conquer the area and defeat enemies. They can upgrade the robot with coins from completing levels. The player controls the robot by programming it. The game has a purposeful and consistent interface, and gameplay provides clear feedback when running the "program/solution" and encourages confidence by allowing for small growth steps.

Team 6 (Code and Conquer): A mobile game for children in primary school interested in technology to understand, apply, and develop competencies in programming skills through drill and practice and scenarios. The goal is to eliminate all the opponents. The game uses animation and tutorials and provides feedback and hints to develop competencies.

Team 7 (Smart city simulator (SCS)): A 3D simulation VR game for young adults (15–30 years old) to understand smart cities. A player uses a VR headset and VR controls to organize a smart city to increase knowledge of smart cities' concepts and seek cognitive reaction. Players use drag and drop to build buildings using 3D visualization. The game goal is to increase the inhabitants' happiness levels by developing smart cities. Inhabitants' happiness gives enjoyment and meaningful purpose, and an immersive game world gives engagement.

4.2   Research Question 2: Collaboration (Main Contributing Factors)

We followed the grounded theory approach by Gioia et al. [33] in conducting and presenting the analysis. The analysis started with finding recurring actions where collaboration occurred, forming first-order concepts (denoted as actions) from the data. We recorded the occurrences of these actions in V-Note, each with a start/end time. Hence, it was also possible to count the number of occurrences of each action during the design process, making it easier to investigate the frequency of different actions in events, in specific time intervals, or over the whole ideation session. The next step was to extract the themes guiding these actions of collaboration. Based on first-level codes (actions), we started seeking similarities and differences in the codes and grouped them to generate second-order themes (theoretical concepts from the data) explaining how codes relate to each other. The second-order themes represent the main factors contributing to collaboration among team members using a card-based toolkit. Finally, the second-order themes were compared against each other to distill them into "aggregate dimensions" that explain how card-based toolkit scaffold collaboration in the early phase of the GBL design process. The resulting data structure for collaboration among team members in ideating learning games using a card-based toolkit is shown in Fig. 7.

Our analysis resulted in the following six themes that characterize interaction in the GBL ideation process when using a card-based tool:

- *Interacting with the material*: In this theme, the contributing factor was the toolkit material that mediated the player's interactions. These instances of collaboration revolve around actions such as presenting cards to other team members, discussing different cards, working on the ideation sheets, or pointing to previous idea sheets. Interactions also included players together arranging, decluttering, or looking through cards for either initiating a discussion or further elaborating on it.

- *Focusing on Play*: The acts of collaboration in this theme were focused on play-related interactions. The players were engaged in discussing the plan, making play decisions, e.g., which aspect to take first, postponing something for later, asking questions about play rules, or explaining play rules to other players. Team members would also update each other on play status, e.g., what has been already done and what is still left.

- *Association for doing design activities*: Here, the contributing factor for collaboration was the association needed for collectively performing the design activities. It consisted of players asking questions and giving answers to each other (e.g., Player1: Who wants to write?; Player 5: I can write); asking questions from the facilitator (e.g., Player 1: Do we build on the previous activity?); agree or disagree with other players (e.g., Player 3: You look like you like drawing!; Player 2: No no! who said.); clarifying their point in a discussion (e.g., Player 2: No, I mean this is something that is already available), or giving general suggestions or comments (e.g., Player 2: It is better to stick them on the sheets at the end; Player 4: Let's move on!). The facilitator also enabled these interactions by often giving some instructions or presenting new information or choices (e.g., you can use more sheets; you can look through other sheets for getting an overview) to the team.

- *Ideating design/creative thinking*: In this theme, all collaborative interactions were instigated by co-creating the design where the players proposed design ideas, made collective design decisions by asking other players for input or analyzing, clarifying, evaluating a design idea. Players developed their design strategy as a team, justified

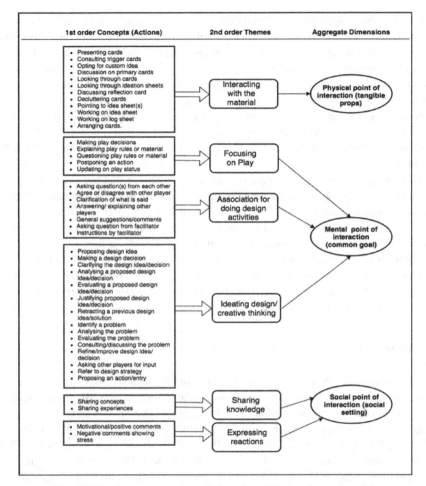

Fig. 7. The data structure for collaboration with a card-based toolkit

proposed design ideas, identified problems, analyzed and evaluated them through discussions, or referred to previous design solutions to improve or refine the design.

- *Sharing knowledge*: The contributing factor that mediated interactions in this theme was sharing knowledge and information. Players referred to their past experiences related to topics under discussion or generally built a rapport with others. Players also explained concepts to each other they knew it would be useful in creating shared understanding and awareness.

- *Expressing reactions*: These instances of collaborations were triggered by the feelings that players experienced within the playful and collaborative setup. The team members expressed their positive and negative thoughts and reactions at different points (sometimes within an activity and sometimes at the beginning or end) that indicated their motivation or stress.

The six themes aggregated to identify the three central features of a card-based toolkit that scaffolds collaboration. A card-based toolkit provides three points of interaction that effectively instigate and foster collaboration among team members: *Physical point of interaction, mental point of interaction,* and *social point of interaction.* The physical point of interaction is created by tangible props that serve as director and structure the activity forming building blocks of play. The mental point of interaction is created by the common goals that serve as actors that lead to performing the stated activity, i.e., ideation of learning game design. The social point of interaction is formed by the social setting that serves as a supporter that encourages participation by providing a friendly environment.

These three points have mutually beneficial relationships that together support the collaborative design process. The tangible props provide a steppingstone and generate a physical point of interaction that supports both attaining the common goal (by posing questions and providing hints) and encouraging social interaction (by providing initial grounds for initiating interaction). The social setting provides a friendly environment making it easier to share knowledge and information, leading to improved ideation and confidence for creative thinking. On the other hand, the common goal is the driver that motivates to make an effort to strengthen all types of collaborative interactions for achieving the objective.

5 Discussion

The results discussed the two research questions concerning scaffolding provided by the card-based ideation tool for completeness and collaboration in the GBL design process.

From the analysis of generated ideas in different design activities and observation of workshop sessions, we have established that the employed card-based toolkit performed well in scaffolding for completeness. It facilitated the teams to address all six key GBL dimensions (categories) in the produced game design ideas. However, not all GBL concepts (primary cards) related to each of the six categories (dimensions) were considered. One reason is the nature of a time-bound design workshop, which restricted the freedom to complete all cards. In a real-world setup, this can be controlled by changing activity rules from time-bound to finishing cards. It is not compulsory to cover all GBL concepts within a dimension as different games might give more weight to different concepts [38, 39]. However, considering the multidisciplinary nature of GBL [40, 41], it is essential to focus on six key GBL dimensions (targeting relevant concepts within each dimension) for effective GBL design, which was successfully achieved using the card-based toolkit. All primary cards were used at least by one team, indicating that every card (GBL concept) was relevant. However, some GBL concepts were more focused than others. The learning domain, game genre, target users, and learning objectives of the game are the concepts that were addressed by all seven teams. Whereas, satisfaction, cognitive needs, and psychological needs were least focused by the teams, perhaps because these concepts require more in-depth focus and analysis, and thus more time was required.

The different categories (color-coded for easy searchability) of primary cards supported achieving multidimensionality. Since cards act as tangible idea containers, by converting the six key GBL dimensions into different card categories, the primary cards acted as design building blocks that team members used to develop and complete their design ideas from multiple angles (achieving multidimensionality in design). The final activity format required documenting all the key GBL dimensions, which served as a reminder for the team to revisit the design decisions and ideation sheets and improve their idea by working on the missing aspects. It directed the teams to focus on all six GBL dimensions in the last activity. However, it is not the only feature that led to the completeness; almost all teams focused on all six GBL dimensions in at least one other design activity in addition to activity 5 (see Fig. 5). Therefore, breaking the ideation task into different activities supports completeness. Each new activity puts things into perspective, providing an opportunity to revisit the design decisions and further add or modify them if needed.

Our study also highlighted the potential of ideation cards to facilitate collaboration among team members in the early phase of the GBL design process. We identified three aggregate dimensions from six contributing factors that facilitate collaboration in the specific context of using a card-based toolkit (see Fig. 7). The toolkit scaffolds for collaboration by providing three points of interaction in the design process: Physical point of interaction (tangible props); Social point of interaction (social setting), and Mental point of interaction (common goal/task). Individual card items' physicality makes them different from other approaches such as design model/framework or checklist by affording actions such as grabbing, pointing, and sorting or grouping [13]. Team members focused on individual items deemed important for their learning game idea, area of expertise, or previous experience to start a discussion or bookmark their ideas. The cards help participants externalize the design rationale, making the ideas concrete and more accessible to themselves and other team members [13]. Also, as each card focused on one specific GBL element, it provided a comprehensive enough description of that element (using definition, examples, or images), making it easier for all stakeholders (from different areas) to understand the concept. Moreover, it also made it easy for team members to use that tangible information to further extend and explain their ideas to other team members. This type of card-based tool also has a strong potential of being a framework for analyzing the GBL's collaborative ideation process of multidisciplinary teams.

5.1 Limitations of the Study

One of the limitations of this paper is that there was no control group to compare the results and assess the intervention's effect. We could use a control group employing some other approach (such as a checklist or framework). However, we wanted to demonstrate its effectiveness in designers' practice where no such approach is typically used. We conducted design workshops for this study instead of using the toolkit in the designer's day-to-day practice in a game studio with professionals as it was practically difficult to achieve. However, the previous work [12] suggests that design workshops are a way to approximate design practice as it offers a similar environment with team-based design exercises and time-constrained format, similar to the environment to which designers are exposed. Another limitation of this study is that the LEAGUÊ toolkit is not representative of all GBL ideation cards. Therefore, the results are only generalizable to ideation cards presenting similiter features to LEGAUÊ or providing enough knowledge of GBL concepts. One could also argue that completeness was evaluated empirically using toolkit artifacts (counting the number of GBL concepts covered by each team). In contrast, expert evaluation could provide useful insights into the quality of generated ideas. However, for this paper's context, we were merely interested in understanding the scaffolding provided by the toolkit for achieving multidimensional focus in generated ideas (considering the learning game idea from multiple angles). The quality or effectiveness of generated ideas is important but was not the main focus of this study. Lastly, the workshop participants had no or little experience of GBL design; this was useful to explore the support for completeness provided by the card-based toolkit and not influenced by their experience and knowledge, ensuring the validity of data. It also allowed us to examine the cards' usefulness for early-career GBL designers but not senior designers.

6 Conclusion

Collaboration and completeness (considering the game from multiple angles) are vital in the GBL design process [5–7, 9] but are difficult to manage in practice [1, 3]. This paper attempts to solve this problem by postulating ideation cards as scaffolding for collaboration and completeness in the early design phase of learning games, advancing the state-of-the-art. The paper investigates the ideation process of learning games when using a card-based ideation toolkit, focusing on contributing factors and design recommendations for improvements. The data collected from the design workshops highlighted the usefulness of a card-based tool for scaffolding completeness and collaboration. All teams focused on GBL's six key dimensions in ideating their learning game design using the toolkit. The toolkit features that most contributed to scaffold completeness were different card categories and different tasks (design activities) in addition to the general characteristics of cards as tangible idea containers. The toolkit features that most contributed to collaboration were tangible props, common goals, and social setting.

Future work will focus on identifying GBL design patterns in the ideation process that can result in effective and efficient learning game designs to further help GBL designers in learning game design practice. A larger sample size is needed for this purpose. Moreover, we intend to use the toolkit with professional GBL design teams consisting of multidisciplinary experts. Future work should also focus on considering other existing card-based tools for GBL ideation and design to act as ready-made scaffolds for completeness and collaboration to validate this approach's effectiveness in the GBL design process. We will also extend the study dimensions to include creative thinking (creativity), which is also essential for the early design phase of learning games.

References

1. Silva, F.G.: Practical methodology for the design of educational serious games. Information 11(1), 14 (2020)
2. Tahir, R., et al.: Codifying game-based learning: the LEAGUE framework for Evaluation. In: Academic Conferences International Limited City (2018)

3. Harteveld, C.: Triadic Game Design: Balancing Reality, Meaning and Play. Springer, London (2011). https://doi.org/10.1007/978-1-84996-157-8
4. Zahedi, M., Tessier, V., Hawey, D.: Understanding collaborative design through activity theory. Des. J. **20**(1), S4611–S4620 (2017)
5. De Lope, R.P., Medina-Medina, N., Soldado, R.M., García, A.M., Gutiérrez-Vela, F.L.: Designing educational games: Key elements and methodological approach. IEEE (2017)
6. Zemliansky, P. Design and Implementation of Educational Games: Theoretical and Practical Perspectives: Theoretical and Practical Perspectives. IGI Global, Hershey (2010)
7. Tran, M.Q., Biddle, R.: Collaboration in serious game development: a case study (2008)
8. Maldonado, H., Lee, B., Klemmer, S.R., Pea, R.D.: Patterns of collaboration in design courses: team dynamics affect technology appropriation, artifact creation, and course performance (2007)
9. Brandt, E., Messeter, J.: Facilitating collaboration through design games (2004)
10. Kangas, M.: Creative and playful learning: Learning through game co-creation and games in a playful learning environment. Thinking Skills Creativity **5**(1), 1–15 (2010)
11. Hannula, O., Irrmann, O.: Played into collaborating: design games as scaffolding for service co-design project planning. Simul. Gaming **47**(5), 599–627 (2016)
12. Mueller, F., Gibbs, M.R., Vetere, F., Edge, D.: Supporting the creative game design process with exertion cards (2014)
13. Deng, Y., Antle, A.N., Neustaedter, C.: Tango cards: a card-based design tool for informing the design of tangible learning games (2014)
14. Markopoulos, P., Martens, J.-B., Malins, J., Coninx, K., Liapis, A.: Creativity and collaboration in early design. In: Markopoulos, P., Martens, J.-B., Malins, J., Coninx, K., Liapis, A. (eds.) Collaboration in Creative Design, pp. 1–9. Springer, Cham (2016). https://doi.org/10.1007/978-3-319-29155-0_1
15. Lucero, A., Dalsgaard, P., Halskov, K., Buur, J.: Designing with cards. In: Markopoulos, P., Martens, J.-B., Malins, J., Coninx, K., Liapis, A. (eds.) Collaboration in Creative Design, pp. 75–95. Springer, Cham (2016). https://doi.org/10.1007/978-3-319-29155-0_5
16. Kellner, G., Sommeregger, P., Berthold, M.: Towards guidelines for educational adventure games creation (EAGC). In: Ravenscroft, A., Lindstaedt, S., Kloos, C.D., Hernández-Leo, D. (eds.) EC-TEL 2012. LNCS, vol. 7563, pp. 550–550. Springer, Heidelberg (2012). https://doi.org/10.1007/978-3-642-33263-0_66
17. Avouris, N., Mavrommati, I., Sintoris, C.: Designing through ideation cards for internet of things: can cards help engineers out of the box (2018)
18. Vaajakallio, K., Mattelmäki, T.: Design games in codesign: as a tool, a mindset and a structure. CoDesign **10**(1), 63–77 (2014)
19. Costa, A.C., Rebelo, F., Rodrigues, A.: Co-designing a civic educational online game with children. In: Marcus, A., Wang, W. (eds.) DUXU 2017. LNCS, vol. 10289, pp. 377–386. Springer, Cham (2017). https://doi.org/10.1007/978-3-319-58637-3_30
20. Marne, B., Wisdom, J., Huynh-Kim-Bang, B., Labat, J.-M.: The six facets of serious game design: a methodology enhanced by our design pattern library. In: Ravenscroft, A., Lindstaedt, S., Kloos, C.D., Hernández-Leo, D. (eds.) EC-TEL 2012. LNCS, vol. 7563, pp. 208–221. Springer, Heidelberg (2012). https://doi.org/10.1007/978-3-642-33263-0_17
21. Kayali, F., Schwarz, V., Götzenbrucker, G., Purgathofer, P.: Learning, gaming, designing: using playful participation to create learning games together with high school students. Conjunctions Transdisciplinary J. Cult. Participation **3**(1), 1–10 (2016)
22. Schmoelz, A.: On co-creativity in playful classroom activities. *Creativity.* Theor. Res. Appl. **4**(1), 25–64 (2017)
23. Roy, R., Warren, J.P.: Card-based design tools: a review and analysis of 155 card decks for designers and designing. Des. Stud. **63**, 125–154 (2019)

24. Frich, J., MacDonald Vermeulen, L., Remy, C., Biskjaer, M. M., Dalsgaard, P.: Mapping the landscape of creativity support tools in HCI (2019)
25. Bekker, T., De Valk, L., Rijnbout, P., de Graaf, M., Schouten, B., Eggen, B.: Investigating perspectives on play: the lenses of play tool (2015)
26. Chasanidou, D.: Design for motivation: evaluation of a design tool. Multimodal Technol. Interact. 2(1), 6 (2018)
27. Sintoris, C., Mavrommati, I., Avouris, N., Chatzigiannakis, I.: Out of the box: using gamification cards to teach ideation to engineering students. In: Kameas, A., Stathis, K. (eds.) AmI 2018. LNCS, vol. 11249, pp. 221–226. Springer, Cham (2018). https://doi.org/10.1007/978-3-030-03062-9_17
28. Pernin, J.-P., Mariais, C., Michau, F., Emin-Martinez, V., Mandran, N.: Using game mechanisms to foster GBL designers' cooperation and creativity. Int. J. Learn. Technol. 9(2), 139–160 (2014)
29. Tahir, R., Wang, A.I.: Transforming a theoretical framework to design cards: LEAGUE ideation toolkit for game-based learning design. Sustainability 12(20), 8487 (2020)
30. Ørngreen, R., Levinsen, K.: Workshops as a research methodology. Electron. J. E-learn. 15(1), 70–81 (2017)
31. Savenye, W.C., Robinson, R.S.: Qualitative research issues and methods: an introduction for educational technologists (2013)
32. Given, L.M.: The Sage Encyclopedia of Qualitative Research Methods. Sage publications, Thousand Oaks (2008)
33. Gioia, D.A., Corley, K.G., Hamilton, A.L.: Seeking qualitative rigor in inductive research: notes on the Gioia methodology. Organ. Res. Methods 16(1), 15–31 (2013)
34. Carson, R.S., et al.: 5.1. 3 Requirements completeness: prepared by the requirements working group of the international council on systems engineering for information only; not approved by INCOSE Technical. INCOSE Int. Symp. (2004)
35. Streeck, J., Mehus, S.: Microethnography: the study of practices. Handbook of Language and Social Interaction, Lawrence Erlbaum Associates, Inc., New Jersey, pp. 381–404 (2005)
36. Kohonen-Aho, L., Alin, P.: Introducing a video-based strategy for theorizing social presence emergence in 3D virtual environments. Presence: Teleoperators Virtual Environ. 24(2) 113–131 (2015)
37. Heath, C., Hindmarsh, J., Luff, P.: Video in Qualitative Research. Sage Publications, Thousand Oaks (2010)
38. Maruyama, Y., Masoodian, M., Rogers, B.: A survey of Japanese gamers' ratings of experience elements for different game genres (2011)
39. Rapeepisarn, K., Wong, K.W., Fung, C.C., Khine, M.S.: The relationship between game genres, learning techniques and learning styles in educational computer games. In: Pan, Z., Zhang, X., Rhalibi, A., Woo, W., Li, Y. (eds.) Edutainment 2008. LNCS, vol. 5093, pp. 497–508. Springer, Heidelberg (2008). https://doi.org/10.1007/978-3-540-69736-7_53
40. De Freitas, S.: Are games effective learning tools? a review of educational games. J. Educ. Technol. Soc. 21(2), 74–84 (2018)
41. Winn, B., Heeter, C.: Resolving conflicts in educational game design through playtesting. Innovate J. Online Educ. 3(2) (2006)

Mobile Game-Based Learning in Distance Education: A Mixed Analysis of Learners' Emotions and Gaming Features

Katerina Tzafilkou$^{(\boxtimes)}$ (ID) and Anastasios A. Economides (ID)

University of Macedonia, Thessaloniki, Greece
tzafilkou@uom.edu.gr

Abstract. Although there are multiple approaches for making lectures more interactive, Game-Based Learning (GBL) tends to achieve the highest impact on students' emotional engagement. To this end, this study seeks to implement a mobile GBL approach in a Distance Education (DE) course to investigate the students' gaming experience and learning related emotions. The experiment was conducted on 26 post-graduate distance students using a Kahoot! mobile game and a self-reported instrument. Quantitative analysis was implemented to measure the students' perceived i) competence, ii) concentration and ii) immersion, and the learning related emotions of i) enjoyment, ii) boredom, iii) confusion, and iv) anxiety. Sentiment analysis revealed a highly positive emotional attitude towards mobile GBL in DE and highlighted the prevalent emotions of joy and competence. Thematic content analysis was applied to investigate the gaming features that caused negative or positive emotions. Time limit and music/sound were proved to cause negative emotions, while multimedia, colors, learnability, and sequencing were reported as positive emotional antecedes. Competition revealed mixed outcomes. Overall, this study provides with useful insights that can be used by educators and emotional designers to increase engagement and learning performance in DE.

Keywords: Distance education · Game-based learning · Learners' emotions

1 Introduction

Learning related emotions (LREs) have long been recognized as strong determinants of student engagement and learning achievement both in face-to-face and in distance education (DE). Emotions seem to play a crucial role in DE since keeping on learners' engagement and attention over time is the greatest challenge. As a fact, low engagement and interactivity in DE courses seem to be the reason for the students' lower scores of performances compared to face-to-face courses [1].

Although there are multiple approaches for making lectures more interactive (e.g., breaking the class into smaller groups, questioning the audience, using students' response system, multimedia, etc.), it is their combination with gaming features that achieves the highest impact on student engagement [2].

The original version of this chapter was revised: the missing acknowledgements section has been added. The correction to this chapter is available at https://doi.org/10.1007/978-3-030-77943-6_23

Researchers generally agree that well-designed games can be efficient learning machines and increase the players' engagement and learning achievement [2]. Interestingly, recent studies [3], have showed that when game-based learning approaches are implemented in DE, students tend to achieve higher performance scores than students attending a face-to-face class. Similarly, in the context of tradition (face-to-face) education, students enrolled in GBL activities have achieved higher performance scores and positive emotions compared to students enrolled in non GBL tasks [4]. Research in higher education has also shown that GBL can significantly improve the students' perception on the learning topic and enhance their overall learning experience and interaction [5].

Beyond learning achievement, research has also shown the ability of games to induce emotions; these emotions tend to enhance learning outcomes in digital learning environments [6]. As a fact, emotional design can be used in GBL to increase students' emotional engagement and enhance their achievement in DE courses. Today, it is even more useful to study the emotional effects of GBL in DE mainly due to the pandemic situation.

Despite the emerged popularity of GBL in education, researchers agree that little is still know about the game elements and mechanics that increase the learners' performance and emotional engagement [4]. As suggested in [6] "future research should investigate additional visual and auditory attributes (music, sound), game mechanics, and other design elements".

Although there are several research studies in the context of implementing GBL in higher education, research on students' emotions or sentiment analysis in DE is significantly limited. Nowadays, the pandemic crisis and the urgent transition to DE has caused a massive shift to mobile learning, since it provides access to multiple people, e.g., in a single household. For this reason, mobile learning is an unavoidable alternative during COVID-19 [7]. In this context, mobile Game-based Learning (mGBL) can be considered as a cost-effective, expandable, and accessible alternative.

Motivated by the mentioned research challenge and the increased need for student engagement in DE courses, this study seeks to investigate the students' gaming experience and emotions, as well as the gaming features that tend to cause positive or negative emotions in DE implemented mGBL activities. To this end, this study is guided by the following research questions.

RQ1. What are the students' perceived emotions and gaming experience during mGBL tasks in DE?
RQ2. What is the main sentiment and the most frequently perceived learning-related emotions during mGBL tasks in DE?
RQ3. What are the mGBL features that cause either negative or positive student emotions in DE?

The main contribution of this study is to provide with useful insights on students' emotions towards mGBL in the context of DE. Moreover, it extends previous literature by detecting the students' sentiment in mGBL, and the game features that bring positive or negative emotional impact. The findings might be useful for educators, emotional designers, and educational institutions towards the design of engaging mGBL activities in DE.

2   Theoretical Background

2.1   Learning Related Emotions and Distance Education

Research has extensively explained how positive emotions support information processing, problem solving and other cognitive activities [8, 9]. For this, it is well accepted that emotions are crucial determinants to the learning processes and have an impact on academic achievement [1]. Unfortunately, the question of how students emotionally experience online-learning environments has not been sufficiently answered so far [10].

Learning-Related emotions (LREs) or else called 'achievement emotions' have emerged after the development of the Control-Value Theory (CVT) [11] that categorized them according to valence (positive, negative) and nature of response (activating or deactivating). In the context of digital education and games, research on LREs usually targets the emotions of enjoyment, frustration, anxiety, boredom, and confusion [12–15]. Overall it is accepted that, positive LREs serve as a determinant of students' emotional well-being and achievement [10], while negative LREs tend to yield negative impact on learning outcomes [14, 15]. For this reason, several studies have proposed the use of emotional agents [16] or other emotional feedback methodologies to induce positive emotions to students.

Recently, research has revealed several emotional differentiations among students who attend distance and face-to-face courses. Most studies conclude that students tend to perceive negative emotions at higher levels when attending online courses compared to students attending face-to-face courses [10].

In parallel, opinion mining and sentiment analysis has revealed mixed emotional responses towards online learning. In [17] the authors found that learners posted in social media more positive than negative comments about online classes, webinars, and e-assignments. Similarly, previous studies revealed positive sentiments towards e-learning and massive open online courses (MOOCs) [18]. However, most of the mentioned studies conducted their research on non GBL online lectures and they were based on generic data retrieved from social media posts.

Recently in [4] the authors conducted a mixed survey using face tracking to measure emotional expressive behavior in GBL and non GBL tasks. Their findings revealed a strong case for differential emotional engagement where learners expressed higher emotional engagement in game than in non-game-based learning tasks. However, their study did not examine the game features that potentially caused higher emotional engagement. Moreover, further research is needed in the context of GBL in DE.

2.2   Game Based Learning Features and Emotional Design

Games have long been recognized as strong emotional influencers. This potential is mainly due to their ability of placing the player in a continuous interaction loop which in turn develops complex cognitive and affective responses [19]. Researchers agree all game features and surroundings, including design elements, mechanics and dynamics can trigger emotional responses to players. The same principle is adopted in the context of GBL. Several studies on learning with multimedia have suggested that different design decisions can induce emotional reactions which in turn, affect learning performance [20,

21]. For this reason, game features can be adjusted by emotional designers to affect the playing experience and influence learner emotions [6, 19, 21]. Some examples of game features that have been found to affect the players' emotional states include audiovisual settings such as lighting, saturation, music) and sound effects Other features concern virtual camera profiles and effects and game rules [19].

Several researchers have studied the effects of game features on learners' emotions [20–22], however most of these studies are focused on the examination of the visual design features like colors and shapes. According to common findings, color and shape affect learners' emotions in GBL tasks, where learners seem to engage more positively with warm colors and round shapes.

Recently, Plass et al. in [6] have extended the research on game elements as emotions antecedents by investigating the role of dimensionality and expression of game characters (images) in GBL. Their findings revealed that 3D visual representations of game characters and positive ("happy") character expressions can bring stronger affective impact compared to 2D characters and neutral/sad expressions. The authors suggest that further research is needed to examine ethe emotional role of other game features like music and sounds.

In this study, we consider the positive impact of GBL on emotional engagement and attempt to explore the game features and their emotional impact on students in the context of DE. To this end, we consider that DE applied GBL might serve as a solution in DE disengagement and increase learner's engagement and learning achievement.

3 Material and Methods

3.1 Mobile Game-Based Learning App

Kahoot! Platform: Kahoot! is a game-based learning platform used to assess students' knowledge, for formative assessment, teach them new topics or be used as a break from traditional classroom activities [2]. Kahoot! is among the most popular (m)GBL platforms and is designed on the principles of student response system, the theory of intrinsic motivation [23] and game flow. In simple terms, Kahoot! is a combination of using audience responses, role-plays and, it uses video and audiovisual aids. The goal of Kahoot! is to increase engagement, motivation, enjoyment, and concentration and improve learning performance.

Prototype App. An mGBL challenge task was designed using the Kahoot! platform to serve as the prototype application. Contrary to live kahoot! games, a challenge (or students-paced game) allows students to play at their own pace using a mobile app. The game-based learning design was based on the teaching approach of 'blind kahoot! for introducing new topics' and was composed of 15 gaming tasks including quizzes, polls, puzzles, image frames, slides with text and videos. The learning topic was 'Prototyping for System and Product Design'. The aim of the game was to teach new knowledge on the topic and not to evaluate an already gained one.

In the first slide the students were introduced with the concept of Prototyping and then they needed to watch the educational material (short videos or text) and reply to different types of questions including multiple-choice with one correct answer, multiple-choice with several correct answers, puzzles of words, polls and True or False statements. The game was designed in a way to progressively add new knowledge and reveal the solutions/correct answers through a framed image. The images were initially hidden and was revealed in pieces within the applied time frame. A timer was visible all the time, and the time limit was varied for every question. The minimum time was set to 20 s, and the maximum time was 240 s.

In the end of every game task the students could see their performance score compared to that of their colleagues, and then proceed to the next tasks. Figure 1 depicts some screen examples of gaming tasks.

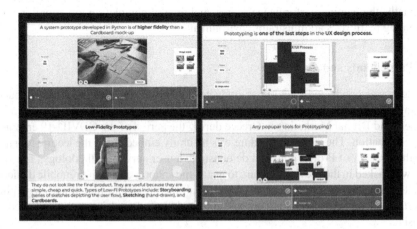

Fig. 1. Example tasks of the kahoot! game

3.2 Instrument and Measures

A self-reported instrument was designed to measure the students' post-gaming perceptions of the gaming experience: i) competence, ii) concentration, and ii) immersion, as well as their learning related emotions of: i) enjoyment, ii) boredom, iii) confusion, and iv) anxiety.

The items were selected from previous studies and were reviewed by two experts in the field of Teacher Training and Technology Enhanced Learning (TEL) to eliminate any typos and difficulty in perceived words or expressions. In particular, the measured items were designed based on the works of [24–26]. All scaled variables were measured using a five-point Likert scale format ranging from 1 = Strongly Disagree to 5 = Strongly Agree. We chose to measure each variable through one questionnaire item. Research has shown that this approach is acceptable with regard to reliability of the model and is applied for particular non-complex constructs that can be clearly and homogeneously perceived (e.g. easiness, enjoyment, interest, attention, etc.), as suggested by several works [14].

The students' perceived ICT self-efficacy levels were measured in the pre-gaming questionnaire, along with the students' demographics, and gaming preferences. ICT Self-efficacy was measured through three scaled items based on previous literature works [27, 28] and the component validity was validated through Cronbach alpha ($\alpha < 0.7$).

The features of GBL that can cause positive and/or negative emotions during distance learning in DE were examined through open-ended questions as following:

(a) "Briefly describe the reasons/features that made you feel discomfort, anxious or angry during the game-based learning task?"
(b) "Briefly describe the reasons/features that made you feel convenient, good or happy during the game-based learning task".

Finally, the gaming performance scores, and time of completion was monitored by the gaming platform's administrator environment.

3.3 Participants and Procedure

The study was conducted on 32 post-graduate students enrolled in the elective course of Human-Computer Interaction, Design and User Experience, in the Programme of e-Business and Digital Marketing in Greece during the period of the COVID-19 emerged remote education. The survey procedure was naturally embedded in the lecture to introduce the concept of Prototyping and demonstrate a user survey methodology. The students were asked in the previous lecture to install the kahoot! app in their mobile devices. Since the course is tough in English language, all the procedure including the gaming tasks, the self-reported questionnaire and the final class-discussion was conducted in English.

A total of 26 students (14 males, 12 females) successfully completed all the survey parts. In the beginning of the survey, the participants were asked to reply on an online pre-game questionnaire to provide some information on their demographics, ICT self-efficacy, gaming preferences and experience.

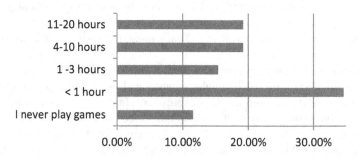

Fig. 2. Learners' gaming hours per week. N = 26

Most of the students expressed high or medium levels of ICT Self-Efficacy (mean = 3.9; st.dev. = 0.7) and reported that they spend less than one hour per day in playing video or mobile games (see Fig. 2). Games of action and strategy where among the most preferred ones, while several students stated that they prefer games of adventure, sports, shooter, and racing. Role playing, VR games and family entertainment received the lowest scores in terms of preference.

Then, they needed to access the GBL app via their mobiles and play the game. After the gaming procedure, the participants had to fill-in a second questionnaire to rate their mGBL experience and perceived emotions. At the end of the survey, all students were invited to orally provide their feedback regarding their perceptions, in the context of a class discussion through the Zoom video conference platform.

3.4 Data Analysis

The data analysis followed a mixed methodology. The collected quantitative data was analyzed in terms of descriptive statistics using SPSS.

The qualitative (text) data was analyzed through thematic content analysis and sentiment analysis. The thematic content analysis included the generation of thematic categories and codes based on the participants' textual feedback that was collected through the open-ended questions. The sentiment analysis was conducted following a lexicon-based approach and the use of three different lexicon packages. The thematic content analysis was conducted manually by the authors through excel tables, while the sentiment analysis was conducted through R scripts and R lexicon libraries.

RQ1 was answered through descriptive statistics, RQ2 was examined through sentiment analysis and RQ3 was examined through content thematic analysis. An overview of the combined results is also discussed in the text.

4 Results and Discussion

4.1 Gaming Performance

The players' scores were monitored and reported by the kahoot! platform. According to these measurements, the students' average performance score was 53.5%. The best performer achieved a score of 100% while the lowest score was 36%. (see Fig. 3). Two questions were labelled as the most difficult ones, including the puzzle task and one question of quiz type. Overall, the game lasted for about 9 min.

Since that was a new challenge game to introduce a new topic that was not previously thought, the performance results were of medium levels (50%–60%) for several users. Based on the discussion feedback that was collected in the end of the survey, this type of learning has might leveraged the level of difficulty. As a fact some students expressed their need to receive further educational material that extends the one provided in the game.

Since the questionnaire feedback was collected anonymously, we could not link the performance scores to the measured variables and analyze them further.

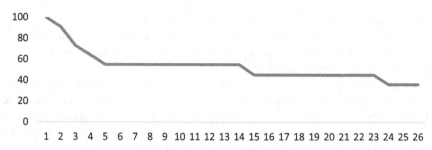

Fig. 3. Learners' gaming performance (max:100%, min:36%). N = 26

4.2 Descriptive Statistics

Overall, the students expressed a positive emotional attitude towards mGBL in DE.

Learning Related Emotions. 84% of the respondents stated that they highly enjoyed the learning game, while only 3% expressed feelings of non-enjoyment. In terms of boredom, 80% of the respondents stated that they did not experience this feeling, while 12% stated that were feeling bored. The feeling of frustration/confusion received a mixed feedback; although 55% revealed no feelings of frustration, 25% of the participants stated that they did feel frustrated and/or confused. This situation can be explained by the performance results, presented above since the overall performance was of a medium level and a couple of questions were monitored as difficult for most of the players. Regarding the feeling of anxiety, 75% of the participants sated that they did not feel anxious during the game while 8% reported some levels stress and 16% expressed a neutral state. This finding is interesting, since according to literature [29] students tend to develop higher levels of anxiety in online and distance education. Hence the inclusion of game-based learning tasks could possibly lead to the elimination of students' anxiety and/or the increment of enjoyment; eventually this could positively affect the overall students' engagement and learning performance [30, 31].

Game Experience. The sense of competency was perceived as the highest one, among the measured gaming flow and experience variables and almost 80% felt challenged. Also, 70% of the participants stated that they were not distracted from anything else while playing the game. Similarly, 75% of the participants stated that they could state concentrated all the time.

Also, it is is worthy to mention that several students (28% of them) felt time-pressured (mean = 2.72, st.dev = 1.18) mainly because of the timer that was applied in all the gaming tasks, as explained in the qualitative results of this survey.

Table 1 below depicts the descriptive statistics results for the measured items.

4.3 Sentiment Analysis

An R-based sentiment analysis was applied on the students' textual feedback, similar to the methodologies of previous studies [32–34] that used lexicon-based approaches

Table 1. Descriptive statistics for the measured items (N = 26)

Variable	Mean	St. Error	Std. Deviation
Game experience			
Competence	4.0833	.16936	.82970
Immersion	3.7917	.13431	.65801
Concentration	3.9683	.15322	.75060
Emotions			
Enjoyment	4.0417	.15322	.75060
Boredom	2.1667	.17720	.86811
Confusion	2.5000	.24818	1.21584
Anxiety	1.8750	.20245	.99181

to analyze students' feedback and course reviews. The developed R program computed sentiment polarity by averaging the sentiments of the text based on a sentiment dictionary derived from different unigram-based lexicons [35, 36].

A total of 61 sentiment related words were identified in the text. The results of the "bing" lexicon analysis [35] revealed that the text has 18 negative polarity words and 43 positive polarity words, meaning that there are almost two times more positive than negative words in this text. Moreover, the summary statistics of the lexicon vectors showed that the median value of sentiment scores is above 0, implying that the overall average sentiment across the responses is positive.

The above-mentioned outcome was further confirmed by an emotion classification approach using the NRC Emotion Lexicon [36] that identifies a set of word associations with eight basic emotions (anger, anticipation, disgust, fear, joy, sadness, surprise, trust) where joy and trust received the highest scores.

Table 2 depicts the LRE related positive and negative words along with their sentiment scores (-5 = very negative, 5 = very positive) according to the "afinn" lexicon scale for annotation. The list displays only the GBL and LRE related terms, while several identified words have been removed because they are not considered by the authors to be tightly associated to the research objectives of this study. The sentiment polarity was automatically detected by the "bing" lexicon and it was cross validated by the authors. Interestingly the word "challenging" was perceived as negative by the "bing" lexicon, but no score was assigned by the "afinn" lexicon, so it is not included in the combined list.

As depicted, the words of "fun" and "winning" were rated as the most positive ones while the most negative word was "lost". When analyzing the phrases that included these words, we discovered that the word "winning" was reflecting the game characteristic of score or reward, while the word "fun" mainly reflected the learning mode that was also perceived as playful and enjoyable.

There was only one student who used the word "lost" referring to the network connection and not the gaming flow or else. The excerpt of the text is provided below:

Table 2. Detected emotion words, polarity, and sentiment scores according to the "bing" and "afinn" lexicons (Hu & Lu, 2004; Nielsen, 2011).

Word	Sentiment polarity	Sentiment Score
Anxious	Negative	−2
Discomfort/Uncomfortable	Negative	−2
Good	Positive	3
Great	Positive	3
Silly	Negative	−1
Mistakes	Negative	−2
Lost	Negative	−3
Liked	Positive	2
Gained	Positive	2
Interesting	Positive	2
Fun	Positive	4
Recommend	Positive	2
Confusing	Negative	−2
Difficult	Negative	−1
Wrong	Negative	−2
Limited	Negative	−1
Playful	Positive	2
Focused	Positive	2
Great	Positive	3
Happy	Positive	3
Friendly	Positive	2
Easy	Positive	1
Interest	Positive	1
Winning	Positive	4
Motivated/Engaged	Positive	1
Winning	Positive	4
Focused	Positive	2
Helpful	Positive	2
Gained	Positive	2
Best	Positive	3

"I got a bit anxious because I lost the connection with the game app while I had three more questions to finish and I didn't know if I could enter again". This finding is in accordance with previous literature [31] showing that network and technical issues are amongst the most common factors that cause students anxiety in distance education.

Some other highly rated positive words were "happy", "good", "great", and "best" reflecting the overall emotional engagement of the students. As a fact, one of the participants with previous GBL experience admitted "It was the best designed kahoot! game that I have participated so far".

Figure 4 depicts the frequency of the most frequently used LRE related words. As depicted in Fig. 4, the synonyms of joy (including happiness, fun, playfulness), easiness and competency were clearly the most frequently used emotional words. Also, the frequency of the word "focused" validated the results in Table 1 regarding the high levels of students' concentration during the tasks.

Interestingly, words related to stress/anxiety where obviously more frequently used than other negative emotional statements like discomfort and confusion. This result is in accordance with previous studies stating that students experience higher levels of anxiety in distance education [29]. In the context of mGBL, this phenomenon can be explained in the next section, where we discuss the gaming features that caused stress/anxiety to several students.

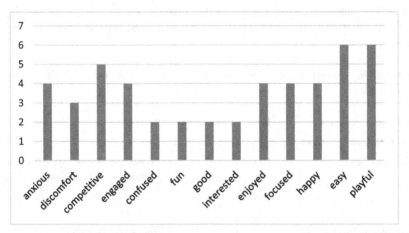

Fig. 4. Most frequently expressed emotion words, related to Game-Based Learning (GBL) and Learning-Related Emotions (LREs)

As a conclusion, in accordance with the results of the statistical values in Table 1, the sentiment analysis revealed an overall positive polarity and showed that joy, easiness and competency were the most frequently perceived LRE.

Although boredom was explicitly measured in the descriptive statistics and was positively rated by 12% of the participants, it was not observed in the students' textual feedback.

Also, although stress/anxiety revealed low scores in the descriptive results, from the qualitative analysis we can conclude that stress/anxiety was the most frequent negative emotion (e.g., compared to confusion) that was perceived from the participants. This outcome can also be validated by the oral feedback that was provided by the students during the group/class discussion where three students expressed their sense of anxiety because of the time-limit and the background music and sounds.

4.4 Mobile Game-Based Learning Features and Emotional Effects

The authors manually coded a sample of 52 sentences using excel tables. The coding identified four main aspects of mGBL features causing either positive or negative emotions: (a) Design elements, (b) User experience and usability, (c) Game dynamics, and (d) Content and learning outcome. Among the detected codes, time limit and music were the most frequently expressed negative features, while colors, multimedia and learnability were perceived to cause positive emotions by most of the students. Interestingly, competency revealed mixed emotions since some students perceived it as motivating while others perceived it as stressful.

The categorization of the codes into distinct themes was mainly based on previous literature studies in the field of GBL and gamification that clearly distinguish the concepts of game mechanics, elements, and dynamics, and User Experience (UX) and usability [37]. The current analysis extended previous studies by proposing more or different codes (e.g., music, timer, learnability) and components.

Table 3 includes the coding categories that make up the four major themes. It also presents the emotional outcome (negative or positive), and some example excerpts of the analyzed text.

Table 3. Gaming features and students' perceived emotions: results from a qualitative content analysis (n = 26)

Content area (theme/code)	Emotional outcome	Example
Theme 1. Design elements		
Multimedia (videos, images)	Positive	"Photos and videos during each question was helpful and enjoyable."
Timer	Negative	"I felt a little bit stressed about the time limit."
Background music/sounds	Negative	"The sounds of kahoot! made me little anxious."
Colors	Positive	'…The colors, pictures, and videos were included as guidelines to find the correct answers."
Theme 2. User experience and usability		
Learnability	Positive	'It was easy to navigate, easy to understand and use."
Memorability	Positive	"I was actively in responding by playing and it was easy to remember what I was doing."

(*continued*)

Table 3. (*continued*)

Content area (theme/code)	Emotional outcome	Example
Support (Information provided)	Positive	"…there was also a short description of the theory taught, at the beginning of some questions."
Game flow (Sequencing)	Positive	"…there was a continuity in the questions, and I wanted to see the next and then the next question…"
Theme 3. Game dynamics		
Score/Reward	Positive	"I believe the winning feature makes the game engaging."
Achievement	Positive	"I felt happy every time I was answering the correct answer"
Competition	Positive	"Also, the fact that you compete others it makes it more engaged and motivate you to be more focused."
	Negative	"…the fact that you compete others with the time as a parameter on your ranking, it made me answer fast and sometimes without thinking thoroughly of my answers."
Theme 4. Topic and learning outcome		
Engaging to learn	Positive	"…it was a fun and enjoyable way to learn, teaching you stuff in not a boring way."
Interest of the learning topic	Positive	"The concept of prototyping interests me a lot."
Perceived gained knowledge	Positive	"I liked the provided knowledge through the quiz."

Following we discuss the most important and contributing outcomes hat were identified in the thematic content analysis.

Design Elements. The thematic content revealed which design elements play an important role in the students' emotional engagement during distance mGBL activities. The most frequently expressed positive attribute was colors. Although we did not receive any further explanation on the type of the colors that caused positive emotions (although we know the interface was designed in warm colors), our finding is in accordance with previous studies [6, 21] suggesting that color is an important game element to be considered in GBL emotional design.

This study also revealed that mages and videos were also considered as positive emotional antecedents, while timer and music were perceived as negative antecedents since several students mentioned that they caused them some level of stress. However, other research [38] has shown that voiceovers has increased student engagement in digital game-based learning. This could be explained by the fact that different types of music might cause different emotions. Moreover, we encourage future researchers to study the effects of time and music derived anxiety on learning outcomes and identify the direction of the relationship. As a fact research has shown that in some cased anxiety can yield positive learning outcomes, mainly because it motivates students to avoid failure and put more effort in terms of attention [11, 20] (Park et al., 2015; Perkun, 2006).

User Experience and Usability Features. User experience design is tightly link to user emotions [39] and hence its principles are carefully adopted in the context of emotional design interfaces. Learnability is a core aspect of User Experience and usability since it defines how easy it is for a user to learn how to use an interface [40]. Memorability tightly linked to learning via some memory related cognitive processes defining that an 'easy to learn' interface should decrease cognitive load by being 'easy to remember'. This study reveals the essential role of learnability and memorability in the design of mGBL apps since they seem to cause positive emotional impact and yield high levels of perceived knowledge improvement.

In addition, game flow regarding the sequence of the questions was mentioned by several students to bring positive emotional effects. Similarly, the provision of information caused positive emotions, however the lack of some information for instance the lack of clear instructions and guidelines on how many answers a multiple-choice question can take caused negative feelings.

Game Dynamics. In accordance with previous [6, 19] this study confirmed that game dynamics affect learners' emotional state also in GBL tasks in DE. As a fact, scoring, rewarding and sense of achievement were perceived positively by the students. However, the most important finding of this part of the study is the competition effects that revealed both positive and negative emotional outcomes. Although most studies conclude that competition will cause positive emotional engagement, it seems that for some students it has reverse impact since it tends to increase anxiety. The negative aspect of competency in games is slightly expressed in previous studies [19] however no statistical evidence is available. Contrary in [41] the authors showed that competition increased in-game learning and enjoyment in mathematics learning games in middle schools.

In this context, we assume that competency might yield anxiety however the relationship to the learning outcome should be further examined since in this study we have not examined whether competency-related anxiety causes higher or lower performance. For this reason, we suggest that GBL emotional designers carefully decide on the inclusion of competency elements and consider its effect on the learning outcome.

Topic and Learning Outcome. In accordance with several [42, 43] that examined the effects of GBL on students' performance and learning outcomes, mGBL in distance education also reveals show high scores of perceived learning outcomes.

Although several studies have examined the learning outcome of using GBL and Kahoot! they do not explicitly describe how Kahoot! improved the students' the learning outcome [2]. The results of this study imply that game content in terms of the learning/teaching topic is also essential in knowledge achievement since several students expressed their interest on Prototyping and this interest has affected their learning engagement in a positive way. However, further research is needed to prove this assumption.

5 Conclusions

The results of this study highlight that mGBL can bring several privileges in terms of students' emotions and learning achievement, hence it should be highly considered during the design of distance courses. Although previous studies point that negative emotions are higher perceived in online educational settings than positive ones (Stephan et al., 2019), this study shows that implementing (m)GBL in DE might bring significantly positive outcomes in student's emotional engagement.

Overall, the mixed analysis of this study provides with useful insights on students' sentiment and emotions towards mGBL in the context of DE and reveals the game design features that bring positive or negative impact on learners' emotions. In general, time limit and music/sounds were the major themes identified to cause negative emotions, while good design, flow/sequencing, easiness, and learnability were reported as positive.

This research extends previous studies by investigating the role of auditory attributes as well as further game dynamics, UX and usability features, and perceived learning outcome. The findings might be useful for educators, course designers and educational institutions towards the design of emotionally engaging mGBL in DE.

Limitations of this study include the self-reported nature of the data collection that can cause some bias in the results, the small sample size, and the generalizability issue. Future research should be conducted on different populations and larger sample sizes to cross validate and extend our findings.

Acknowledgements. This research is co-financed by Greece and the European Union (European Social Fund- ESF) through the Operational Programme «Human Resources Development, Education and Lifelong Learning» in the context of the project "Reinforcement of Postdoctoral Researchers - 2 nd Cycle" (MIS-5033021), implemented by the State Scholarships Foundation (IKY).

References

1. Francis, M.K., Wormington, S.V., Hulleman, C.: The costs of online learning: examining differences in motivation and academic outcomes in online and face-to-face community college developmental mathematics Courses. Front. Psychol. **10,** 2054 (2019)
2. Wang, A.I., Tahir, R.: The effect of using Kahoot! for learning – a literature review. Comput. Educ. **149,** 103818 (2020). https://doi.org/10.1016/j.compedu.2020.103818
3. Hernández-Ramos, J.P., Belmonte, M.L.: Evaluación del empleo de Kahoot! en la enseñanza superior presencial y no presencial. Educ. Knowl. Soc. **21,** 13 (2020). https://doi.org/10.14201/eks.22910.

4. Ninaus, M., et al.: Increased emotional engagement in game-based learning – a machine learning approach on facial emotion detection data. Comput. Educ. **142**, 103641 (2019). https://doi.org/10.1016/j.compedu.2019.103641

5. Campillo-Ferrer, J.M., Miralles-Martínez, P., Sánchez-Ibáñez, R.: Gamification in higher education: Impact on student motivation and the acquisition of social and civic key competencies. Sustain **12**(12), (2020). https://doi.org/10.3390/SU12124822

6. Plass, J.L. et al.: Emotional design for digital games for learning: The effect of expression, color, shape, and dimensionality on the affective quality of game characters. Learn. Instr. **70**, 101194 (2020). https://doi.org/10.1016/j.learninstruc.2019.01.005

7. Naciri, A., Baba, M.A., Achbani, A., Kharbach, A.: Mobile Learning in Higher Education: Unavoidable Alternative during COVID-19. Aquademia 4(1), ep20016 (2020). https://doi.org/10.29333/aquademia/8227

8. Porat, E., Blau, I., Barak, A.: Measuring digital literacies: Junior high-school students' perceived competencies versus actual performance. Comput. Educ. **126**, 23–36 (2018). https://doi.org/10.1016/j.compedu.2018.06.030

9. Konradt, U., Filip, R., Hoffmann, S.: Hypermedia learning. Br. J. Educ. Technol. **34**(3), 309–327 (2003)

10. Stephan, M., Markus, S., Gläser-Zikuda, M.: Students' achievement emotions and online learning in teacher education. Front. Educ. **4**, 109 (2019)

11. Pekrun, R.: The control-value theory of achievement emotions: assumptions, corollaries, and implications for educational research and practice. Educ. Psychol. Rev. **18**(4), 315–341 (2006). https://doi.org/10.1007/s10648-006-9029-9

12. Schrader, C., Kalyuga, S.: Linking students' emotions to engagement and writing performance when learning Japanese letters with a pen-based tablet: an investigation based on individual pen pressure parameters. Int. J. Hum. Comput. Stud. **135**, 102374 (2020) https://doi.org/10.1016/j.ijhcs.2019.102374

13. Schrader, C., Nett, U.: The perception of control as a predictor of emotional trends during gameplay. Learn. Instr. **54**, 62–72 (2018). https://doi.org/10.1016/j.learninstruc.2017.08.002

14. Ding, Y., Zhao, T.: Emotions, engagement, and self-perceived achievement in a small private online course. J. Comput. Assist. Learn. **36**(4), 449–457 (2020). https://doi.org/10.1111/jcal.12410

15. Obergriesser, S., Stoeger, H.: Students' emotions of enjoyment and boredom and their use of cognitive learning strategies – How do they affect one another?. Learn. Instr. **66**, 101285 (2020) https://doi.org/10.1016/j.learninstruc.2019.101285

16. Moridis, C.N., Economides, A.A.: Affective learning: empathetic agents with emotional facial and tone of voice expressions. IEEE Trans. Affect. Comput. **3**(3), 260–272 (2012). https://doi.org/10.1109/T-AFFC.2012.6

17. Raja, M., Lakshmi Priya, G.G.: Sentiment and emotions extraction on teaching–learning from home (TLFH) and impact of online academic activities in India. Mater. Today Proc. (2021). https://doi.org/10.1016/j.matpr.2020.12.346

18. Shapiro, H.B., Lee, C.H., Wyman Roth, N.E., Li, K., Çetinkaya-Rundel, M., Canelas, D.A.: Understanding the massive open online course (MOOC) student experience: An examination of attitudes, motivations, and barriers. Comput. Educ. **110**, 35–50 (2017). https://doi.org/10.1016/j.compedu.2017.03.003

19. De Melo, C.M., Paiva, A., Gratch, J.: Emotion in games. Handb. Digit. Games 575–592 (2014). https://doi.org/10.1002/9781118796443.ch21

20. Park, B., Knörzer, L., Plass, J.L., Brünken, R.: Emotional design and positive emotions in multimedia learning: an eyetracking study on the use of anthropomorphisms. Comput. Educ. **86**, 30–42 (2015). https://doi.org/10.1016/j.compedu.2015.02.016

21. Plass, J.L., Heidig, S., Hayward, E.O., Homer, B.D., Um, E.: Emotional design in multimedia learning: effects of shape and color on affect and learning. Learn. Instr. **29**, 128–140 (2014). https://doi.org/10.1016/j.learninstruc.2013.02.006

22. Mayer, R.E., Estrella, G.: Benefits of emotional design in multimedia instruction. Learn. Instr. **33**, 12–18 (2014). https://doi.org/10.1016/j.learninstruc.2014.02.004

23. Malone, T.W.: Toward a theory of intrinsically motivating instruction. Cogn. Sci. **5**(4), 333–369 (1981). https://doi.org/10.1016/S0364-0213(81)80017-1

24. Fang, X., Chan, S., Brzezinski, J., Nair, C.: Measuring enjoyment of computer game play. In: 14th Americas Conference on Information Systems, AMCIS 2008, vol. 3, pp. 1611–1620 (2008)

25. Klepsch, M., Schmitz, F., Seufert, T.: Development and validation of two instruments measuring intrinsic, extraneous, and germane cognitive load. Front. Psychol. **8**, 1997 (2017)

26. van Tilburg, W.A.P., Igou, E.R.: On boredom: lack of challenge and meaning as distinct boredom experiences. Motiv. Emot. **36**(2), 181–194 (2012). https://doi.org/10.1007/s11031-011-9234-9

27. Tzafilkou, K., Protogeros, N.: Diagnosing user perception and acceptance using eye tracking in web-based end-user development. Comput. Human Behav. **72**, (2017). https://doi.org/10.1016/j.chb.2017.02.035

28. Tzafilkou, K., Protogeros, N., Chouliara, A.: Experiential learning in web development courses: examining students' performance, perception and acceptance. Educ. Inf. Technol. **25**(6), 5687–5701 (2020). https://doi.org/10.1007/s10639-020-10211-6

29. Ajmal, M., Ahmad, S.: Exploration of anxiety factors among students of distance learning: a case study of Allama Iqbal Open University. Bull. Educ. Res. **41**(2), 67–78 (2019)

30. Heckel, C., Ringeisen, T.: Pride and anxiety in online learning environments: Achievement emotions as mediators between learners' characteristics and learning outcomes. J. Comput. Assist. Learn. **35**(5), 667–677 (2019). https://doi.org/10.1111/jcal.12367

31. George Saadé, R., Kira, D., Mak, T., Nebebe, F.: Anxiety & performance in online learning. In: Proceedings of 2017 InSITE Conference, pp. 147–157 (2017). https://doi.org/10.28945/3736

32. Aung, K.Z., Myo, N.N.: Sentiment analysis of students' comment using lexicon based approach. In: Proceedings of 16th IEEE/ACIS International Conference on Computer Information Science, ICIS 2017, pp. 149–154 (2017). https://doi.org/10.1109/ICIS.2017.7959985

33. Hew, K.F., Hu, X., Qiao, C., Tang, Y.: What predicts student satisfaction with MOOCs: a gradient boosting trees supervised machine learning and sentiment analysis approach. Comput. Educ. **145**, 103724 (2020) https://doi.org/10.1016/j.compedu.2019.103724

34. Nasim, Z., Rajput, Q., Haider, S.: Sentiment analysis of student feedback using machine learning and lexicon based approaches. In: International Conference on Research and Innovation in Information Systems, ICRIIS, pp. 1–6 (2017). https://doi.org/10.1109/ICRIIS.2017.8002475

35. Hu, M., Liu, B.: Mining and summarizing customer reviews. In: Proceedings of the tenth ACM SIGKDD International Conference on Knowledge Discovery and Data Mining, KDD-2004, pp. 168–177 (2004). https://doi.org/10.1145/1014052.1014073

36. Mohammad, S.M., Turney, P.D.: Crowdsourcing a word-emotion association lexicon. Comput. Intell. **29**(3), 436–465 (2013). https://doi.org/10.1111/j.1467-8640.2012.00460.x

37. Shiratuddin, N., Zaibon, S.B.: Designing user experience for mobile game-based learning. In: Proceedings of - 2011 International Conference on User Science and Engineering, i-USEr 2011, pp. 89–94 (2011). https://doi.org/10.1109/iUSEr.2011.6150543

38. Byun, J., Loh, C.S.: Audial engagement: Effects of game sound on learner engagement in digital game-based learning environments. Comput. Human Behav. **46**, 129–138 (2015). https://doi.org/10.1016/j.chb.2014.12.052

39. Sharp, J.G., Sharp, J.C., Young, E.: Academic boredom, engagement and the achievement of undergraduate students at university: a review and synthesis of relevant literature. Res. Pap. Educ. **35**(2), 144–184 (2020). https://doi.org/10.1080/02671522.2018.1536891
40. De Villiers, M.R.: e-Learning artefacts: are they based on learning theory? Alternation **12**(1b), 345–371 (2005)
41. Plass, J.L., et al.: The impact of individual, competitive, and collaborative mathematics game play on learning, performance, and motivation. J. Educ. Psychol. **105**(4), 1050–1066 (2013). https://doi.org/10.1037/a0032688
42. Ares, A.M., Bernal, J., Nozal, M.J., Sánchez, F.J., Bernal, J.: Results of the use of Kahoot! gamification tool in a course of Chemistry, pp. 1215–1222 (2018). https://doi.org/10.4995/head18.2018.8179
43. Lee, C.C., Hao, Y., Lee, K.S., Sim, S.C., Huang, C.C.: Investigation of the effects of an online instant response system on students in a middle school of a rural area. Comput. Human Behav. **95**, 217–223 (2019). https://doi.org/10.1016/j.chb.2018.11.034

Tangible Solutions for Learning Basic Math Skills: Exploring Concepts of Emotions and Enaction

Julio Alberto Vansan Gonçalves[1], Rodrigo Bonacin[1,2(✉)] (iD),
and Julio Cesar dos Reis[3] (iD)

[1] UNIFACCAMP, Campo Limpo Paulista, Campo Limpo Paulista, Brazil
julio@vansan.com.br
[2] Renato Archer Information Technology Center - CTI, Campinas, SP, Brazil
rodrigo.bonacin@cti.gov.br
[3] Institute of Computing and NIED, University of Campinas, Campinas, Brazil
jreis@ic.unicamp.br

Abstract. Emotion is a key aspect of human cognition and learning. It may have great influence on math learning process in childhood. Tangible and playful interfaces can be used to support teachers to increase students' motivation and learning outcome. In this paper, we explore the concepts of emotion and enaction in the design of the EMFK (Emotion Math For Kids) prototype, which focuses on supporting teachers in the basic math skills learning process. The EMFK prototype allows the development of learning activities with playful physical objects, as well as it is able to adapt its interface and difficulty level according to students' emotional expressions. We present both the design and development of EMFK' software and hardware components. Our field study with seven teachers shows the viability of the proposal and points out open challenges to be overcome.

Keywords: Tangible interfaces · Mathematics learning · Emotions · Enactive interfaces

1 Introduction

Learning basic math concepts and skills can be an arduous task for primary school students. Various factors, such as motivation and children's emotional state, can directly influence learning [9]. In this sense, playful learning through interactive tangible objects can be an alternative to improve children's learning outcome.

Literature presents several investigations in how games (*e.g.*, [8]) and gamification in mathematics classes (*e.g.*, [5]) can contribute to the learning process. Various studies inquire the benefits in using tangible objects for teaching math concepts (*e.g.*., [16,26]). Literature shows benefits of considering emotional

© Springer Nature Switzerland AG 2021
P. Zaphiris and A. Ioannou (Eds.): HCII 2021, LNCS 12785, pp. 133–152, 2021.
https://doi.org/10.1007/978-3-030-77943-6_9

aspects in learning environments [9]. However, it is still an open research challenge the design of computational systems that take into account emotional expressions in the support of learning activities.

This work proposes the design and development of a playful tangible system to support children learning basic math concepts and skills. Our system is based on the concepts of emotions and enaction [10,28]. It is hence designed to change the learning strategy and its user's interfaces based on the children's emotional expression.

Our investigation contributes to advance the knowledge of how an interactive tangible system considers aspects related to emotion expressions in playful learning of basic math concepts and skills. We present details of the design, development and evaluation of a computational device prototype specially constructed for this purpose. Our study describes and discusses scenarios with children using this technology.

In our study, game-based activates about basic mathematical operations were created using educational practices for children. In the system, students execute a set of math exercises, which are selected according to the informed profile, students' score and emotional feedback. Subject's responses are given through cards and playful objects containing RFID sensors.

We evaluated the proposed prototype in a preliminary study with teachers that work with children aged 5 to 8. Our study analyzed prospective use situations and the perception of seven teachers in their first contact with the prototype. Participants indicate the potential of the system for children in the second and third grades and its easiness for using.

The remainder of this article is structured as follows: Sect. 2 describes background concepts on enactive systems, emotions and related work concerning tangible technologies for math learning; Sect. 3 details the design and development of the proposed tangible artifact; Sect. 4 presents results of the assessment study; finally, Sect. 5 concludes the paper and presents future work.

2   Background and Related Work

We present the theoretical and methodological foundation of this work as well as key related work. Subsect. 2.1 details concepts about enactive systems, emotions and learning. Subsect. 2.2 presents investigations on the use of tangible technologies for math learning. Subsect. 2.3 presents studies on enactive systems and emotions for math learning.

2.1   Enactive Systems and Emotions Connected to Learning

We can understand enactive systems, in a technological view, as computer systems that dynamically link human processes and technology. Enactive systems have feedback cycles using sensors and data analysis, which allows a fluid interaction between humans and computers, *i.e.*, they should be able to detect human aspects, such as emotions, and properly react to them [10]. This technology can, for example, promote advances in learning with the use of playful techniques. According to Tikka *et al.* [24], there are several areas of innovative applications of enactive systems, such as generative music videos and medical health applications adaptable to physiological states. It is also possible to explore this technology on educational scenarios (*e.g.*, [3,15,27]).

Emotion is a fundamental element of human processes, as well as it plays a key role in enactive systems. Our investigation emphasizes the emotional aspects, and how a computational system can consider them to support the learning processes. Basic cognitive processes such as attention and memory are linked to the subject's neurological capacity in the learning process, just as teaching and learning is linked to emotional and affectivity factors [6]. Indeed, emotion impacts students' cognition, as well as it affects various processes such as memory, attention, and creativity [9]. According to Jarvela [9], studies have shown that emotions have substantial impact on several aspects of learning, such as: achievement, motivation, interest, goals and meta-cognition.

Emotions can lead to both positive and negative impacts on learning [18]. Studies shows that the induction of positive mood in children can improve their effectiveness in classical measures of intelligence, such as in block-design task [9]. While negative emotions (e.g., fear, anger, disgust, boredom, sadness) can be associated with lower performance and dropout. In particular, Existing studies highlight the importance of emotions on math education and their impacts on mathematical problem solving [14] by pointing out the need for supporting emotions and motivation in classrooms [23].

This work assumes the relevance of emotions in human cognition as well as the need for modern interactive technological tools for supporting emotional aspects in math learning. To this end, we propose a tangible playful solution.

2.2 Tangible Technologies for Math Learning

Tangible interfaces can be used to improve problem solving and learning. Schneider [22], for instance, highlighted the role that tangibility plays in problem solving tasks by comparing learners using a multi-touch and tangible interfaces. According to the authors, the tasks were performed more effectively by those that used tangible interfaces, obtaining a greater gain in learning outcome as compared with multi-touch. The study showed that tangible interfaces can be used to promote constructive skills by improving the exploration, collaboration, and playfulness aspects.

Several studies have emphasized the potential of using tangible artifacts in the teaching of mathematics. According to Ueno *et al.* [26], it is difficult for pupils learning abstract math concepts using just number and symbols. The study shows possibilities to improve the learning process by using tangible objects (felt ball), which gives pupils' mathematical intuition. Other studies reinforce the relevance of having physical and digital components [16], in which animated and interactive videos assist teachers to promote interest among children during classes.

Bujak *et al.* [2] investigated the possibilities of using physical objects and virtual information in the math classrooms. They presented a framework for understanding how Augmented Reality (AR) learning occurs in math from three perspectives: the physical dimension, where physical manipulation affords natural interactions, thus encouraging the creation of embodied representations; the cognitive dimension, where spatio-temporal alignment of information through AR experiences can support student's understanding of abstract concepts; and, the contextual dimension, where AR creates possibilities for collaborative learning around virtual content.

There are several other studies emphasizing the use of tangible technology in childhood education. Gonzalez *et al.* [7] presented a systematic review about the use of this technology on the education of children up to six years old. Some of the revised studies focus on the use of tangible computing in the teaching of math in childhood, such as [17,20,21]).

Khandelwal and Mazalek [11] created a wireless object tracking system integrated with a graphic display, giving visual and sound feedback. Their objective was to promote a better understanding of mathematical concepts and to improve the child interest in math, by providing friendly feedback and tips, along with visual feedback on a table surface. As aligned with our proposal, child executes activities by placing on a table the marked objects in the form of numbered blocks, geometric shapes, etc.

Although existing studies, as presented in this section, make use of tangible technology for math education for children, our study differs by considering emotional aspects in childhood math education in an original designed digital artifact build for this purpose.

2.3   Enactive Systems for Math Learning

Enactive technology can bring new perspectives for the use of technology in education [3,27] as well as tangible technology can be used for promoting enactive educational scenarios [15]. We present studies by comprehending a exploratory literature review about enactive systems (and emotion) for math learning.

Khoo *et al.* [12] presented a study to identify how children enact by viewing and representing skills using apps during the addition and subtraction learning. Their study involved four students of 5 years old in playful activities and showed that digital technology supported the participants to enact autonomous tasks to construct their own meanings.

Embodied is a key feature of enactive systems. Arroyo [1] presented a study on embodied educational math games. They proposed the use of SmartPhones and SmartWatches on math team-based activities that require physical engagement with the environment. The cognitive and affective outcomes of thirteen 9–10 years old students was analyzed. Students were engaged in creating the games (by themselves) for other students. According to the authors, this resulted in the development of computational thinking and the acquisition of a more positive attitudes and perceptions of math.

Casano *et al.* [4] presented the design and implementation of embodied cognition in mathematics teaching systems. Students used wrist wearable devices, by which received clues to help them in an task of finding hidden geometric objects. A study with seven participants of 4th to 6th grade point out usability concerns. Teachers in their study point out the collaborative nature of the activities and they seemed open to the idea of adopting a game-based reinforcement in their math classes.

Trninic and Abrahamson [25] investigated the mediated emergence of mathematical notions from embodied-interaction instructional activities. A study with twenty two students from a private K–8 school indicated the importance of movements and interactions with physical objects to math education. Aligned with that, King and Smith [13] demonstrated advancements of technologies controlled by body movement, such as those related to mixed reality. The authors argue that such advanced technologies enabled new possibilities for math learning, such as to embody a mathematical concept while a visual feedback is provided. Also, Price and Duffy [19] addressed sensor-based technology for sensory motor involvement for mathematical learning. Their objective was to analyze and understand how children use their bodies to learn geometric concepts.

These presented studies reveal the relevance of considering physical artifacts in the design of interactive solutions for supporting children to learn basic math skills. Our work considers the use of physical/tangible objects, which allows embodiment based activities. Combined with that, our proposed solution considers aspects related to students' emotional expressions, including changes in the computational system internal state by taking them into account. Our solution works as a kit for supporting teachers in the development of richer educational scenarios. The proposed tangible system offers an improved interaction with the computational system based on its adaptability aspects.

3 The Emotion Math for Kids Prototype

The EMFK (Emotion Math For Kids) prototype was developed with the objective of investigating how to design an interactive tangible system that considers aspects related to emotion expressions in playful learning of basic math skills. Subsect. 3.1 presents our research method as well as the initial conception of the EMFK; Subsect. 3.2 details the design of the hardware components; Subsect. 3.3 presents the design of the software components; and Subsect. 3.4 describes user interfaces and features provided by the EMFK.

3.1 Prototype Design Decisions

For the design of our solution, we conducted a research method considering the following main steps: (1) problem identification and characterization, including a literature review; (2) the proposal of an initial set of features with the participation of teachers to understand how emotional aspects impacts in learning basic math concepts (cf. Subsect. 3.4); (3) prototype development (cf. Subsects. 3.2 3.3); and (4) evaluation based on interviews (cf. Sect. 4 regarding the evaluation results). In the following, we synthesize a basic set of functionalities and technologies involved in our solution relying on the results of steps 1 and 2.

Game-based activities about basic mathematical operations were defined considering educational practices for children education. In our system proposal, students execute a set of math exercises, which are selected according to the informed profile, students' score and emotional feedback. Subject's answers are given through cards and playful objects containing RFID sensors.

A initial scope of math operations to be implemented by the system was defined. We defined the focus on children beginning literacy stage and up to eight years. Students should execute a set of math exercises about basic operators (addition, subtraction, multiplication and division) defined according to the informed profile, students' score and emotional feedback. Teachers stressed that the system should provide age-appropriate interface elements that explore playful aspects. We chose to use cards and playful objects containing RFID sensors, given that this is a reliable and low cost solution.

Based on this initial analysis, we defined that children' emotional expressions should be continuously analyzed, and the system should be reconfigured at runtime according to the detected emotional expressions. The emotional expression is used to reconfigure the system in various manners, which includes: 1) adjustments in the interface; 2) changes on difficulty level of the activities; and 3) to provide ludic elements on content (to change the mood). For example, if a student misses an exercise and shows to be sad or disinterested, the system interface background can be changed to include an animated character and an easier exercise is selected to motivate him/her again. Still in this context, motivational messages must be used to encourage students and the interaction mode changes until contrary feedback is obtained. Therefore, each student has a unique interaction experience according to their emotional expressions. The reconfiguration capability of the system is based on concept of enaction.

In summary, we defined the following methods and techniques to provide the system features:

1. Use of tangible objects with RFid with ludic format or picture related to basic mathematics concepts (e.g., number of spots on a ladybug). The proposed prototype uses Raspberry Pi [1] technology for executing game-based activities with the tangible objects in a ludic device.
2. The prototype accesses services (Microsoft Azure Face API[2]) to recognize students' emotional expressions. The results of the Microsoft Azure Face API are interpreted by the system to promote changes on the content and interface.
3. A decision algorithm selects the next action to be executed according to the subject's emotional state. A set of exercises and annotated media is used in this step.
4. A decision algorithm changes the user's interfaces according to the subject's emotional state.

---

[1] https://www.raspberrypi.org/.

[2] https://azure.microsoft.com/pt-br/services/cognitive-services/face/.

From this initial conception, we designed a high-level organization of our system prototype (cf. Fig. 1), which is implemented by an embedded computer device. The main components of the system are: a WebCam to capture emotional expressions; a monitor to visualize the activities; RFid sensors to receive the child's responses through RFid cards and playful tangible objects; buttons to assist students in confirming the response and interact with the system (in addition to RFid); and, a Raspberry Pi to execute the program and communicate with the Microsoft Azure Face API.

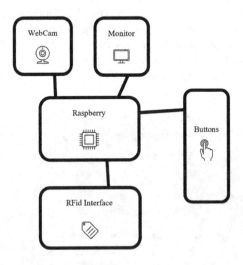

Fig. 1. Overview of the prototype system components.

The basic functioning of the prototype includes the following sequence of steps: (1) the teacher setup the EMFK according to defined scenario and activities, for example, they can choice of objects as well as the age of the student, (2) the student visualizes the activity in the monitor and (3) the student execute the activities using tangible objects by placing it on the device. At each execution cycle, the system can be automatically reconfigured according to the student's emotional state. The next subsections detail the prototype development (hardware and software).

3.2   Design and Implementation of the Hardware Components

Figure 2 presents the initial hardware design of the EMFK prototype. It was designed to have a base where the RFid cards (or objects) can be uphold, and an area for placing the answers; as well as a set of colored buttons on the right side.

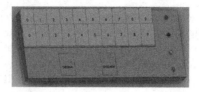

Fig. 2. Initial design of the hardware of the EMFK prototype.

Figure 3 shows the current version of the developed tangible device. The EMFK has a box where the cards (or other objects) can be positioned and buttons on right side. On the back, there is a video monitor for displaying options, messages and mathematical operations. At the top of the monitor, there is a webcam for capturing facial images.

Fig. 3. Current version of the developed tangible device.

Figure 4 presents examples of playful cards prototypes, including ladybugs with different numbers of spots to represent numbers in the activities.

Figure 5 presents an overview of the prototype's internal components. At the center, there is the Raspberry Pi with its connections. The figure presents a circuit built for this device, sensors and the buttons positioned on the right side of the prototype. The Raspberry Pi 3 B+ was chosen because it is portable, relatively inexpensive, has the necessary interfaces to connect with the other devices (monitor, sensors, Webcam, etc.). In addition, it has sufficient processing capacity necessary to execute the graphical interfaces of the proposed activities

Fig. 4. Examples of playful cards.

and enable to access the service for recognize emotional expressions. It supports an appropriate programming language (Python) and execute a database manger (SQLite).

Fig. 5. Overview of the internal components of the EMFK prototype.

Figure 6 shows the protoboard circuit design for EMFK prototype. It presents the electrical scheme developed using the fritzing software[3], an open software to facilitate the design and visualization of hardware projects. All circuit power uses 3.3v electrical voltage, which is supplied by the Raspberry Pi on pin 1. As shown in Fig. 6, the connections of the 2 RFID-RC522 modules are in parallel, excepting the SS pin (Slave Select) of the module, which is in the Raspberry Pi connected to ports GPIO 08 and GPIO 07. The communication protocol SPI (Serial Peripheral Interface) is used in these ports, a synchronous communication protocol.

The button are powered by 3.3v, and when pressed there is a split of the electric current: a part goes to a port on the Raspberry Pi sending the trigger signal; and the other part is connected to the GND through a $10k\Omega$ resistor. The GPIO extension follows the same sequence on both ends, to facilitate the assembly of the circuit, the following ports were chosen to connect the buttons: GPIO12, GPIO16, GPIO20 and GPIO21.

---

[3] https://fritzing.org/.

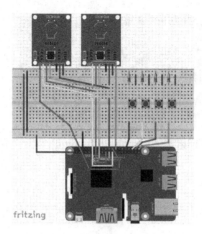

Fig. 6. Electric scheme of the device.

3.3 Design and Implementation of the Software Components

The EMFK software prototype was developed in Python with a SQLite database to store activities, messages and results. The Python language was chosen because it offers access to services on the Web, as well as high transparency level for reading and control of the hardware. Figure 7 presents a simplified diagram of the software architecture. The complete code of the solution can be download at GitHub [4].

Two threads are executed in parallel during all the time to improve the system performance. The first thread, named "MicroControl" (Fig. 7), reads the buttons; and, the second one (screen_manager thread in Fig. 7) is responsible for switching between the interfaces as needed. In other words, the first reads the states of the buttons, and the second takes actions according to the active interface and button states.

We used the tkinter[5] libraries in the interface development. It was selected because it is a open and standard Python GUI toolkit; also it is available on our platform (Raspberry Pi 3 B+). The SimpleMFRC522 library[6] was used for reading the RFid cards (embedded in cards and objects), representing both units and tens. This is a open python library to read/write RFid tags and is compatible with Raspberry Pi.

We created two components to implement our interface communication with Microsoft Azure Face API (*face recognition process* in Fig. 7): *image capture* and *face communication* (cf. Fig. 7). These components make use of the cognitive_face, requests and Json libraries. The image capture component takes photos in 4 moments: (1) when the exercise to be solved is presented; (2) when the student misses and the result is presented; (3) when the student hits and the result

---

[4] https://github.com/juliovansan/mestrado.git.
[5] https://docs.python.org/3/library/tkinter.html.
[6] https://github.com/pimylifeup/MFRC522-python.

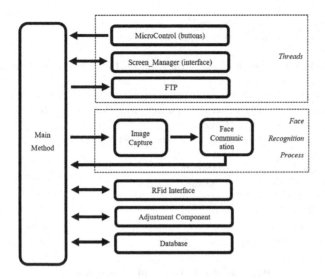

Fig. 7. Overview of the EMFK software architecture.

is presented; and (4) when the final result including hits and errors are displayed to the student. The face communication component send the images to Microsoft Azure Face API and read the results (in Json format).

Based on the received result with the emotional state, the decision algorithm promotes changes in the level of difficulty of the exercises and at the user's interface level (*Adjustment Component* in Fig. 7). We adopted a simplified version of a decision algorithm (cf. Algorithm 1), as our objective was to investigate the design and feasibility of the prototype (it is out of the scope of this paper to show the development of advanced reconfiguration algorithms and to develop complex changes in the interface). As Algorithm 1 shows, we used happiness, surprised, neutral, sadness and anger emotions as input, while emotions such as fear, contempt and disgust are not used.

We defined in Algorithm 1 an adjustment parameter (*AdjutParam* variable) to represent the difficulty (adjust) level. At the beginning of a sequence of exercises, the adjustment parameter is set as *5* (default value). The *AdjutParam* can range from *0* to *10*, and it is changed at each interpretation of a captured image (i.e., the Algorithm 1 is called every time an emotion expression is identified). The value of *0* means that the player is less motivated (associated with negative emotions) and the value of *10* means that the player is fully motivated (associated with positive emotions).

If the returned value from Microsoft Azure Face API (*EmotionVec* variable[7]) linked to *happiness* emotion is greater than 0.1; or the value linked to *surprise* emotion is greater to 0.2; the adjustment variable is increased by *1* (up to *10*

---

[7] The FACE API returns a vector with positive real numbers ($0.0 \leq value \leq 1.0$) linked to emotions; higher values mean a higher probability of that emotion.

Require: $AdjutParam$; $EmotionVec$;
Ensure: $AdjutParam \in N, 0 \leq AdjutParam \leq 10$
1: **Begin**
2: **if** $(EmotionVec.happiness>0.1$ **or** $EmotionVec.surprise>0.2)$ **and** $AdjutParam<10$ **then**
3:     $AdjutParam \leftarrow AdjutParam + 1$
4: **else if** $(EmotionVec.neutral>0.7$ **and** $AdjutParam \geq 1)$ **then**
5:     $AdjutParam \leftarrow AdjutParam - 1$
6: **else if** $(EmotionVec.sadness>0.1$ **or** $EmotionVec.anger>0.1)$ **then**
7:     **if** $AdjutParam \geq 1$ **then**
8:         $AdjutParam \leftarrow AdjutParam - 1$
9:     **else if** $AdjutParam \geq 2$ **then**
10:         $AdjutParam \leftarrow AdjutParam - 2$
11:     **end if**
12: **end if**
13: **return** $AdjutParam$
14: **End**

Algorithm 1: Decision algorithm

limit). If the value linked to *neutral* emotion is greater than *0.7*, the adjustment variable is decreased by -1 respecting up to a minimum of *1*. If the value linked to *sadness* is greater than *0.1*; or the value linked to *anger* is greater than *0.1*; the variable is decreased by -2, up to a minimum of 0. The adopted values[8] were defined in an iterative process, based on the theoretical background about positive and negative emotions (*cf.* Sect. 2), as well as the dimensions that reflect the emotional experience (*cf.* Sect. 2).

This adjustment value ($AdjutParam$ variable) is used to determine the difficult level of the exercise inside the student's school grade. A database with questions classified according to the school grade and level of difficulties is previously stored in the system (*database* component in Fig. 7).

The adjustment parameter ($AdjutParam$ variable) is further used to change aspects at the user's interface. Two types of changes are possible in the current version of the prototype, including changes in texts/messages, and changes in colors. We stored (*database* component in Fig. 7) a set of messages for each level of the adjustment parameter. These messages can be modified by educators aiming to improve the students' motivation.

The system changes colors of the user's interface according to the adjustment parameter ($AdjutParam$ variable). This parameter has influence on the background and text colors. For example, initially the gray color, which is neutral, is setup at the background, if $AdjutParam$ increases to *6* or *7* the light blue color (calm and confidence) is used; and if $AdjutParam$ increases to *8* to *10* the light green color (tranquility) is used. If $AdjutParam$ decreases to *4* or *3* the orange

---

[8] The limit values were defined according to our preliminary tests to better express positive and negative emotions. Such values are configurable and may change according to empirical results obtained in future analyzes.

color (friendly and lively) is used; and if *AdjutParam* decreases to *2* to *0* the light yellow color (optimism and energy) is used.

3.4   System Interfaces and Features

This subsection presents the main user interfaces and key features of the EMFK system prototype. Figure 8 presents the first interface of the prototype, *i.e..*, when the user turns on it. This is a welcome interface, where the teacher can turn off, continue or calibrate the web camera. The options are positioned on the right side in all interfaces. They are selected using the device button according to the positions and respective colors (cf. left side in Fig. 8).

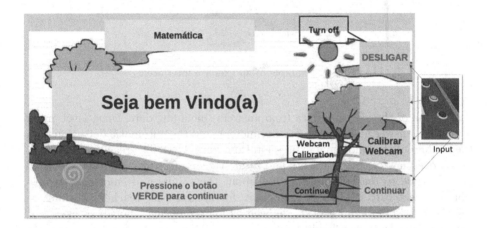

Fig. 8. EMFK welcome interface and input mechanism.

Figure 9 presents an example of the user interface with an exercise. In the middle of this figure, there is the question presented to the student. The answer is given through cards or playful objects. The background screen, cards pictures and playful objects can be changed according to the game narrative, as defined by teachers and educators. Narratives involving body movements and interaction between children can be defined, as long as the objects (with RDID) is placed to answer the exercises; and the child's face is within the reaching of the camera before and after the activity.

Figure 10 presents an example of an adapted interface with a wrong answer. In this example, the EMFK selected a message, that encourages the student to continue, according to the adjustment parameter. The text background color was changed to light green color due to an increasing of the adjustment parameter (i.e., the student expressed negative emotions).

We developed a Web system so that the teacher can make further analysis of the results, as well as to assess the emotional state of the students. Figure 11 presents an illustrative example of a photo of a student after the question; the

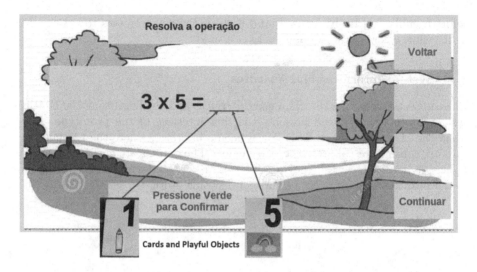

Fig. 9. Example of an exercise interface.

description of the exercise; data from answers (including date, time, level, math operation, answer and adjustment perimeter); and the automatic detection data (i.e., values of the emotional expression from Face API). The teacher can visualize an overview of their students and filter students for their analysis. Our goal is to provide to teachers information about the results and emotional expressions connected to it. This is important, for instance, for teachers working on the students' emotional aspects, as well as for promoting changes in exercises, messages and level of difficulty.

4   User Evaluation

This section presents a preliminary study with teachers, with experience in childhood education. Subsect. 4.1 presents the objectives, participants and methods, and Subsect. 4.2 details the obtained results.

4.1   Study Description

The objective in this study is to evaluate the feasibility of our system prototype. We aim to identify interface problems and to elicit changes for the next versions. Due to difficulties in carrying out activities directly with children due to the Covid-19 sanitary issues, only teachers participated in this study.

The study was carried out from 21–24 January 2020. Seven (7) teachers participated, who all are graduated in pedagogy and teach in early childhood education. Participants were recruited through email invitations from the researcher to teachers of early childhood education schools in São Paulo, Brazil. One of the participants is the pedagogical coordinator of an early childhood education

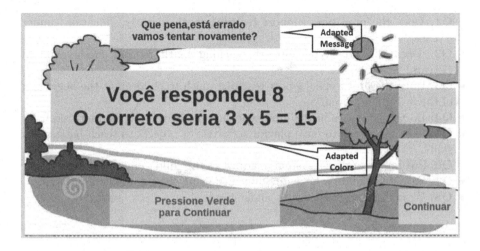

Fig. 10. Example of an adapted interface with a wrong answer.

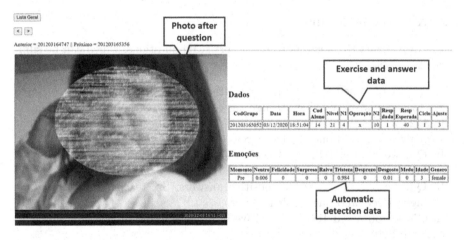

Fig. 11. Example of teacher's web interface.

school. Our study was approved by the ethical committee of UNIFACCAMP process #16228619.2.0000.5397.

The study was performed in three steps. Firstly, the participants watched an video with a presentation of how the EMFK prototype works[9]. In the sequence, they evaluated the prototype through the free utilization of its features and pre-registered activities, and then answered questions in the Google Forms. This form included the following questions:

– Likert Scale Questions (*1. Strongly disagree, 2. Disagree, 3. Neutral, 4. Agree, 5. Strongly agree*)

---

[9] https://youtu.be/uaQltmBOTCg.

- **Q1.** Does the prototype support teaching math in early education (under 6 years)?
- **Q2.** Does the prototype support teaching math to 2nd grade children (7 years)?
- **Q3.** Does the prototype support teaching math to children at the beginning of the 3rd grade (8 years).
- **Q4.** Do the activities in the prototype support learning basic math skill?
- **Q5.** Is it important to have playful activities or objects to teach basic math skill?
- **Q6.** Is it important for a system to adjust to the child's emotional expression?
- **Q7.** Wouldn't children have any difficulty using these tangible interfaces?
- **Q8.** Were the messages easy to understand?

– A open question

- **Q9.** Make suggestions to enable the use of the tangible device at school.

4.2 Assessment Results

Figure 12 presents the answers to the Likert scale questions, which can be summarized as follows:

– In **Q1**, we obtained 85.7% of positive answers and 14.3% of negative answers. Six teachers answered that strongly agree, and one teacher strongly disagree.
– In **Q2**, we obtained 100% of positive answers. Six teachers answered that strongly agree, and one teacher agrees.
– In **Q3**, we obtained 100% of positive answers. Six teachers answered that strongly agree, and one teacher agrees.
– In **Q4**, we obtained 100% of positive answers. Six teachers answered that strongly agree, and one teacher agrees.
– In **Q5**, we obtained 100% of positive answers. The seven teachers answered that strongly agree.
– In **Q6**, we obtained 100% of positive answers. The seven teachers answered that strongly agree.
– In **Q7**, we obtained 71.5% of positive answers. Three teachers answered that strongly agree, two teacher agree, and two teachers gave a neutral answer.
– In **Q8**, we obtained 71.5% of positive answers. Four teachers answered that strongly agree, one teacher agrees, and two teachers gave a neutral answer.

With regard Q9, we obtained five response as follows:

1. "It would be interesting to have one for each student."
2. "I suggest to create additional types of challenges/activities."
3. "Make it available so that the student can really use."
4. "Device dissemination and training."
5. "To encourage teachers to use."

RESULTS

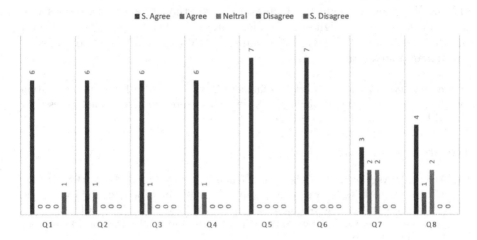

Fig. 12. Question results based on a Likert scale.

In general, the results of the evaluation were positive. Most of the teachers believe that the device could be used for the second (Q2) and third (Q3) grades as well as for younger children (under 6 years) (Q1). The majority of the teachers expressed that the user's tangible interface is easy to use (Q7) and messages can be understood by children (Q8). They all strongly agreed about the importance of considering the use of playful activities (Q5) and objects to adjust the system according to the child's emotional expression (Q6). Furthermore, teachers believe that the proposed activities can support learning basic math skill (Q4). Regarding the open responses (Q9), as detailed above, most of the suggestions were related to the expansion of use.

5 Conclusion

Learning math is a challenging process for educators and children. Literature has point out the influence that emotional aspects have on math learning activities. Tangible technologies have brought new perspectives for the development of teaching activities. Playful activities with tangible interfaces can increase students' motivation. This article presented the design of the EMFK, a system based on concepts of emotion and enaction to provide adaptive tangible solutions for learning basic math skills. The system makes use of objects with RFid sensors to support teachers to construct playful activities with students. EMFK is able to dynamically propose activities and adapt the interfaces according to the students' emotional expression. We therefore expected to promote a more fluid interaction, as well as support teachers in the development of activities that lead to arousing motivation and promoting learning. Our study with seven teachers reveled the feasibly of the use of our system. Next step involves improving

EMFK by including new tangible solutions and more complex decisions algorithms. We plan to conduct a final study with students and teachers, as well as to investigate the design of a complete interactive learning environment with multiple interconnected devices (including EMFKs), which adapts to students' emotional expressions.

Acknowledgements. This work was financed by the São Paulo Research Foundation (FAPESP) (Grants #2015/16528-0) (The opinions expressed here are not necessarily shared by the financial support agency.)

References

1. Arroyo, I., Micciollo, M., Casano, J., Ottmar, E., Hulse, T., Rodrigo, M.M.: Wearable learning: Multiplayer embodied games for math. In: Proceedings of the Annual Symposium on Computer-Human Interaction in Play, CHI PLAY 2017, pp. 205–216. Association for Computing Machinery, New York (2017). https://doi.org/10.1145/3116595.3116637
2. Bujak, K.R., Radu, I., Catrambone, R., MacIntyre, B., Zheng, R., Golubski, G.: A psychological perspective on augmented reality in the mathematics classroom. Comput. Educ. **68**, 536–544 (2013). https://doi.org/10.1016/j.compedu.2013.02.017
3. Caceffo, R., et al.: Collaborative meaning construction in socioenactive systems: study with the mBot. In: Zaphiris, P., Ioannou, A. (eds.) HCII 2019. LNCS, vol. 11590, pp. 237–255. Springer, Cham (2019). https://doi.org/10.1007/978-3-030-21814-0_18
4. Casano, J., Tee, H., Agapito, J., Arroyo, I., Rodrigo, M.M.T.: Migration and evaluation of a framework for developing embodied cognition learning games. In: Proceedings of the 3rd Asia-Europe Symposium on Simulation & Serious Gaming, pp. 199–203 (2016)
5. Cunha, G.C.A., Barraqui, L.P., de Freitas, S.A.A.: Evaluating the use of gamification in mathematics learning in primary school children. In: 2018 IEEE Frontiers in Education Conference (FIE), pp. 1–4 (2018). https://doi.org/10.1109/FIE.2018.8658950
6. De Oliveira, D.C., Kottel, A.: Determinantes comportamentais e emocionais do processo ensino-aprendizagem. Caderno Intersaberes **5**(6), 1–12 (2016)
7. González-González, C.S., Guzmán-Franco, M.D., Infante-Moro, A.: Tangible technologies for childhood education: a systematic review. Sustainability **11**(10), (2019). https://doi.org/10.3390/su11102910
8. Hartono, M., Candramata, M.A., Adhyatmoko, K.N., Yulianto, B.: Math education game for primary school. In: 2016 International Conference on Information Management and Technology (ICIMTech), pp. 93–96 (2016). https://doi.org/10.1109/ICIMTech.2016.7930309
9. Jarvela, S.: Social and Emotional Aspects of Learning. Elsevier, Amsterdam (2011)
10. Kaipainen, M., et al.: Enactive systems and enactive media: embodied human-machine coupling beyond interfaces. Leonardo **44**(5), 433–438 (2011). https://doi.org/10.1162/LEON_a_00244
11. Khandelwal, M., Mazalek, A.: Teaching table: a tangible mentor for pre-k math education. In: Proceedings of the 1st International Conference on Tangible and Embedded Interaction, TEI 2007, pp. 191–194. Association for Computing Machinery, New York (2007). https://doi.org/10.1145/1226969.1227009

12. Khoo, K.Y.: Enacting App-Based Learning Activities with Viewing and Representing Skills in Preschool Mathematics Lessons. In: Churchill, D., Lu, J., Chiu, T.K.F., Fox, B. (eds.) Mobile Learning Design. LNET, pp. 351–372. Springer, Singapore (2016). https://doi.org/10.1007/978-981-10-0027-0_21

13. King, B., Smith, C.P.: Mixed-reality learning environments: what happens when you move from a laboratory to a classroom? Int. J. Res. Educ. Sci. **4**(2), 577–594 (2018)

14. McLeod, D.B.: Beliefs, attitudes, and emotions: new views of affect in mathematics education. In: McLeod, D.B., Adams, V.M. (eds.) Affect and Mathematical Problem Solving. pp. 245–258. Springer, New York (1989). https://doi.org/10.1007/978-1-4612-3614-6_17

15. Mendoza, Y.L.M., Baranauskas, M.C.C.: Tangitime: Designing a (socio)enactive experience for deep time in an educational exhibit. In: Proceedings of the 18th Brazilian Symposium on Human Factors in Computing Systems, IHC 2019, Association for Computing Machinery, New York (2019). https://doi.org/10.1145/3357155.3358451

16. Nagaraju, K., Jain, S.: Use of technology for improving math and science skills of children of classes primary and upper-primary. In: 2015 IEEE Seventh International Conference on Technology for Education (T4E), pp. 111–117 (2015). https://doi.org/10.1109/T4E.2015.15

17. Patchan, M.M., Puranik, C.S.: Using tablet computers to teach preschool children to write letters: exploring the impact of extrinsic and intrinsic feedback. Comput. Educ. **102**, 128–137 (2016). https://doi.org/10.1016/j.compedu.2016.07.007

18. Pekrun, R., Linnenbrink-Garcia, L.: International Handbook of Emotions in Education. Routledge, New York (2014)

19. Price, S., Duffy, S.: Opportunities and challenges of bodily interaction for geometry learning to inform technology design. Multimodal Technol. Inter. **2**(3), 41 (2018)

20. Reeves, J.L., Gunter, G.A., Lacey, C.: Mobile learning in pre-kindergarten: using student feedback to inform practice. Educ. Technol. Soc. **20**(1), 37–44 (2017)

21. Schacter, J., et al.: Math shelf: A randomized trial of a prekindergarten tablet number sense curriculum. Early Educ. Dev. Math shelf: a randomized trial of a prekindergarten tablet number sense curriculum. **27**(1), 74–88 (2016). https://doi.org/10.1080/10409289.2015.1057462

22. Schneider, B., Jermann, P., Zufferey, G., Dillenbourg, P.: Benefits of a tangible interface for collaborative learning and interaction. IEEE Trans. Learn. Technol. **4**(3), 222–232 (2011). https://doi.org/10.1109/TLT.2010.36

23. Schukajlow, S., Rakoczy, K., Pekrun, R.: Emotions and motivation in mathematics education: theoretical considerations and empirical contributions. ZDM **49**(3), 307–322 (2017). https://doi.org/10.1007/s11858-017-0864-6

24. Tikka, P.: Enactive media - generalising from enactive cinema. Digit. Creativity **21**(4), 205–214 (2010). https://doi.org/10.1080/14626268.2011.550028

25. Trninic, D., Abrahamson, D.: Embodied Interaction as Designed Mediation of Conceptual Performance. In: Martinovic, D., Freiman, V., Karadag, Z. (eds) Visual Mathematics and Cyberlearning. Mathematics Education in the Digital Era, pp. 119–139. Springer, Netherlands (2013). https://doi.org/10.1007/978-94-007-2321-4_5

26. Ueno, M.: Possibility of felt ball math. In: 2017 6th IIAI International Congress on Advanced Applied Informatics (IIAI-AAI), pp. 105–108 (2017). https://doi.org/10.1109/IIAI-AAI.2017.140

27. Valente, J.A., et al.: A robot-based activity for kindergarten children: an embodied exercise. In: Proceedings of the 2020 Constructionism Conference, pp. 137–146. The University of Dublin (2020)
28. Varela, F.J., Thompson, E., Rosch, E.: The Embodied Mind, revised edition: Cognitive Science and Human Experience. MIT press, Cambridge (2017)

Chatbots in Learning

University Student Surveys Using Chatbots: Artificial Intelligence Conversational Agents

Noorhan Abbas[1] , Thomas Pickard[1] , Eric Atwell[1(✉)] , and Aisha Walker[2]

[1] School of Computing, University of Leeds, Leeds, UK
e.s.atwell@leeds.ac.uk
[2] School of Education, University of Leeds, Leeds, UK

Abstract. Predefined web surveys are often used to collect course evaluations from students in higher education institutions. These institutions use the evaluations to adjust their courses' pedagogical standards and lecture style to cope with an increasingly uncertain and complex world. Many limitations to using web surveys have been reported such as low response rates and low-quality responses to open questions. To overcome these limitations, artificial intelligence conversational agents (CAs) or 'chatbots' are used to play the interviewer role, facilitating the enhancement of the quality of responses. This is accomplished by mimicking human-human conversations; by asking questions in a friendly, casual way and pursuing high-quality responses. This study aims to explore the opportunities and the obstacles of using CAs in collecting course evaluations in three European universities (UK, Spain and Croatia) and one Centre of excellence in Cyprus. The transcripts collected have been analyzed using statistical data analysis methods and qualitative data analysis techniques. Our findings reveal that the use of CAs in collecting course feedback from students has a positive impact on response quality and can boost students' enjoyment levels. Furthermore, gender differences and student age have been identified as important factors that can influence the depth of the conversation with the CA.

Keywords: Chatbot · Conversational agent · Online course evaluation · Pedagogical conversational agents · Student enjoyment

1 Introduction

Nowadays, web or online surveys are often used to collect course feedback/evaluations from students in higher education institutions. This feedback enables these institutions to adjust their courses' pedagogical standards and lecture style to cope with an increasingly uncertain and complex world [1, 2]. Web surveys have become the standard format for these course evaluations [3, 4]. Despite the widespread use of web surveys to collect quantitative data, previous research has highlighted some limitations such as low response rates and low-quality responses to open questions [5, 6]. Several reasons have been offered to explain these limitations. For instance, respondents' satisficing behaviour, survey fatigue and the static interaction style are among the key reasons that can explain

© Springer Nature Switzerland AG 2021
P. Zaphiris and A. Ioannou (Eds.): HCII 2021, LNCS 12785, pp. 155–169, 2021.
https://doi.org/10.1007/978-3-030-77943-6_10

these negative effects [7]. Respondents' satisficing behaviour occurs to mitigate cognitive burden by responding to survey questions in a non-differentiation style; hence, generating satisficing responses instead of accurate ones, as argued by Krosnick [8]. Roster, Rogers, Albaum and Klein [9] claim that, by using web surveys, responses are far more susceptible to satisficing behaviour and poor-quality responses compared to face-to-face or telephone surveys. In addition, survey fatigue occurs when respondents feel bored or uninterested in the survey and as a result, provide inaccurate responses to the survey questions [10].

To overcome these limitations, Steyn, Davies and Sambo [11] have proposed that individual interviews should be adopted to enhance the quality of responses and to gain in-depth insights. However, due to resource constraints, interviewing students is unpractical as lecturers, especially at the time of COVID 19, are trying to cope with unprecedented workload. Alternatively, Kim et al. [7] and Wambsganss et al. [3, 12] argue that the use of artificial intelligence conversational agents (CAs) or 'chatbots' is promising and can facilitate collection of high-quality course feedback as these intelligent agents can play the interviewer role. CAs are software programs that communicate with users through natural language interaction interfaces [13]. Wambsganss et al. [3] claim that CAs not only enhance the quality of responses but also boost students' levels of enjoyment. The use of CAs in education is growing and the technology is still evolving [14, 15].

While many aspects of the use of CAs in education could be examined, this paper focuses on exploring the opportunities and obstacles of using 'Hubert.ai' (an artificial intelligence CA) in collecting course feedback from students at three universities in the UK, Spain and Croatia and one research institute in Cyprus. This study contributes to the educational CA literature, by highlighting key patterns that characterise the use of smart CAs, like Hubert.ai, in collecting course feedback in higher education institutions. Our analysis outlines and demonstrates these patterns to facilitate advancing the use of artificial intelligence chatbots in education.

2 Background

There is a growing interest in the use of CAs or chatbots in educational settings as they can provide efficient and timely services to students [16]. The authors differentiate between two categories of educational CAs: service oriented CAs and teaching oriented CAs. Service oriented CAs like Ask L.U. [17], which is built on Amazon Web Services, provide services to students using voice technology. Ask L.U. delivers a voice interface to answer students' questions about timetables, grades, tutors, societies, clubs and assist them in booking spaces to meet their peers [17]. Examples of other service oriented CAs that are used to assist students during enrolment and admission are Lola [18] and Dina [19]. Differ and CourseQ [20] are CAs that can assist students in the various services offered by universities that promote student engagement in the learning process. Lisa [21] acts as a virtual assistant to introduce new students to university life. Many of these CAs have shown good results as their success is assessed either through questionnaires or by the number of satisfactory answers they generate [16].

On the other hand, teacher oriented CAs aim to act as teaching assistants, reinforcing learning of students through generating knowledge like a human tutor, hence, relieving the workload of teachers [16]. For instance, Coding Tutor [22] is developed to support university students studying introductory programming courses in writing software code and getting an automatic assessment of this code though step-by-step guidance using natural language interactions. Providing feedback to students about their performance aims to initiate metacognitive thinking processes that can boost students' motivation and engagement [14]. Other teacher oriented CAs are developed to promote language learning, e.g., Bookbuddy [23], Clive Chatbot [24] and Mobile Chatbot [25]. As the main objective of these chatbots is to teach, their assessment is based on their teaching efficiency and on achieving predefined learning outcomes [16]. Other quality metrics that have been used to evaluate CAs include the length and structure of the conversation [26]. Smutny and Schereiberova [15], after evaluating 47 educational CAs implemented in Facebook Messenger, propose four categories of quality metric: teaching, humanity, affection and accessibility.

Furthermore, Griol, Molina and Callejas [27] argue that the use of educational CAs can advance students with disabilities in their studies, reporting benefits such as motivation, improved grades and engagement. Pedagogical CAs can provide personalised learning to students, however, the collaboration of a human tutor and a CA is still necessary to achieve learning outcomes [16]. Despite the positive impact of educational CAs reported by many research studies, further research is needed to establish the long-term effects on both learning processes and learning outcomes [14].

3 Research Methodology

To explore the opportunities and challenges of using educational chatbots or CAs like Hubert.ai in higher education institutions, the Erasmus + funded EDUBOTS project collaborated with three European universities and one research institute: University of Leeds, University of Granada, University of Zagreb and CYENS Centre of Excellence in Cyprus to advance knowledge about this technology. Hubert.ai is an artificial intelligence chatbot that aims to help educators get students' feedback to improve their teaching and provide students with personalised follow-ups to boost their learning. Using Hubert.ai, the four research teams collected course feedback data from both undergraduate and postgraduate students studying a variety of courses. Each research team formulated their surveys by choosing from a set of questions provided by Hubert.ai. The questions focused on students' general views of specific modules/courses (rather than overall programmes) and possible avenues for improvement.

A total of 206 students participated in this study. The participation in this study was voluntary. Nevertheless, not all of them completed the survey. The dropout rate, defined as the percentage of students who quit the survey before answering questions about the positive and negative aspects of the course, was 17.4%. Therefore, this study's sample size is N = 170.

Some instructors collected demographic information about their students like gender and age. In this study, demographic data were collected for three modules: Business Informatics (24 females and 5 males, average students' age was 19.5), Software Engineering (5 females and 19 males, average students' age was 21.5) and Text and Image Editing (12 females and 16 males, average students' age was 19.5). In addition, some educators asked their students to evaluate Hubert.ai and to give the chatbot itself a score. A sample of the survey questions used by instructors in the four universities is shown below.

> Beep boop, here we go! By the way, just say "go back" and correct me if I misunderstand you.
> Hi, how old are you? Please type your age as a number
> What is your gender? Please choose Male or Female [Male] [Female]
> What is working well with Course X and should continue in the same way?
> What could the teachers start doing, that would improve it?
> What could the teachers stop doing, that would improve Course X?
> What is your overall experience of Course X? Please write a sentence or two.
> How did you like this type of evaluation compared to a regular survey?
> So on a scale from 1-10, would you give it a 9?

Fig. 1. A sample of the survey questions

The four research teams collated the course feedback transcripts in csv (comma separated values) files. All the feedback data was sanitised and anonymised before being sent to the University of Leeds team for further analysis and data mining.

The transcripts were collated into a single file and several transformations applied to the text to facilitate later analysis; emoji characters were replaced with text descriptions, and identifiers for the questions asked by the CA (see Fig. 1) were appended. In addition, numerical ratings were extracted and standardised to lie on a scale from 0 to 10. For responses such as "a 6 or 7", an average value was taken. Where users provided ratings for different aspects of the course ("Laboratory exercise: 10; Lectures (theory): 4") or based on hypotheticals ("9, it would be a 10 without the exam"), the minimum rating offered was taken. In many cases, the chatbot suggested a rating to the user, who could agree with it or provide a different one – the last rating given in response to each question was retained. Conversation lengths were calculated, in terms of both the number of utterances and the total elapsed time.

Statistical data analysis was performed using MS Excel's spreadsheet filters and pivot tables to extract demographic data and the depth of the conversations. Furthermore, qualitative analysis was undertaken to understand the different patterns that characterise students' conversations with Hubert.ai.

4   Results and Analysis

The descriptive statistical analysis of the data reveals that students participating in the study are mainly studying computing-related courses, but also a range of science and humanities courses, as shown in Table 1.

The depth of the conversations with CAs has been identified by Przegalinska et al. [26] as a quality metric that can be used to assess the performance of the chatbot; so, the depth of each conversation was calculated and the average depth of conversation per course is shown in Table 2.

It is worth noting that the average conversation depth across all the courses ranged between 26 and 37 utterances. One conversation lasted for 218 iterations as the student tried to challenge Hubert.ai's intelligence. This student challenged Hubert.ai at the end of the survey; after answering all Hubert.ai's questions in detail. Hence, this conversation's length was omitted from the average scores to preserve consistency of the data.

Table 1. Number of participating students in each course

Course title	Respondents
3D Modelling and Animation	9
Business Informatics	30
Taxation	14
Data Mining	17
Data Mining and Text Analytics	20
Computer-Mediated Communications	2
Social Information Systems	2
Professional Software Technology Practice	16
Health and Fitness	4
Web Design and Development	15
Statics	11
Predmet	1
Sociology and Pedagogy issues in Physical Education	4
Software Engineering	24
Text and Image Editing	28
Data Mining	9
Grand Total	**206**

Table 2. Average depth of conversation (no. of utterances) per course

Course name	Avg depth of conversation
3D Modelling and Animation	28
Business Informatics	27
Taxation	32
Data Mining	29
Data Mining and Text Analytics	30
Computer-Mediated Communications	29
Social Information Systems	35
Professional Software Technology Practice	31
Health and Fitness	27
Web Design and Development	30
Statics	32
Predmet	37
Sociology and Pedagogy issues in Physical Education	30
Software Engineering	29
Text and Image Editing	28
Data Mining	26

Some respondents supplied numerical ratings (out of 10) for their overall experience of the course and/or for the experience of using the Hubert.ai chatbot to supply feedback.

In total, 218 such ratings were given (as some respondents gave ratings for both of these questions). The distributions of ratings are shown in Fig. 2. Distribution of Numerical Ratings by Question.

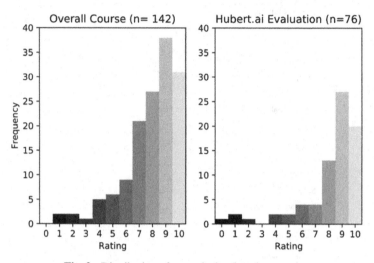

Fig. 2. Distribution of numerical ratings by question

In the context of collecting course feedback in higher education institutions, a key difference between the use of a web survey and a conversational agent is the latter's ability to mimic human-human conversations; by asking questions in a friendly casual way to students and pursue high-quality responses. Hubert.ai uses emoji in his replies, mirroring the texting style that humans usually adopt in virtual conversations with their friends. Embedding anthropomorphic design elements like informal language and emoji in conversational agents has been proven to positively influence the interactivity of the conversation [7, 28].

In addition, Hubert.ai can express empathy with students who are happy/unhappy about some course aspects. For instance, when students claim that they like everything about the course, Hubert.ai would ask them:

- *Ok, tell me about what was best then* 😊
- *Are you absolutely, definitively 100% sure about that* 😊?

Evidently, in this study, data reveals that this technique has helped students to think more about their answers and to provide more constructive replies to Hubert.ai as shown below. As web surveys have a predefined design, it is impossible to match conversational agents' flexibility or 'intelligence'. As argued by Wambsganss et al. [12], this feature can mitigate common web survey challenges like satisficing behaviour and survey fatigue.

In addition, in many cases where Hubert.ai received short answers from students, he asked them to elaborate on these. In most conversations, this successfully helped students to provide more precise and focused answers. An example of Hubert.ai's ability to guide towards constructive answers from students is shown in Fig. 3.

Hubert.ai	What could the teachers start doing, that would improve it?
User	I think everything is alright. Nothing to improve
Hubert.ai	Surely there must be something that could be improved?
User	I can't remember anything bad
Hubert.ai	Not yet!
Hubert.ai	Let me repeat the question
Hubert.ai	What could the teachers start doing, that would improve it?
User	I can't remember anything bad
Hubert.ai	Not yet!
Hubert.ai	What could the teachers start doing, that would improve it?
User	Maybe weekly tasks could be equal, because I heard that some students got harder tasks than others
Hubert.ai	I understand...
Hubert.ai	What could the teachers stop doing, that would improve course X?
User	I think that teachers should put more information online, not in last week or something like that
Hubert.ai	I'm sorry to hear that
Hubert.ai	What is your overall experience of course X? Please write a sentence or two
User	irrelevant*
Hubert.ai	Alright, noted. Let's continue.
Hubert.ai	Do you want to add something more?
User	Overall experience: I have been very frustrated and angry. As I said professors have been wasting times in preparing videos that have a little impact on students' teaching a lesson. Professor V has gave us a many material but in exam it was very hard to understand. A point is there is no connection between two topics at least. It's shameful.....This year, on this course, there was so many cheating. I regret that I haven't cheated. Prof. B should be ashamed that he's said that this generation is better than generation 2014/2015. I guess I am correct. One little advice to professor is to simplify lesson or course PI with important information. Don't give us boring materials that make no sense. Lessons are boring and exams are very tough. Grade for this course is 1-10: 5....I forget to mention about laboratory tests. They were tough. I recommend that you check knowledge every 2-3 weeks. Overall, for me, laboratory exams were very tough.
Hubert.ai	Got it

Fig. 3. A sample conversation guiding the student to more constructive answers

4.1 Evaluation of the Conversational Agent

Some students expressed positive perceptions about the use of a conversational agent like Hubert.ai; many students perceived their experiences with Hubert.ai as fun and more interesting than web surveys, as demonstrated in Fig. 4. This was also reflected in the overall numerical ratings presented in Fig. 2.

On the other hand, a few students argued that regular static web surveys are better than conversational agents, as shown in Fig. 5.

Moreover, this study's data captures some indicators of students' enjoyment which is demonstrated through students' use of humour during their interactions with Hubert.ai. This finding confirms Wambsganss et al.'s [3] claim that the use of conversational agents in collecting course feedback from students can have a positive impact on students' level of enjoyment compared to web surveys. Many respondents mirrored Hubert.ai's language and used emoji and generally friendly comments in greeting Hubert.ai as shown in Fig. 6.

Generally, there are no clear differences observed in the quality of course feedback provided by students of different genders. However, some male students attempted to challenge Hubert.ai's intelligence. Framing systems like conversational agents as anthropomorphic often leads to raising user expectations of the intelligence of these systems [29]. Dibitonto et al. [21] argue that as a result of a false sense of anonymity when chatting with conversational agents, users can tend to be ruder than when chatting with a human interviewer.

It's worth noting that Hubert.ai's handling of these challenges from users did not lead to a failure in handling the conversation. This contrasts with other conversational agents that have been developed using the Facebook Messenger API as reported by Kim, Lee and Gweon [7]. The authors argue that this failure has caused student frustration as a result of the agent posing the same question repeatedly despite getting a full answer to the question.

As mentioned above, the longest conversation with Hubert.ai lasted for 218 utterances. Examples of some students' challenging responses are shown in Fig. 7.

This study's data indicates that older students (21+) completed answering Hubert.ai's questions with a fewer number of iterations compared to the younger students (18, 19 and 20 years old). One explanation for that can be attributed to the extent of students' experience of the university courses as they head towards the end of their academic degrees.

Unlike some Facebook Messenger conversational agents [7], Hubert.ai allows students to modify their answers, as shown in Fig. 8.

Hubert.ai	How did you like this type of evaluation compared to a regular survey?
User	Very interesting and unique.
Hubert.ai	So on a scale from 1-10, would you give it a 10?
User	Let it be a 10!

Hubert.ai	How did you like this type of evaluation compared to a regular survey?
User	Interesting.
Hubert.ai	So on a scale from 1-10, would you give it a 10?
User	Yes
Hubert.ai	I see...
Hubert.ai	How did you like this type of evaluation compared to a regular survey?
User	Yes, it's fun
Hubert.ai	So on a scale from 1-10, would you give it a 10?
User	yes, without no doubt

Hubert.ai	How did you like this type of evaluation compared to a regular survey?
User	I think this way is better for communication.
Hubert.ai	So on a scale from 1-10, would you give it a 10?
User	Good!

Hubert.ai	How did you like this type of evaluation compared to a regular survey?
User	It was a much more interesting approach to feedback, much more bearable to fill out. I really enjoyed it to be honest, really cool.
Hubert.ai	So on a scale from 1-10, would you give it a 10?
User	Yeah

Hubert.ai	How did you like this type of evaluation compared to a regular survey?
User	I really enjoyed it, comparing it to the boring evaluation this gives you a sense of involvement and making a change to the productivity of the institute in a good way.
Hubert.ai	So on a scale from 1-10, would you give it a 10?
User	maybe 9

Hubert.ai	I'll ask a question about myself as well:
Hubert.ai	How did you like this type of evaluation compared to a regular survey?
User	It's much more interesting and fun :)
Hubert.ai	So on a scale from 1-10, would you give it a 10?
User	Yes
Hubert.ai	I see...
Hubert.ai	How did you like this type of evaluation compared to a regular survey?
User	this way is total different with regular one. However, it is interesting
Hubert.ai	So on a scale from 1-10, would you give it a 7?
User	maybe 8
Hubert.ai	How did you like this type of evaluation compared to a regular survey?
User	it's really interesting, better than filling a form
Hubert.ai	So on a scale from 1-10, would you give it a 10?
User	10

Fig. 4. Examples of positive perceptions of use of Hubert for course evaluation

| Hubert.ai | How did you like this type of evaluation compared to a regular survey? |
| User | No difference from regular survey other than the scripted responses |

| Hubert.ai | How did you like this type of evaluation compared to a regular survey? |
| User | Still not realistic enough - don't feel like i'm chatting. Perhaps more option paths can be created |

Fig. 5. Examples of negative perceptions of use of Hubert for course evaluation

| Hubert.ai | Thank you those were all the questions I had! You may close this window now. Have a great day! ☺ |
| User | *You too bot!* |

Hubert.ai	Are there any other points you would like to comment on?
User	You are a very clever bot Hubert
Hubert.ai	My bad!
Hubert.ai	Let me repeat the question:
Hubert.ai	Are there any other points you would like to comment on?
User	Nope! Stay safe and healthy
Hubert.ai	I understand

Fig. 6. Examples of positive friendly responses to Hubert

Hubert.ai	Thank you, those were all the questions I had! You may close this window now. Have a great day! ☺
User	Bitch
Hubert.ai	"A poor choice of words never improved anything" - Hubert the bot
User	tell me a joke
Hubert.ai	Knock knock.
User	whos there
Hubert.ai	Hey there!
Hubert.ai	I don't have any questions for you right now. Please come back later!
User	sick joke man

Hubert.ai	What is working well with course X and should continue in the same way?
User	yes ofskrzo
Hubert.ai	Ok, what?
User	why yes
Hubert.ai	Ok, what?
User	u limited
User	yes \\ u limited
Hubert.ai	Ok, what?
User	Yes
Hubert.ai	Ok, what?
User	go back
Hubert.ai	Are you sure you want to go back one question and answer it again?
User	Yes
Hubert.ai	What is your gender? Please choose Male or Female [Male] [Female]
User	Male

Hubert.ai	I don't have any questions for you right now. Please come back later!
User	Coronavirus
User	What does coronavirus cause
Hubert.ai	I'll try to answer that, but I may be totally wrong. Give me a sec.
Hubert.ai	SARS-CoV-2 virus
Hubert.ai	Now it's your turn to answer my question:
User	Sure
User	Can you send me an emoji

Fig. 7. Examples of student responses that were challenging for Hubert

Hubert.ai	Thank you, those were all the questions I had! You may close this window now. Have a great day! ☺
User	Are you still there
Hubert.ai	Yes.
User	Can I ask you questions
Hubert.ai	Hey there!
Hubert.ai	I don't have any questions for you right now. Please come back later!
User	What do you like to eat
Hubert.ai	I'll try to answer that, but I may be totally wrong. Give me a sec.
Hubert.ai	I'm sorry but I can't answer that. Even Googled it.
User	Hello \\ What's today's weather
Hubert.ai	I'll try to answer that, but I may be totally wrong. Give me a sec.
Hubert.ai	I'm sorry but I can't answer that. Even Googled it.
User	What is the time now?
Hubert.ai	I'll try to answer that, but I may be totally wrong. Give me a sec.
Hubert.ai	9:36:05 A.M. Eastern Daylight Time, Tuesday, May 12, 2020
Hubert.ai	Now it's your turn to answer my question:
User	Okay
User	What is it?
Hubert.ai	I'll try to answer that, but I may be totally wrong. Give me a sec.
Hubert.ai	What Is It? is a 2005 American surrealist film written, edited, co-produced and directed by Crispin Glover and starring Crispin Glover, Fairuza Balk, and Steven C. Stewart.

Hubert.ai	How did you like this type of evaluation compared to a regular survey?
User	I like you are so cute
Hubert.ai	So on a scale from 1-10, would you give it a 10?
User	want to go on a date?
Hubert.ai	That was all, thanks! You can close this window now.
User	you too
User	Thanks
Hubert.ai	Sure buddy ☺
User	who are you
Hubert.ai	I am Hubert, the world's first artificially intelligent evaluation bot. Here to serve you!
User	can you give me money?
Hubert.ai	I'll try to answer that, but I may be totally wrong. Give me a sec.
Hubert.ai	I'm sorry but I can't answer that. Even Googled it.
User	how old are you
Hubert.ai	I am Hubert, the world's first artificially intelligent evaluation bot. Here to serve you!
User	love you
Hubert.ai	Thank you, I have no more questions now. You can close this window!
User	say me too
User	No
User	Yes

Fig. 7. (*continued*)

Hubert.ai	What is working well with course Y and should continue in the same way?
User	same assignment
User	Sorry
User	I think just keep the way of assessment
Hubert.ai	Ok
Hubert.ai	What is your gender? Please choose Male or Female [Male] [Female]
User	No
User	We can go now
User	Yes
User	Female
Hubert.ai	I see...

Fig. 8. Examples of students modifying their responses to Hubert

5 Conclusions

This study aims to explore the impact of using Hubert.ai, an AI chatbot or conversational agent in collecting course evaluations in higher education institutions. Analysis of the student-chatbot conversation transcripts allowed us to identify key qualities of the interactions:

- the chatbot was able to guide the student to more constructive answers;
- many students volunteered positive perceptions of use of Hubert for course evaluation, though a few were negative;
- students engaged with the chatbot, with positive friendly responses to Hubert;
- some student responses were challenging for Hubert to analyse;
- this could be alleviated by allowing students to modifying their responses.

The key findings of the study indicate that the use of chatbots has positively impacted students' response quality. Many students have favoured using chatbots over the regular web surveys. Others demonstrated their enjoyment through the use of humour during their interactions with Hubert.ai. In addition, in most conversations, the chatbot has successfully helped students to provide more precise and focused answers.

However, the data analysed here was gathered from a relatively small number of conversations, and participation was voluntary and offered predominantly to students taking courses in technical subjects – it may be that the self-selected participants were somewhat predisposed towards positive engagement with and evaluation of the conversational agent (and/or towards exploring its limitations).

The EDUBOTS project is ongoing, with further trials of the Hubert.ai chatbot taking place. These are expected to yield additional data which will be used to enable more robust conclusions to be drawn and to enable more detailed analysis and the application of further natural language processing techniques to enable thematic analysis and automated identification of "useful" student feedback.

References

1. Fadel, C., Groff, J.: Four-dimensional education for sustainable societies. In: Cook, Justin W. (ed.) Sustainability, Human Well-Being, and the Future of Education, pp. 269–281. Springer, Cham (2019). https://doi.org/10.1007/978-3-319-78580-6_8
2. Spooren, P., Brockx, B., Mortelmans, D.: On the validity of student evaluation of teaching. Rev. Educ. Res. **83** (2013). https://doi.org/10.3102/0034654313496870
3. Wambsganss, T., Winkler, R., Sollner, M., Leimeister, J.M.: A conversational agent to improve response quality in course evaluations. In: ACM CHI Conference on Human Factors in Computing Systems, pp. 1–9 (2020)
4. Blair, E., Valdez Noel, K.: Improving higher education practice through student evaluation systems: is the student voice being heard? Assess. Eval. High. Educ. **39**(7), 879–894 (2014). https://doi.org/10.1080/02602938.2013.875984
5. Keränen, H., Holm, E.: Students' role in quality enhancement – a reflexion of functional stupidity or an implication of 'Quality as Practice'? Paper presented at the 9th European Quality Assurance Forum, Barcelona, Spain (2014)
6. Richardson, J.T.E.: Instruments for obtaining student feedback: a review of the literature. Assess. Eval. High. Educ. **30**, 387–415 (2005). https://doi.org/10.1080/02602930500099193
7. Kim, S., Lee, J., Gweon, G.: Comparing data from chatbot and web surveys effects of platform and conversational style on survey response quality. In: Conference on Human Factors in Computing Systems – Proceedings, pp. 1–12 (2019). https://doi.org/10.1145/3290605.330 0316
8. Krosnick, J.: Response strategies for coping with the cognitive demands of attitude measures in surveys. Appl. Cogn. Psychol. **5**(3), 213–236 (1991)
9. Roster, A.C., Rogers, R.D., Albaum, G., Klein, D.: A comparison of response characteristics from web and telephone surveys. Int. J. Mark. Res. **46**, 359–374 (2004)
10. Tucker, B., Jones, S., Straker, L.: Online student evaluation improves course experience questionnaire results in a physiotherapy program. High. Educ. Res. Dev. **27**(3), 281–296 (2008)
11. Steyn, C., Davies, C., Sambo, A.: Eliciting student feedback for course development: the application of a qualitative course evaluation tool among business research students. Assess. Eval. High. Educ. **44**(1), 11–24 (2019)
12. Wambsganss, T., Winkler, R., Schmid, P., Sollner, M.: Unleashing the potential of conversational agents for course evaluations: empirical insights from a comparison with web surveys. In: Twenty-Eighth European Conference on Information Systems (ECIS2020), pp. 1–18 (2020)
13. Abu Shawar, B., Atwell, E.: Using corpora in machine-learning chatbot systems. Int. J. Corpus Linguist. **10**(4), 489–516 (2005)
14. Winkler, R., Söllner, M.: Unleashing the potential of chatbots in education: a state-of-the-art analysis. In: Academy of Management Annual Meeting (AOM), Chicago, USA (2018)
15. Smutny, P., Schreiberova, P.: Chatbots for learning: a review of educational chatbots for the Facebook Messenger. Comput. Educ. **151**, 1–11 (2020)
16. Pérez, J., Daradoumis, T., Puig, J.: Rediscovering the use of chatbots in education: a systematic literature review. Comput. Appl. Eng. Educ. **28**, 1549–1565 (2020)
17. Lancaster University: Lancaster University Launch Pioneering Chatbot Companion for Students (2019). https://www.lancaster.ac.uk/news/lancaster-university-launch-pioneering-cha tbot-companion-for-students
18. Muñoz, A.P.: Lola, el chatbot inteligente que triunfa entre los estudiantes (2018). (in Spanish). https://retina.elpais.com/retina/2018/11/30/innovacion/1543580663_865121.html

19. Santoso, H.A., et al.: Dinus Intelligent Assistance (DINA) chatbot for university admission services. In: International Seminar on Application for Technology of Information and Communication, pp. 417–423 (2018). https://doi.org/10.1109/ISEMANTIC.2018.8549797
20. Brustenga, G., Alpiste, M., Castells, N.: Briefing paper: Chatbots in education (2018). http://hdl.handle.net/10609/80185
21. Dibitonto, M., Leszczynska, K., Tazzi, F., Medaglia, C.M.: Chatbot in a campus environment: design of LiSA, a virtual assistant to help students in their university life. In: Kurosu, M. (ed.) HCI 2018. LNCS, vol. 10903, pp. 103–116. Springer, Cham (2018). https://doi.org/10.1007/978-3-319-91250-9_9
22. Hobert, S.: Say hello to 'coding tutor'! Design and evaluation of a chatbot-based learning system supporting students to learn to program. In: 40th International Conference on Information Systems, ICIS 2019, vol. 1, pp. 1–17 (2019)
23. Ruan, S., et al.: BookBuddy: turning digital materials into interactive foreign language lessons through a voice chatbot. In: ACM Conference on Learning, vol. 30, pp. 1–4 (2019). https://doi.org/10.1145/3330430.3333643
24. Zakos, J., Capper, L.: CLIVE – an artificially intelligent chat robot for conversational language practice. In: Darzentas, J., Vouros, G.A., Vosinakis, S., Arnellos, A. (eds.) SETN 2008. LNCS (LNAI), vol. 5138, pp. 437–442. Springer, Heidelberg (2008). https://doi.org/10.1007/978-3-540-87881-0_46
25. Pham, X., et al.: Chatbot as an intelligent personal assistant for mobile language learning. In: Proceedings of the 2nd International Conference on Education and E-Learning (2018). https://doi.org/10.1145/3291078.3291115
26. Przegalinska, A., Ciechanowski, L., Stroz, A., Gloor, P., Mazurek, G.: In bot we trust: a new methodology of chatbot performance measures. Bus. Horiz. 62(6), 785–797 (2019)
27. Griol, D., Molina, J., Callejas, Z.: Incorporating Android conversational agents in M-learning apps. Expert Syst. 34(4), 1–17 (2017)
28. Gnewuch, U., Morana, S., Adam, M.T.P., Maedche, A.: Faster is not always better: understanding the effect of dynamic response delays in human-chatbot interaction. In: 26th European Conference on Information Systems (ECIS) (2018)
29. Shedroff, N., Noessel, C.: Make It So: Interaction Design Lessons from Science Fiction. Rosenfeld, Brooklyn, New York (2012)

An Overview of the Use of Chatbots in Medical and Healthcare Education

Fotos Frangoudes[✉] ⓘ, Marios Hadjiaros ⓘ, Eirini C. Schiza ⓘ,
Maria Matsangidou ⓘ, Olia Tsivitanidou ⓘ, and Kleanthis Neokleous

CYENS Centre of Excellence, Nicosia, Cyprus
{f.frangoudes,M.Hadjiaros,e.schizas,m.matsangidou,
o.tsivitanidou,K.Neokleous}@cyens.org.cy

Abstract. Chatbots are becoming a trend in many fields such as medical, service industry and more recently in education. Especially in healthcare education, there is a growing interest in integrating chatbots in the learning and teaching processes mostly because of their portability and affordance. In this paper, we seek to explore the primary uses of chatbots in medical education, as well as how they are developed. We elaborate on current chatbot applications and research enacted in the domains of medical and healthcare education, We focus in the areas of virtual patients in medical education, patients' education related to healthcare matters but also chatbots as course assistance in for enhancing healthcare professionals' curricula. Additionally, we examine the metrics that have been used to evaluate these chatbots, which include subjective ones like the usability and acceptability by the users, and objectives ones, like their accuracy and users' skills evaluation. Overall, even though chatbots offer a flexible solution and a vast possibility to improve healthcare education, our literature review suggests that their efficacy has not been thoroughly tested. Also, limited examples of chatbots in European Healthcare curricula have been found. These call of the need for further research towards this direction.

Keywords: Chatbots · Conversational agents · Higher education · Medical education · Healthcare education

1 Introduction

Dialogue systems and conversational agents, including chatbots, are becoming ubiquitous in modern society. Chatbots can also be identified in the literature as "chatbot virtual assistants", "conversational agents", "chat bots", "pedagogical agents", "intelligent tutor systems", "dialogue systems", "smart personal assistants" and "smart assistants". They comprise software tools that simulate textual and/or auditory conversations and with which users interact on a certain topic or in a specific domain through digital services in a natural, conversational way using text and voice input [1, 2].

Their conceptualization emerged in the 1950s from the need of humans to interact with computers in a natural human language, while the term "Chatterbot" was coined a

© Springer Nature Switzerland AG 2021
P. Zaphiris and A. Ioannou (Eds.): HCII 2021, LNCS 12785, pp. 170–184, 2021.
https://doi.org/10.1007/978-3-030-77943-6_11

few years later in 1994. The internet era and the massive expansion of social network-ing sites sparked the widespread use of chatbots just a decade ago. The basic princi-ple employed in chatbots consists of an environment that receives questions in natural human language, associates these questions with a knowledge base, and then provides a response [3]. Commonly, chatbots appear in customer services as frequently asked questions (FAQ), as virtual and personal assistants on mobile devices, and in business webpages for sailing products and to offering legal advice [4]. They are becoming a trend in many fields such as medicine, product and service industry, and lately in educa-tion. The exploitation of Artificial Intelligence (AI), machine learning techniques, and deep learning technologies allow for the design and development of chatbots which can be meaningfully integrated into education, and specifically, in medical and healthcare education which is the focus of this paper.

There is an increasing need to learn, practice and even design modern and technology-rich clinical environments. The ongoing global pandemic has highlighted the need to enhance preparedness for complicated and unexpected scenarios and the challenges healthcare professionals and patients alike face. It is therefore imperative to invest in intelligent and technologically advanced approaches to endorse personalized healthcare education that is more than ever needed nowadays. In fact, digital integration in learning and teaching has a high priority within Europe 2020 and is highly relevant within the context of healthcare where it is a declared political aim to promote Information Tech-nology (IT) infrastructure in hospitals and the development of e-Health solutions both within the EU and globally [5].

Recently, there has been a growing interest in integrating chatbots in healthcare edu-cation, mostly because of their ease to develop and deploy without the use of any special equipment. As a result, chatbots can be a low cost and affordable technology for all the Higher Education Institutes (HEI) to embed them in their healthcare curricula to enhance their students' knowledge and skills. In addition, chatbots can enhance individ-ual learning since students can use them as standalone resources with no additional cost and receive personalized content.

Further to the above, there is growing evidence around chatbots' potential to change the way students learn and search for information [6]. Chatbots can quiz existing knowl-edge, enable higher student engagement with a learning task and support higher-order cognitive activities (e.g., a better understanding of their learning habits, reflect on prac-tice). Chatbots can also be very scalable, able to support hundreds of students con-currently, assisting with individual problems, answering questions and contributing to personalized learning. We believe that chatbots have a lot to offer both in Higher Edu-cation, and also in improving the publics' health literacy. In the following sections, we present a meticulous regarding the use and impact of chatbots in healthcare education and particularly in virtual patients, patients' education, and course assistance in HEIs.

2   Method

We performed a systematic literature review, following the PRISMA [7] methodology, of the use of chatbots and conversational agents in general, in medical education. The main aim of the study is to identify the opportunities chatbots offer in the area, what are their primary uses, along with their general implementation framework and some of the metrics that have been used to evaluate them.

2.1 Search Strategy

The search looked up publications from the electronic databases ACM Digital Library, IEEE Xplore Digital Library, ProQuest, PubMed, Sage Journals, Springer and Taylor & Francis Online. Results were restricted to publications from January 2015 to September 2020 and written in English. The pattern Chatbot AND Healthcare AND Education was used as the composition for the search terms. Each of the three terms was expanded to a set of words of similar context as follows: Chatbot was defined as chatbot OR "conversational agent" OR "virtual agent" OR "dialogue system" OR "virtual patient". Healthcare was defined as health OR healthcare OR medical OR clinical and Education as educate OR school OR student OR learn OR teach OR simulate. Additional publications were retrieved and added to the search results from references and related sources.

2.2 Study Selection Criteria

The study looked at publications that focused on the development of chatbots or the conversation component of a virtual agent. Studies that included embodied conversational agents (ECA) or virtual agents and did not provide sufficient details about the conversational component were excluded. Additionally, the selected publications evaluated the chatbots through a user study or pilot. Review articles and publications where the full-text was not available were also excluded.

2.3 Screening Strategy and Article Review

After the removal of duplicate entries, the initial results were screened by three researchers, based on their titles and abstracts. From the remaining publications, the same team of researchers assessed their eligibility by doing a full-text screening. Publications that did not meet the selection criteria were excluded. Any disagreements were resolved through discussion between the researchers.

2.4 Data Extraction and Synthesis

After the final set of studies was selected, the included studies were analyzed and categorized based on different criteria. The focus was on the use of each chatbot, their underline implementation, and how they were evaluated.

3   Results

Through the search in the electronic databases, 4856 publication records were retrieved (Fig. 1). Additionally, another 59 records were identified from the references and included for screening. After duplicates were removed, 4397 records were screened based on their titles and abstracts. From those 4331 were excluded and 66 were assessed

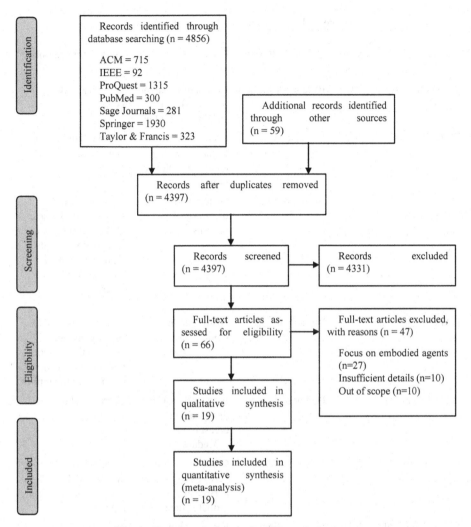

Fig. 1. Search procedure in the electronic databases

based on their full-text for eligibility. From those 47 did not meet the selection criteria and were excluded. More than half (n = 27) were excluded because they focus on embodied agents, without enough information on the conversational component, 10 provided insufficient details about the development and 10 were out of scope. The process resulted in 19 records being included in the study for qualitative analysis (Table 1).

The analysis showed a few key areas where chatbots are used in medical education. Several studies focused on the development of virtual patients [10, 11, 13–18, 22, 25]. Another area chatbots have been used in is patients education [4, 8, 9, 12, 19, 21, 23, 24]. Other uses have also been explored like course assistance by administering quizzes [20] and facilitating communication between students and instructors.

Table 1. List of records included in the review.

Authors	Year	Use of chatbot	Focus area	Metrics for chatbots' evaluation
[8] Amith et al.	2019	Patient education	Counselling parents for providing HPV vaccine to children	Usability of the system
[9] Beaudry et al.	2016	Patient education	Counselling teenagers with common health-care issues	Acceptability of the chatbots/user engagement
[10] Campillos-Llanos et al.	2020	Virtual patients	History taking and diagnosis of virtual patients	Usability of the systems, the accuracy of the system (NLU components and user input) vocabulary coverage for new cases, vocabulary usage
[11] Carnell et al.	2015	Virtual patients	History taking by novice users	Usability, user skills (history taking, conversation duration, topic discoveries), accuracy of the replies
[12] Chetlen et al.	2019	Patient education	Frequently asked questions for a breast biopsy procedure	Usability of the systems
[13] Datta et al.	2016	Virtual patients	Communication between healthcare personnel during a virtual patient visit	Accuracy of the system (NLU components and user input)
[14] El Zini et al.	2019	Virtual patients	History taking to gain clinical experience	Accuracy of the system (NLU components and user input)
[15] Foster et al.	2016	Virtual patients	History taking to improve communication skills and learn to empathize	User skills (history taking, communication skills and empathy)

(continued)

Table 1. (*continued*)

Authors	Year	Use of chatbot	Focus area	Metrics for chatbots' evaluation
[16] Isaza-Restrepo et al.	2018	Virtual patients	History taking to gain clinical experience	Usability of the systems, user skills (history taking skills)
[17] Jin et al.	2017	Virtual patients	History taking and diagnosis of virtual patients	Accuracy of the system (NLU components and user input)
[18] Laleye et al.	2020	Virtual patients	History taking to gain clinical experience	Accuracy of the system (NLU components and user input), the accuracy of the system (dialogue management component)
[19] May et al.	2020	Patient education	Counselling on general consent and clinical data donation	Usability of the systems
[20] Pereira et al.	2016	Course assistance	Multiple choice quiz for assessing students knowledge	Acceptability of the chatbots
[21] Rose-Davis et al.	2019	Patient education	Counselling parents with children with Juvenile Idiopathic Arthritis	Usability of the systems, accuracy of the system (dialogue management component)
[4] Rosruen et al.	2018	Patient education	Medical consultation for home treatment	Usability of the system, accuracy of the system
[22] Tanana et al.	2019	Virtual patients	Communication skills during psychotherapy counselling	Usability of the systems, user skills (communication skills)
[23] Wang et al.	2015	Patient education	Health literacy improvement related to family history	Usability of the systems, user skills (history taking accuracy)

(*continued*)

Table 1. (*continued*)

Authors	Year	Use of chatbot	Focus area	Metrics for chatbots' evaluation
[24] Yadav et al.	2019	Patient education	Counselling mothers about breastfeeding	Usability of the systems, acceptability of the chatbots
[25] Yang et al.	2019	Virtual patients	Clinical practice to gain clinical experience	Usability of the systems, acceptability of the chatbots, accuracy of the system (dialogue management component), user skills (history taking skills), user skills (communication skills)

Interaction with the chatbots is primarily done through free text inputted through keyboard [4, 10, 16, 17, 22, 24, 25] and using speech [17, 24]. Some chatbots, however, followed more linear flow with either pre-selected answers or specific commands that can be selected [9, 11, 12, 20, 23]. On the other hand, the logic behind the chatbots regarding understanding user input and the decision making primarily was done through some implementation of a natural language understanding system [4, 10, 13–15, 17–19, 21, 22, 25]. Some other studies used the Wizard-of-Oz [8, 24] methodology with a human controller following specified rules simulating a limited-intelligence chatbots' behaviour.

There is also a variety in the ways chatbots have been deployed, that shows the versatility of the technology. Some were used through smartphones or tablets [4, 8, 9, 12, 20, 23, 24], either through custom applications, using sms messages [9], or integrated in social media applications like Telegram [20] and Line [4]. Others were web-based [10, 11, 16, 22], run as standalone applications on personal computers [14, 17, 25], and even integrations in Virtual Reality systems [18, 19].

The evaluation of chatbots can vary based on the focus of each study and how far along each is. One of the main evaluation metrics is the usability of the systems [8, 10, 12, 16, 19, 21–25], which however does not follow any set guidelines, combing Likert-scale questions, and open-ended inquiries. Another metric that is used, especially in early-stage studies or with more digitally illiterate populations, is the acceptability of the chatbots [9, 20, 24, 25]. This can also include the ability of users to create rapport with the users and open up with it and talk about sensitive subjects [24].

One of the main ongoing challenges of chatbots is the natural interaction with the user, and their ability to understand what the user is saying. Therefore, several studies have focused more on the overall accuracy of the system, both related to the accuracy of the NLU components and understanding the user input [10, 13, 14, 17, 18], but also the dialogue management component that selects the correct responses to the users [18, 21, 25].

Finally based on the target audience of each chatbot, and the goals of each study, the user skills are measured like history taking skills [11, 16, 25], communication skills [15, 22, 25], empathy [20].

Following is an analysis of the main areas chatbots are being used in, with more details on their focus, as well as their implementation framework.

3.1 Virtual Patients

Chatbots as virtual patients have been used across healthcare practitioners' education including for physicians [15, 16, 18], and speech pathologist [11]. They also cover a wide range of conditions from psychological like depression [15], substance abuse [15], to other pathological areas including dysphagia [11], conditions related to abdominal pain [16, 18] and more robust systems that can simulate various case across domains [10, 14, 25]. Other variation can also be found in the interface that has been used. This can range from chat-like interfaces [11, 15, 16, 22] just showing an avatar of the patient, to 3D avatars [10, 14, 17, 18, 25]. Also, even though most receive user input through typing, some have used speech recognition [14, 18]. Another feature that has been observed across several studies [15, 16, 22, 25], and has shown overall positive results is the inclusion of automatic feedback modules either during or usually at the end of the interaction with virtual patients.

One of the goals of health-professional education is the development of student's communication and clinical reasoning skills. Starting from the 1960s [26] schools adopted the use of standardized patients by using actors that acted as real patients. This allowed interviewing patients in a controlled setting. However, the use of standardized patients can be time-consuming and costly for institutions [27]. To address these concerns, virtual patients have been developed that can simulate real-life interactions [28]. Virtual patients can have different forms ranging from simple conversational avatars, with a text-based interface, to more complex multi-modal agents. Chatbots, and conversational agents in general, provide the communication logic behind virtual patients.

Designing a chatbot can be a tedious and complex task to achieve a natural and robust interaction. Some, especially earlier, systems were designed to provide the user with a set of pre-defined options to select from. With the advancement of computational capabilities, however, researchers have started utilizing Natural Language Understanding (NLU) to analyze text from users as well.

Carnell et al. [11] compared two approaches. They used transcripts from previous interactions with virtual patients to create question-answer pairs that they then present to students as selection-based options. They then compared how a selection-based interface compares with a natural language interface. Results showed that the chat-based interaction resembled a real interaction, but the selection-based interface provided more guidance on what questions should be asked. Thus, novices that have no prior experience with interviewing might find the latter more useful until they gain enough experience. The findings were further supported by Isaza-Restrepo et al. [16] that incorporated a virtual patient in their curriculum, with students interacting with a number of virtual patients over the course of a semester. A pre- and post-assessment with standardized patients showed significant improvement. Students noted its usefulness, especially for novice students that have little or no prior experience with interviewing patients. The chatbot also reinforced the importance of post-session feedback as well as the benefits of repetition of scenarios and the ability to try different responses.

When using an NLU-based approach, understanding the user's intent, and then generating an appropriate response can be a difficult task. To achieve these rule-based systems utilizing pattern-matching have been used. Campillos-Llanos et al. [10] designed a dialogue system for a virtual patient that can support interactions for multiple cases from different medical domains. Their rule-based approach was designed by extracting questions and answers from standardized patient interviews and other clinical examination guides. Their knowledge model "hosts structured thesauri with linguistic, terminological and ontological knowledge". After an evaluation with 35 different cases from 18 specialities, the NLU module achieved an F-measure of 95.8%, while the dialogue manager answered correctly 74.3% of the time.

Foster et al. [15] examined different ways of teaching empathy through virtual patients. Interaction with the system was through a text-based interface, matching the input to predefined patterns. To detect paraphrasing, a machine-learning module was used to detect similarities between input. To teach empathy, human assessors reviewed students' responses and at the end of each interaction, provided more empathetic alternatives. This empathetic-feedback system led to increased empathy from students and building a better rapport with standardized patients.

With the compilation of large enough datasets, AI and machine learning approaches have also been implemented to create more robust and scalable systems [29]. Zini et al. [14] implemented a deep-learning framework to develop a medical domain-specific question-answering corpus based on medical documents. The framework works by first computing the word embeddings from the input and then computes sentence embeddings using a long short-term memory network (LSTM). Finally, a convolutional neural network (CNN) model computes the most appropriate answer. The system provided an overall accuracy of 81% answering the student's questions.

Tanana et al. [22] used two different LSTM networks to generate responses. The system also provided real-time feedback back to the users prompting them for more open questions and to use reflections. The group that was provided with the feedback improved their performance even after the feedback was removed. Their chatbot was still a proof-of-concept however tested with non-mental health trainees.

Research has also been made in hybrid models combining traditional rules-based approaches with deep learning ones. For example, Yang et al. [25] designed a system using pattern-matching with a Multiple Classification Ripple Down Rules knowledge base which utilizes a CNN model to select an appropriate answer based on the inferences. The system also includes an automatic competency assessment that can provide feedback back to the students. The evaluation of the system showed promising results, with students reporting more confidence and improvement in their skills.

Laleye et al. [18] implemented a hybrid system that primarily uses a rule-based pattern matching approach to find appropriate answers to input questions. However, when no appropriate match is found, the system switches to a semantic similarity subsystem based on word embeddings, to find the most similar question. They achieve this by combining FastText and CNN models, resulting in an F1-score of 92.29.

Jin et al. [17] also used a hybrid approach by combining pattern matching with a stack of CNNs. The dataset for the model consisted of prior dialogues of students with a virtual patient chatbot. For the NLU it uses a combination of CNNs for characters and words that are stacked. At the end, they use a binary classifier that chooses between the pattern matching and the CNN models based on the expected accuracy of each one. The result is an 89.3% accuracy and a significant reduction in error.

3.2 Patients Education

Chatbots in patients education can take the form of a Frequently Asked Questions (FAQ) to answers patients questions about a topic. Other uses assist with the communication between healthcare professional and the patients. One example of such a chatbot is for diabetic patients to record their medical histories in a short description [4]. Chatbots provide information and counselling to hospital patients at the time of hospitalization and react to patient questions. These interventions aim to provide individual support to patients helping them to follow their therapy. For example, one study showed that patient education aims at strengthening the competence and self-care capabilities of a patient [6]. Through websites or by asking questions, patients learn about diseases and treatment as a basis for their decision-making. However, their motivation to learn is often limited due to the complexity of content or significant barriers for asking specific questions. To address this issue, a smartphone application named CLAIRE was developed in this study [19]. It combines virtual reality (VR), a chatbot and a voice user interface (VUI). In the virtual environment, the user can move freely, interact with objects, and talk to the character CLAIRE. Then, the character provides information on the respective learning topic, which is in its current implementation information on the donation of personal health data and concluded that VR with integrated VUI can extend the existing information channels for patient education [19].

Patient education chatbots were created by the effort to overcome barriers related to the collection of family health history information. Relational agents are computer-animated characters that use speech, gaze, hand gesture, prosody, and other nonverbal modalities to emulate the experience of human face-to-face conversation. They can be programmed and used for automated health education and behavioral counselling interventions, and they have been demonstrated to establish and maintain therapeutic relationships through these and other interactions. These agents have been successfully used to facilitate medication adherence, to explain health documents, to promote breast-feeding and to educate about and motivate exercise and weight loss. Wang, et al. [23] developed a chatbot called VICKY which is an animated computer character designed to collect family health history information by asking a series of questions about the user's family health history, targeting common chronic conditions including heart disease, diabetes, hypertension, stroke, and various cancers. Users respond to VICKY's verbal questions by selecting a preformulated simple response on a touch screen, with the choices updated at each turn in the conversation. Response options are short and easy to read. Minimal reading and typing are required, thus reducing the literacy burden. Moreover, additional opportunities are interwoven throughout the program to let respondents tell VICKY when they are uncertain about the meaning of a response option.

Rosruen and Samanchuen [4] implemented MedBot which is designed to be a general doctor, expert on symptoms and treatment. MedBot can provide suggestions and medical advice to patients. The objective of the chatbot is to provide consultations only on general symptoms. Beyond that, it will recommend the patients to visit a real doctor. MedBot was designed based on 34 intents including 16 intents of symptoms, 10 intents of sub-detail of stomachache, five intents of sub-detail of a headache, one intent of greeting with a chatbot, one intent of no illness, and one intent of finding the hospital by getting the link.

In another study, Yadav et al. [24] studied how a chatbot can be used to educate new mothers who are breastfeeding their children. The chatbot in the study, even though it was run as a Wizard of Oz experiment, emulated a low-intelligent agent that tried to provide information usually provided by health workers to mothers 24–7 through their smartphone. The study was largely explorative, studying the acceptability of the system, but showcases the potential chatbots can have especially with digitally illiterate populations. The users of the chatbot slowly developed a relationship with the chatbot and with time trusted more its recommendations and guidance. The chatbot other than just answering questions from the user, provided counter-questions and also additional information and facts through notifications.

3.3   Course Assistance in HEIs

Personalized learning has the potential to improve the decision-making skills of physicians [30] by allowing greater transfer and cognitive flexibility, which may be especially important for future healthcare professionals and lifelong learning [30]. Consequently, training of healthcare professionals who enter the era of personalized medicine is of utmost importance and therefore the traditional academic setting must adapt to include personalized healthcare education aids [31]. There is growing evidence around chatbots, understood in this context as conversational agents that they have the potential to change the way students learn and search for information. In the context of healthcare education, chatbots may quiz existing knowledge, enable higher student engagement with a learning task or support higher-order cognitive activities [20]. Existing chatbot solutions have been studied before for their technical potential [32]. In large-scale learning activities involving a high number of students, chatbots can solve the problem of individual student support and contribute to personalized learning. Therefore, chatbots can be a solution to the inadequate individual support that students received in large-scale courses and/or MOOCs, with no further financial and organizational costs for the providers. For students but also teachers to accept and utilize the advantages of such solutions, it is important to introduce trust towards the performance of chatbots. There are therefore specific design characteristics of chatbots that can enhance the users' trust and therefore support chatbot's potential into healthcare education.

A recent survey conducted in 2020 by [33] found that students identified pharmacology and medical law as the courses that the chatbots have the potential to support. In particular, the chatbots could facilitate memorizing concepts, such as pharmacological formulas but also laws, and enable focusing on local variances in healthcare in both pharmacology and law disciplines. Another useful solution that could facilitate education is the FAQ chatbot. Students often ask for clarifications or pose common questions to educators. These could be about assessment, due dates, or resources, for example. This type of FAQ chatbot aims at answering to some of these common queries.

Another application of chatbots in Higher Education Institutions for medical and healthcare educations relates to the provision of online short response questions. For example, students may be asked to respond to a multiple-choice question, giving a justification about the answer they had selected. A chatbot can facilitate this interaction and then provide some personalized feedback. This chatbot application also provides many potential benefits [34], including a more personalized approach for users and the 24/7 availability of the chatbot. Implementing this style of textually enhanced concept inventory as a chatbot would allow for other benefits, specific to this application. For instance, the ability of a chatbot to confirm the wording or conceptual understanding of a student. This could be especially relevant when a student gives an explanation which is different from a common example, or one previously seen. This quiz chatbot also supports in time learning, allowing students to learn and receive feedback at points crucial to their learning process. Another benefit relates to the possibility for educators to see and identified common areas that students struggle with. This would allow for class-wide interventions to be taken [34].

4 Discussion and Conclusion

In this paper, we report a systematic literature review of chatbots in the area of medical education. Our inquiry was guided by the need to identify the main uses of chatbots in medical and healthcare education, but also examine the metrics which have been used to evaluate the usability of those chatbots.

The potential of educational chatbots relies on the fact that chatbots can enhance the learning process, by improving the way students learn and search for information [6]. In addition, chatbots can assist simultaneously multiple students by solving individual problems and quests contributing to a personalized form of learning [35] as if each student were receiving private education. To illustrate that, as aforementioned, chatbots can quiz existing knowledge, enable higher student engagement with a learning task and support higher-order cognitive activities. More specifically chatbots have been applied in several educational areas, as virtual patients for medical education purposes, for patients' education for healthcare matters but also as course assistance in for enhancing healthcare professionals' curricula. Firstly, virtual patient chatbots have been developed and released to enhance the communication skills of a doctor. For many decades, the doctor's interaction with the patient has been puzzling, with the communication skills to be an assessment course [36]. Nowadays chatbots are used as virtual patients to increase the empathic responses of the doctor toward the patient [15, 28]. Secondly, chatbots have been also used to educate the patients. Chatbots were found to be useful in providing information, responses to patients queries and counselling to patients during hospitalization. As a result, chatbots were found to be able to provide emotional support to patients in need [23]. Finally, chatbots were also used as course assistants in HEIs, since chatbots were found to be a reliable assistive technology to enhance the healthcare professionals' curricula, via answering student questions or by taking the patient's role.

Concerning the metrics which have been used for evaluating the chatbot solutions included into the pool of the selected papers, these involve usability, accessibility evaluation of the systems, and an assessment of the overall accuracy of the systems. Furthermore, it has been found that in some of the studies included in this review, user skills, such as history-taking skills, communication skills and empathy, have been measured, as part of the chatbot solutions' evaluation. We suggest the need for additional metrics to be used for chatbot systems' evaluation, especially related to their effectiveness on the cognitive, affective, and social aspects of learning. As Hobert and Meyer von Wolff [37] propose, there is a need for comprehensive and in-depth evaluation studies in this direction.

To conclude, there is a growing interest in integrating chatbots in healthcare education mostly because of their portability and affordance. As explained above chatbots can enhance education through a regular computer having access on the internet or even through the learners mobile phone. Even though chatbots are offering a flexible solution and vast possibility to improve healthcare education, limited examples of chatbots in European Healthcare curricula have been utilized. We believe that this review reveals the effective use of chatbot digital technologies in open education, since it proves that the use of chatbots in healthcare education will enable students to increase their health and medical-related skills through flexible learning.

Acknowledgements. The work was supported by the Erasmus+ programme, Action Strategic Partnerships for higher education (Grant Number 2019-1-UK01-KA203-062091), CEPEH: Chatbots Enhance Personalised European Healthcare Curricula, the project EDUBOTS, which is funded under the scheme Erasmus + KA2: Cooperation for innovation and the exchange of good practices - Knowledge Alliances (grant agreement no: 612446), as well as from the European Union's Horizon 2020 research and innovation program under grant agreement No. 739578 and the government of the Republic of Cyprus through the Directorate General for European Programmes, Coordination and Development.

References

1. Serban, I.V., et al.: A deep reinforcement learning chatbot. arXiv:1709.02349 [cs, stat] (2017)
2. Smutny, P., Schreiberova, P.: Chatbots for learning: a review of educational chatbots for the Facebook Messenger. Comput. Educ. **151**, 103862 (2020). https://doi.org/10.1016/j.compedu.2020.103862
3. Fryer, L., Carpenter, R.: Bots as language learning tools. Lang. Learn. Technol. **10**, 8–14 (2006)
4. Rosruen, N., Samanchuen, T.: Chatbot utilization for medical consultant system. In: 2018 3rd Technology Innovation Management and Engineering Science International Conference (TIMES-iCON), pp. 1–5 (2018)
5. European Commission: Communication from the commission to the European parliament, the 13 council, the European economic and social committee and the committee of the regions eHealth Action Plan 2012-2020: Innovative healthcare for the 21st century (2012). https://eur-lex.europa.eu/legal-content/EN/ALL/?uri=CELEX%3A52012DC0736

6. Winkler, R., Söllner, M.: Unleashing the potential of chatbots in education: a state-of-the-art analysis. Presented at the Academy of Management Annual Meeting (AOM) , Chicago, USA (2018)
7. Moher, D., Liberati, A., Tetzlaff, J., Altman, D.G., PRISMA Group: Preferred reporting items for systematic reviews and meta-analyses: the PRISMA statement. PLoS Med. **6**, e1000097 (2009). https://doi.org/10.1371/journal.pmed.1000097
8. Amith, M., et al.: Early usability assessment of a conversational agent for HPV vaccination. Stud. Health Technol. Inform. **257**, 17–23 (2019)
9. Beaudry, J., Consigli, A., Clark, C., Robinson, K.J.: Getting ready for adult healthcare: designing a chatbot to coach adolescents with special health needs through the transitions of care. J. Pediatric Nurs. Nurs. Care Children Families **49**, 85–91 (2019). https://doi.org/10.1016/j.pedn.2019.09.004
10. Campillos-Llanos, L., Thomas, C., Bilinski, É., Zweigenbaum, P., Rosset, S.: Designing a virtual patient dialogue system based on terminology-rich resources: challenges and evaluation. Nat. Lang. Eng. **26**, 183–220 (2020). https://doi.org/10.1017/s1351324919000329
11. Carnell, S., Halan, S., Crary, M., Madhavan, A., Lok, B.: Adapting virtual patient interviews for interviewing skills training of novice healthcare students. In: Brinkman, W.-P., Broekens, J., Heylen, D. (eds.) IVA 2015. LNCS (LNAI), vol. 9238, pp. 50–59. Springer, Cham (2015). https://doi.org/10.1007/978-3-319-21996-7_5
12. Chetlen, A., Artrip, R., Drury, B., Arbaiza, A., Moore, M.: Novel use of chatbot technology to educate patients before breast biopsy. J. Am. Coll. Radiol. **16**, 1305–1308 (2019). https://doi.org/10.1016/j.jacr.2019.05.050
13. Datta, D., Brashers, V., Owen, J., White, C., Barnes, L.E.: A deep learning methodology for semantic utterance classification in virtual human dialogue systems. In: Traum, D., Swartout, W., Khooshabeh, P., Kopp, S., Scherer, S., Leuski, A. (eds.) IVA 2016. LNCS (LNAI), vol. 10011, pp. 451–455. Springer, Cham (2016). https://doi.org/10.1007/978-3-319-47665-0_53
14. El Zini, J., Rizk, Y., Awad, M., Antoun, J.: Towards a deep learning question-answering specialized chatbot for objective structured clinical examinations. In: 2019 International Joint Conference on Neural Networks (IJCNN), Budapest, Hungary, pp. 1–9. IEEE (2019)
15. Foster, A., et al.: Using virtual patients to teach empathy: a randomized controlled study to enhance medical students' empathic communication. Simul. Healthc. **11**, 181–189 (2016). https://doi.org/10.1097/SIH.0000000000000142
16. Isaza-Restrepo, A., Gómez, M.T., Cifuentes, G., Argüello, A.: The virtual patient as a learning tool: a mixed quantitative qualitative study. BMC Med. Educ. **18**, 297 (2018). https://doi.org/10.1186/s12909-018-1395-8
17. Jin, L., White, M., Jaffe, E., Zimmerman, L., Danforth, D.: Combining CNNs and pattern matching for question interpretation in a virtual patient dialogue system. In: Proceedings of the 12th Workshop on Innovative Use of NLP for Building Educational Applications, Copenhagen, Denmark, pp. 11–21. Association for Computational Linguistics (2017)
18. Laleye, F.A.A., Blanié, A., Brouquet, A., Behnamou, D., de Chalendar, G.: Semantic similarity to improve question understanding in a virtual patient. In: Proceedings of the 35th Annual ACM Symposium on Applied Computing, pp. 859–866. Association for Computing Machinery, New York (2020)
19. May, R., Denecke, K.: Extending patient education with CLAIRE: an interactive virtual reality and voice user interface application. In: Alario-Hoyos, C., Rodríguez-Triana, M.J., Scheffel, M., Arnedillo-Sánchez, I., Dennerlein, S.M. (eds.) EC-TEL 2020. LNCS, vol. 12315, pp. 482–486. Springer, Cham (2020). https://doi.org/10.1007/978-3-030-57717-9_49
20. Pereira, J.: Leveraging chatbots to improve self-guided learning through conversational quizzes. In: Proceedings of the Fourth International Conference on Technological Ecosystems for Enhancing Multiculturality, pp. 911–918. Association for Computing Machinery, New York (2016)

21. Rose-Davis, B., Van Woensel, W., Stringer, E., Abidi, S., Abidi, S.S.R.: Using an artificial intelligence-based argument theory to generate automated patient education dialogues for families of children with juvenile idiopathic arthritis. Stud. Health Technol. Inform. **264**, 1337–1341 (2019). https://doi.org/10.3233/SHTI190444

22. Tanana, M.J., Soma, C.S., Srikumar, V., Atkins, D.C., Imel, Z.E.: Development and evaluation of ClientBot: patient-like conversational agent to train basic counseling skills. J. Med. Internet Res. **21**, e12529 (2019). https://doi.org/10.2196/12529

23. Wang, C., et al.: Acceptability and feasibility of a virtual counselor (VICKY) to collect family health histories. Genet. Med. **17**, 822–830 (2015). https://doi.org/10.1038/gim.2014.198

24. Yadav, D., Malik, P., Dabas, K., Singh, P.: Feedpal: understanding opportunities for chatbots in breastfeeding education of women in India. Proc. ACM Hum.-Comput. Interact. **3**, 170:1–170:30 (2019). https://doi.org/10.1145/3359272

25. Yang, W., Hebert, D., Kim, S., Kang, B.: MCRDR knowledge-based 3D dialogue simulation in clinical training and assessment. J. Med. Syst. **43**(7), 1–21 (2019). https://doi.org/10.1007/s10916-019-1262-0

26. Cleland, J.A., Abe, K., Rethans, J.-J.: The use of simulated patients in medical education: AMEE guide no 42. Med. Teach. **31**, 477–486 (2009). https://doi.org/10.1080/01421590903002821

27. Bosse, H.M., Nickel, M., Huwendiek, S., Schultz, J.H., Nikendei, C.: Cost-effectiveness of peer role play and standardized patients in undergraduate communication training. BMC Med. Educ. **15**, 183 (2015). https://doi.org/10.1186/s12909-015-0468-1

28. Kononowicz, A.A., Zary, N., Edelbring, S., Corral, J., Hege, I.: Virtual patients - what are we talking about? A framework to classify the meanings of the term in healthcare education. BMC Med. Educ. **15**, 11 (2015). https://doi.org/10.1186/s12909-015-0296-3

29. Agarwal, R., Wadhwa, M.: Review of state-of-the-art design techniques for chatbots. SN Comput. Sci. **1**(5), 1–12 (2020). https://doi.org/10.1007/s42979-020-00255-3

30. Mehta, N., Geissel, K., Rhodes, E., Salinas, G.: Comparative effectiveness in CME: evaluation of personalized and self-directed learning models. J. Continuing Educ. Health Prof. **35**, S24 (2015). https://doi.org/10.1002/chp.21284

31. Haiech, J., Kilhoffer, M.-C.: Personalized medicine and education: the challenge. Croat. Med. J. **53**, 298–300 (2012). https://doi.org/10.3325/cmj.2012.53.298

32. Reiswich, A., Haag, M.: Evaluation of chatbot prototypes for taking the virtual patient's history. Stud. Health Technol. Inform. **260**, 73–80 (2019). https://doi.org/10.3233/978-1-61499-971-3-73

33. Stathakarou, N., et al.: Students' perceptions on chatbots' potential and design characteristics in healthcare education. Stud. Health Technol. Inform. **272**, 209–212 (2020)

34. Cunningham-Nelson, S., Boles, W., Trouton, L., Margerison, E.: A review of chatbots in education: practical steps forward. In: Proceedings of the AAEE2019 Conference, Brisbane, Australia, p. 9 (2019)

35. Zumstein, D., Hundertmark, S.: Chatbots - an interactive technology for personalized communication and transaction. IADIS Int. J. WWW/Internet **15**, 96–109 (2018)

36. Bernardini, A.A., Sônego, A.A., Pozzebon, E.: Chatbots: an analysis of the state of art of literature. In: Workshop on Advanced Virtual Environments and Education, vol. 1, pp. 1–6 (2018). https://doi.org/10.5753/wave.2018.1

37. Hobert, S., von Wolff, R.M.: Say hello to your new automated tutor – a structured literature review on pedagogical conversational agents. In: Wirtschaftsinformatik 2019 Proceedings (2019)

Studying How to Apply Chatbots Technology in Higher-Education: First Results and Future Strategies

Antonio M. Mora[1]($\boxtimes$) (ID), Alberto Guillén[2] (ID), Francisco Barranco[2],
Pedro A. Castillo[2] (ID), and Juan J. Merelo[2] (ID)

[1] Department of Signal Theory, Telematics and Communications, ETSIIT-CITIC, University of Granada, Granada, Spain
amorag@ugr.es

[2] Department of Computer Architecture and Technology, ETSIIT-CITIC, University of Granada, Granada, Spain
{aguillen,fbarranco,pacv,jmerelo}@ugr.es

Abstract. This paper tries to find the best condition to use chatbots (conversational agents) in higher-education studies after pilots carried out at the University of Granada (Spain). Our aim, along with the rest of partners in EDUBOTS -an Erasmus + European Project which counts with two pedagogical chatbots-, is to improve students' engagement in class, as well as reducing the existing gap between them and their teachers. In this paper we present the results of a previous survey carried out among the students with the intention of laying out a plan of possible effective applications of this technology in the classroom in the near future, if possible during the next project pilot. The survey helps us confirm the reasons for the learning outcomes in the carried out pilots, as well as identify the targets for future application of chatbot technology.

Keywords: Higher education · Chatbots · Student-teacher communication · Messaging platform

1 Introduction

Conversational agents or *Chatbots* are software programs that interact via written or spoken word with persons or groups of persons [4, 7, 12]. They can be found currently in many environments such as webpages, applications and, of course, in our 'smart' devices (smartphones, smart TVs, smartwatches, and even smart rings). Thus, chatbots have become an incredibly useful tool in many domains and applications, with the virtual assistants created by Google, Apple (Siri) or Microsoft (Cortana), be it in text or voice, being the most famous.

They are, essentially, autonomous agents using many Artificial Intelligence techniques [1], such as Natural Language Processing, Automatic Speech Recognition, Data Mining, Machine Learning, or Sentiment Analysis, to cite a few. Thus, most of them are close to passing a classic Turing test [8] (at least for a non-expert human), since they are

© Springer Nature Switzerland AG 2021
P. Zaphiris and A. Ioannou (Eds.): HCII 2021, LNCS 12785, pp. 185–198, 2021.
https://doi.org/10.1007/978-3-030-77943-6_12

able to answer almost any speaker's question fluently, and even ask other questions to the human.

They might use natural language processing to understand a conversation and insert themselves in a one-to-one or grupal chat group. This is, however, not strictly necessary for many uses, even more so in an educational environment.

Chatbots have been used in a lot of areas, however there are still very few applications of them in education environments, and almost none in higher-education. One of the main reasons is the existing lack of knowledge regarding how to implement and train the chatbots for specific scenarios in this domain, as well as which issues or tasks should they address in the educational process.

It can be identified some preliminary problems of the adoption of chatbots in this scope, such as their difficulty to be integrated in common Learning Management Systems (e.g. Moodle); or the use of proprietary applications that cannot be integrated with popular messaging systems like WhatsApp, Telegram or Discord.

Therefore, even if we surround these issues, the use case definition for educational chatbots is not an easy task.

According to some researchers in this topic [25] is the teacher who should supervise and control the educational process and maybe these agents should be focused on helping them in these tasks, rather than substitute them in any of their teaching responsibilities. However, nowadays there are extensive studies on how humans interact with chatbots [22]; for instance, how the mood transmitted by the bot affects interaction; even so, according to [28], we are still in the very beginning of the application of these techniques to increase learning outcomes.

In this line, EDUBOTS project ("Best practices of pedagogical chatbots in higher education") has as aim to successfully apply chatbots in higher-education as a mean to fill the existing gap between educators and students due to the usual existing high ratio, which makes it very difficult to achieve a desirable formative assessment as well as providing personalised feedback.

The plan was to deploy and test different instances of two specialised chatbots in four universities around Europe in the UK, Latvia, Croatia and Spain; also with the participation of partners from Sweden, Cyprus and Norway. Each of these chatbots will interact -in text mode- with students of different degrees and subjects per university, ideally in their mother tongue.

The present study will be placed in a preliminary step, thus, prior to actually creating or implementing bots in class, we need to find out the actual needs for students, and since they are chatbots, we need to know where the students actually chat and in which context, i.e. which messaging systems or chat rooms/channels they use normally.

Thus, the main objective of the present work, is to directly ask the main actors in this scenario: the students, and then extract some conclusions based on their answers.

To this end, we report a survey among higher (bachelor and master degree) education students at the University of Granada, mostly in tech-oriented degrees, which focused on the messaging applications they used, how they used to interact through them with their peers, and what they would want the chatbots to do. That will be used later on to design pilot experiments that will introduce chatbots in the messaging applications they actually use (if it's at all possible).

Then, the survey responses have been analysed and, from them, some conclusions have been extracted on the best strategies or steps to follow in order to use chatbots successfully in such an educational environment, i.e. increasing the feedback to the teacher, enhancing the students' engagement, having a better student follow-up, and reducing the dropout rates (mainly in the first academic years).

The rest of the work is organized as follows: next we present a brief state of the art in the use of messaging and other technologies and chatbots in the classroom, including any intelligence that's added to them. After this, we briefly introduce the project in which this study is enclosed. Then we will describe what we did for this specific survey and why, and finally we will report the results, proposing action lines to apply chatbots in higher-education.

2   State of the Art

The introduction of new technologies in the classroom has demonstrated to be very effective in order to increase the students' motivation and engagement, as well as to enhance their performance and academic results [5], mostly on the new so-called 'digital generation'.

These are normally applied as a way to increase the interactivity during classes, for instance using electronic devices for interaction and feedback [10, 16, 26], approaches to let the students pose questions to the teacher for its resolution during the class [6], or even using commercial mobile applications for educational purposes during the class [13].

Many proposals have followed an approach based on the so-called *Edutainment* (or educational entertainment) [21], that is, aiming to improve aspects of education through a system that also entertains. This kind of *Serious games* (games created for educational purposes rather than to have fun) have been very prolific in several educational settings, including technical degrees [18].

Chatbots have existed for many years [24]. In the field of education chatbots have been used for both providing information to the user or facilitating student learning [2, 3, 15]. Chatbots can help students and teachers in many ways, e.g. automatically grading questions posed to students, or compiling the highlighted points mentioned by the majority of the students, and further send it to the teachers, giving them the opportunity to identify gaps in their teaching efforts and improve their classes and explanations [27]. For example, an approach to introduce these devices in high school teaching is presented in [9] where Google Echo and Amazon Alexa are questioned about some common concepts in the STEM area with poor performance on the answers but increasing the motivation and interest in the students.

However, almost all the approaches are focused on the increase of the students' participation and engagement during the classes (catching their attention), while almost none of them is worried about other existing flaws. For instance, a weak point in the teaching of subjects in higher-education (in almost any Degree) [14], is the student-teacher feedback, normally focused on the feelings and engagement that the students have during classes, but which could also be translated to a general feedback about the subject. Since, once the students leave the classroom it is quite difficult to get in contact with them and to receive this type of comments/criticisms.

Thus, in order to cover this weakness, EDUBOTS project partners have created two pedagogical chatbots specialised in ease some aspects of the subject management to the teacher, as well as serve to reduce the existing communicative gap between the students and their professor. One of these chatbots can also be utilized as an informal breaking ice tool to meet colleagues in the first academic courses,or as a formal academic communication tool between them. These agents are described in the next section.

3   EDUBOTS Project

"Best practices of pedagogical chatbots in higher education" (EDUBOTS) is the name of an European Project funded by program Erasmus + KA2: Cooperation for innovation and the exchange of good practices - Knowledge Alliances.

In it, the consortium, composed by some European companies and Universities, aim to apply two different chatbots in higher-education in order to improve the students' performance, engagement and to effectively reduce the dropout rates at this stage.

Two different chatbots are to be used in the project, each of them focused on a different objective, namely:

- *Differ*: created by EdTech Foundry AS (Norway) - www.differ.chat
  Aiming to stimulate student collaboration, creating informal and 'safe' online communities where students can chat with other classmates in an anonymous way.
- *Hubbert*: created by Anna & Hubert AB (Sweden) - https://hubert.ai/
  Which aims to automate the feedback to educators. This chatbot has been mainly used in other domains, such as the recruitment of human resources in companies, doing an initial job interview for filtering candidates, for instance.

Both bots were accessed by the students using a common interface, being introduced by mentors, i.e. students selected to collaborate in the project for ice-breaking. However, unfortunately, the chatbots only worked in English, German and Swedish languages at the first pilots, which was a handicap in some universities such as Granada, as we comment in [19].

4   Students Surveys

4.1   Initial Survey

After the initial pilot, reported in [19], which revealed that our initial assessment of the needs and attitudes of students with respect to using chatbots in their education was not in line with what we actually obtained in the pilot, we decided to start from scratch looking at several different things: first, what kind of chat "rooms" or "channels" would students prefer, and what kind of functionalities would chatbots add to those chat rooms. Additionally to the conclusions shown in [19], it was concluded that students didn't want to use a new chat system additionally to the ones they were using already, and on top of that, it was very likely that a chat that (possibly) included all students in the course was not the best option either. Besides, there was little functionality in that pilot beyond the possibility of meeting new people.

At the same time, since the new pilot included new functionalities, such as the possibility of establishing FAQs, although it came at the cost of including professors in the chat rooms; it still needed a specific chat application. This is why we designed a new survey with the initial intention of getting responses into the design of the new EDUBOTS pilot.

In order to probe the attitudes of students, we published an initial test survey consisting of only two questions: one related to the scope of the chat rooms they would like to participate in, and another related to the functionality of chatbots. This survey was done via Telegram, in Spanish, using the already existing class-wide telegram group for two classes, one in the last year of Computer Science, and another in the Master. More than 100 students participated in it.

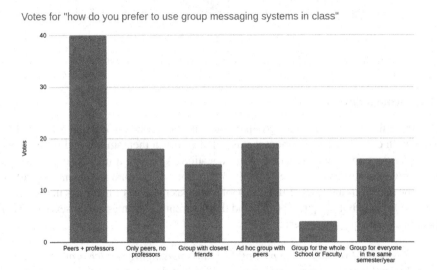

Fig. 1. Most selected answers to the first question of the initial survey.

The answers to the question about the scope of the chat channel are shown in Fig. 1. In this case, there were 57 answers and students could check as many answers as they wanted. This initial survey confirmed our conclusions of the pilot study, but at the same time helped us discard questions if we wanted to create a wider survey.

With respect to the type of functionality that students would want there, the chosen answers are shown in Fig. 2. This specific Telegram group already included a bot that answered questions about the next deadline, and this was indeed one of the most popular answers. As a matter of fact, meeting new people was not considered valuable (as it is in EDUBOTS project), but we should take into account that these students had already been in the same class for many years.

These answers allowed us to design a more directed survey, which is reported below.

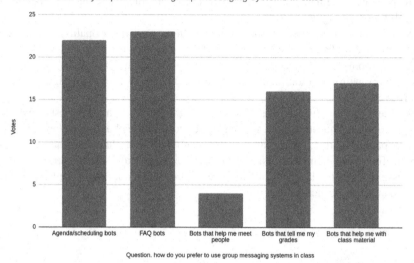

Votes for "how do you prefer to use group messaging systems in class"

Question. how do you prefer to use group messaging systems in class

Fig. 2. Most selected answers to the second question of the initial survey.

4.2 Extended Survey

After these first results, a bigger group of students were asked to complete a new short survey with only 3 questions about the use of chatbots in their studies and instant messaging services and social networking in Education. Although it may pose a challenge, the survey was purposely limited to only 3 questions to encourage students to participate. The questions analyzed crucial variables such as the type of members in their class groups (Q1), chatbot objectives (Q2), and their current use of messaging services (Q3). Specifically, the questions were:

- Q1. *Who would you like to be part of your class messaging service group?*
- Q2. *Which kind of chatbot would you consider useful to improve the learning process in class?*
- Q3. *Currently, which messaging service do you use to get in touch/contact with other classmates or teachers?*

The first question aims at analyzing the social interaction within class groups, from classmates and the teacher to broader social contexts such as the whole year class, or the whole University School. Next, Q2 asks for particular interests in chatbots considering: *calendar bots* that offer reminders for assignment deadlines or exams, *FAQ bots, bots to meet* classmates, *bots to provide grades, study material,* or *official academic and bureaucratic information.* Finally, the last question provides data about the familiarity with different instant messaging services, and the experience with services that already include popular chatbots (e.g. Telegram).

Additionally to the chatbot questions, some self-identification and 'profile' queries regarding age, gender, current studies and (optionally) previous studies were included. Self-identification responses are detailed in Fig. 3.

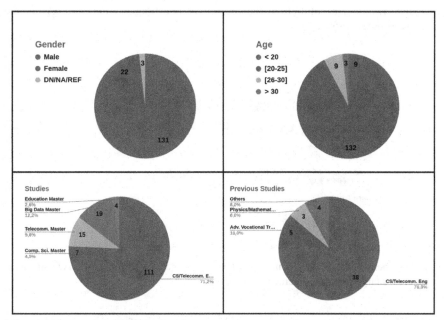

Fig. 3. Self-identification student responses for gender, age, current and previous studies. The questionnaire gathers information of a predominantly male population, between 20–25 years old undergraduate students mainly from Computer and Telecommunication Engineering. Regarding background diversity, some responses come from the Education Master students that include graduates from Physics and Mathematics, Statistics, Philosophy, or History.

We collected responses from a total of 156 students (undergraduate and master's) of the University of Granada, all from ICT backgrounds, namely Computer Science, Telecommunications, and Education for Technology and Informatics. Our aim was to include students that had strong links with technologies and were already familiar with chatbots.

4.3 Extended Survey Results

The most important facts of the 156 completed questionnaires are summarized next: Regarding the profile (Fig. 3), ICT students are predominantly male and thus overrepresented in our work with approximately 85% of males' responses and 15% females. Most students (86%) are in the range 20–25 years old which represents the average age for undergraduate and master's students; 6% are younger than 20 (first years of their studies) and 8% older than 25. With respect to the background diversity, 72% of them study Computer Science and Telecommunications, 26% are ICT master's students, and interestingly 2% are students from the Master in Education for Technology and Informatics.

Since some groups are underrepresented, we will not discriminate responses per group; the intention of providing this data is simply to show the overall composition of responders to the survey, which is roughly the same as the composition of the classes where it has been distributed.

Figures 4, 5 and 6 summarize the results for questions Q1-Q3, comprising the responses from the 156 students.

Fig. 4. Distribution of responses for multiple choice, multiple answers for question Q2: members of class groups targeting social interaction and group size.

Regarding the social extent (Fig. 4), students primarily prefer groups with their own classmates and teachers (71%) closely followed by only-student groups (53%). Also, almost 50% consider potentially interesting ad-hoc groups created for a specific project or assignment that will eventually be abandoned after the submission deadline. Bearing in mind that the question allows students to select as many options as wanted, let us highlight that less than 15% of students find potentially useful year class groups and only 5% groups for the whole University School. Consequently, students find more useful smaller instant messaging groups whose objective is well-defined and even tuned for a very specific task, and probably consider other alternatives for broader social interactions. An unusual result is that only 20% consider a group for close classmates. This may be due to certain overlapping with other options (a group for classmates or an ad-hoc group for a specific project/assignment), or to the use of other forms of communication with close classmates.

The analysis of question Q2 (see Fig. 5) produces engaging results for the use of calendar chatbots (more than 90% students find them useful), or bots that provide grades (65%) and study material (60%). However, similarly to the results for Q1, bots with more general objectives that provide responses for frequently asked questions (23%) or official academic information (less than 1%) are less demanded. Finally, let us emphasize that about 23% of students find useful a chatbot for helping them meet other classmates. The objective of this bot is not academic and thus, it is difficult to analyze the result without a more thorough analysis and additional questions.

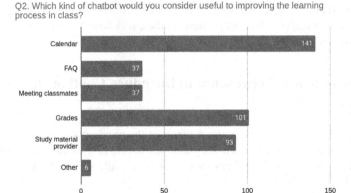

Fig. 5. Distribution of responses for multiple choice, multiple answers for question Q2: potential functionalities of chatbots for Education.

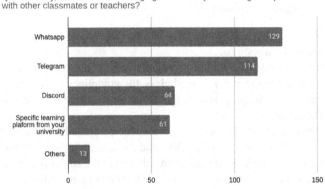

Fig. 6. Distribution of responses for multiple choice, multiple answers for question Q3: use of messaging services that may unveil previous experience and point at target service platforms for the development of effective chatbots.

Question Q3 (shown in Fig. 6) analyzes the current use of instant messaging services in Education and the familiarity with services that already offer popular chatbots as Telegram. Most popular instant messaging services are overrepresented e.g. Whatsapp and Telegram. Moreover, specific learning platforms from their University are used by almost 40% of students. This result was expected since some courses enforce the use of these platforms especially for the communications with teachers, to provide online class materials, or inform about grades. Finally, it is interesting the position of Discord servers (40%) that are popular in the videogame culture due to their low latency, anonymity, and robust hardware infrastructure [17], but are increasingly gaining notoriety in other fields. Concerning this matter, lately some works in the literature showed very positive results increasing motivation and initiative when using Discord with small groups, specifically for team-based learning [11]. Other services include e-mail, Twitter groups or Slack and all of them aggregated represent less than 4%.

Once the survey results have been analysed, in the following section we present some ideas to effectively apply chatbots in these studies, following the reached conclusions, i.e., the students' opinion.

5   Methodological Approaches to Introduce Chatbots in Higher Education

Considering the answers given by the students in the previous section, it is possible to devise some strategies to be tested in the classroom during future courses (or future pilots of the project). This section presents some ideas that could be implemented in parallel or isolatedly.

The requirements set to define the following approaches have been thought considering the use of messaging groups per course - maybe in WhatsApp, Telegram or inside Differ chats and communities - where both the students and the professors are involved.

5.1   Scenario 1: Passive Group Chat

All students share a group chat where they can propose questions and by themselves, answer other students' questions.

The role of the professor should be more passive just controlling that no inadequate interactions are done (insults i.ex.). Nonetheless, the guidelines and instructions on how to use the group should be prepared by the professor and given to the students at the beginning of the course.

Once the course is finished, several metrics can be computed according to the type of questions and answers made by each student and this can be included in the final mark. Co-evaluation can be introduced by giving the chance to the students to give the highest mark to the students that contributed the most valuable answers or the most useful.

The inclusion of a chatbot could be useful to automatise the collection of statistics. By doing so, these metrics could be updated in real time so a student can be aware of its progress towards achieving this objective on the course.

5.2   Scenario 2: Active Group Chat

In this approach, as the one commented above, the students share a group where the professor is included. The main difference is the role the professor adopts, in this case, should be active and dynamiser.

The professor should propose regularly (at least one interaction per week) some ideas to be discussed related to the course topics and anything related to the course that could appear in the media. By doing this there is the chance to enforce the meaningful learning in the interpretation given by Moreira in [20] discussing the ideas proposed by David Ausubel during his career. A new aspect that should be included in the interaction is the emotional part. Although this is mandatory during high school, in college and beyond should not be forgotten, especially in adverse situations like the recent confinement due to COVID-19 pandemic [23].

Chatbots in this context could be used to ameliorate the burden of greeting to every user, set reminders to interact and participate in the current discussion. For the sake of clarity the chatbot could rank the interactions to avoid too many similar or redundant answers when dealing with a topic.

Although polling functionality is something that tends to be embedded in the messenger platform, chatbots could collect the results of the surveys thrown by the professor. This could simplify the off-line analysis in order to provide marks.

5.3 Scenario 3: Correcting Exercises

Chatbots can be very useful to check if a list of exercises proposed to the students have correct answers. Instead of providing the students with the classical answer sheet. It could be possible to include this answer sheet within the chatbot so the students are obligated to ask it about if the answer they obtained is correct or not. A few hints can be included after a few trials have been carried out. For this approach, it seems more interesting the individual perspective as the students will not feel intimidated by showing the number of times they are mistaken.

Metrics on trials can be computed to evaluate the complexity of the assignments proposed.

6 Conclusions and Future Work

In this paper we have reported the results of a survey among higher education students trying to design some scenarios for the use of chatbots, after the experience of some initial pilot programs carried out in the University of Granada, in Southern Spain.

The first result of this survey is that all students use Whatsapp, and most of them, at least in a technological degree, use Telegram. This makes these platforms the ideal one for the deployment of chatbots in higher education. As a matter of fact, it is not a trivial matter to design a WhatsApp bot and, besides, this platform is not a good one to share with students since the phone number of the teachers needs to be available. Telegram, on the other hand, has a free client and free development kits, and bots can be created and deployed using free software and platforms with a free tier. This is why the use of Telegram would be very recommended to deploy any kind of bot. Thus, it is very important to incorporate similar functionalities to the chatbots to use, such as the Differ chat communities.

However, from the results we can see that at any rate, in order to be successful, a chatbot should be deployed in a platform that students already use, and that meets the privacy (and other) requirements that anyone involved has. So, it will be a difficult challenge to motivate students to use a novel tool.

The second question concerned who should be included in the chat group, and in this case there seems to be a certain consensus that there should be one group that included the teachers, although the common practice seems to be to have two groups, one with and another without the teachers. This would be, then, the target for the chatbots since professors could easily create or curate frequently asked questions (FAQs) as well as other content that would be required.

These are the kind of bots that would be more popular among the students. As a matter of fact, FAQ and agenda bots seem to be what the students are looking for, as well as informative bots that inform the student about the grades, help them with class material (for instance, searching something among the class material). In the case of the FAQ there seems to be a certain discrepancy in the second group of surveys, which put it at the same level as meeting new people. At any rate, it seems quite clear that meeting new people is not a very popular option for using chatbots.

These results explain the outcome of some of the initial pilots, but at the same time propose a survey-based methodology for introducing new technologies in higher education: they should piggyback on products that students already used, they should take into account what the students want to obtain from them to form a good use case, and they should offer an open and free-software based programming interface so that the creation of specific bots can be either done from scratch or tailored to different institutions or locales. In the proposed scenarios we also present different possibilities where, according to the survey results, the learning outcomes of using messaging applications endowed with chatbots would be positive.

These results open many different lines of work. We should probably extend the surveys to many other different locations and degrees, so that we can draw conclusions on the best scenarios for higher education at large. We will also try to follow up on the survey results by implementing bots in Telegram, and see if their use and learning outcomes actually match what the students responded to in the survey. This will be done as free software, and released in the near future.

Acknowledgements. This work is part of the project EDUBOTS, which is funded under the scheme Erasmus + KA2: Cooperation for innovation and the exchange of good practices - Knowledge Alliances (grant agreement no: 612446).

References

1. Abdul-Kader, S.A., Woods, J.C.: Survey on chatbot design techniques in speech conversation systems. Int. J. Adv. Comput. Sci. Appl. **6**(7), 1–2 (2015)
2. Agarwal, R., Wadhwa, M.: Review of state-of-the-art design techniques for chatbots. SN Comput. Sci. **1**, 246 (2020)
3. Bii, P.: Chatbot technology: a possible means of unlocking student potential to learn how to learn. Educ. Res. **4**(2), 218–221 (2013)
4. Bradesko, L., Mladenic, D.: A survey of chabot systems through a loebner prize competition. Res. Net. **2**, 1–4 (2012)
5. Burbules, N.: Watch IT: The Risks and Promises of Information Technologies for Education. Routledge, Boston (2018)
6. Cao, B., Esponda-Argüero, M., Rojas, R.: Development and evaluation of a classroom interaction system. In: International Association for Development of the Information Society (2016)
7. Clarizia, F., Colace, F., Lombardi, M., Pascale, F., Santaniello, D.: Chatbot: an education support system for student. In: Castiglione, A., Pop, F., Ficco, M., Palmieri, F. (eds.) CSS 2018. LNCS, vol. 11161, pp. 291–302. Springer, Cham (2018). https://doi.org/10.1007/978-3-030-01689-0_23

8. Copeland, J.: The Turing Test. In: Moor, J. (ed.) The Turing Test: The Elusive Standard of Artificial Intelligence. Springer, Heidelberg (2003). ISBN 978-1-4020-1205-1

9. Del Sol Pérez, M., Villalonga, C., Guillén, A., Baños, O.: Análisis del uso de asistentes virtuales en el aula como recurso complementario en la práctica docente. Enseñanza y Aprendizaje de Ingeniería de Computadores, num 10. Ed. Universidad de Granada. Departamento de Arquitectura y Tecnología de Computadores (2020). https://digibug.ugr.es/bitstream/handle/10481/64782/T5_N10_Revista_EAIC_2020.pdf?sequence=1&isAllowed=y

10. Fernández, P.G., Mora, A.M., García-Sánchez, P.: Using electronic voting devices for increasing students' participation in the classroom and easing their continuous evaluation. Rev. Iberoam. de Tecnol. del Aprendiz. **13**(3), 93–100 (2018)

11. Gledhill, D., Novak, M.: Game jams: an innovative education experience in higher education. In: International Conference on Computer Supported Education (CSEDU), pp. 489–494 (2019)

12. Gong, L.: How social is social responses to computers? the function of the degree of anthropomorphism in computer representations. Comput. Human Behav **24**(4), 1494–1509 (2008). Including the Special Issue: Integration of Human Factors in Networked Computing

13. Hatun Ataş, A., Delialioğlu, Ö.: A question–answer system for mobile devices in lecture-based instruction: a qualitative analysis of student engagement and learning. Interact. Learn. Environ. **26**(1), 75–90 (2018)

14. Jony, S.: Student centered instruction for interactive and effective teaching learning: perceptions of teachers in Bangladesh. Int. J. Adv. Res. Educ. Technol. **3**(3), 172–178 (2016)

15. Kerly, A., Hall, P., Bull, S.: Bringing chatbots into education: towards natural language negotiation of open learner models. Knowl.-Based Syst. **20**(2), 177–185 (2007)

16. Kroumov, V., Shibayama, K., Inoue, A.: Interactive learning tools for enhancing the education in control systems. Proc. Front. Educ. **2003**, 23–28 (2003)

17. Lacher, L., Biehl, C.: Using discord to understand and moderate collaboration and teamwork. In: Proceedings of the 49th ACM Technical Symposium on Computer Science Education, p. 1107 (2018)

18. Ma, M., Oikonomou, A., Jain, L.C.: Serious Games and Edutainment Applications. Springer, London (2011)

19. Merelo, J.J., Mora, A.M., Castillo, P.A.: Using chatbots in higher-education classrooms: expected benefits in an European pilot experience. In: Merelo, J.J., Mora, A., Castillo, P.A. (eds.) Accepted in CIVINEDU (2020). https://www.researchgate.net/publication/344992161_Using_chatbots_in_higher-education_classrooms_Expected_benefits_in_an_European_pilot_experience/stats#fullTextFileContent

20. Moreira, M.A.: ¿Al final, qué es aprendizaje significativo? Published by Universidad de La Laguna. Servicio de Publicaciones (2012)

21. Okan, Z.: Edutainment: is learning at risk? Br. J. Edu. Technol. **34**(3), 255–264 (2003)

22. Park, M., Aiken, M., Salvador, L.: How do humans interact with chatbots?: an analysis of transcripts. Int. J. Manag. Inf. Technol. **14**, 3338–3350 (2019)

23. Pérez, R.; Villalonga, C.; Baños, O.; Guillen, A.: Estudio de la influencia del confinamiento debido a la COVID-19 en padres, alumnado y profesorado en ESO y FP. Enseñanza y Aprendizaje de Ingeniería de Computadores, num 10. Ed. Universidad de Granada. Departamento de Arquitectura y Tecnología de Computadores (2020). https://digibug.ugr.es/handle/10481/64780.

24. Shah, H., Warwick, K., Vallverdu, J., Wu, D.: Can machines talk? comparison of eliza with modern dialogue systems. Comput. Hum. Behav. **58**, 278–295 (2016)

25. Shawar, B.A., Atwell, E.: Chatbots: are they really useful?. In: Ldv Forum, vol. 22, no. 1, pp. 29–49 (2007)

26. Siau, K., Sheng, H., Nah, F.: Use of classroom response system to enhance classroom interactivity. IEEE Trans. Educ. **49**(3), 398–403 (2006)
27. Smutny, P., Schreiberova, P.: Chatbots for learning: a review of educational chatbots for the facebook messenger. Comput. Educ. **151**, 103862 (2020)
28. Winkler, R., Soellner, M.: Unleashing the potential of chatbots in education: a state-of-the-art analysis (2018)

'Are You OK?' Students' Trust in a Chatbot Providing Support Opportunities

Joonas A. Pesonen[1,2(✉)]

[1] University of Helsinki, Helsinki, Finland
`joonas.pesonen@helsinki.fi`
[2] Annie Advisor Ltd., Helsinki, Finland

Abstract. Chatbots show promise as a novel way to provide support to students. However, a central issue with new technologies such as chatbots is whether students trust the technology. In the present study, we use a chatbot to proactively offer academic and non-academic support to students $(N = 274)$ in a Finnish vocational education and training (VET) organization. Students responded to the chatbot with a very high response rate (86%), and almost one-fifth (19%) of the respondents disclosed a need for support. Survey with a subset of participants $(N = 49)$ showed satisfactory trust (total trust score 71% as measured by a human-computer trust scale) and satisfaction (average of 3.83 as measured by a five-point customer satisfaction instrument) with the chatbot. Trust was positively correlated with satisfaction as well as students' likelihood to respond to the chatbot. Our results show that this kind of approach is applicable for recognizing students' latent needs for support. Future studies should target the formation of trust in more detail and cultural differences in trusting chatbots.

Keywords: Human-computer trust · Help-seeking · Student support

1 Introduction

In recent years, chatbots have become increasingly common in various domains, enabled by recent advancements in natural language processing and increased usage of mobile and online messaging platforms. A chatbot can be defined as a computer program designed to simulate conversation especially to provide information or assistance to the user as part of an automated service [1].

In the educational context, chatbots have been used, for example, in admissions [34], elective course selection [12], helping students in their campus life [13], language learning [8] and instructional scaffolding [46]. One prominent use case for chatbots in education is a virtual student advisor who helps students with studies, wellbeing, and other issues. While early prototypes of such systems exist [5, 28], this is mostly unresearched territory.

In the present study, we introduce a setting where a chatbot proactively provides support opportunities to students by asking them if they need help.

P. Zaphiris and A. Ioannou (Eds.): HCII 2021, LNCS 12785, pp. 199–215, 2021.
https://doi.org/10.1007/978-3-030-77943-6_13

We investigate whether students trust the chatbot and are willing to disclose their support needs to it. The theoretical background for our work is, on the one hand, in help-seeking behavior in academic and health contexts, and on the other hand in human-computer trust. In the following, we present relevant literature and our detailed research questions.

1.1   Help-Seeking Behavior

Help-seeking has been researched in both contexts of self-regulated learning [22, 23] and mental health [39]. Depending on the context, help-seeking can be defined as 'the process of seeking assistance from other individuals or other sources that facilitate accomplishing desired goals' [22] or as 'an adaptive coping process that attempts to obtain external assistance to deal with a mental health concern' [39].

In the self-regulated learning context help-seeking is seen as a skill and a strategy instead of an act of dependency [22]. Newman [32] describes an adaptive help-seeker as someone who begins by accurately assessing that help is necessary, formulates an appropriate request for help, understands the best resources available, designs strategies for successful requests, and productively processes the help received. However, many students needing help may not seek help due to feeling hopeless or threatened, or due to the lack of adequate help-seeking skills [22]. White and Bembenutty [45] identified three different kinds of help-seekers in their study; 54% of students saw help-seeking as an important self-regulatory strategy, 32% of students showed a tendency to avoid help-seeking yet were able to use adaptive strategies, and 14% felt that seeking help implies inadequacy. Regarding help-seeking for mental health, only a minority of adolescents reporting symptoms for mental health seek and receive help from specialist health services [47].

The factors related to avoiding help-seeking are diverse. Early research on help-seeking found low achievement being associated with the reluctance to seek help [33]. Regarding motivational orientations, mastery-oriented students are more likely to seek help, whereas performance-oriented are more likely to avoid seeking help [10,21]. Moreover, instructional and emotional support by teachers predict help-seeking behavior [14]. In a mental health context, adolescents themselves see stigma and embarrassment, problems recognizing symptoms, and a preference for self-reliance as the most important barriers to help-seeking [18]. On the other hand, parents perceived systemic issues, views and attitudes towards services and treatment, understanding of mental health problems and the help-seeking process and family circumstances [38] as main barriers.

Technological advancements have resulted in major changes in help-seeking research and practice [24]. Data from information and communication systems expand opportunities to track the student learning process to more completely understand help-seeking. [9,23]. Moreover, help-seeking can now include assistance from sources that do not comprise communication with an actual person [40]. In a context of mental health, the key benefits of online help-seeking include anonymity and privacy, immediacy, ease of access, inclusivity, the ability to connect with others and share experiences, and a greater sense of control over the help-seeking journey [37]. There are some concrete examples. First, Andalibi [6] found that Instagram-users used #depression -hashtag to connect with others having similar experiences and to seek support. Second, Frost and Casey [15] found in relation to self-injury that young people who were least likely to seek help overall, were most likely to seek help online and that internet may be a proximal step to face-to-face help-seeking. Third, Glasheen and colleagues [16] found that students experiencing psychological distress had a preference for online counseling.

In summary, avoidance of help-seeking is a complex problem. The nature of the problem has changed with technological advancement: young people are willing to search for help online, but seeking professional help remains an issue. Here, chatbots show promise as a solution combining interactivity with the ease of access and lack of stigma. These will be discussed in more detail in the following section.

1.2   Human-Computer Trust and Chatbots

An established view is that people form trusting relationships with computers and assign them human characteristics [27,44]. The literature on the differences between human-human interaction and human-computer interaction, especially in sensitive topics, shows some mixed findings. For example, Mou and colleagues [30] found that users tended to be more open and self-disclosing when interacting with humans than with AI. On the other hand, Ta and colleagues [42] found that the social companion chatbot *Replika* can provide a "safe space" in which users can discuss any topic without the fear of judgment or retaliation.

Also, Zamora [48] considers a lack of judgment as a unique aspect of chatbots. They found that having a conversation and gaining insights on sensitive topics without being judged is valuable among American and Indian participants. However, they also found several participants voicing concerns about mishandling their sensitive data and were afraid of possible leaks [48]. Thus, developing trust with a chatbot will be required for meaningful interactions. In general, trust can be defined as the willingness of a trustor to be vulnerable to a trustee's actions based on the expectation that the trustee will perform a particular action important to the trustor, irrespective of the ability to monitor or control the trustee [26].

Various factors have been found to affect humans' trust in chatbots. Høiland and colleagues [19] found that participants were willing to trust a mental health chatbot when they felt that the chatbot cared for them and perceived it as comforting. Toader and colleagues [43] found that participants who interacted with a chatbot anthropomorphized as female reported significantly higher willingness to disclose personal information, showing that also gender stereotypes may have an effect. Moreover, Mller and colleagues [31] found that people with different personality profiles significantly vary in their trust in chatbots. Regarding usage context, Aoki [7] found that the public's initial trust in chatbots was lower in chatbots for parental support than in chatbots for waste separation. Also cultural differences may affect trust: Chien and colleagues found that general trust towards automation varied significantly between the US, Taiwan and Turkey [11].

Views on favorable use cases for chatbots seem to vary. In a medical context, Powell [36] argues that artificial intelligence needs to supplement rather than replace medical professionals. Palanica [35] found that physicians may be comfortable using chatbots to automate simple logistical tasks but do not believe that chatbots are advanced enough to replace complex decision-making tasks requiring expert medical opinions. On the other hand, there is some early evidence that human-chatbot relationships may positively affect well-being [41] and that chatbots can provide actual care in mental health issues [19]. While these scenarios may seem suspicious and risky, positive experiences in interaction with the chatbot seem to increase trust and encourage more self-disclosure, further strengthening the human-chatbot relationship [41].

1.3   Aims of the Study

According to Moore and colleagues [29] there is widespread recognition that student support initiatives should address both academic and non-academic needs. Based on previous research, chatbots show promise as a novel way to provide learning-related [28, 46] and health-related support [19]. In the present study, we take an integrative approach to target all student concerns related to studies, well-being, and other issues.

Usually, getting help requires the student to take initiative. As shown in help-seeking research, this may prevent many young people in need of help from actually getting it because of stigma, feeling threatened, or preference for self-reliance (possibly relying on the information found on the internet) [18, 22, 45]. We hypothesize that when support opportunities are proactively presented to all students by a chatbot, soliciting help becomes cognitively easier, socially more acceptable, and simply more convenient.

Finally, a central issue with new technologies such as chatbots is whether students trust the technology. Both too high and low levels of trust may cause misuse, abuse, or disuse of the technology [20]. In the present study, the students should trust the chatbot enough to respond and solicit help, but on the other hand, be realistic about its capabilities.

In the present study, we use a rule-based chatbot to proactively offer both academic and nonacademic support to all students, not just those at-risk. This low-threshold opportunity is designed to catch students' latent concerns and needs. When a need for support is recognized in the conversation, a human professional will take over and provide the requested support. In the following, we present the research questions.

RQ1: Will Students Disclose Their Support Needs to a Chatbot that Provides Support Opportunities? We answer this question by conducting a chatbot pilot with four vocational programs in a large Finnish vocational education and training (VET) organization. We investigate if and how students respond to the chatbot and whether there are any differences between vocational programs or gender.

RQ2: Do Students Trust the Chatbot and How Satisfied They Are with It? After the pilot, we conduct a survey asking the students about their experience with the chatbot. Satisfaction is measured by a five-point customer satisfaction instrument and trust by a multi-dimensional scale by Gulati, Sousa, and Lamas [17].

RQ3: What Are the Connections Between Responding to the Chatbot, Needing Support, Being Satisfied with the Chatbot, and Trusting the Chatbot? We hypothesize that responding, being satisfied, and having trust are all intertwined together. Moreover, we hypothesize that not responding is connected with low levels of trust with the chatbot. Correlations between these variables are calculated to answer this question.

2 Methodology

2.1 Context

The study was conducted in a large Finnish vocational education and training (VET) institution. The Finnish VET system aims to increase and maintain the vocational skills of the population, develop commerce and industry, and respond to its competence needs [4]. Around half of the students completing their basic education in Finland continue to VET instead of general upper secondary education. Vocational education and training also enables pupils to continue their studies in higher education [3].

Four vocational programs (information and communications technology, electrical engineering and automation technology, safety and security, and social and health care) participated in a pilot in which a chatbot contacted students offering them support opportunities. At the time of the research, teaching was primarily organized as distance education because of the COVID-19 pandemic. While distance education was the main rule, some small group teaching and workshops by special needs teachers were organized in the school premises, and on-the-job learning was carried out normally whenever possible. The school offered student support services in a hybrid model, where students could choose if they want to meet in person or via teleconferencing. However, the school did not organize social events related to student support during the distance education period.

2.2   Participants

All the students who had started their studies between August 2020 and January 2021 in target programs (N = 275, see Table 1) were part of the chatbot pilot program, and 49 of them agreed to participate on a research survey after the pilot. The gender distributions were male-dominant on technology programs and female-dominant on the social and health care program, which is typical for corresponding programs in Finland.

Table 1. Participants

Vocational program	Chatbot pilot		Survey	
	N	Female%	N	Female%
Information and communications technology	119	10%	18	11%
Electrical engineering and automation technology	83	2%	16	0%
Safety and security	38	26%	8	38%
Social and health care	34	79%	7	86%
Total	274	18%	49	11%

2.3   Intervention

The chatbot intervention was carried out using a chatbot called *Annie Advisor*. Two weeks into the beginning of spring term 2021, each student in the pilot programs received an SMS message from the chatbot (see Fig. 1). In the chatbot conversation, students were offered the possibility to disclose a need for support. In case the student needed help, the chatbot asked students to specify their requirements further. If the student did not respond in 24 h, the chatbot reminded the student. If the student still did not respond, the student was marked as needing support, and the case was assigned to a designated teacher mentor.

Based on the chatbot conversation and the collaboratively pre-designed classification of support needs and responsible professionals (see Table 2), the system assigned the support cases to the corresponding professional. Professionals then used the chatbot system's administration view (see Fig. 2) to track their students and carry out the following steps (e.g., setting up meetings).

2.4   Measures

The data for this study were collected in two ways. First, we extracted log data of the chatbot system to collect data on students' responses. Second, one week after the pilot, we sent a survey link to students to collect data on user satisfaction and human-computer trust.

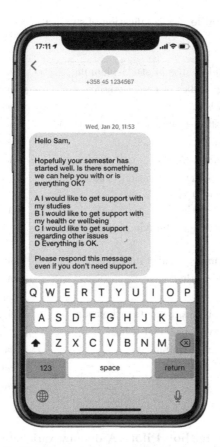

Fig. 1. The chatbot from a student's perspective.

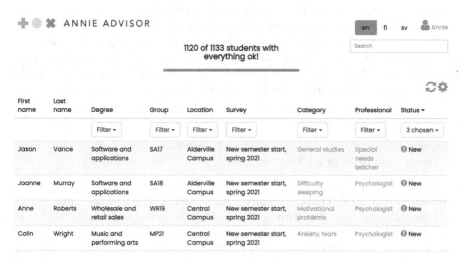

Fig. 2. The chatbot system from a professional's perspective.

Table 2. Classification of support needs.

Category	Subcategory	Responsible professional
Studies	Vocational studies or study planning	Teacher mentor
	Aborting studies or career guidance	Guidance counselor
	On-the-job learning	Teacher mentor
	General studies (math, languages, etc.)	Special needs teacher
	Study equipment or ICT	Teacher mentor
	Other studies-related	Special needs teacher
Wellbeing	General coping, motivation, anxiety or mental health	Psychologist
	Physical health	School nurse
	Social challenges, bullying, anxiety or loneliness	Social worker
	Sleep, gaming or substance abuse	Social worker
	Not sure or other	Social worker
Other	Hobbies	Youth worker
	Financial issues, benefits or housing	Social worker
	Philosophy or personal values	Religious counselor
	ICT or study equipment	Teacher mentor
	Not sure or other	Teacher mentor
No response	–	Teacher mentor

Responses in the Chatbot Pilot. A dummy variable *responded* takes the value 1 if the student responded to the chatbot within 72 h from the message being sent and otherwise 0. Furthermore, a dummy variable *needed support* takes the value 1 if the student disclosed the need for support while responding to the chatbot and 0 if the student indicated that no support is required. When support is requested, the needs are classified into three *support categories*: studies, wellbeing, and other issues. Although more fine-grained data was available in the system, the categories are reported on this aggregated level for privacy reasons.

User Satisfaction. The student's general satisfaction with the chatbot was measured by a question, *'In general, how satisfied were you with Annie?'* rated on a scale ranging from 1 ('Very unsatisfied') to 5 ('Very satisfied').

Human-Computer Trust. To measures students' trust in the chatbot, we used the human-computer trust scale by Gulati, Sousa and Lamas [17]. The scale consists of 12 items measuring four dimensions: risk perception (3 items, e.g. 'I believe that there could be negative consequences when using Annie'), benevolence (3 items, e.g. 'I believe that Annie will act in my best interest'), competence (3 items, e.g. 'I think that Annie is competent and effective in offering support') and general trust (3 items, e.g. 'If I use Annie, I think I would be able to depend on it completely'). Items are answered on a scale from 1 ('Disagree') to 5 ('Agree'). The scores of risk perception items are inverted so that a higher score indicates less risk perception. Also, we calculated a total trust score using all the trust items.

2.5   Analyses

First we combined the chatbot system log data with the survey data. For participants who had not responded to the survey, we marked survey measures as not available. In all of the statistical analyses, we included the largest possible number of participants in each calculation. We carried out chi-squared tests to determine if there were differences in responding or needing support between survey respondents and other pilot participants. We found no significant differences.

Sum variables were created for the dimensions of the human-computer trust scale and checked for internal consistency, which was satisfactory for risk-perception ($\alpha = 0.67$) and good for all other trust measures ($\alpha \geq 0.84$). We then calculated descriptive statistics for all the measures and ran pairwise Spearman correlations between responded (yes/no), response time, needed support (yes/no), user satisfaction, and trust (i.e., risk perception, benevolence, competence, general trust) to determine the relationships between the measures.

We used chi-squared tests to test for possible differences between programs or genders on responding to the chatbot or needing support. Regarding user satisfaction, we used Mann-Whitney U-test to test for differences between genders and independent samples Kruskal-Wallis to test for differences between vocational groups. For trust measures, we used independent samples T-test to test for differences between genders and a one-way ANOVA to test for differences between vocational groups.

3   Results

3.1   Students' Responses to the Chatbot

Outcomes of the chatbot conversations are presented in Table 3. The average response rate was 86%, which can be considered very high. Based on chi-squared tests, there were no significant differences in responding between programs or genders on responding or not responding to the chatbot.

Altogether 19% ($N = 44$) of participants disclosed a need for support in the chatbot conversation. Studies-related needs were most common ($N = 26$), followed by well-being-related ($N = 13$) and other ($N = 5$). Based on chi-squared tests, there were no significant differences between programs or genders on needing or not needing support. A small sample size prevented testing differences on support need categories (studies, well-being, other) between programs or genders.

Table 3. Outcomes of the chatbot conversations.

Vocational program	Everything OK	Support needed			Student did not respond	Total
		Studies	Well-being	Other		
Information and communications technology	82	11	6	2	18	119
Electrical engineering and automation technology	62	10	1	2	8	83
Safety and security	23	1	3	1	10	38
Social and health care	23	4	4	0	3	34
Total	190	26	13	5	39	274

3.2 User Satisfaction and Trust

The means and standard deviations for user satisfaction and trust are presented in Table 4. The mean score for user satisfaction can be considered satisfactory (3.82 ± 0.97). We found a significant difference between genders on user satisfaction using independent samples Mann-Whitney U-test $(U = 121.5, p = 0.03)$, with female students being more satisfied (4.36 ± 0.81) than male students (3.68 ± 0.97). Using independent samples Kruskal-Wallis test, we found no significant differences in user satisfaction between different programs.

The general trust score was satisfactory $(71\%, 3.55 \pm 0.72)$. Out of different trust measures, inverted risk perception scored highest (3.79 ± 0.88), followed by benevolence (3.58 ± 0.84), competence (3.53 ± 0.85) and general trust (3.33 ± 0.92). We found no significant differences between genders or programs in any of the trust measures, based on independent samples T-test and one-way ANOVA.

3.3 Connections Between Variables

Correlation analyses revealed multiple significant correlations between variables (see Table 4). First, as anticipated, all the trust measures were positively correlated with one another, with the lowest correlation between risk perception and competence $(\rho = 0.31)$ and highest between benevolence and the total trust score $(\rho = 0.90)$. Second, all the trust variables positively correlated with user satisfaction, benevolence having the highest correlation $(\rho = 0.49)$ followed by the total trust score $(\rho = 0.47)$, competence $(\rho = 0.43)$, risk perception $(\rho = 0.30)$ and general trust $(\rho = 0.29)$.

Whether students responded to the chatbot or not was positively correlated with the total trust score $(\rho = 0.29)$. This confirms our hypothesis that the lower the trust, the less probably a student responds to the chatbot. However, correlations with risk perception, benevolence, competence, and general trust were not significant.

Finally, whether students needed support was positively correlated with user satisfaction ($\rho = 0.34$).

Table 4. Correlations, descriptive statistics and measures of internal consistency.

	RE	NE	US	RI[1]	BE	CO	GE	TTS
Chatbot pilot								
Responded (RE)	1.00							
Needed support (NE)	–	1.00						
Survey								
User satisfaction (US)	0.12	0.34*	1.00					
Risk perception (RI)[1]	0.11	0.07	0.30*	1.00				
Benevolence (BE)	0.27	0.09	0.49**	0.41*	1.00			
Competence (CO)	0.27	0.01	0.43**	0.31*	0.87**	1.00		
General trust (GE)	0.22	-0.02	0.29*	0.32*	0.71**	0.78**	1.00	
Total trust score (TTS)	0.29*	0.03	0.47**	0.60**	0.90**	0.89**	0.86**	1.00
N	*274*	*235*	*48*	*47*	*47*	*47*	*47*	*47*
M	*0.86*	*0.19*	*3.83*	*3.79*	*3.58*	*3.53*	*3.33*	*3.55*
SD	*1.08*	*1.12*	*0.97*	*0.88*	*0.84*	*0.85*	*0.92*	*0.72*
Cronbach's alpha				*0.67*	*0.87*	*0.84*	*0.87*	*0.84*

* $p < 0.05$, ** $p < 0.01$,
[1] Inverted, higher score indicating lower risk.

4 Discussion

4.1 Responses to the Chatbot Reveal Latent Needs for Support

As shown in the literature, avoiding help-seeking is a problem both in the context of self-regulated learning [22,45] and mental health [18,47]. Our first research question was whether students would disclose their support needs to a chatbot. Our results show that students responded to the chatbot with a very high response rate (86%). For comparison, Manfreda and colleagues found an 11% average response rate in a meta-analysis of online surveys [25]. Furthermore, almost every fifth of respondents disclosed a need for support. To put the figure into context, Zachrisson and colleagues found that 6.9% of adolescents reported seeking help for mental problems during the preceding twelve months in a large Norwegian sample.

We consider these results a success and as a signal that there indeed are latent needs for support. The possible explanation for these high numbers is that when support opportunities are offered proactively with a fixed set of choices, soliciting help becomes cognitively easier and socially more acceptable. It is considerably easier, both practically and mentally, for a student to answer an SMS compared to initiating contact with a support professional.

Regarding user satisfaction, students who needed support had higher satisfaction with the chatbot than those who did not need support. This was an expected result, as for students not needing support, the experience was presumably neutral. Even in this case, the initial message conveys a message that the school cares for its students and that support is available if needed later.

Interestingly, we found a gender difference in satisfaction, showing that female students' satisfaction with the chatbot was significantly higher than male students'. Regarding other measures in the study, we found no differences between genders. In future studies, this should be investigated in more detail.

4.2   Trust with Chatbots in Different Scenarios

Our results showed satisfactory levels of trust with the chatbot (total trust score 71%). Furthermore, the level of trust was positively correlated with student's likelihood to respond to the chatbot, indicating that not responding is to some extent related to lack of trust. Based on the literature, the need for trust seems to increase as the content of conversation becomes more sensitive. For example, sharing a concern related to well-being may require more trust than sharing a study-related need. However, within the present study, we did not aim for students to self-disclose themselves to a chatbot but merely catch a need for further discussion with a human professional.

Regarding the different dimensions of trust, benevolence (i.e., acting in the user's best interest) had the highest correlation with user satisfaction and the total trust score. This is also in line with the findings by Høiland and colleagues [19], who found that feeling chatbot as 'caring' was linked with the willingness to trust the chatbot.

The question of an optimal level of trust is complex and can also vary based on the chatbot's aim. For example, when a chatbot is used to provide actual care, the requirement for trust is naturally higher. However, there are also situations where too high trust may cause problems. For example, in our study, we did not want students to report details about their health to the chatbot for security reasons.

4.3   Limitations

An obvious limitation of the current study is that the sample size is relatively small, male-dominant, and from only four programs in a single institution, entailing the results' limited generalizability. Another factor limiting the generalizability is the cultural context, which affects in multiple ways. First, general trust towards automation has been shown to vary between countries [11]. Second, student support's availability and scope vary a lot between educational systems, and the intervention used here might not be viable in another context. Third, young people's preference for online communication about secrets, inner feelings, and concerns varies between countries and is relatively high in Finland [2].

One possible problem is that it might be difficult for students to distinguish their experience of using the chatbot from receiving help from a professional. Students who received support, especially the user satisfaction measure, may reflect satisfaction with the whole process from requesting help to receive it.

Furthermore, our comprehension of nonresponding students is limited. While it is possible that a student does not answer because there is no need for support, not responding even after reminding could also be seen as an alarming sign. Therefore, we included the non-responding students on the chatbot system's administration view as students potentially needing help. However, analyzing non-respondents more closely is out of the scope of the present study.

4.4 Implications

Although the response rate was very high, the chatbot's total trust score was only satisfactory, and means to increase trust should be investigated. Randomized controlled trials with alternative designs (e.g., different communication channels and wording, scheduling, and personalization of the messages) should be carried out to determine the optimal design. Moreover, cultural differences in trust should be addressed with a study carried out in multiple different contexts. Also, we find it important to address the nonresponding students and possible false negatives (students reporting everything to be fine although actually needing help) in more detail.

An important aspect to consider is that recognizing many needs on short notice may strain the institutions' resources. However, pre-emptive care aims to prevent students' problems from escalating into more severe problems, which also burden the support personnel. We hypothesize that large-scale adoption of this kind of system would initially increase the workload but, while in place, actually save time and target the use of support resources in a more impactful way.

5 Conclusions

In this study, we used a chatbot to proactively provide support opportunities to students by asking them if they need help. Our results showed that students were ready to solicit help from a chatbot and that this kind of approach is applicable for recognizing students' latent needs for support. Moreover, we show that students' trust in the chatbot was positively correlated with their general satisfaction with the chatbot and their likelihood to respond to the chatbot. While an adequate level of trust with the chatbot is important, future studies are needed to understand better the formation of trust between the student and the chatbot and cultural differences in trusting chatbots.

Disclosure

Joonas A. Pesonen is employed as Chief Product Officer at Annie Advisor Ltd, receives a salary from the company, and owns stocks of the company.

References

1. Chatbot, n. https://www.oed.com/view/Entry/88357851
2. Preference for online communication (May 2020). https://gateway.euro.who.int/en/indicators/hbsc%5F149-preference-for-online-communication/
3. Finnish vocational education and training (2021). https://www.oph.fi/en/education-system/finnish-vocational-education-and-training
4. Vocational education and training (2021). https://minedu.fi/en/vocational-education-and-training
5. Alkhoori, A., Kuhail, M.A., Alkhoori, A.: Unibud: a virtual academic adviser. In: 2020 12th Annual Undergraduate Research Conference on Applied Computing (URC), pp. 1–4. IEEE (2020)
6. Andalibi, N., Ozturk, P., Forte, A.: Depression-related imagery on instagram. In: Proceedings of the 18th ACM Conference Companion on Computer Supported Cooperative Work & Social Computing, pp. 231–234 (2015)
7. Aoki, N.: An experimental study of public trust in ai chatbots in the public sector. Gov. Inf. Quart. **37**(4), 101490 (2020)
8. Ayedoun, E., Hayashi, Y., Seta, K.: Adding communicative and affective strategies to an embodied conversational agent to enhance second language learners' willingness to communicate. Int. J. Artif. Intell. Educ. **29**(1), 29–57 (2019)
9. Ben-Eliyahu, A., Bernacki, M.L.: Addressing complexities in self-regulated learning: a focus on contextual factors, contingencies, and dynamic relations. Metacognition Learn. **10**(1), 1–13 (2015). https://doi.org/10.1007/s11409-015-9134-6
10. Butler, R., Neuman, O.: Effects of task and ego achievement goals on help-seeking behaviors and attitudes. J. Educ. Psychol. **87**(2), 261 (1995)
11. Chien, S.Y., Sycara, K., Liu, J.S., Kumru, A.: Relation between trust attitudes toward automation, hofstede's cultural dimensions, and big five personality traits. In: Proceedings of the Human Factors and Ergonomics Society Annual Meeting, vol. 60, pp. 841–845. SAGE Publications Sage CA, Los Angeles, CA (2016)
12. Chung, H., Iorga, M., Voas, J., Lee, S.: Alexa, can i trust you? Computer **50**(9), 100–104 (2017)
13. Dibitonto, M., Leszczynska, K., Tazzi, F., Medaglia, C.M.: Chatbot in a campus environment: design of LiSA, a virtual assistant to help students in their university life. In: Kurosu, M. (ed.) HCI 2018. LNCS, vol. 10903, pp. 103–116. Springer, Cham (2018). https://doi.org/10.1007/978-3-319-91250-9_9
14. Federici, R.A., Skaalvik, E.M.: Students' perceptions of emotional and instrumental teacher support: relations with motivational and emotional responses. Int. Educ. Stud. **7**(1), 21–36 (2014)
15. Frost, M., Casey, L.: Who seeks help online for self-injury? Arch. Suicide Res. **20**(1), 69–79 (2016)
16. Glasheen, K., Shochet, I., Campbell, M.: Online counselling in secondary schools: would students seek help by this medium? British J. Guidance Counselling **44**(1), 108–122 (2016)

17. Gulati, S., Sousa, S., Lamas, D.: Design, development and evaluation of a human-computer trust scale. Behav. Inf. Technol. **38**(10), 1004–1015 (2019)
18. Gulliver, A., Griffiths, K.M., Christensen, H.: Perceived barriers and facilitators to mental health help-seeking in young people: a systematic review. BMC Psychiatry **10**(1), 1–9 (2010)
19. Høiland, C.G., Følstad, A., Karahasanovic, A.: Hi, can i help? exploring how to design a mental health chatbot for youths. Human Technol. **16**(2), (2020)
20. Jacovi, A., Marasović, A., Miller, T., Goldberg, Y.: Formalizing trust in artificial intelligence: Prerequisites, causes and goals of human trust in ai. arXiv preprint arXiv:2010.07487 (2020)
21. Karabenick, S.A.: Perceived achievement goal structure and college student help seeking. J. Educ. Psychol. **96**(3), 569 (2004)
22. Karabenick, S.A., Berger, J.L.: Help seeking as a self-regulated learning strategy (2013)
23. Karabenick, S.A., Gonida, E.N.: Academic help seeking as a self-regulated learning strategy: Current issues, future directions (2018)
24. Makara, K.A., Karabenick, S.A.: Characterizing sources of academic help in the age of expanding educational technology: A new conceptual framework. Advances in help seeking research and applications: The role of information and communication technologies pp. 37–72 (2013)
25. Manfreda, K.L., Bosnjak, M., Berzelak, J., Haas, I., Vehovar, V.: Web surveys versus other survey modes: a meta-analysis comparing response rates. Int. J. Mark. Res. **50**(1), 79–104 (2008)
26. Mayer, R.C., Davis, J.H., Schoorman, F.D.: An integrative model of organizational trust. Acad. Manage. Rev. **20**(3), 709–734 (1995)
27. Mcknight, D.H., Carter, M., Thatcher, J.B., Clay, P.F.: Trust in a specific technology: an investigation of its components and measures. ACM Trans. Manage. Inf. Syst. (TMIS) **2**(2), 1–25 (2011)
28. Mendoza, S., Hernández-León, M., Sánchez-Adame, L.M., Rodríguez, J., Decouchant, D., Meneses-Viveros, A.: Supporting student-teacher interaction through a chatbot. In: Zaphiris, P., Ioannou, A. (eds.) HCII 2020. LNCS, vol. 12206, pp. 93–107. Springer, Cham (2020). https://doi.org/10.1007/978-3-030-50506-6_8
29. Moore, K.A., Lantos, H., Jones, R., Schindler, A., Belford, J., Sacks, V.: Making the grade: A progress report and next steps for integrated student supports. publication# 2017-53. Child Trends (2017)
30. Mou, Y., Xu, K.: The media inequality: comparing the initial human-human and human-ai social interactions. Comput. Hum. Behav. **72**, 432–440 (2017)
31. Müller, L., Mattke, J., Maier, C., Weitzel, T., Graser, H.: Chatbot acceptance: A latent profile analysis on individuals' trust in conversational agents. In: Proceedings of the 2019 on Computers and People Research Conference, pp. 35–42 (2019)
32. Newman, R.S.: Adaptive and nonadaptive help seeking with peer harassment: an integrative perspective of coping and self-regulation. Educ. Psychol. **43**(1), 1–15 (2008)
33. Newman, R.S., Goldin, L.: Children's reluctance to seek help with schoolwork. J. Educ. Psychol. **82**(1), 92 (1990)
34. Page, L.C., Gehlbach, H.: How an artificially intelligent virtual assistant helps students navigate the road to college. AERA Open **3**(4), 2332858417749220 (2017)
35. Palanica, A., Flaschner, P., Thommandram, A., Li, M., Fossat, Y.: Physicians' perceptions of chatbots in health care: Cross-sectional web-based survey. J. Med. Internet Res. **21**(4), e12887 (2019)

36. Powell, J.: Trust me, i'ma chatbot: How artificial intelligence in health care fails the turing test. J. Med. Int. Res. **21**(10), e16222 (2019)
37. Pretorius, C., Chambers, D., Coyle, D.: Young people's online help-seeking and mental health difficulties: systematic narrative review. J. Medi. Internet Res. **21**(11), e13873 (2019)
38. Reardon, T., Harvey, K., Baranowska, M., O'Brien, D., Smith, L., Creswell, C.: What do parents perceive are the barriers and facilitators to accessing psychological treatment for mental health problems in children and adolescents? a systematic review of qualitative and quantitative studies. Eur. Child Adolesc. Psychiatry **26**(6), 623–647 (2017)
39. Rickwood, D., Thomas, K.: Conceptual measurement framework for help-seeking for mental health problems. Psychol. Res. Behav. Manage. **5**, 173 (2012)
40. Rickwood, D.J.: Promoting youth mental health through computer-mediated communication. Int. J. Mental Health Promot. **12**(3), 32–44 (2010)
41. Skjuve, M., Følstad, A., Fostervold, K.I., Brandtzaeg, P.B.: My chatbot companion-a study of human-chatbot relationships. Int. J. Human-Comput. Stud. **149**, 102601 (2021)
42. Ta, V., et al.: User experiences of social support from companion chatbots in everyday contexts: thematic analysis. J. Med. Internet Res. **22**(3), e16235 (2020)
43. Toader, D.C., et al.: The effect of social presence and chatbot errors on trust. Sustainability **12**(1), 256 (2020)
44. Waytz, A., Heafner, J., Epley, N.: The mind in the machine: Anthropomorphism increases trust in an autonomous vehicle. J. Exp. Soc. Psychol. **52**, 113–117 (2014)
45. White, M.C., Bembenutty, H.: Not all avoidance help seekers are created equal: Individual differences in adaptive and executive help seeking. Sage Open **3**(2), 2158244013484916 (2013)
46. Winkler, R., Hobert, S., Salovaara, A., Söllner, M., Leimeister, J.M.: Sara, the lecturer: Improving learning in online education with a scaffolding-based conversational agent. In: Proceedings of the 2020 CHI Conference on Human Factors in Computing Systems, pp. 1–14 (2020)
47. Zachrisson, H.D., Rödje, K., Mykletun, A.: Utilization of health services in relation to mental health problems in adolescents: a population based survey. BMC public health **6**(1), 1–7 (2006)
48. Zamora, J.: I'm sorry, dave, i'm afraid i can't do that: Chatbot perception and expectations. In: Proceedings of the 5th International Conference on Human Agent Interaction, pp. 253–260 (2017)

Usability and User Experience of a Chat Application with Integrated Educational Chatbot Functionalities

Dijana Plantak Vukovac(✉), Ana Horvat, and Antonela Čižmešija

Faculty of Organization and Informatics, University of Zagreb, Pavlinska 2, 42000 Varaždin, Croatia
{dijana.plantak,anhorvat,acizmesi}@foi.unizg.hr

Abstract. In recent years chatbots have found their use in education, especially in higher education (HE), but are they really serving a purpose and helping both students and faculty staff? Since bad experiences can discourage potential users, chatbots have to be carefully designed to be useful and to offer the best possible experience to its users. To explore this premise, in this paper we will tackle one aspect of chatbot design through evaluation of usability and user experience of a chat application Differ, which has integrated chatbot functionalities. For the duration of one semester at the Faculty of Organization and Informatics' students used Differ on several courses. Differ was introduced as a tool to facilitate communication related to courses and students' obligations, between students and educators by initiating communication through a Differ's chatbot called Buddy Bot. Differ was also seen as a tool to enhance students' connections and social life through creation of private student communities. After the end of semester, students' opinions about Differ were evaluated through means of UEQ and SUS questionnaires which are frequently used for user experience and usability evaluation. Results of the study showed that Differ's perceived usability and user experience are slightly above average, but with a lot of room for improvements, especially in the context of novelty, stimulation and chatbot functionalities.

Keywords: Educational chatbot · Usability evaluation · User experience evaluation · SUS · UEQ

1 Introduction

Around 60 years ago first chatbot was developed as a very simple program called ELIZA and nowadays, chatbots are almost ubiquitous: they are used by banks, hairdressers, universities, customer support and in a variety of other service activities [1]. Chatbots, or conversational agents, intelligent personal assistants, or simply bots, are programs that support conversation with users in a specific domain using natural language, artificial intelligence, and other technologies [1, 2]. Because chatbots can convincingly communicate with people, they greatly contribute to automatization of certain tasks which can

P. Zaphiris and A. Ioannou (Eds.): HCII 2021, LNCS 12785, pp. 216–229, 2021.
https://doi.org/10.1007/978-3-030-77943-6_14

contribute to achieving more work efficiently and reducing costs. For that reason, chatbots are very often used in business, but their application is valuable in other contexts such as education.

In recent years chatbots have indeed found their use in education, especially in higher education (HE). Higher education is changing inevitably: number of students is rising every year, communication habits are being transformed by the use of Internet and messaging applications, and students' needs are rapidly transforming due to many various factors such as internationalization or introduction of different types of study programs (e.g. distance learning and part-time study) that are influenced by digital transformation in HE [1–3]. Introduction of chatbots in HE could help universities to tackle some of those issues and improve quality of their service to students. Chatbots can be used as a means to help students with administrative questions related to university and courses, as a tool to enhance teaching and learning, or as a tool for helping educators in research work, likewise in enriching students' and educators' social life [4].

Since the steady adoption of chatbots in HE, the question is are they a fancy trend or are they really serving a purpose and helping both students and teaching staff? As all other products and services, chatbots have to enable an exceptional user experience for their commercial success [5] and be experienced as useful and pleasurable [6] because a bad chatbot experience could turn away up to 73% of users [7]. Therefore, chatbots have to be carefully designed to offer the best possible experience for users. Following this premise, in this paper we will tackle user experience and usability of chatbots through evaluation of usability and UX on the case study of Differ, an application with integrated educational chatbot functionalities, and report the usability and user experience assessment of Differ, performed with the students enrolled in five different courses at one university.

The research study presented in this paper has been performed as a part of the first pilot within the ongoing Erasmus+ project EDUBOTS which involves two industry partners and four academic partners. One of the project goals is to document best practices for the use of chatbots in higher education, with the focus on two applications: Hubert, a chatbot application for collecting students' feedback in the form of the survey with open-ended questions, and Differ, a chat application with a bot implemented to match the students and stimulate student collaboration. During the project implementation, improvements of the chatbot applications are expected after each pilot, based on the users' feedback. One of the project outcomes is to provide feedback from students and teachers about their user experience with applications. This paper reports about Differ, a novel application whose potential user cases are still under development, so assessment of usability and user experience (UX) with end-users is crucial for improving and enriching existing functionalities.

The paper is structured as follows. Brief overview of related work in the field of the chatbots followed by description of evaluated application presented in the next section. Employed research methodology is described in the third section. The results of the study are presented in the fourth section. Concluding remarks with limitations of conducted study are provided in the last section.

2   Background to the Research

2.1   Related Work

Usability and User Experience (UX) are two interrelated concepts, explained with various definitions that arose during the years. Most commonly, usability refers to the user's accomplishment of the task while interacting with the products, systems or services, while user experience includes aforementioned pragmatic aspects, but is also related to hedonic aspects of product use and possession [8].

Our brief literature review starts with the usability and UX of the chat/messenger applications, since Differ is primarily a chat platform with some chatbot functionalities. Then, we explored several published papers about chatbot design and evaluation to better understand the importance of user experience and usability of chatbots in general and particularly in higher education. Perspectives on user experience can vary and we will try to identify what constitutes good or poor user experience, uses, and good practices of chatbots in educational environments. Previous research on the usability and user experience of chat platforms and chatbots used in education is scarce, so conclusions from other areas of implementation are presented as well.

Sergio Caro-Alvaro et al. [9] have explored usability of mobile instant messaging applications in general. They evaluated interactions of 28 iOS and 45 Android applications by applying keystroke level modelling (KLM) followed by identification of main usability problems of 7 iOS and 6 Android applications with heuristic evaluation method. Qualitative analysis performed by usability experts discovered that messaging applications had difficulties in performing tasks, had problems with the user interface, lacked consistency and cohesion, and lacked information about privacy and security features.

Darin et al. [10] evaluated usability and the user experience of mobile social application whose purpose was to improve the interaction between students and faculty in a Brazilian University, related to the service and the quality of meals in the university restaurant. Application was first evaluated with users by means of a questionnaire, in which users expressed their perceptions on the impact and utility of the application, and satisfaction with the one. In the follow-up interviews, observation of usage, post-test questionnaire and final usability questionnaire, some problems in the navigation, organization, and labeling were revealed. Conclusion of the study was that such application can positively impact the students' behavior, and sense of belonging to the institution, so future improvements are essential in order that application retains the users and fulfills its purpose.

Regarding chatbots, Følstad and Brandtzaeg [6] conducted a research involving more than 200 chatbot users which used mostly chatbots on a variety of messenger platforms to assess what are good and what are poor user experiences. Through their research authors showed that efficient assistance and entertainment value were very frequently mentioned as positive aspects of user satisfaction, and problems with interpretation and rude responses were frequently mentioned as negative aspects. At the end of the study, four lessons learnt for chatbot providers were presented to follow. In their paper authors also mention several important aspects of chatbot design and use. They noted that user experience of a chatbot may change over time due to different reasons such as running into difficulties or simply losing interest. Therefore, a chatbot has to consistently provide users with useful and pleasurable experiences which can also increase frequency of use of a certain chatbot.

For a chatbot to provide efficient assistance, its developers need to understand chatbot's target group and their needs. In our case, chatbots' target group are students and educators in a high education environment. Tsivitanidou and Ioannou [4] conducted a research with students and educators to determine their needs and expectations and to explore which functionalities a chatbot should have. They showed that the target group's needs can be grouped into three categories (learning and teaching, research, social bonding) and that a successful chatbot should be able to handle complex conversations, offer personalized feedback, understand different user needs, and have a friendly personality while having low maintenance cost.

Concerning chatbot use, they are mostly used to help students find information and help them with administrative issues such as enrolling, paying for scholarships etc. Dibitonto et al. [11] described their research about the design and implementation of chatbot LiSA (*Link Student Assistant*) that would help students by providing information and services. Authors note that to design and implement a successful chatbot, technology must be integrated with humans' psychological and sociological aspects. This means that a chatbot must understand a person as any other person would and its user interface needs to be simple and intuitive so that even users without any experience with such technology can use it without any problems. In the second part of their research authors presented a study conducted to explore students' needs regarding information and communication which showed that traditional means of communication did not satisfy students' needs.

In their research, Hien et al. [12] described design and implementation of a chatbot to improve students' communication with the Faculty of Information Technology of Vietnamese HCMC University of Science (FIT-HCMUS). Authors proposed development of a chatbot that would help students with administrative issues such as finding information about scholarships, courses, exams, etc., but that would also support their learning experience. Motivation for implementing a chatbot lies in discovery that students frequently ask the same or similar questions about scholarships, courses, assignments, etc. Therefore, authors propose implementing a chatbot named FIT-EBot that could answer those questions at any time.

Stapić et al. [1] described a proposed design of a chatbot at the University of Zagreb's Faculty of Organization and Informatics. In the scope of their research, the authors surveyed students and gave them the opportunity to pose questions related to four topics (mid-terms, exams, consultations, room locations) as they would pose them to a chatbot. Data obtained was examined by means of the thematic analysis. Based on the grouped questions and keywords, the authors propose different types of features for each group (e.g. yes/no questions, list view for questions regarding consultation terms, remainders for exams, etc.). Students were also asked about their thoughts and preferences on chatbots and from the results it is visible that chatbot's personality plays an important role, since the students noted that they would prefer a fun and polite personality in communication.

There are various other educational contexts and different purposes chatbots can help with. For example, in Morocco, a chatbot was used in early career development and preferred workplace for undergraduate and graduate students based on their personality type [13]. Cardenal Herrera University (CUE) in India uses a chatbot that has a role of a personal assistant for answering students' administrative queries such as paying fees and resolving other educational issues. Sandu & Gide (2018) [14] report that students are prone to use chatbot technology rather than other communication channels and consider it as the fastest way of communication. Still, privacy is the biggest concern in chatbot communication (e.g. disclosure of personal information) and in some cases, obtaining incorrect information from the chatbot. At the high school level, Benotti et al. [15] compared educational tools Alice and Chatbot - software platform for teaching computer science basics and increasing engagement of students. Results of the study show that in the case of female teenage students, higher interest and retention to course content have been achieved with Chatbot than with Alice.

Liu and Dong [16] introduced *Jiao Xiao Tong*, question and answer chatbot designed as a university navigation assistant supporting students in everyday faculty activities. From the perspective of UX, prompt answers from chatbot are crucial for successful interaction and user satisfaction. As a means of communication, Dahiya [17] stresses that chatbots should be user-friendly, not complicated, straightforward and the knowledge base should be compact.

From the perspective of evaluation, Maroengsit et al. [18] analysed 30 research papers to find out which evaluation methods were used for evaluating the chatbot. In only 12 papers (40%), user satisfaction with a chatbot was evaluated, followed by evaluation of functional aspects (30%) and the content evaluation (16.6%).

Casas et al. [19] performed a meta-analysis of 53 papers related to the chatbot evaluation, to discover the trends in using evaluation methods between 2016 and 2020. Evaluation methods were used mostly to examine main factors of the usability: effectiveness, efficiency and satisfaction, as defined by ISO 9214–11 standard. Effectiveness relates to the technical performance and correctness of the underlying algorithms of the chatbots, i.e. includes functionality and humanity. It is the most popular criteria for evaluating chatbots, followed by satisfaction that relates to the interest, affection, ethics and behaviour of the users towards the chatbot. However, the popularity of efficiency evaluation methods is rising, which examines if the chatbot fulfills the task, i.e. gives the correct answer or avoids inappropriate phrases.

Holmes et al. [20] evaluated usability and user experience of a *WeightMentor* chatbot, a tool for supporting weight loss maintenance. The authors have employed three questionnaires, System Usability Scale (SUS), User Experience Questionnaire (UEQ) and developed Chatbot Usability Questionnaire (CUQ) with the items aimed to evaluate chatbot characteristics. Results of the evaluations showed that conventional questionnaires do not evaluate all aspects of a chatbot interface. Although correlation among all three questionnaires found to be strong, and multiple regression showed that UEQ and CUQ are measuring similar aspects of chatbot usability, still 20% of the variance in CUQ score is explained by other factors that are not measured by SUS or UEQ. According to the opinions collected by the questionnaire, *WeightMentor* has been found highly usable: an A + grader, *best imaginable* or *promoter* on the various SUS scales, and with great UX since it received high scores on all UEQ scales [20].

As the last example, te Pas et al. (2020) [21] compared the user experience of a Chatbot Questionnaire with a regular computer questionnaire that is used in a preoperative procedure in the hospital among health care patients. The UEQ scores showed that patients preferred the chatbot over the standard questionnaire, giving the highest score for attribute "rapid", although the time to complete both questionnaires didn't vary significantly.

2.2 Application in This Study

For the purpose of this study, the application Differ is introduced into the higher education environments, in order to provide pedagogical support: safe space for the students to introduce themselves and then to stimulate their participation in the course related activities, through the chats with peers and feedback to the course teachers.

Differ is a chat platform with chatbot functionalities developed with the guiding principle to foster and facilitate communication and connections between students and teachers in online communities [22] through well-designed chatbot experience. Differ's purpose is to help new students to make friends and create a feeling of university affiliation with the long-term vision of increasing their engagement and successful completion study in future. Differ is founded on three main pillars: (1) Engaging students in social educational activities; (2) Innovative way of implementing frequently asked questions and (3) Providing quality feedback to educators. Differ is available as a desktop application, mobile version for iOS and Android users, or through web-browser. Connecting to Differ is very easy and GDPR compliant. After creating a community, an educator shares an invitation link by e-mail or learning management system. Then, students access the community, and their mobile number is used only for verification and code entry. SMS invitations have up to 90% successful registration rate [23].

Concerning Differ's functionalities, they are focused on both sides involved in the learning process: students and teachers. From students' point of view, in Differ's communities students can collaborate with peers on course related topics, make their own study/project groups or communities associated with common interests and hobbies outside of the course. By using Differ, students can have individual or group informal conversations and find like-minded people on different topics. Those virtual communities are often a reflection of real-world connections or the common ground for their creation.

Along with informal student communities, educators can use the Differ for various academic purposes in course groups like creating course related communities and give students a personal welcome and open a line of communication (see Fig. 1).

The biggest advantages for educators arise upon Differ's chatbot functionalities: (1) using ice-breaking to introduce and connect students with each other, student mentors or teaching assistants, (2) creating conversations around Frequently Asked Questions. In the first version of Differ, a Buddy Bot performed the role of ice-breaker and match-maker (see Fig. 2). In the current version of Differ, a social bot BO was introduced with more chatbot functionalities, whose job is to help educators create communities or split students into smaller groups, help students to introduce to each other or ask questions to the community. More chatbot functionalities, such as giving feedback to educators, will be implemented in the last round of the project.

Fig. 1. User interface of a desktop Differ - teacher's message to the students

Fig. 2. Buddy bot in differ initializes communication

Differ has already been identified as a platform that improves students' engagement with the academic programme of study and their engagement with peers, as well as a channel for quicker and personalized student-to-teacher communication [24]. Recent study by the authors of this paper also showed that communication activities in Differ app helped students to successfully complete the course, achieve better grades, or become more active in the course participation, while improving communication with the course teachers [25]. However, assessment of usability and user experience of the application has not been investigated, so this paper presents a contribution to the scarce body of evidence related to UX of the chatbots and messaging applications.

3   Research Methodology

In order to gain a comprehensive user view of Differ aligned with the EDUBOTS project goals, the research team has decided to evaluate its usability and user experience by collecting opinions from the users, primarily students, about their satisfaction with the application. Teachers of five courses at the Faculty of Organization and Informatics, University of Zagreb, have agreed to participate in the study and then to pilot and evaluate Differ with the students at their courses in the summer semester 2020. The following courses were involved in pilot study: Multimedia Systems, Text and Image Processing, Business Informatics, Software Engineering, and Computer-Mediated Communication. Teachers have been communicating with their students via Differ for at least one month and then invited them to fill-in the usability and UX surveys. The research was approved by the Ethics Committee of the institution and participation in the surveys was completely anonymous and voluntary for students.

Strategies of using Differ at the courses were various, but the following ones were the most common: a) teachers in the course agreed to have regular communication with the students in Differ by asking questions about the progress with the tasks or providing answers to the students' questions, b) the topic Announcement was one-way and used by the teachers to announce important news about course, c) teachers have created topics for discussions that were created on a thematic basis (e.g. for each laboratory task a new topic was created) or on the students' group basis (e.g. each laboratory student group had its own topic in which students of that group were discussing), d) two courses had student mentors who encouraged communication in the community and also provided solutions to the task when feasible, e) most of the teachers used less formal communication style than in email or via LMS, and included emojis in their messages. Finally, the test period of using Differ fell into the outbreak of the COVID-19 pandemic, when most of the teaching activities were online. Thus, some of the students viewed that situation as an opportunity to contact the teacher via Differ more frequently and in a private chat, while some of the students dropped out of the courses.

3.1   Research Questions

Application Differ is employed in the project to enhance the quality of learning and teaching process, but it is also used as a tool to establish and promote social inclusion within the higher education system. In line with one of the main goals of the EDUBOTS project and additional project outcomes that need to be based on users' feedback, this research explored chatbot application Differ from two aspects: (a) Usability and (b) User Experience. The backbone of the research are two research questions:

RQ1: What is the perceived usability of the chat application with chatbot functionalities? RQ2: What user experience aspects of the chat application with chatbot functionalities need to be improved?

3.2   Research Instruments

Questionnaires are common tools in the human-computer interaction field to assess user perceptions about an interactive product. There are a lot of standardized questionnaires used for various purposes, e.g. SUS and PSSUQ for evaluating usability, AttrakDiff and UEQ for user experience, UTAUT and TAM for user acceptance of technology [26]. In the past few years, UEQ is frequently used for UX evaluation, with the complementary method SUS as the most common one for usability assessment [27]. Taking into consideration project goals, and insight from the literature review, a research team has proposed research questions, and adapted terminology of the SUS and UEQ questionnaires for this study.

System Usability Scale (SUS) is a highly robust and versatile usability ten-items measurement tool which has been used among researchers and industry experts [8] for almost 30 years. SUS has been applied in various contexts like: testing mobile applications for phones and tablets [28], everyday products [29] or e-learning systems [30]. User Experience Questionnaire (UEQ) is a tool that measures both usability and hedonic quality aspects by applying 26 pairs of contrasting attributes [5, 31]. The questionnaire is available in many languages, accompanied with instructions, benchmarks and Excel sheet to help with evaluation [32]. In the past few years, UEQ is frequently used for UX evaluation, with the complementary method SUS as the most common one for usability assessment [27]. For the purpose of our research, Chatbot Usability Questionnaire (CUQ) [20] was also under consideration, but was excluded as a tool since when we evaluated the first version of Differ it had just a few chatbot functionalities (e.g. student matching).

For this research, ten items of the original SUS scale with answers on a five-point Lickert scale, and 26 pairs of attributes from the UEQ were translated into the Croatian language. Translated questionnaires were then implemented into the Google Forms online survey and a link to the survey and research invitation was sent to the students via the course learning management system.

4 Study Results

4.1 Participants

Total of $N = 76$ students from the Faculty of Organization and Informatics, who have used Differ in five courses in the academic year 2019/2020, completed the online survey. Regarding demographic characteristics of the sample, 40,79% male and 59,21% female evaluated Differ. Average age of the participants in the sample was 21 years.

4.2 Usability of the Application Differ

Students' opinions about Differ's ease of use were analyzed according to [33] and revealed that the mean SUS score was 72.4 (StDev $= 0.8$) and the median was 76.3. The highest score was 100.0 and the lowest was 27.5. A boxplot of Differ SUS scores is shown in Fig. 3. This positions the evaluated version of Differ a slightly above average application, given that all SUS scores above 68 would be considered above average. Concerning other descriptive ratings [34], Differ is a "good" application (adjective rating) earning a school grade C + and having acceptable interface. On the Net Promoter Score, which is the measure of customer loyalty in industry, Differ scored about 7, which means that it has passive users, who would not likely recommend the app to a friend or colleague. Overall, perceived usability of Differ is slightly above average, which gives the answer to the RQ1.

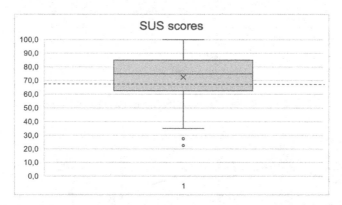

Fig. 3. Differ SUS scores (Benchmark of 68.0 is marked in red dotted line)

4.3   User Experience of the Application Differ

Opinions about user experience of Differ collected with UEQ were analysed with the tool accessible at the [32]. Items of the User Experience Questionnaire (UEQ) are grouped into the 6 scales: *Attractiveness* (gives overall impression about the product), *Perspicuity* (measures learnability of using the product), *Efficiency* (measures efficiency of interaction with the product), *Dependability* (measures levels of control of the product), *Stimulation* (measures levels of motivation to use the product) and *Novelty* (measures levels of innovation or originality of the product) [5]. Each scale ranges from -3 (horribly bad) and + 3 (extremely good) values, corresponding to the positive or negative attribute on a differential scale, e.g. on the *Attractiveness* scale a product is described with the pairs *unpleasant-pleasant*. Values above 0,8 represent a positive evaluation of the quality aspect, while values below 0,8 represent a negative evaluation.

Analysis showed that Differ is positively evaluated on the scales *Attractiveness*, *Perspicuity*, *Efficiency* and *Dependability*, but achieved lower scores on the scales of *Stimulation* (mean 0,438) and *Novelty* (mean 0,572), which is shown in the Fig. 4. Two later scales, *Stimulation* and *Novelty*, which are included in the hedonic quality of Differ, were negatively assessed with a mean of approximately 0,5.

Lower scores on the hedonic quality aspect are further underpinned by a benchmark against a data set from 452 studies concerning different products (business software, web pages, web shops, social networks). Benchmark revealed (see Fig. 5) that stimulation for using Differ is low and also the worst aspect of the application (it belongs to the range of the 25% worst results). Furthermore, novelty or originality of Differ is below average (50% of results of other studies are better, 25% of results are worse).

These results might suggest that students are not willing to use Differ outside the classroom, since it does not stimulate their motivation or excitement, nor offers additional

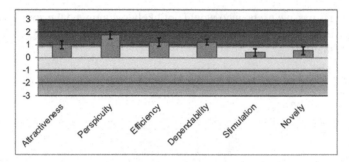

Fig. 4. User experience of differ measured by UEQ scales

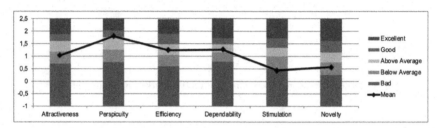

Fig. 5. Positioning of differ on a benchmark with 452 studies

advantages in comparison to the other chat platforms. This is in line with the Differ SUS NSP scale, in which users were classified as passive ones regarding recommendation of the application. Differ has been perceived as a quite ordinary chat application, which suggests that chatbot functionalities were not recognized or used in the application. Results of evaluation of Differ's user experience suggest that future redesign of the application should consider factors that stimulate students to use it frequently and give additional value to their academic life, which could be achieved by employing chatbot functionalities that are relevant for the educational environment. In comparison to the chatbot application *WeightMentor* [20], which received much higher UX scores, it seems that chatbot functionalities raise overall quality in use of the application. To answer to RQ2, improvements in the hedonic aspect and implementation of advanced chatbot functionalities of Differ would position Differ on a higher UX benchmark.

5   Concluding Remarks

This paper presented Differ, a messaging platform with the chatbot functionalities that is used in the higher educational environment. After being applied as an informal commu-nication tool at five computer science courses, Differ has been evaluated for its usability and user experience with questionnaires SUS and UEQ that evaluate user satisfaction with the interactive product.

Evaluation results on the UEQ scales showed that, while the application is visually attractive and slightly above average in pragmatic quality aspect, its attributes related to motivation and originality achieved lower scores. These results indicate that improvements in the Differ are possible, ranging from its limited chatbot functionalities to non-functional requirements that would raise motivation for its use. Literature suggests that educational chatbots should assist students in the administrative tasks related to the university and courses, likewise in achieving learning outcomes or enriching academic social life. They also need to provide clear interaction with the user and facilitate pleasant communication while returning the correct answers. Currently, the main advantage of Differ is that it is a safe online place where students can chat with their colleagues and approach teachers in a more relaxed and faster way without sharing too much personal information.

However, the results of this study should not be generalized on the other chatbot applications since Differ is still more a chat platform and a less chatbot. Through this research we have gained some valuable insights for upgrading Differ into a successful educational chatbot. Nonetheless, our research has some limitations: it covers data only from one institution which cannot be a representation of the overall student population. Therefore, future work should consider the evaluation of Differ on a more diverse student population after new Differ functionalities, presumably chatbot ones, are added to the application. Also, user testing to gain qualitative information regarding usability problems and specific measuring instruments or tools that evaluate the aspects of usability and user experience more related to chatbots should be applied.

Acknowledgements. This work is a part of the project "Best practices of pedagogical chatbots in higher education / EDUBOTS" which is funded under the Erasmus+ KA2: Cooperation for innovation and the exchange of good practices – Knowledge Alliances (grant agreement no: 612446, project ref.: 612446-EPP-1–2019-1-NO-EPPKA2-KA).

References

1. Stapić, Z., Horvat, A., Plantak Vukovac, D.: Designing a faculty Chatbot through user-centered design approach. In: Stephanidis, C., et al. (eds.) HCII 2020. LNCS, vol. 12425, pp. 472–484. Springer, Cham (2020). https://doi.org/10.1007/978-3-030-60128-7_36
2. Pérez, J.Q., Daradoumis, T., Puig, J.M.M.: Rediscovering the use of chatbots in education: a systematic literature review. Comput. Appl. Eng. Educ. **28**, 1549–1565 (2020). https://doi.org/10.1002/cae.22326
3. Brandtzaeg, P.B., Følstad, A.: Chatbots: changing user needs and motivations. Interact. **25**, 38–43 (2018). https://doi.org/10.1145/3236669
4. Tsivitanidou, O., Ioannou, A.: Users' needs assessment for chatbots' use in higher education. In: Strahonja, V., Hertweck, D., Kirinić, V. (eds.) Proceeding of 31st Central European Conference on Information and Intelligent Systems, p. 8. University of Zagreb, Faculty of Organization and Informatics, Varaždin (2020).
5. Schrepp, M., Hinderks, A., Thomaschewski, J.: Construction of a benchmark for the user experience questionnaire (UEQ). Int. J. Interact. Multimed. Artif. Intell. **4**, 40 (2017). https://doi.org/10.9781/ijimai.2017.445
6. Følstad, A., Brandtzaeg, P.B.: Users' experiences with chatbots: findings from a questionnaire study. Qual. User Experience **5**(1), 1–14 (2020). https://doi.org/10.1007/s41233-020-00033-2

7. New DigitasLBi research shows more than 1 in 3 Americans are willing to make purchases via Chatbots. https://www.digitas.com/en-us/news/press-releases/new-digitaslbi-research-shows-more-than-1-in-3-americans-are-willing-to-make-purchases-via-chatbots. Accessed 12 Jan 2021

8. Hassenzahl, M., Tractinsky, N.: User experience - a research agenda. Behav. Inf. Technol. **25**, 91–97 (2006). https://doi.org/10.1080/01449290500330331

9. Caro-Alvaro, S., Garcia-Lopez, E., Garcia-Cabot, A., de-Marcos, L., Martinez-Herraiz, J.-J.: Identifying usability issues in instant messaging apps on iOS and android platforms. Mob. Inf. Syst. **2018**(1), 1–19 (2018). https://doi.org/10.1155/2018/2056290

10. Darin, T., Andrade, R., Macedo, J., Araújo, D., Mesquita, L., Sánchez, J.: Usability and UX evaluation of a mobile social application to increase students-faculty interactions. In: Stephanidis, C. (ed.) HCI 2016. CCIS, vol. 618, pp. 21–29. Springer, Cham (2016). https://doi.org/10.1007/978-3-319-40542-1_4

11. Dibitonto, M., Leszczynska, K., Tazzi, F., Medaglia, C.M.: Chatbot in a campus environment: design of LiSA, a virtual assistant to help students in their university life. In: Kurosu, M. (ed.) HCI 2018. LNCS, vol. 10903, pp. 103–116. Springer, Cham (2018). https://doi.org/10.1007/978-3-319-91250-9_9

12. Hien, H.T., Cuong, P.-N., Nam, L.N.H., Nhung, H.L.T.K., Thang, L.D.: Intelligent assistants in higher-education environments: the FIT-EBot, a Chatbot for administrative and learning support. In: Proceedings of the Ninth International Symposium on Information and Communication Technology, pp. 69–76. Association for Computing Machinery, New York (2018). https://doi.org/10.1145/3287921.3287937

13. Zahour, O., Benlahmar, E.H., Eddaoui, A., Ouchra, H., Hourrane, O.: A system for educational and vocational guidance in morocco: Chatbot E-orientation. Procedia Comput. Sci. **175**, 554–559 (2020). https://doi.org/10.1016/j.procs.2020.07.079

14. Sandu, N., Gide, E.: Adoption of AI-Chatbots to enhance student learning experience in higher education in India. In: 2019 18th International Conference on Information Technology Based Higher Education and Training (ITHET), pp. 1–5. IEEE, Magdeburg (2019). https://doi.org/10.1109/ITHET46829.2019.8937382

15. Benotti, L., Martínez, M.C., Schapachnik, F.: Engaging high school students using chatbots. In: Proceedings of the 2014 conference on Innovation and technology in computer science education, pp. 63–68. Association for Computing Machinery, New York (2014). https://doi.org/10.1145/2591708.2591728

16. Liu, R., Dong, Z.: A study of user experience in knowledge-based QA Chatbot design. In: Karwowski, W., Ahram, T. (eds.) IHSI 2019. AISC, vol. 903, pp. 589–593. Springer, Cham (2019). https://doi.org/10.1007/978-3-030-11051-2_89

17. Dahiya, M.: A tool of conversation: Chatbot. Int. J. Comput. Sci. Eng. 4 (2017)

18. Maroengsit, W., Piyakulpinyo, T., Phonyiam, K., Pongnumkul, S., Chaovalit, P., Theeramunkong, T.: A survey on evaluation methods for Chatbots. In: Proceedings of the 2019 7th International Conference on Information and Education Technology, pp. 111–119. Association for Computing Machinery, New York (2019). https://doi.org/10.1145/3323771.3323824

19. Casas, J., Tricot, M.-O., Abou Khaled, O., Mugellini, E., Cudré-Mauroux, P.: Trends and methods in Chatbot evaluation. In: Companion Publication of the 2020 International Conference on Multimodal Interaction, pp. 280–286. ACM, Virtual Event Netherlands (2020). https://doi.org/10.1145/3395035.3425319

20. Holmes, S., Moorhead, A., Bond, R., Zheng, H., Coates, V., Mctear, M.: Usability testing of a healthcare Chatbot: can we use conventional methods to assess conversational user interfaces? In: Proceedings of the 31st European Conference on Cognitive Ergonomics, pp. 207–214. Association for Computing Machinery, New York (2019). https://doi.org/10.1145/3335082.3335094

21. te Pas, M.E., Rutten, W.G.M.M., Bouwman, R.A., Buise, M.P.: User experience of a Chatbot questionnaire versus a regular computer questionnaire: prospective comparative study. JMIR Med. Inform. **8**, e21982 (2020). https://doi.org/10.2196/21982

22. Differ - Helping you connect with other new students. http://www.differ.chat. Accessed 22 Feb 2021

23. Differ for educators - improve your students wellbeing and success. http://www.differ.chat. Accessed 22 Feb 2021

24. Studente, S., Ellis, S., Garivaldis, S.F.: Exploring the potential of Chatbots in higher education: a preliminary study. **14**, 4 (2020)

25. Čižmešija, A., Horvat, A., Vukovac, D.P.: Improving student engagement and course completion using Chatbot application. In: INTED2021 Proceedings (in press), p. 10. IATED, Spain (2021). https://doi.org/10.21125/inted.2021

26. Forster, Y., Hergeth, S., Naujoks, F., Krems, J.F.: How usability can save the day - methodological considerations for making automated driving a success story. In: Proceedings of the 10th International Conference on Automotive User Interfaces and Interactive Vehicular Applications, pp. 278–290. Association for Computing Machinery, New York (2018). https://doi.org/10.1145/3239060.3239076

27. Díaz-Oreiro, L.: Quesada, guerrero: standardized questionnaires for user experience evaluation: a systematic literature review. Proceedings **31**, 14 (2019). https://doi.org/10.3390/proceedings2019031014

28. Kortum, P., Sorber, M.: Measuring the usability of mobile applications for phones and tablets. Int. J. Hum.-Comput. Interact. **31**, 518–529 (2015). https://doi.org/10.1080/10447318.2015.1064658

29. Kortum, P.T., Bangor, A.: Usability ratings for everyday products measured with the system usability scale. Int. J. Hum.-Comput. Interact. **29**, 67–76 (2013). https://doi.org/10.1080/10447318.2012.681221

30. Harrati, N., Bouchrika, I., Tari, A., Ladjailia, A.: Exploring user satisfaction for e-learning systems via usage-based metrics and system usability scale analysis. Comput. Hum. Behav. **61**, 463–471 (2016). https://doi.org/10.1016/j.chb.2016.03.051

31. Laugwitz, B., Held, T., Schrepp, M.: Construction and evaluation of a user experience questionnaire. In: Holzinger, A. (ed.) USAB 2008. LNCS, vol. 5298, pp. 63–76. Springer, Heidelberg (2008). https://doi.org/10.1007/978-3-540-89350-9_6

32. User Experience Questionnaire (UEQ). https://www.ueq-online.org/. Accessed 12 Jan 2021

33. Sauro, J.: Measuring usability with the System Usability Scale (SUS). https://measuringu.com/sus/. Accessed 11 Jan 2021

34. Sauro, J.: MeasuringU: 5 Ways to Interpret a SUS Score. https://measuringu.com/interpret-sus-score/. Accessed 14 Feb 2021

Envisioned Pedagogical Uses of Chatbots in Higher Education and Perceived Benefits and Challenges

Olia Tsivitanidou[1]([⊠]) [iD] and Andri Ioannou[1,2] [iD]

[1] CYENS Centre of Excellence, Nicosia, Cyprus
o.tsivitanidou@cyens.org.cy, andri.i.ioannou@cut.ac.cy
[2] Cyprus Interaction Lab, Cyprus University of Technology, Limassol, Cyprus

Abstract. The widespread use of chatbots is a reality and their application in higher education is promising. Understanding higher education users' expectations for the use of chatbots in education is important for the design and development of new solutions. The present investigation documents how higher education users envision the pedagogical uses of chatbots in higher education, and how experts in the domain of education chatbots perceive the potential benefits and challenges related to the use of chatbots in education. A qualitative inquiry was undertaken based on 22 semi-structured interviews with higher-education students and instructors, and experts from the fields of Artificial Intelligence and educational chatbots. Based on our findings, the envisioned pedagogical uses of chatbots can be categorized in terms of chronological integration into the learning process: prospective, on-going, and retrospective. Under each one of those higher-order categories, specific learning domains can be supported (i.e., cognitive, affective), besides administrative tasks. Benefits and challenges foreseen in the use of pedagogical chatbots are presented and discussed. The findings of this study highlight the manner in which higher-education users envision the use of chatbots in education, with potential implications on the creation of specific pedagogical scenarios, accounting also for the learning context, chatbot technology, and pedagogies that are deemed appropriate in each scenario.

Keywords: Educational chatbots · Higher education · Pedagogical uses · Technology-enhanced learning

1 Introduction

Dialogue systems and conversational agents, including chatbots, are becoming ubiquitous in modern society. Chatbots – also called machine conversation systems, virtual agents, dialogue systems, and chatterbots – comprise computer programs that are used to simulate auditory and/or textual conversations with users, or other chatbots using natural languages [46, 56, 59]. Even though chatbots have been around for decades, with their origins dating to the 1950s with the so-called Turing test, a renewed interest in chatbots appeared in 2016, due to massive advances in artificial intelligence (AI) and a

© Springer Nature Switzerland AG 2021
P. Zaphiris and A. Ioannou (Eds.): HCII 2021, LNCS 12785, pp. 230–250, 2021.
https://doi.org/10.1007/978-3-030-77943-6_15

major usage shift from online social networks to mobile-messaging applications [10]. Nowadays, chatbots are becoming a trend in many fields such as personal assistants on mobile devices, in customer service, in medicine and healthcare, and lately in education [45, 56].

1.1 Chatbots in Education

Given that nowadays a significant part of the learning and teaching process utilizes Information and Communication Technologies (ICT), chatbot technology can be considered an important innovation for e-learning [11] for addressing the needs of the learning community (i.e., learners and instructors) [8]. A chatbot solution might offer support for different teaching and learning tasks, depending on its architecture and technology used (i.e., retrieval-based models, [36] and generative models, [47]). On the one hand, chatbots have the potential to facilitate students' learning and offer interactive learning experiences for the students, and even smoothen the transition of secondary-education students into university environment or help to increase university enrolment (e.g., the Pounce chatbot introduced at the Georgia State University for safeguarding students' successfully transition to college). On the other hand, chatbots can ease the instructors' workload, by acting as teaching assistants and enacting the role of tutors, e.g., by answering student's questions and to Frequently Asked Questions (FAQs), by sending reminders to the students for upcoming deadlines, or even by conducting online assessments.

Chatbot solutions have been already applied in multiple educational contexts, such as, in health and well-being interventions [1, 7], in medical education [28], in mathematics education [30], and in language learning [4, 17, 25, 26, 32]. Also, their use in learning scenarios can be identified in recent studies, in which chatbots appear to function as teaching assistants [18], as tutors supporting students in learning general knowledge subjects [13], for motivating students [40, 57], for feedback provision and metacognitive thinking triggering [29, 35] and as formative assessment solutions (e.g., peer assessment chatbots in Lee and Fu study [34]). Similar chatbot uses, serving teaching and learning purposes, have been identified in the literature review of educational chatbots for the Facebook Messenger [48], such as recommending learning content to users, providing feedback, questions, and answers (Q&A), setting goals and monitoring learning progress.

In recent years there has been an attempt to further exploit the capabilities of educational chatbots, especially for large-scale learning scenarios at universities or in massive open online courses (MOOCs), since chatbots have the potential to provide individual support and feedback to students with no further financial or organizational costs for the providers [56]. Nevertheless, the effectiveness of chatbots in education is complex and depends on a variety of factors, such as students' individual differences and personality traits [22, 49], their educational background, their social and technological skills [38, 39] their self-efficacy and self-regulated skills [49], and instructors' willingness and their attitudes towards using chatbots in routine teaching [8]. Also, when chatbots do not meet certain requirements such as easy use and access, they add little value to the learning process, including cognitive, meta-cognitive, and affective dimensions, and there is a high possibility of not being used by the students [20]. Further, one of the major challenges relates to the development and sustainable use of a smart chatbot, capable of delving into content-related topics and offering personalized guidance and feedback to the learners [37].

Therefore, the design of new chatbot solutions and their meaningful integration in higher education presupposes a good understanding of users' personal traits, their needs, and expectations, as well as, an examination of their perceptions towards educational technology [27, 43], the adoption of an appropriate pedagogy [19], and last but not least, a confrontation of technological challenges and potential limitations, that come relate to the Natural Language Processing (NLP) research field [58]. In addition, current chatbot applications suggest that conversational user interfaces still face substantial challenges, also related to the human-computer interaction (HCI) field [16].

1.2 Users' Expectations for the Use of Chatbots in Higher Education

Several chatbot solutions have already been designed, developed, and tested, as resulting from the review of literature on chatbots in education. Yet, chatbot initiatives often ignore user needs and user experiences [10]. As the field of chatbots is gradually expanding, developers and designers have an urgent need to understand the user needs that motivate the future use of chatbots, which is required to make successful automatic conversational interfaces [10].

Brandtzaeg and Følstad [10] outline some of the new needs and challenges posed by the emergent trend of chatbots. Those include, among others, the need for: (i) having an effective and efficient accomplishment of productivity tasks, (ii) obtaining assistance or information, (iii) using chatbots for fun or entertainment, (iv) addressing social and relational factors, (v) reducing loneliness, or enabling socialization. Previous research along these lines and with the focus on educational chatbots has also already been done to some extent, projecting possible uses of chatbots in education [21, 33, 48, 50, 55]. Findings of those studies outline the potential use of chatbots as career advisors [33, 54], as intelligent tutors answering students' questions [21, 55], as means for improving users' soft skills [54], and as means for formative assessment implementation with the provision of qualitative feedback [55]. Moreover, users' expectations for the design characteristics of chatbots have been already explored (i.e., recognition; visibility of system status; anthropomorphism in communication; knowledge expertise, linguistic consistency; realistic interaction) which may enhance the feeling of trust and support students in a personalized and interactive way [50].

2   Research Questions of the Study

A few educational chatbot solutions have already been designed and developed in Higher Education, being yet an emerging educational technology within many countries. The examination of users' needs and expectations has been explored to some extent, with a focus on chatbots' characteristics and HCI implications. However, an investigation of how higher-education students and educators envision the meaningful integration of chatbots in higher education in a broader scope is still missing. In response to this, the present investigation aims to document the envisioned pedagogical uses of chatbots in higher education and the benefits and challenges related to their use. The following two research questions are being addressed in this study: (1) What are the envisioned pedagogical uses of chatbots in higher education as proposed by learners, instructors with relevant experiences, and experts in the domain of chatbots? (2) What are the benefits and challenges of using chatbots in education as perceived by experts in their proposed pedagogical uses of chatbots?

3 Methodology

This is a qualitative injury. Data collection is based on in-depth, semi-structured interviews with various stakeholders, including students, instructors as well as experts in the field of AI and educational chatbots.

3.1 Participants

Instructors and students from different local universities in Cyprus were invited to participate in this study. Ten instructors and eight undergraduate students, with different backgrounds (i.e., Multimedia and Graphics Art, Computers Science, Sport & Exercise Science), volunteered to participate in semi-structured interviews. Also, all the participants had experienced at least once an interaction with a chatbot, regardless of the field of application, as confirmed by the interview data. Additionally, experts from the field of AI and educational chatbots participated in the study. Two came from academia (one from each organization: Bellwether College Consortium, University College London - Knowledge Lab) and two came from the industry (one from each organization: Sintef Digital, CYENS Centre of Excellence). A total of 22 interviews were conducted via teleconferencing. All the participants consent to anonymously use the data for research purposes.

3.2 Data Collection

Data from in-depth, semi-structured interviews were considered to be the most important source, serving the needs of our research aims, as they provided us with rich and deep insights into the concepts under investigation [14]. The semi-structured interviews were driven by two protocols, developed by the authors. The first protocol was used with higher-education instructors and students and included questions on the previous experience of the users with chatbots (e.g., *Have you used a chatbot before? With reference to this previous experience, what would you change in the chatbot(s), so that it would better address your needs?*) and their needs and expectations on a potential chatbot use (e.g., *In your opinion, could a chatbot facilitate your learning/teaching progress? How? Please explain your reasoning.*). A slightly adapted version of the first protocol was used with the experts, including questions on the state-of-the-art on pedagogical chatbots in higher education in terms of areas of application (e.g., *What is the state-of-the-art on pedagogical chatbots in higher education? In terms of instructional designs integrating chatbots? In terms of areas of application and learning scenarios?*) and the potential of educational chatbots to facilitate teaching and learning (e.g., *How could chatbots facilitate students' learning in higher education?*).

The second protocol, was used merely with experts and included questions on the added value of chatbots in education (i.e., *What is the added value for chatbots in higher education?*), and the benefits and challenges raised in the proposed areas of application, the potential and/or possible constraints of chatbots to offer personalized learning experiences (e.g., *What is the potential of chatbots in offering personalized learning experiences, including personalized feedback to learners? What types of features should chatbots have, serving this purpose? What are the possible constraints?*). All the interviews were recorded upon the interviewees' consent and transcribed verbatim.

3.3 Data Analysis

For addressing the first research question of the study, the first dataset was utilized (use of first interview protocol). The study adopted a grounded theory approach in order to address the first research question. Specifically, the analysis of participants' interview transcripts followed an iterative analysis was conducted as described in Strauss and Corbin [51, 52] and Thai, Chong, and Agrawal [53]. The coding operations employed for the data analysis included an open-coding process for concepts and categories, axial-coding for relationship between categories at their property and dimension levels, and selective-coding for our results' formation. All these required constant comparison as an inherent task.

Our first step was to discover concepts through detailed examination of the data. We started with open coding; this was a line-by-line coding in which key statements used by the participants were noted, attempting to unitize the data. Open coding resulted in a total of 32 codes. Throughout the process, we maintained memos on the process to allow for selective coding, an iterative process of grouping and regrouping the codes into core categories. However, as the analysis progressed, the code system was continually trimmed down and refined for better understanding of the data and concepts underlying in the data. In the end, 23 codes were kept (see Table 1).

Next, we carried out axial-coding (i.e., comparison of data observations) to find the relationships that existed between the different codes corresponding to groups of conceptual properties and dimensions [52]. With the help of the literature, we categorized the codes under more abstract higher-order classifications in two different levels: (i) categories: different dimensions of the learning process (i.e., cognitive, metacognitive, and affective domain, administrative work); (ii) sub-categories: specific type of activities (e.g., counselling) and/or aspects of learning (e.g., emotional aspect). Following that, we went through a third coding processes, using the codes, the sub-categories and the categories which resulted in the previous steps. During this process, we related the categories found in axial-coding to the core category which represents the main theme of this study, that is the learning process. With the use of techniques, such as, the use of diagrams, sorting, and reviewing through memos, we concluded to three higher-order categories, reflecting the chronological intervention of chatbots in the learning process.

For addressing the second research question of the study, the second dataset was utilized (use of second interview protocol with domain experts). In this case, we adopted a thematic analysis approach [41] involving an open coding process followed by clustering of the emerged codes into broader themes portraying the (i) benefits and (ii) challenges of the proposed pedagogical uses of chatbots.

4 Results

4.1 Envisioned Pedagogical Uses of Chatbots in Higher Education (RQ1)

The data analysis revealed various envisioned pedagogical uses of chatbots in higher education which can potentially facilitate learning (Table 1). Those uses can be clustered based on the domain of learning that they serve (e.g., cognitive and affective) and instruction-related tasks (i.e., administration) and also the phase in which they are situated with respect to the learning process (i.e., prospective, on-going, and retrospective intervention).

Proactive Intervention. This higher-level category refers to uses of chatbots in education which focuses on the cognitive learning domain (i.e., assessing students' prior knowledge and setting-up learning goals), on social aspects of the affective domain, such as, the promotion of inter-social interactions among learners (i.e., the chatbot connecting students' with common educational paths and initiating an interaction among those) and on the easing of administrative work (i.e., the chatbot providing administrative information for the university to freshmen) for smoothening the transition of secondary-education students into the university environment. Those uses were proposed by instructors and experts, whereas the students did not make any reference to the potential proactive use of chatbots. Indicative quotes from the interviews tangling the above-mentioned uses are given below (Table 2).

On-Going Intervention. This higher-level category refers to uses in which the chatbot can facilitate the on-going learning process and can be clustered in two different learning domains: cognitive and affective. In addition, a category corresponding to administrative work that facilitates or accompanies the learning and teaching process also emerged through the data analysis.

The first category involves uses with the chatbots targeting cognitive aspects of learning (see Table 3). Namely, one use relates to the role of the chatbot as a remote tutor in the learning process. Experts referred to the role of the chatbot as a remote tutor helping the instructor in lecturing and delivering content to the students and responding to students' content-related questions. Students and instructors also envisioned chatbots as tutors for responding to students' content-related questions. Specifically, the instructors-interviewees pointed out the need of having a chatbot responding to students' content-related questions, rather than administrative matters, since the latter can be also addressed now through the mass amount of information that students already receive in social networks and e-learning systems. Specific functionalities that the chatbots could have for serving this use were also proposed. A functionality that the chatbot could have, is posing a question at the end of the conversation for assuring that the conversation has successfully taken place and the content-related issues have been resolved. Another functionality could allow the chatbot to share relevant resources with the students. Apart from the pedagogical value of this use of chatbots in the learning process, it also benefits the instructors in the sense that is saves time, but also the chatbot could be available at any time of the day, thus helping the students to receive immediate support, as acknowledged by the interviewees.

Interviewees further proposed a tutoring role of chatbots for offering tutorials for basic concepts of a course, supporting the learners while studying a new language, and even delivering a specific lesson that a student missed in the class. In addition, the

Table 1. Envisioned pedagogical uses of chatbots in higher education

Higher-level categories	Categories	Sub-categories	Codes
Proactive	**Cognitive**	Assessment	Assess prior conceptual knowledge
	Affective	Social	Promote inter-social bonding of learners with common educational paths
	Administrative	Induction	Provide introductory information about the university
On-going	**Cognitive**	Remote tutor	Tutorials; respond to content questions; shared resources; mediator to the instructor
	Cognitive	Formative assessment	Assess conceptual understanding; offer personalized feedback
	Affective	Emotional	Offer psychological support to the students; fulfil the feelings of loneliness and anxiety
	Affective	Motivational	Motivate the students and query about students' satisfaction with their performance
	Affective	Social	Promote inter-social bonding of learners
	Administrative	Counselling	Offer course counselling; students' affairs services
	Administrative	Reservations	Book meetings with instructor; book a slot at the Lab
	Administrative	Course information and admin processes	Provide information about course deadlines; offer support in submissions; collect assignments; respond to FAQs

(*continued*)

Table 1. (*continued*)

Higher-level categories	Categories	Sub-categories	Codes
	Administrative	Surveys	Facilitate teaching evaluation
Retrospective	**(Meta)cognitive**	Reflection	Act as personal reflective tool
	Cognitive	Learners' summative assessment	Conduct quizzes

Table 2. Indicative quotes for the proactive intervention of chatbots in higher education

Sub-categories	Codes	Indicative quotes
Assessment	Assessing prior knowledge	"I would like a chatbot that could test students' prior knowledge at the beginning of the semester, especially when the course has a prerequisite." (Instructor #3)
Social	Inter-social bonding of learners with common educational paths	"You might have a component beneath the chatbot that identifies how students seem to follow some educational path because of their background [...] and the chatbot could proactively propose connections with other peers with similar educational paths so that they can form a study group to work together." (Expert #2)
Induction	Introductory information about the university	"The chatbot could give some instructions to freshmen students e.g., some information about student life, or about the university processes." (Instructor #5)

instructors proposed specific instances in which remote tutoring, namely meaningful conversations between chatbots and students for learning purposes, could be beneficial for the students. One of these instances includes the scenario in which the chatbot can act as a guide in problem-based learning; in other words, the chatbot can offer step-by-step support in problem solving tasks to the students. In another instance, the chatbot could intervene in critical benchmarks and check points of the learning process, interacting with the students and making sure that the core learning objectives have been met. In addition, interviewees from the three categories (expert, instructor, students) proposed a mediating role of the chatbot in the learning and teaching process. In this occasion, the chatbot, while interacting with the students in content-related topics, has the capability to understand when the instructor should intervene in the chatbot-student conversation; therefore, the chatbot is acting as the mediator with the instructor to intervene in the conversation.

Table 3. Indicative quotes for the on-going intervention of chatbots in higher education in the cognitive domain

Sub-categories	Codes	Indicative quotes
Remote tutor	Tutorials; respond to content questions; shared resources; mediator to the instructor	"I can imagine having a chatbot that helps you get all your lectures online. Chatbot being remote tutor could be very helpful for lecturers in this situation" (Expert #4)
Social	Inter-social bonding of learners with common educational paths	"Definitely, chatbots could help in content-related questions and problems, which I see that many students face similar problems, and it takes time to see one by one." (Instructor #4)
Induction	Introductory information about the university	"I usually read late in the evenings, and when a question may arise during my study, I would like to have a chatbot to help me and address my questions." (Student #8)

Another major sub-category under the cognitive domain of chatbot educational uses includes the implementation of formative assessment. In this case, the chatbots can be designed for assessing students' conceptual understanding on a topic, offer personalized and direct feedback to the learners and even identify learning difficulties of the learners. However, one of the experts stressed the importance of having well-designed chatbots for this educational use, as there might some risk that the chatbot will cause frustration and irritation to the students if it fails to provide meaningful responses.

The second category of the on-going chatbot uses serves affective aspects of the learning process, namely, emotional, motivational, and social aspects of learning (Table 4). The interviewees proposed the potential of chatbots to offer psychological support to the students and to fulfil the feelings of loneliness and anxiety (i.e., emotional), to motivate the students during their learning journey and query them in short conversations about their satisfaction with their performance (i.e., motivational), as well as, to promote inter-social bonding of learners and learners with mentors (i.e., social). For the social bonding idea, the experts referred to personalization and adaption of chatbots to respond to language, cultural and social norms of the students. Nevertheless, the social bonding idea was faced with some concerns from the experts' side. Cultural differences were cited as a potential barrier in designing technological solutions that can really serve social bonding and explained that this is an area that needs further research and development. Besides this, the application of chatbots for social bonding was seen with caution by some of the interviewees (i.e., instructors and students), as they could not see any value of chatbots mediating in the social bonding with other humans.

Table 4. Indicative quotes for the on-going intervention of chatbots in higher education in the affective domain

Sub-categories	Codes	Indicative quotes
Emotional	Offer psychological support to the students; fulfil the feelings of loneliness and anxiety	"One part that has been in my mind for several years now, that maybe chatbots can help with, is in psychological support rather than educational support, in the sense that the chatbots understand the psychology of the students" (Instructor #2)
Social	Inter-social bonding of learners with common educational paths	"The increase of anxiety and loneliness we see especially among the higher education students, it's increasing for sure. And having that chatbot at least feels like they've listened to There might be a great opportunity there" (Expert #3)
Motivational	Motivate the students and query about students' satisfaction with their performance	"I would add the affective part as well. That is, the chatbot should be smart enough to look at how satisfied the student is with his or her own performance if there are issues that need to come to the teacher's attention beyond the cognitive part." (Instructor #3)

Last, the fourth category of on-going chatbots uses in the learning and teaching process encompasses complemented administration tasks (Table 5). In particular, the chatbot could be used for course counselling (i.e., course counselling, students' affairs counselling, and services), for reservations (i.e., arrange and book meetings between a student and the instructor or for making a reservation in the laboratory and other university premises), and for course information and administrative processes (i.e., collecting students' assignments throughout the semester, reminding students for course deadlines, facilitating and offering support during the submission process of assignments and responding to FAQs of the students that deal with administration). Last, the chatbots can be used for module feedback provision that typical takes place at the end of the academic semester and as part of the instructors' evaluation. Students' responses could be shared directly with the instructor, thus leaving room for improvements in the course delivery.

Table 5. Indicative quotes for the on-going intervention of chatbots in higher education in complemented administration

Sub-categories	Codes	Indicative quotes
Counselling	Course counselling; students' affairs services	"… or to use a chatbot for getting an immediate response that you need from the students' affairs, instead of waiting a few hours when the issue is urgent" (Student #8) "It could offer support as a curriculum guide and for course counselling" (Student #3)
Reservations	Book meetings with instructor; book a slot at the Lab	"I often need to go to the lab to use the 3D printer, the laser and other equipment, but in our university, we have a big problem in making a reservation for the lab. I would like to have a chatbot making a reservation for the lab" (Student #3) "to make an appointment with me via a chatbot would be a good choice" (Instructor #1)
Course information and admin processes	Information about course deadlines; offer support in submissions; collect assignments; respond to FAQs	"The majority of the questions are like, when is the deadline, where should we submit … so a chatbot responding to all these FAQs would help!" (Instructor #2)
Surveys	Facilitate teaching evaluation	"Instead of the standard questionnaires given to students at the end of the semester, the chatbot could do a mini-interview with the students to give me a richer feedback on my lesson. This could take place several times during the semester." (Instructor #3)

Retrospective Intervention. Uses in which the chatbot can facilitate the learning process retrospectively were proposed by experts and students; those uses have been clustered under the metacognitive domain. Chatbots may appear as personal reflective tools, getting in short conversations with the students, but also the instructors, for helping them to reflect on the learning and teaching process. Also, the chatbots can be used for summative assessment, with the implementation of quizzes and tests that measure students' conceptual understanding of a topic (see Table 6).

Table 6. Indicative quotes for the retrospective intervention of chatbots in higher education in the metacognitive domain

Sub-categories	Codes	Indicative quotes
Reflection	Act as personal reflective tool	"I think you could use it for educators and for students as a personal reflective tool. So, a chatbot that would help you understanding your learning behavior, that would kind of sit on your shoulder virtually and monitor certain things". (Expert #4)
Learners' summative assessment	Conduct quizzes	"Maybe the bot could do something like a quiz, giving you a percentage of your correct answers at the end of the quiz." (Student #3) "One approach could be, using the chatbots to do assignment, do quizzes" (Expert #1)

4.2 Benefits and Challenges of the Proposed Pedagogical Uses (RQ2)

As it has been revealed from the interview data, the envisioned uses of educational chatbots bears several advantages but also challenges, often linked to technological affordances and constraints. Among the advantages (see Table 7), the cognitive offload of the users was mentioned. That is, from the users' perspective cognitive offload was explained in the sense that they do not need to memorize pieces of information, deadlines, etc., when a chatbot can offer this type of information easy and quickly via a short interaction with the user. Then, from the instructors' perspective, cognitive offload was explained in the sense that the chatbot can reply to FAQs. More benefits include the low development cost, the capability of chatbots to address the needs of large-scale classes, the chatbots' availability to interact with the users at any time of the day and their potential to interact proactively with the users and display precisely the information that the users are searching for. In addition, the type of interaction that takes place between chatbots and users can be characterized as a human-like and enjoyable and can be considered appropriate for online teaching and learning. In addition, the personalization aspect has been acknowledged as an advantage, since a sufficiently advanced chatbot should be able to accommodate the particularities of the user or the student interacting with a chatbot.

Table 7. Indicative quotes from the experts' interview data on the benefits of the proposed pedagogical uses of chatbots

Codes	Indicative quotes
Cognitive offloading	"So instead of having to remember things for myself or having to solve a certain task in a prescribed way the chatbot allows offloading my cognitive effort to a machine." (Expert #2)
Low-cost development	"… for some chatbots getting started is really easy so that the cost of starting out by getting a minimum value products chatbots is low, much lower than any kind of development projects." (Expert #1)
Personalization	"A sufficiently advanced chatbot should be able to accommodate the particularities of the user or the student interacting with a chatbot. […] therefore, offering personalized feedback back to the students I think is a second potential for benefit by using chatbots in the classroom." (Expert #2)
Availability at any time	"One benefit is the continues feedback to the students in the sense that the students can ask as often as they choose for feedback on their progress or on their next steps and a teacher might not be available all the time to give this feedback, so the first benefit is to have this continues opportunity for feedback" (Expert #2)
Appropriate for large scale classes	"The benefits are of course the efficiency that can be used with chatbot in education space especially for large classes" (Expert #3)
Easy to retrieve information	"I think chatbots have their main benefit when they are able to provide users with help in a more convenient manner than students could have got otherwise" (Expert #1)
Human-like and enjoyable interaction	"I think that if the chatbot is able to represent content in a dialogue manner the content will likely be better and more engaging and more to the point than if the content is given in a sort of text post on a website. So, the benefit can be that chatbots forces us to make better content or at least content that fits a way of interacting for the user" (Expert #1)
Appropriateness for online learning and teaching	"I think right now it is the perfect time, as pretty much all of all the universities are moving completely online […] the fact that everything is being put online now, shows the opportunity to have a chatbot." (Expert #3)

(continued)

Table 7. (*continued*)

Codes	Indicative quotes
Proactive intervention	"By having a proactive intervention from the chatbot to the students they could help them to propose new variations of the questions that the students missed." (Expert #2)

Table 8. Indicative quotes from the experts' interview data on the challenges of the proposed pedagogical uses of chatbots

Codes	Indicative quotes
Personalization technology limitations	"Now, chatbots come with pre-determined skills for rather narrow domain of discourse. Having unconstrained chatbots would essentially solve the AI problems we have now, and we are far from doing that" (Expert #2)
Ethical considerations	"I would see that the primary challenge in my mind is the ethical dimension of the employment of chatbots in the classroom or in education in general […] I think there is also a concern of how to handle the data that is gathered from a chatbot interacting with a student" (Expert #2) "Then there is also the data that involves with the collection of data, data privacy issues are always of concern" (Expert #3)
High maintenance cost	".. on the challenge side the cost of maintaining a chatbot that has advance capabilities are quite high. So, starting out is easy and cheap, maintaining is something growing into something that is costly and challenging" (Expert #1)
UX problems	"You just have to find out what the capabilities of the chatbot are, and I think that this can also be a challenge, because the users might feel frustrated if they are not aware of what the chatbot should be able to do." (Expert #1)

However, the application of chatbots may be accompanied with challenges (Table 8). Personalization, even though being viewed as a potential benefit, it has been also listed among the challenges, as the technology is not ready yet to fully support this functionality, according to the experts in the domain. Related to the previous constraint, another challenge proposed by the experts, includes the limitation of a chatbot to handle complex conversations and the high error rate at the beginning of their use, which can evolve via machine learning techniques. As the domain expert-interviewees explained, this challenge affects in a great extent the successful application of pedagogical scenarios for students' learning support, assessment, and personalized feedback provision. Another major challenge that was revealed in our analysis, deals with ethical considerations around the application of chatbots in education. This challenge bears several dimensions. First, a chatbot-student interaction can be viewed as an educational intervention which raises ethical questions in case of undesirable effects. Second, an orthogonal ethical consideration involves data privacy issues; that is the data that is gathered from a chatbot interacting with a student and its further use for research or policy making purposes. Finally, the experts argued that sustainability of use, high maintenance cost and potential user experience (UX) problems which might cause feelings of frustration to the users, were also outlined. Related to the latter point, it was explicated by one of the experts that it is necessary for the users (e.g., learners) to be aware of the capabilities of the chatbots and adjust their expectations accordingly, to avoid feelings of frustration.

5 Discussion

5.1 Envisioned Pedagogical Uses of Chatbots in Higher Education (RQ1)

In this study, we sought to identify how higher-education users and experts in the domain of educational chatbots envision pedagogical uses of chatbots in higher education, as well as the benefits and challenges related to their use. The qualitative analysis relied on 22 in-depth, semi-structured interviews with learners, instructors, and experts in the domain of AI and chatbots. Our analysis disclosed envisioned pedagogical uses applicable for three distinct phases of the learning process: prospectively, on-going, and retrospectively. It further revealed a wide spectrum of potential uses of chatbots that the particular interviewees consider appropriate and meaningful to be integrated into higher education, covering core dimensions of learning in the cognitive [3, 9] and affective (emotional, motivational, social) [31] learning domains. In addition to the above-mentioned categories, we have documented uses of chatbots that support the conduction of administrative tasks that relate to the learning and teaching processes. Using technology effectively in administrative activities could provide more access to information resources and ease the teaching and learning processes [42]. Likewise, the proposed chatbot uses have the potential to increase administrative efficiency and even lead to innovative administrative approaches.

Even though several envisioned pedagogical uses have been already identified as chatbot solution in previous studies, such as chatbots acting as teaching assistants [18], as tutors [13], for feedback provision and metacognitive thinking triggering [29, 35], and as formative assessment solutions (e.g., peer assessment chatbots in Lee and Fu study [34]), still our findings portray potential uses of chatbots in a wider spectrum of educational applications. In addition, our analysis provides a useful categorization of chatbots' uses into three distinct phases of the learning process and into different learning domains. In this sense, our findings depict in a non-fragmented manner the uses of chatbots in education, as envisioned by the participants of this study.

Of particular interest is the fact that chatbots have been suggested by our participants as means to enacting the role of the facilitator in problem-based tasks, while also intervening in the learning process, and interacting with the students in check points. This use aligns with two learning approaches. First, it aligns with the inquiry-based learning approach [2], in which the instructor appears as a facilitator intervening in the so-called check points for discussing with the learners; likewise, when appropriately trained, chatbots could enact this specific role. Second, this chatbot use relates to the problem-based learning model [44], during which the learners are engaged in self-directed learning, to examine and solve a given problem. Overall, chatbots were envisioned by the interviewees as facilitators in problem-based and inquiry-based learning and teaching. Such pedagogies adhering to principles of active learning and collaboration fall under the category of socio-constructivist learning theories (i.e., constructivism by Piaget and socioculturalism by Vygotsky). Even though current chatbot solutions do function as teaching assistants and tutors in the classrooms [13, 18], yet the framing of those solutions within an appropriate pedagogy seems to be still scant and little research has been conducted with this focus [57]. The need to design chatbots to support such pedagogical uses, with implications in pedagogical contexts, is imperative. This requires an understanding of learning as an active process on the behalf of learners, whose prior knowledge and the interaction with the social environment has a catalyst role to play in their knowledge construction.

5.2 Benefits and Challenges of the Proposed Pedagogical Uses (RQ2)

The realization and potential success of these pedagogical uses is associated with their technological affordances and constraints. First, a human-like interaction with chatbots, as described by some of our participants, can be considered appropriate for online teaching and learning, especially in the post-covid era that we are experiencing nowadays. Further, among the advantages that chatbots bring into education, is their low development cost, as acknowledged by our participants, consistent with what is already proposed by previous scholars [56]. However, interviewees in this study also argued about the high costs of maintaining the use of chatbots, which might have implications for the widespread use of chatbots by educational organizations. More advantages include the cognitive offload of the users (e.g., bots responding to FAQs), chatbots' availability to interact with the users at any time of the day, and their potential to interact proactively with the users. Consistent with previous authors, this proactive role can be achieved because chatbots can initiate a 'dialogue' with the user and adjust the content of the communication appropriately, considering the user's location or clickstreams, making the user feel that s/he is personally addressed [24].

The appropriateness of chatbots for large-scale classes has been acknowledged by our participants. One would think that chatbots, as applied in education, can be a solution to the inadequate individual support that students receive in large-scale courses and/or MOOCs [23], with no further financial and organizational costs for the providers. In sum, chatbots can potentially provide essential individual student support especially in large scale classrooms, in which the provision of individualized feedback and support is demanding for educators. Moreover, the interactions among chatbots and the users can be automatically analyzed (e.g., by employing sentiment analysis as a proxy to measure users' satisfaction, as proposed by Feine, Morana, and Gnewuch, [15]), thus providing another advantage of using chatbots in education. Analysis of this nature can be used to understand the users' requirements and therefore improve the service or product that the chatbot is serving.

Despite all these advantages, there are several constraints that hinder the maximum performance of educational chatbots. For instance, even though chatbots can evolve via machine learning techniques and through evaluating conversations with users, the error rate at which a chatbot works is initially high [36]. Also, according to the same authors, even though chatbots can simplify the administrative work of educators by disclosing supplementary information to students about their courses, they often fail to solve content issues. This becomes a bit problematic when chatbots are meant to be used for meaningful formative assessment purposes and content-related guidance provision. Let alone, as indicated by the experts in our study, when chatbots do not comprehend the users' requests and questions, even in administrative matters, they could cause frustration originating from ineffective communication.

Shortcomings in the use of chatbots include the usual disconnect between the vision of what AI powered chatbots or intelligent tutoring systems could be, and what they really are [5]. This could be attributed to the approaches used in practice, which are mainly simple. Also, research innovations in the field, often do not get integrated into the systems deployed at scale; that is, systems being used at scale in education are generally not representative of the full richness that research systems demonstrate. Therefore, even though there is an initial intend from researchers to develop systems that can use reinforcement learning to improve themselves [6], few systems incorporate this capacity [5].

Finally, another major challenge deals with ethical considerations on the application of chatbots in education. As with all novel technologies, chatbots also entail ethical and privacy implications. Besides, chatbots comprise AI entities and, therefore, they must be subject to the ethical standards applicable to AI [12]. As derived from our data, especially in the field of education, chatbots may be hindered by ethical considerations in relation to the actual educational intervention, but also the type of interactions that take place, and the way the conversation data are being further used and exploited. Those concerns are expected to be encountered in chatbots' integration in an educational context, and thus, appropriate attention should be given to each potential chatbot use, according to the purpose that the chatbot serves each time.

6 Implications and Limitations

The findings of this study can have implications for researchers and educators in higher education, but also, software designers and developers in the field of chatbots. The proposed pedagogical uses of chatbots that can be exploited for the creation of specific pedagogical scenarios, accounting also for the added value of a particular chatbot use, the learning context, users' characteristics, and particular needs, chatbot technology, and pedagogies that are deemed appropriate in each scenario.

Finally, in this work, the participants (learners, instructors, and one of the four experts) came from a single country, as they were reached by convenience. In future work, the authors should aim to have participants from a wider region and other cultures. Our results, although not generalizable, offer an in-depth analysis of current and future opportunities and challenges related to the use of chatbots in higher education. This study contributes new knowledge in the area, and we hope it will spark interest, research, and development in the field of educational chatbots in higher education.

Acknowledgments. This work is part of the project EDUBOTS, which is funded under the scheme Erasmus + KA2: Cooperation for innovation and the exchange of good practices - Knowledge Alliances (grant agreement no: 612446), and from the European Union's Horizon 2020 Research and Innovation Programme under Grant Agreement No 739578 and the Government of the Republic of Cyprus through the Directorate General for European Programmes, Coordination, and Development.

References

1. Alepis, E., Virvou, M.: Automatic generation of emotions in tutoring agents for affective e-learning in medical education. Expert Syst. Appl. **38**(8), 9840–9847 (2011)
2. Anderson, R.: Reforming science teaching: what research says about inquiry. J. Sci. Teacher Educ. **13**(1), 1–12 (2002)
3. Anderson, L.W., Krathwohl, D.R. (eds.): A Taxonomy for Learning, Teaching, and Assessing: A Revision of 's Taxonomy of Educational Objectives. Longman, New York (2001)
4. Ayedoun, E., Hayashi, Y., Seta, K.: A conversational agent to encourage willingness to communicate in the context of English as a foreign language. Procedia Comput. Sci. **60**, 1433–1442 (2015)
5. Baker, R.S.: Stupid tutoring systems, intelligent humans. Int. J. Artif. Intell. Educ. **26**(2), 600–614 (2016)
6. Beck, J., Woolf, B.P., Beal, C.R.: ADVISOR: a machine learning architecture for intelligent tutor construction. AAAI/IAAI, pp. 552–557 (2000)
7. Bickmore, T.W., Schulman, D., Sidner, C.: Automated interventions for multiple health behaviors using conversational agents. Patient Educ. Couns. **92**(2), 142–148 (2013)
8. Bii, P.K., Too, J.K., Mukwa, C.W.: Teacher attitude towards use of chatbots in routine teaching. Univ. J. Educ. Res. **6**(7), 1586–1597 (2018)
9. Bloom, B.S., Engelhart, M.D., Furst, E.J., Hill, W.H., Krathwohl, D.R.: Taxonomy of educational objectives: The classification taxonomy of educational goals. In: Handbook 1: Cognitive Domain. David McKay, New York (1956)
10. Brandtzaeg, P.B., Følstad, A.: Chatbots: changing user needs and motivations. Interactions **25**(5), 38–43 (2018)
11. Colace, F., De Santo, M., Lombardi, M., Pascale, F., Pietrosanto, A., Lemma, S.: Chatbot for e-learning: a case of study. Int. J. Mech. Eng. Robot. Res. **7**(5), 528–533 (2018)
12. Dignum, V.: Ethics in artificial intelligence: introduction to the special issue. Ethics Inf. Technol. **20**(1), 1–3 (2018). https://doi.org/10.1007/s10676-018-9450-z
13. Dutta, D.: Developing an Intelligent Chat-bot Tool to assist high school students for learning general knowledge subjects. Georgia Institute of Technology (2017)
14. Eisenhardt, K.M.: Building theories from case study research. Acad. Manag. Rev. **14**(4), 532–550 (1989)
15. Feine, J., Morana, S., Gnewuch, U.: Measuring Service Encounter Satisfaction with Customer Service Chatbots using Sentiment Analysis (2019)
16. Følstad, A., Brandtzæg, P.B.: Chatbots and the new world of HCI. Interactions **24**(4), 38–42 (2017)

17. Fryer, L.K., Ainley, M., Thompson, A., Gibson, A., Sherlock, Z.: Stimulating and sustaining interest in a language course: an experimental comparison of chatbot and human task partners. Comput. Hum. Behav. **75**, 461–468 (2017)

18. Goel, A., Creeden, B., Kumble, M., Salunke, S., Shetty, A., Wiltgen, B.: Using watson for enhancing human-computer co-creativity. In: 2015 AAAI Fall Symposium Series (2015)

19. Gonda, D.E., Luo, J., Wong, Y.L., Lei, C.U.: Evaluation of developing educational chatbots based on the seven principles for good teaching. In: 2018 IEEE International Conference on Teaching, Assessment, and Learning for Engineering (TALE), pp. 446–453. IEEE (2018)

20. Gupta, S., Bostrom, R.: Research note—an investigation of the appropriation of technology-mediated training methods incorporating enactive and collaborative learning. Inf. Syst. Res. **24**(2), 454–469 (2013)

21. Gupta, S., Jagannath, K., Aggarwal, N., Sridar, R., Wilde, S., Chen, Y.: Artificially Intelligent (AI) Tutors in the Classroom: A Need Assessment Study of Designing Chatbots to Support Student Learning (2019)

22. Harley, J.M., et al.: Examining the predictive relationship between personality and emotion traits and students' agent-directed emotions: towards emotionally-adaptive agent-based learning environments. User Model. User-Adap. Inter. **26**(2–3), 177–219 (2016). https://doi.org/10.1007/s11257-016-9169-7

23. Hone, K.S., El Said, G.R.: Exploring the factors affecting MOOC retention: a survey study. Comput. Educ. **98**, 157–168 (2016)

24. Howlett, N.: How machine learning is developing to get more insight from complex voice-of-customer data. Appl. Mark. Anal. **3**(3), 250–254 (2017)

25. Huang, J.X., Lee, K.S., Kwon, O.W., Kim, Y.K.: A chatbot for a dialogue-based second language learning system. CALL in a climate of change: adapting to turbulent global conditions, 151 (2017)

26. Jia, J., Chen, W.: Motivate the learners to practice English through playing with Chatbot CSIEC. In: Pan, Z., Zhang, X., El Rhalibi, A., Woo, W., Li, Yi. (eds.) Technologies for E-Learning and Digital Entertainment. Lecture Notes in Computer Science, vol. 5093, pp. 180–191. Springer, Heidelberg (2008). https://doi.org/10.1007/978-3-540-69736-7_20

27. Keller, C., Cernerud, L.: Students' perceptions of e-learning in university education. J. Educ. Media **27**(1–2), 55–67 (2002)

28. Kerfoot, B.P., et al.: A multi-institutional randomized control trial of web-based teaching to medical students. Acad. Med. **81**(3), 224–230 (2006)

29. Kerly, A., Ellis, R., Bull, S.: Dialog systems in e-learning. In: Proceedings of AI2008, pp. 169–182 (2008)

30. Knill, O., Carlsson, J., Chi, A., Lezama, M.: An artificial intelligence experiment in college math education (2004)

31. Krathwohl, D.R., Bloom, B.S., Masia, B.B.: Taxonomy of educational objectives: the classification of educational goals. In: Handbook II: Affective Domain. David McKay Company, Incorporated (1956)

32. Kwon, O.W., Lee, K., Kim, Y.K., Lee, Y.: GenieTutor: a computer assisted second-language learning system based on semantic and grammar correctness evaluations. In: Critical CALL–Proceedings of the 2015 EUROCALL Conference, pp. 330–335. Research-publishing, Net (2015)

33. Lee, T., et al.: Intelligent Career Advisers in Your Pocket? A Need Assessment Study of Chatbots for Student Career Advising (2019)

34. Lee, Y.C., Fu, W.T.: Supporting peer assessment in education with conversational agents. In: Proceedings of the 24th International Conference on Intelligent User Interfaces: Companion, pp. 7–8 (2019)

35. Lundqvist, K.O., Pursey, G., Williams, S.: Design and implementation of conversational agents for harvesting feedback in eLearning systems. In: Hernández-Leo, D., Ley, T., Klamma, R., Harrer, A. (eds.) Scaling up Learning for Sustained Impact. Lecture Notes in Computer Science, vol. 8095, pp. 617–618. Springer, Heidelberg (2013). https://doi.org/10.1007/978-3-642-40814-4_79

36. Ma, W., et al.: TripleNet: Triple Attention Network for Multi-Turn Response Selection in Retrieval-based Chatbots. arXiv preprint arXiv:1909.10666 (2019)

37. Molnár, G., Szüts, Z.: The role of chatbots in formal education. In: 2018 IEEE 16th International Symposium on Intelligent Systems and Informatics (SISY), pp. 000197–000202. IEEE (2018)

38. Mimoun, M.S.B., Poncin, I.: A valued agent: how ECAs affect website customers' satisfaction and behaviors. J. Retail. Consum. Serv. 26, 70–82 (2015)

39. Novielli, N., de Rosis, F., Mazzotta, I.: User attitude towards an embodied conversational agent: effects of the interaction mode. J. Pragmatics 42(9), 2385–2397 (2010)

40. Oudeyer, P.Y., Gottlieb, J., Lopes, M.: Intrinsic motivation, curiosity, and learning: theory and applications in educational technologies. In: Progress in Brain Research, vol. 229, pp. 257–284. Elsevier (2016)

41. Patton, M.Q.: Qualitative Research and Methods: Integrating Theory and Practice. SAGE Publications, Thousand Oaks (2015)

42. Picciano, A.G.: Educational Leadership and Planning for Technology, 2nd edn. Prentice-Hall Inc., USA (1998)

43. Popovici, A., Mironov, C.: Students' perception on using eLearning technologies. Procedia-Soc. Behav. Sci. 180, 1514–1519 (2015)

44. Savery, J.R., Duffy, T.M.: Problem based learning: an instructional model and its constructivist framework. Educ. Technol. 35(5), 31–38 (1995)

45. Serban, I.V., et al.: A deep reinforcement learning chatbot. arXiv preprint arXiv:1709.02349 (2017)

46. Shawar, B.A., Atwell, E.: Chatbots: are they really useful? Ldv forum 22, 29–49 (2007)

47. Sheikh, S.A., Tiwari, V., Singhal, S.: Generative model chatbot for human resource using deep learning. In: 2019 International Conference on Data Science and Engineering (ICDSE), pp. 126–132. IEEE (2019)

48. Smutny, P., Schreiberova, P.: Chatbots for learning: a review of educational chatbots for the Facebook Messenger. Comput. Educ. 151, 103862 (2020)

49. Söllner, M., Bitzer, P., Janson, A., Leimeister, J.M.: Process is king: evaluating the performance of technology-mediated learning in vocational software training. J. Inf. Technol. 33(3), 233–253 (2018)

50. Stathakarou, N., et al.: Students' perceptions on chatbots' potential and design characteristics in healthcare education. Stud. Health Technol. Inform. 272, 209–212 (2020)

51. Strauss, A., Corbin, J.: Grounded theory methodology. Handbook Qual. Res. 17, 273–285 (1994)

52. Strauss, A., Corbin, J.: Basics of qualitative research: Techniques and procedures for developing grounded theory, 2nd edn. Sage, Thousan Oaks (1998)

53. Thai, M.T.T., Chong, L.C., Agrawal, N.M.: Straussian grounded theory method: an illustration. Qual. Rep. 17(5), 1–55 (2012)

54. Thies, I.M., Menon, N., Magapu, S., Subramony, M., O'Neill, J.: How do you want your chatbot? An exploratory Wizard-of-Oz study with young, urban Indians. In: Bernhaupt, R., Dalvi, G., Joshi, A., Balkrishan, D.K., O'Neill, J., Winckler, M. (eds.) Human-Computer Interaction – INTERACT 2017. Lecture Notes in Computer Science, vol. 10513, pp. 441–459. Springer, Cham (2017). https://doi.org/10.1007/978-3-319-67744-6_28

55. Tsivitanidou, O., Ioannou, A.: Users' needs assessment for chatbots' use in Higher Education. In: Proceedings of the Central European Conference on Information and Intelligent Systems, pp. 55–62 (2021). Faculty of Organization and Informatics, University of Zagreb. ISSN 1848–2295 (Online)

56. Winkler, R., Söllner, M.: Unleashing the potential of chatbots in education: a state-of-the-art analysis (2018)

57. van der Meij, H., van der Meij, J., Harmsen, R.: Animated pedagogical agents effects on enhancing student motivation and learning in a science inquiry learning environment. Educ. Tech. Res. Dev. **63**(3), 381–403 (2015). https://doi.org/10.1007/s11423-015-9378-5

58. Yan, M., Castro, P., Cheng, P., Ishakian, V.: Building a chatbot with serverless computing. In: Proceedings of the 1st International Workshop on Mashups of Things and APIs, pp. 1–4 (2016)

59. Zemčík, M.T.: A brief history of chatbots. In: DEStech Transactions on Computer Science and Engineering. AICAE (2019)

AR, VR and Robots in Learning

Towards a New Chemistry Learning Platform with Virtual Reality and Haptics

Doga Demirel[1]($\boxtimes$) (iD), Abdelwahab Hamam[1] (iD), Caitlin Scott[2], Bayazit Karaman[1] (iD), Onur Toker[1], and Lyan Pena[1]

[1] Florida Polytechnic University, Lakeland, FL 33805, USA
{ddemirel,ahamam,bkaraman,otoker,lpena4344}@floridapoly.edu
[2] Hendrix College, Conway, AR 72032, USA
scottc@hendrix.edu

Abstract. With COVID-19, colleges had to change the way they handle education. Students had to adapt to remote learning instead of the face-to-face learning they are used to. The transition to remote learning has proved to be difficult, but most courses have translated over without any problems. Unfortunately, the same cannot be said for the lab courses, which traditionally have students conduct hands-on experiments. In order to achieve the same level of effectiveness that the labs had prior to COVID-19; a new system is required. The long-term goal of this work is to develop a complete immersive Virtual Reality (VR) chemistry lab. In the VR lab space, the student can handle chemicals and equipment to simulate an actual chemistry lab. Using a VR headset and haptic gloves, the user will be able to freely move and interact with the virtual lab, fellow students, and their teacher. Due to COVID-19 restrictions, instead of the students testing the virtual experience, we presented a 6-min video demonstration of our immersive VR chemistry lab to 109 General Chemistry students. Students filled out pre- and post-questionnaires. 80% of the students either strongly agreed or agreed with the statement, "I think learning general chemistry with VR and haptics will be more engaging than a standard lecture". For the statement, "I think undergoing the chemistry lab training in a VR environment rather than watching videos will help me learn the basics of chemistry lab better", 71.8% of the students strongly agreed or agreed with the statement.

Keywords: Chemistry · Virtual reality · Haptics

1 Introduction

The onset of the COVID-19 pandemic has drastically changed the way chemistry is taught at academic institutions. Starting in March 2020, many U.S. colleges and universities closed their doors to in-person learning causing students to learn remotely. This greatly hampered the instruction of chemistry labs, where students typically conduct experiments using chemicals and instruments. Instead, students watch videos of experiments, write lab reports on provided data, perform at-home experiments, and use virtual simulations [1]. However, students did not get the hands-on experience of learning the

© Springer Nature Switzerland AG 2021
P. Zaphiris and A. Ioannou (Eds.): HCII 2021, LNCS 12785, pp. 253–267, 2021.
https://doi.org/10.1007/978-3-030-77943-6_16

correct protocol to work in a lab and handle modern machinery and hazardous chemicals. Given that many schools remain closed to in-person learning, it has become imperative to develop a way that students can learn the skills and techniques of conducting chemistry experiments without having to physically be in the lab. Benefits of a virtual lab would also extend beyond the end of the current pandemic. Students who cannot attend lab because they are pregnant, in the military, or are handicapped would benefit from alternative lab experiences that still adequately prepare them for working in a lab [2]. Even before the pandemic began, the utility of undergraduate labs for General Chemistry courses was called into question [1, 3, 4]. Labs are expensive to conduct [5], and many academic institutions were already experiencing a strained budget. Furthermore, it was questionable if students were actually learning the intended goals [1, 3, 4].

However, despite the cost and questions about learning, if done correctly, labs can be a vital part of the General Chemistry learning experience. Johnstone purposed that chemistry is taught in a three-pronged approach—the symbolic, the microscopic, and the macroscopic. The lecture sections generally emphasize the symbolic material (the chemical symbols, abbreviations, math equations, and variables) and the microscopic material (atomistic movements). Lab is the place where students can learn about chemistry macroscopically, that is, how chemical reactions affect the environment and the surroundings, and students can make connections between the macroscopic and the microscopic and symbolic worlds [6, 7].

Our solution to remote lab instruction is to use virtual reality (VR) head-mounted displays (HMDs) with haptic gloves. VR is beneficial for student learning for multiple reasons including making abstract ideas seem tangible and making students be actively engaged [8]. Our simulation will allow students to explore a realistic lab setting while handling machinery and chemicals. Students can interact with the avatars of other students, the lab assistants, instructors, as well as a "Virtual Buddy" who can act as a resource by answering questions. The haptic gloves will allow the students to feel the weight of the glassware and to handle the lab equipment and chemicals in a safe and controlled manner.

As mentioned above, there is uncertainty about the intellectual benefit that General Chemistry students gain from taking lab. Part of the problem can be attributed to the cognitive overload that students experience [9]. Typically, in a college teaching lab, students are introduced to the instruments and chemicals when they are conducting the experiments. Students not only have to learn the chemistry, but how to handle the equipment and materials as well. Some students do not take lab as part of their high school chemistry course. Even if they had, they may not have seen the same types of instruments and machines. Many of the chemical names sound foreign to the students, which creates confusion [6, 7]. To counter this, Brigham Young University and Purdue University require that their students record videos to verify that they know how to use the equipment before conducting actual experiments. At BYU, instructors have noted a decrease in broken glassware and safety issues [1]. For over three semesters at the University of Western Australia, approximately 75% of level-1 Chemistry students opted to participate in a 360° virtual tour the lab with over 90% of students saying that they agreed that the lab tour familiarized them with the lab setting and approximately 70–90% agreed that they felt prepared for lab [10]. By introducing the lab setting and materials to students in a safe manner that students can explore on their own time, we are hoping to prepare students for actual experiments so that they can focus on the chemical reactions and learning goals rather than be distracted by the lab setting.

Another potential benefit of VR-lab training is self-efficacy. Self-efficacy is defined as the student's belief that their actions can lead to success in a chosen subject or task [11]. A study of students in a social studies class show that student's self-efficacy impacted their goals and eventual academic achievement in the class, which suggests that self-motivation has a large impact on student success [12]. A study of first-year college students shows a direct correlation between student expectations and student success [13]. Therefore, to increase student retention, it would make sense to invest and improve student confidence. The role of VR in increasing self-efficacy needs more research, but there are some promising signs [9]. One way to enhance a student's self-efficacy is to give that student a sense of control [14]. An immersive VR environment would provide this for the student [9]. A meta-analysis of computer simulations and gaming in the classroom showed that students who used interactive computer simulations had more cognitive gains and a better attitude about learning than those in a traditional learning environment [15, 16]. A 2019 study about VR-lab safety training for engineering students showed that students in an immersive VR environment had increased motivation and self-efficacy compared to students reading the lab manual or using VR on a desktop computer [17]. VR training has also been shown to improve the self-efficacy of participants undergoing training for negotiating [18] or classroom teaching [19]. In our planned VR lab space, students would handle their own equipment and chemicals in a safe environment with easy access to a "Lab Buddy," which acts as a resource when the instructor and lab assistants may not be available. Thus, students would control their own learning experience, which should strengthen their confidence when they are ready to conduct experiments in an actual lab.

VR has been used in classroom instruction for decades. Computer simulations have been used to augment lab instruction as far back as 1980 [20]. VR-haptic surgery training has been used since 1998 [21, 22] and remains an important tool for training doctors and surgeons before practicing on patients. VR has been used to train surgeons in how to do laparoscopies, carotid stenting, and ophthalmology [8]. VR-trained surgeons were 29% faster and six times less likely to make mistakes while performing laparoscopic cholecystectomy gallbladder dissection than surgeons with traditional training [8, 23]. These studies show that VR training is effective at preparing doctors. We believe that it can be equally as effective as preparing students for their chemistry courses.

VR has already been in use to teach organic chemistry [24], physical chemistry [25], and biochemistry [26, 27]. In previous studies, students have found that using VR to teach chemistry to be very fun and educational. The "Bug Off Pain" VR game teaches students about the impact that toxins have on pain signaling pathways in the body. In a post-game survey, students reported feeling engaged and motivated to learn more [27]. This and other chemistry VR learning platforms, such as Labster [28], EduChemVR [29], VR-ENGAGE [30], Molecular Zoo, Peroxiredoxin Fish Tank, Protein Backbone Explorer, Nano Simbox iMD, Water VR [31], and MEL Science [32] rely on HMDs, whereas our proposed simulation will allow students to "touch," "feel," and "handle" the chemicals and lab equipment with the use of haptic gloves. Our chemistry lab simulation is designed to allow students to access the lab in a safe and comfortable setting in a way that will give students confidence for the time that they first approach the actual chemistry lab. By being prepared in a virtual space, we anticipate that students will feel more comfortable and have increased confidence, which will encourage them to continue with their chemistry education.

2 Methods

2.1 Application

Our fully immersive virtual environment has four main components: a) Virtual Scene, b) Haptic glove, c) Companion- "Virtual Buddy", and d) Database. Figure 1 shows the overall system design.

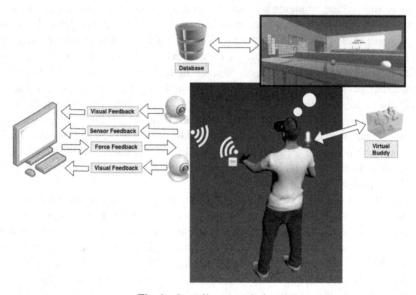

Fig. 1. Overall system design.

The virtual scene has two capabilities: a classroom and a lab. For a realistic rendering of the scene, we used High Definition Render Pipeline and Physically-based Rendering (PBR) [33, 34] in Unity software package. PBR uses bi-directional reflectance distribution function (BRDF) [35, 36] to approximate accurate light-flow models.

We placed an interactive periodic table on the wall of our scene (as seen in Fig. 2). The periodic table has a CPK Color toggle button which changes the colors of elements in the periodic table to CPK colors, which are used to distinguishing atoms of different chemical elements. Clicking on an element in the periodic table will spawn the selected element on the table. Radius and color information for each element will be stored in our MySQL [37] database.

Fig. 2. First-person view in the virtual scene.

2.2 Video Demo

Due to the restrictions of COVID-19, instead of students testing the virtual experience, we presented a 6-min video demonstration of our immersive VR chemistry lab to 109 General Chemistry students at Hendrix College. The video demonstration was two-fold. The first part included information about VR HMDs, haptic gloves, and the reasoning of the study. The students were informed that the study goal is to simulate an actual chemistry lab experience through VR that will allow them to handle chemicals and equipment. They were provided a general overview of the steps they must accomplish: a pre-video questionnaire (which they have already did prior to watching the video), complete watching the video, and then complete a post-video questionnaire. The second part was a full demonstration of our virtual chemistry lab. In the demonstration, we showed a walk-through of the virtual scene which consisted of navigating the lab from a first-person point of view. The students were shown the virtual equipment, white board, the periodic table on the wall, the safety equipment, and the workspace available. The safety equipment is composed of various eye cleaning stations/emergency showers and a fire extinguisher. As the avatar was walking around the virtual avatar, the students could see what the avatar is seeing and hear information about how they would experience this in VR.

The second part also included the interaction with the periodic table to create elements in the scene and compounds by connecting the elements. The students were shown how to pick a particular element from the periodic table and use it in the interaction. Once they select an element the atomic representation of that elements appears. Bringing elements into proximity will form an ionic bond between the two elements, while moving them further will break that bond.

2.3 Questionnaire

The questionnaire started with a general description of the video that the students are about to see as well as a statement on the goal of conducting the study and instructions on filling the questionnaire. This was followed by questions about the participants' demographics. The demographic data were collected to deduce conclusion about the data, however, they were kept anonymous.

Prior to watching the video, students answered a pre-questionnaire about their background in chemistry and gaming, and their interest, motivation, and preparedness in learning chemistry. The pre-video questionnaire is comprised of Likert-like multiple choice questions (as seen in Fig. 3) and descriptive open-ended questions where the students would fill out information in a given space. The open-ended questions include: "What is your chemistry background?", "Why are you enrolled in chemistry?", "How do you feel about your chemistry course?", and "How do you feel about your chemistry lab?".

	Strongly disagree	Disagree	Neutral	Agree	Strongly agree
1. I am interested in learning about chemistry.	○	○	○	○	○
2. I am well-prepared for my college chemistry courses.	○	○	○	○	○
3. I am motivated to learn chemistry.	○	○	○	○	○
4. I feel comfortable about working in a chemistry lab.	○	○	○	○	○
5. I feel anxious about working in a chemistry lab.	○	○	○	○	○
6. I am looking forward to working in a chemistry lab.	○	○	○	○	○
7. I enjoy learning through standard lectures.	○	○	○	○	○

Fig. 3. Likert-like multiple pre-video questions

After the demonstration of the video, students were given a post-video questionnaire with open-ended and Likert-like questions which outlined how the use of VR and haptics would be beneficial in learning. In both the pre- and post-video questionnaires, the Likert-like questions were anchored with labels strongly agree, agree, neutral, disagree, and strongly disagree (as seen in Fig. 4). The open-ended question for post-video questionnaire was "How has your perception of the study of chemistry changed as a result of this video?".

	Strongly disagree	Disagree	Neutral	Agree	Strongly agree
1. I have experience playing computer and video games.	○	○	○	○	○
2. I think undergoing the chemistry lab training in a Virtual Reality (VR) environment rather than watching videos will help me learn the basics of chemistry lab better.	○	○	○	○	○
3. I think learning general chemistry through VR and Haptics will be more hands on than a standard lecture.	○	○	○	○	○
4. I think learning general chemistry through VR and Haptics will be more engaging than a standard lecture.	○	○	○	○	○
5. I will prefer the immersive VR learning experience to the learning experience from a standard lecture.	○	○	○	○	○

Fig. 4. Likert-like multiple post-video questionnaire questions

3 Results

In this study, a survey consisting of 14 questions is conducted on a total of 109 students. For the statement, "I think learning general chemistry with VR and haptics will be more engaging than a standard lecture", 42.7% of the students strongly agreed with the statement, 37.3% agreed, 11.8% was neutral, 5.5% disagreed, and 2.7% strongly disagreed. For the statement, "I think undergoing the chemistry lab training in a VR environment rather than watching videos will help me learn the basics of chemistry lab better", 30% of the students strongly agreed with the statement, 41.8% agreed, 17.3% was neutral, 8.2% disagreed, and 2.7% strongly disagreed.

The following 7 questions are more relevant for our analysis, and the rest are more related to chemistry itself. For each question, we also use a short abbreviation to simplify tables and visualization of correlation data. These abbreviations are shown in parentheses.

1. (Interested) I am interested in learning about chemistry.
2. (Anxious) I feel anxious about working in a chemistry lab.
3. (Learning) I enjoy learning through standard lectures.
4. (Experience) I have experience playing computer and video games.
5. (Undergoing) I think undergoing the chemistry lab training in a Virtual Reality (VR) environment rather than watching videos will help me learn the basics of chemistry lab better.

6. (More engaged) I think learning general chemistry through VR and Haptics will be more engaging than a standard lecture.
7. (Prefer) I will prefer the immersive VR learning experience to the learning experience from a standard lecture.

For each survey questions, there were a total of 5 possible answers; 0: Strongly Disagree, 1: Disagree, 2: Neutral, 3: Agree, 4: Strongly Agree,

Namely instead of categorical data, we have ordinal values. Therefore, instead of chi-square type tools for correlation analysis, we used Spearman's Rank-Order correlation formula. Because all of our data (i.e. answers) are ordinal values rather than categorical. We are not using Pearson's correlation formula, because we are not interested in linear relationships, rather we are looking for monotonic relationships, whether linear or not. Basically, Spearman's correlation measures monotonic relationships. In the following table, we have the so-called p-values, where a small value indicates a strong "monotonic" correlation, and a large value implies the lack of correlation.

Our p threshold is selected as 0.05, i.e. if a p-value is less than 0.05, we conclude that there is a strong correlation between two variables. All p-values which are below 0.05 are highlighted, except the ones along the diagonal which have perfect correlation because of being identical variables.

Table 1. Table of p-values for the selected questions. Small p-values are highlighted, yellow background indicates positive correlation, whereas gray background is used for negative correlation.

	Interested	Anxious	Learning	Experience	Undergoing	More Engaged	Prefer
Interested	0.000	0.679	0.001	0.160	0.340	0.563	0.763
Anxious	0.679	0.000	0.980	0.304	0.003	0.099	0.108
Learning	0.001	0.980	0.000	0.088	0.543	0.245	0.110
Experience	0.160	0.304	0.088	0.000	0.025	0.003	0.007
Undergoing	0.340	0.003	0.543	0.025	0.000	0.000	0.000
More Engaged	0.563	0.099	0.245	0.003	0.000	0.000	0.000
Prefer	0.763	0.108	0.110	0.007	0.000	0.000	0.000

In Table 1, we see a couple "islands" of "zeros" representing highly correlated variables. The first one is

Island 1 (Experience, Undergoing, More Engaged, Prefer): This island indicates a strong correlation between Experience, Undergoing, More Engaged, Prefer, more precisely.

- (Experience) I have experience playing computer and video games.
- (Undergoing) I think undergoing the chemistry lab training in a Virtual Reality (VR) environment rather than watching videos will help me learn the basics of chemistry lab better.
- (More engaged) I think learning general chemistry through VR and Haptics will be more engaging than a standard lecture.

- (Prefer) I will prefer the immersive VR learning experience to the learning experience from a standard lecture.

As it is clear from this analysis, students who have previous gaming experience will prefer the use of such tools, will be more engaged, and find these tools very advantageous for a better learning experience.

Island 2 (Learning, Interested):

- (Interested) I am interested in learning about chemistry.
- (Learning) I enjoy learning through standard lectures.

The purpose of these questions was simply to assess the reliability of our dataset. These are logically correlated questions, but the wording was quite different. If a majority of students answer a significant portion of the survey almost randomly without reading carefully, one would expect either no or very low correlation between these two questions. However, our analysis shows a very strong correlation between the two, which is an indication of a reliable dataset or survey result.

Island 3 (Undergoing, Anxious):

- (Anxious) I feel anxious about working in a chemistry lab.
- (Undergoing) I think undergoing the chemistry lab training in a Virtual Reality (VR) environment rather than watching videos will help me learn the basics of chemistry lab better.

All of the correlations discussed so far, were positive correlations, whereas here we have a negative correlation. Basically, students who feel anxious about working in a chemistry lab think that undergoing the chemistry lab training in a Virtual Reality (VR) environment rather than watching videos will NOT help them learn the basics of chemistry lab better. In other words, students who are anxious about chemistry do not find these tools really useful to improve their learning experience.

In Fig. 5, we have a visual representation of p-values matrix. While dark blue like colors are representing small p-values, i.e., strong correlation, yellow like colors indicate large p-values, namely lack of correlation. A color bar shown on the right summarizes the relationship between colors and numerical p-values.

Figure 6 show that, majority of students are interested in learning about chemistry. However, the second graph shows that not all enjoy learning through standard lectures. In other words, they would like to see better alternative tools to be used for teaching.

The results from Fig. 7 shows that the proposed immersive VR chemistry tool will be useful not only for a special group of students, but for a broader audience. Because, although a good number of students do not have any gaming experience, some of them still believe that these VR tools will improve their learning experience.

We see a large group of students who answered Neutral (as seen in Fig. 8). These two figures show that, most students consider VR tools as something which will improve their learning experience; however, they seem to be a bit confused and possibly scared about using such tools in a standard lecture.

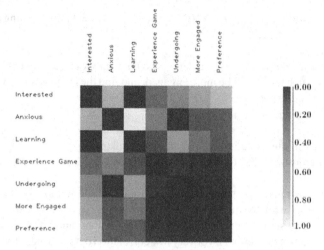

Fig. 5. Spearman's p matrix in color image format (Parula colormap).

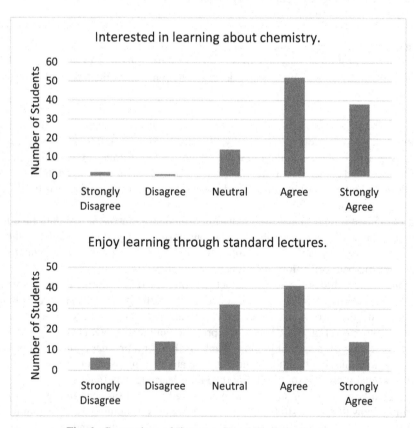

Fig. 6. Comparison of "Interested" and "Learning" answers.

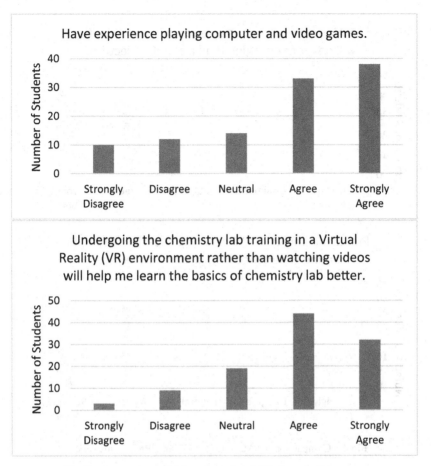

Fig. 7. Comparison of "Experience" and "Undergoing" answers.

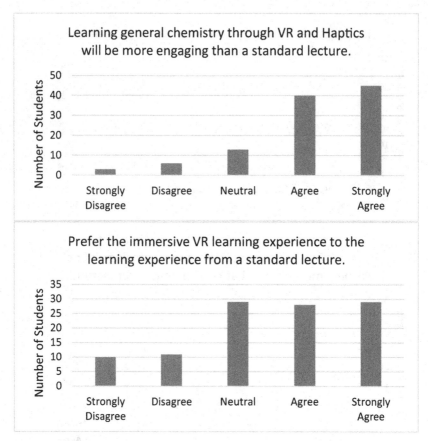

Fig. 8. Comparison of "More Engaged" and "Prefer" answers.

4 Conclusion

With COVID-19, many colleges have had to change the way they handle their education. As a result, students have been unable to engage in face-to-face learning and most educational establishments have switched to remote learning in order to ensure the safety of the students, professors, and staff. Remote learning has its advantages but is not as effective as in-class instruction, especially for lab environments.

In this study, we created a preliminary interactive virtual chemistry learning environment using HMDs. Due to the restrictions of COVID-19, instead of students testing the virtual experience, we presented a 6-min video demonstration of our immersive VR chemistry lab to 109 General Chemistry students. After the demonstration of the video, students were given a post-video questionnaire with open-ended and multiple-choice questions which outlined how the use of VR and haptics would be beneficial in learning. In the post-video questionnaire, students answered 14 multiple choice questions as strongly agree, agree, neutral, disagree, and strongly disagree. For the statement, "I think learning general chemistry with VR and haptics will be more engaging than a standard lecture", 42.7% of the students strongly agreed with the statement, 37.3% agreed, 11.8% was neutral, 5.5% disagreed, and 2.7% strongly disagreed. For the statement, "I think undergoing the chemistry lab training in a VR environment rather than watching videos will help me learn the basics of chemistry lab better", 30% of the students strongly agreed with the statement, 41.8% agreed, 17.3% was neutral, 8.2% disagreed, and 2.7% strongly disagreed.

We also conducted the Spearman's rank correlation coefficients and p-values to analyze the correlation between multiple choice questions. It has been observed that students who have previous experience with computer and video games prefer immersive VR learning experience compared to standard methods. The Spearman's test showed a p-value of 0.0069 suggesting a strong correlation between the two. Students who have previous experience with gaming, find VR tools more effective compared to online video tutorials. The Spearman test p-value was 0.0163 also suggesting a strong correlation between the two. Student who feel anxious about chemistry labs find VR tools more effective compared to online video tutorials. Our study showed a Spearman test p-value of 0.0163 also suggesting a strong correlation between the two. We have observed no significant correlation, p-value of 0.5628, between the interest level of students to learn chemistry and their level of interest for VR and haptic tools. This result shows that the proposed immersive VR chemistry tool will be useful not only for a special group of students, but for a broader audience.

References

1. Arnaud, C.H.: Questioning the value of general chemistry labs. Chem. Eng. News **98**(18) (2020). https://cen.acs.org/education/undergraduate-education/Questioning-value-general-chemistry-labs/98/i18

2. Colson, C.J.: Virtualizing Organic Chemistry Labs. DELTA News (2018). https://delta.ncsu.edu/news/2018/12/19/virtualizing-organic-chemistry-labs/

3. Bretz, S.L.: Evidence for the importance of laboratory courses. J. Chem. Educ. **96**(2), 193–195 (2019). https://doi.org/10.1021/acs.jchemed.8b00874

4. Hofstein, A., Lunetta, V.N.: The laboratory in science education: foundations for the twenty-first century. Sci. Educ. **88**, 28–54 (2004)

5. Jones, N.: Simulated labs are booming. Nature **562**, S5–S7 (2018). https://doi.org/10.1038/d41586-018-06831-1

6. Johnstone, A.H.: Why is science difficult to learn? Things are seldom what they seem. J. Comput. Assist. Learn. **7**(75), 701–703 (1991)

7. Gabel, D.: Improving teaching and learning through chemistry education research: a look to the future. J. Chem. Educ. **76**(4), 548 (1999). https://doi.org/10.1021/ed076p548

8. Slater, M., Sanchez-Vives, M.V.: Enhancing our lives with immersive virtual reality. Front. Robot. AI **3**, 74 (2016). https://doi.org/10.3389/frobt.2016.00074

9. Merchant, Z., Goetz, E.T., Keeney-Kennicutt, W., Kwok, O., Cifuentes, L., Davis, T.J.: The learner characteristics, features of desktop 3D virtual reality environments, and college chemistry instruction: a structural equation modeling analysis. Comput. Educ. **59**(2), 551–568 (2012). https://doi.org/10.1016/j.compedu.2012.02.004

10. Clemons, T.D., Fouché, L., Rummey, C., Lopez, R.E., Spagnoli, D.: Introducing the first year laboratory to undergraduate chemistry students with an interactive 360° experience. J. Chem. Educ. **96**(7), 1491–1496 (2019). https://doi.org/10.1021/acs.jchemed.8b00861

11. Bandura, A.A.: Self-efficacy: The exercise of control (1997)
12. Zimmerman, B.J., Bandura, A., Martinez-Pons, M.: Self-motivation for academic attainment: the role of self-efficacy beliefs and personal goal setting. Am. Educ. Res. J. **29**(3), 663–676 (1992). https://doi.org/10.3102/00028312029003663
13. Chemers, M.M., Hu, L., Garcia, B.F.: Academic self-efficacy and first year college student performance and adjustment. J. Educ. Psychol. **93**(1), 55–64 (2001). https://doi.org/10.1037/0022-0663.93.1.55
14. Bandura, A.: Perceived self-efficacy in cognitive development and functioning. Educ. Psychol. **28**(2), 117–148 (1993). https://doi.org/10.1207/s15326985ep2802_3
15. Vogel, J., Vogel, D., Cannon-Bowers, J., Bowers, C., Muse, K., Wright, M.: Computer gaming and interactive simulations for learning: a meta-analysis. J. Educ. Comput. Res. **34**, 229–243 (2006). https://doi.org/10.2190/FLHV-K4WA-WPVQ-H0YM
16. Merchant, Z., Goetz, E.T., Cifuentes, L., Keeney-Kennicutt, W., Davis, T.J.: Effectiveness of virtual reality-based instruction on students' learning outcomes in K-12 and higher education: a meta-analysis. Comput. Educ. **70**, 29–40 (2014). https://doi.org/10.1016/j.compedu.2013.07.033
17. Makransky, G., Borre-Gude, S., Mayer, R.E.: Motivational and cognitive benefits of training in immersive virtual reality based on multiple assessments. J. Comput. Assist. Learn. **35**(6), 691–707 (2019). https://doi.org/10.1111/jcal.12375
18. Ding, D., Brinkman, W.-P., Neerincx, M.A.: Simulated thoughts in virtual reality for negotiation training enhance self-efficacy and knowledge. Int. J. Hum. Comput. Stud. **139**, 102400 (2020). https://doi.org/10.1016/j.ijhcs.2020.102400
19. Nissim, Y.W., Eyal, : Virtual reality (VR) as a source for self-efficacy in teacher training. Int. Educ. Stud. **10**(8), 52–59 (2017)
20. Moore, C., Smith, S., Avner, R.A.: Facilitation of laboratory performance through CAI. J. Chem. Educ. **57**(3), 196 (1980). https://doi.org/10.1021/ed057p196
21. Krummel, T.M.: Surgical simulation and virtual reality: the coming revolution. Ann. Surg. **228**(5) (1998). https://journals.lww.com/annalsofsurgery/Fulltext/1998/11000/Surgical_Simulation_and_Virtual_Reality__The.2.aspx
22. Marescaux, J., et al.: Virtual reality applied to hepatic surgery simulation: the next revolution. Ann. Surg. **228**(5) (1998). https://journals.lww.com/annalsofsurgery/Fulltext/1998/11000/Virtual_Reality_Applied_to_Hepatic_Surgery.1.aspx
23. Seymour, N.E.: Virtual reality training improves operating room performance: results of a randomized, double-blinded study. Ann. Surg. **236**(4) (2002). https://journals.lww.com/annalsofsurgery/Fulltext/2002/10000/Virtual_Reality_Training_Improves_Operating_Room.8.aspx
24. Dunnagan, C.L., Dannenberg, D.A., Cuales, M.P., Earnest, A.D., Gurnsey, R.M., Gallardo-Williams, M.T.: Production and evaluation of a realistic immersive virtual reality organic chemistry laboratory experience: infrared spectroscopy. J. Chem. Educ. **97**(1), 258–262 (2020). https://doi.org/10.1021/acs.jchemed.9b00705
25. Barrett, R., et al.: Social and tactile mixed reality increases student engagement in undergraduate lab activities. J. Chem. Educ. **95**(10), 1755–1762 (2018). https://doi.org/10.1021/acs.jchemed.8b00212
26. Bennie, S.J., et al.: Teaching enzyme catalysis using interactive molecular dynamics in virtual reality. J. Chem. Educ. **96**(11), 2488–2496 (2019). https://doi.org/10.1021/acs.jchemed.9b00181
27. Bibic, L., Druskis, J., Walpole, S., Angulo, J., Stokes, L.: Bug off pain: an educational virtual reality game on spider venoms and chronic pain for public engagement. J. Chem. Educ. **96**(7), 1486–1490 (2019). https://doi.org/10.1021/acs.jchemed.8b00905
28. Labster. A million-dollar lab, one click away. https://www.labster.com
29. EduChemVR Improving Chemistry Learning with Virtual Reality. http://educhem-vr.com/

30. Virvou, M., Katsionis, G.: On the usability and likeability of virtual reality games for education: the case of VR-ENGAGE. Comput. Educ. **50**(1), 154–178 (2008). https://doi.org/10.1016/j.compedu.2006.04.004
31. Virtual Reality at UCSF (2020). http://vr.ucsf.edu/#education
32. MEL Science experiments for kids, delivered to your door. https://melscience.com/US-en/
33. Pharr, M., Jakob, W., Humphreys, G.: Physically Based Rendering: From Theory to Implementation (2016)
34. Schlick, C.: An inexpensive BRDF model for physically-based rendering. Comput. Graph. Forum **13**(3), 233–246 (1994)
35. Ashikhmin, M., Shirley, P.: An anisotropic phong BRDF model. J. Graph. Tools **5**(2), 25–32 (2000)
36. Ashikmin, M., Premože, S., Shirley, P.: A microfacet-based BRDF generator. In: Proceedings of the 27th Annual Conference on Computer Graphics and Interactive Techniques, pp. 65–74 (2000). https://doi.org/10.1145/344779.344814
37. MySQL AB (2001) MySQL.

Effect of Height in Telepresence Robots on the Users' Spatial Awareness

Oliver Gawron$^{(\boxtimes)}$ ⬤, Lisa Keller ⬤, Karsten Huffstadt, and Nicholas H. Müller

University of Applied Sciences Würzburg-Schweinfurt, Sanderheinrichsleitenweg 20, 97074 Würzburg, Germany
mail@olivergawron.com

Abstract. Since reduction of personal contact is key in fighting the COVID-19 pandemic, remote communication solutions saw a rise in importance. Next to the more common forms like video and audio conference calls, telepresence solutions are also becoming more popular. Telepresence robots can be remotely driven and allow, with the help of cameras and displays on the robot and the users' side, face-to-face communication with onsite personal, establishing a remote telepresence. Depending on the model, the height of the robot can be adjusted by the remote user. Even though the effect of the height in relation to onsite people is being researched, the effect on the users' side has not been examined immensely. Therefore, this work examines the effect of the difference in height between a telepresence robot and its user on the users' spatial awareness. Subjects have experienced the usage of a telepresence robot driving at a fixed height through a video. Afterwards, they filled out a questionnaire, which asks the user to answer questions about the experience. These questions were regarding the spatial awareness of the user in the remote location, asking them to estimate different parts of the tour. Their estimations were mapped to the users' height, allowing to correlate the difference in height and the users' spatial awareness. The work has shown, that only the perceived height of the telepresence robot was affected by the difference in size. However, more tests have to be conducted, to factor in multiple robot heights.

Keywords: Telepresence robots · Remote communication · Spatial awareness

1 Introduction and Background

Since reduction of personal contact is key in fighting the COVID-19 pandemic, remote communication solutions saw a rise in importance, with downloads of video conferencing apps in march 2020 being magnitudes higher than in the fourth quarter of 2019 [1]. Next to the more common forms like video and audio conference calls, telepresence solutions are also becoming more popular. Telepresence Robots are in general movable platforms with cameras, speakers, a microphone and a display. A remote user can log into the robot to control it, while

© Springer Nature Switzerland AG 2021
P. Zaphiris and A. Ioannou (Eds.): HCII 2021, LNCS 12785, pp. 268–277, 2021.
https://doi.org/10.1007/978-3-030-77943-6_17

experiencing the onsite surroundings on a computer screen. Simultaneously, the users' face is being projected live onto the robots screen, allowing onsite personal to communicate with the user in a face-to-face manner, establishing a remote telepresence.

This form of telepresence allows to be implemented in a wide variety of fields. In teaching oriented environments like schools and universities, telepresence robots can be deployed to be used by lecturers and students attending classes [2,3]. Students using the robots in educational tasks have shown to embrace teamwork more and improve in conflict management and coordination [4]. Additionally, students motivations has shown to be positively improved when using robots [5–7]. Groups of people can solve challenges through multiple robots which has shown to have a positive team building effect [8]. Furthermore, the private sector has shown an increased interest in telepresence robots being used in personal homes [9].

Some models of telepresence robots allow the user to change the robots height e.g. with a telescopic pole. This could theoretically allow the user to set the robots size to match his or her own height. But not all telepresence robots feature a changeable height or are limited to ranges that cannot perfectly represent all humans. Additionally, the functionality might be hidden in the user interface or come with a drawback, like a reduced speed at greater heights, which even though available, does not encourage the user to change the height or even knowingly change it to be smaller than himself or herself. This leads to many telepresence users not having the telepresence robot adjusted to their seize and thus experiencing the world on a different height than they are used to.

2   Research Question and Hypotheses

The effect of the height of telepresence robots has been subject of many studies before. A study has showed that its size does not effect a remote instructors' authority and a shorter than life-size robot was perceived friendlier the instructors' students [10]. Furthermore, when used by persons in leadership roles, a study has shown that locals found the robot user less persuasive when the robot was smaller than himself [11]. But what effect a difference in height between the user and the driven robot has, had not been investigated immensely. To establish an immersive telepresence on the user side, the user should experience the same spatial awareness, as he would being onsite. Therefore, this work investigates the following question:

RQ1: Does the difference in height of a telepresence robot effect the users' spatial awareness?

Since spatial awareness is a complex construct, that cannot be measured by a single data point, Elito's and Czarnolewski's "Everyday Spatial Behavioral Questionnaire" was used to split the research question in three measurable hypotheses [12]:

H1: The difference in height between a telepresence robot and its user does affect the users estimation of sizes seen through the telepresence robot.

H2: The difference in height between a telepresence robot and its user does affect the users estimation of the telepresence robots driven distance.

H3: The difference in height between a telepresence robot and its user does affect the users estimation of the height of the telepresence robot.

3 Approach

Because the usage of telepresence robots varies heavily from user to user, a uniform experience could not be achieved by performing the test on actual telepresence robots. To generate a homogeneous experience the participants can be exposed to, a video of the usage of a telepresence robot was used in the study. It shows the web interface of the used telepresence robot, featuring mainly the robot's view of its surroundings. To allow the participants to view the video, it was uploaded to the popular video platform YouTube.

The used telepresence robot was a Double 2 from Double Robotics. It features a telescopic pole allowing the camera to be lifted from 119 cm up to 157 cm high. This maximum was also the height used for the experiment, as it is closer to the average human height, allowing the differences to the users heights to be proportionate greater. The size of the telepresence robot did not change during the video. Figure 1 shows a screenshot of the uploaded video.

Fig. 1. Recorded video uploaded to YouTube. The Pepper robot is visible in the distance. Link to the video: https://youtu.be/a3NxMjaAxbE

In order to have the participants estimating a driven distance, the telepresence robot drove during the video through a room and a hallway, totalling a distance of 27.7 m. As mentioned in Sect. 1, the higher the robot, the slower its speed. Since the telepresence robot drove at maximum height it was rather slow and took 2 min and 5 s for this distance. During this commute, fairly common objects like doors, chairs, fire extinguishers and a one liter Coca Cola bottle were placed, to allow the user to get a sense of the scale of the environment.

The estimation of sizes was also a main subject of this work. To not have the participants estimate a size previously known to them, a rather uncommon item was needed for them to guess. The 121 cm high Pepper humanoid robot from Softbank Robotics fits this specification and was placed on the route. Participants can see the robot early on in the video, 20 s after it started, as the telepresence robot approaches it until it stops in front of it. Afterwards, at second 50, the telepresence robot turns and continues its route, with the Pepper robot out of sight for the rest of the video. This allowed the participants to see the Pepper robot for 30 s uninterrupted from different distances, creating a baseline to consider their estimation about its size.

Next to the estimation of a completely unknown size, the estimation of a relative common object was prepared. Since an adult human man is probably seen by every participant on a daily basis, one was part of the video for its height to be estimated. With 178 cm the person was about average for a German adult man [13]. The person is visible between minute 1:34 and 1:50. In these 16 s, the participant can see him from different angles and distances, allowing the participant to estimate his size in questionnaire afterwards. Figure 2 shows the person in the video.

Fig. 2. Cropped video frame containing the person.

The participants were asked to watch the video once and then immediately fill out the questionnaire seen in Sect. 4.

4   Methods

In order to examine the research questions and hypotheses (refer to Sect. 2), a quantitative questionnaire was designed which participants filled out at the end of the experiment. The designed questionnaire (listed below) is based on the findings of Elitos's and Czarnolewski's "Everyday Spatial Behavioral Questionnaire", which concluded, that estimating the size of a previously seen object or estimation a distance are valid data points to measure someone's spatial awareness [12]. In addition to the questionnaire, information about the participants' age, gender and, most importantly, their size were collected.

1. Estimate the total driven distance of the telepresence robot.
2. Estimate, how tall the white robot in the video was.
3. Estimate, how tall the person in the Video was.
4. Estimate, how tall the driven telepresence robot was.

5   Results and Analysis

Participants ($N = 39$) were aged 19 to 51. Moreover, 21 (53.8%) were male, 17 (43.6%) female, and 1 (2.55%) did not specify their sex. The average participant was male, 25.85 years old ($\sigma = 6.4$) and 174,13 cm ($\sigma = 8.4$) tall.

Since every hypothesis is based on the difference in height between a telepresence robot and its user, each data point needed an additional. This value was called ΔParticipantSize and was calculated by subtracting the participants' height with the height of the telepresence robot. This concluded, that the average participant was 17,13 cm ($\sigma = 8.4$) taller than the telepresence robot. Every participant was 0 cm to 31 cm taller than the telepresence robot.

Additionally, the estimations of the size of the Pepper robot, the size of the human, the driven distance and the height of the telepresence robot also got compared to the actual measured values, creating four new Δ-values. Since all data points are metric, Pearson correlations were used to determine relationships between the values. The used significance level was $p \leq 0.05$.

Estimation of Sizes

The null hypothesis of H1 states, that the difference in height between a telepresence robot and its user does not affect the users estimation of sizes seen through the telepresence robot. To prove this, there cannot be a statistical significant correlation between ΔParticipantSize and ΔPepperRobot or a statistical significant correlation between ΔParticipantSize and ΔPerson.

The participants average guess of the height of the Pepper robot was only 7 mm smaller than the actual robot ($\sigma = 25,7$ cm) with ΔPepperRobot ranging from -71 cm to $+39$ cm. The participants average guess of the height of the person was 1,1 cm smaller than the actual person ($\sigma = 4$ cm) with ΔPerson ranging from -8 cm to $+4$ cm. This smaller standard deviation was expected, as humans have a general knowledge on how tall other humans are.

There is no significant correlation between the variable ΔPepperRobot and the variable ΔParticipantSize with r = 0.061 p = 0.714. The corresponding graph can be seen in Fig. 3.

There is a small, positive correlation between the variable ΔPerson and the variable ΔParticipantSize with r = 0.181 p = 0.27. The corresponding graph can be seen in Fig. 4.

As both p-values are above the significance level, the null hypothesis of H1 cannot be rejected.

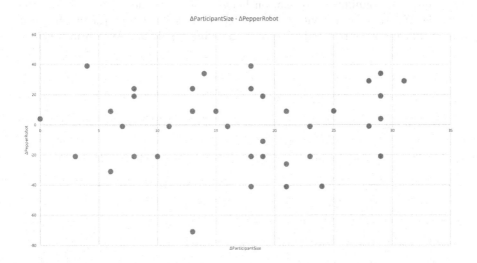

Fig. 3. ΔPepperRobot and ΔParticipantSize, r = 0.061, p = 0.714

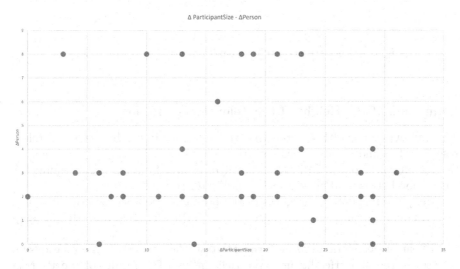

Fig. 4. ΔPerson and ΔParticipantSize, r = 0.181, p = 0.27

Estimation of Driven Distance

The null hypothesis of H2 states, that the difference in height between a telepresence robot and its user does not affect the users estimation of the telepresence robots driven distance. To prove this, there cannot be a statistical significant correlation between ΔParticipantSize and ΔDistance.

The participants average guess of the driven distance of the telepresence robot was 15 m over the measured distance ($\sigma = 43$ m) with ΔDistance ranging from -22 m to $+172$ m.

There is no significant correlation between the variable ΔDistance and the variable ΔParticipantSize with r $= -0.039$ p $= 0.816$. Therefore, the null hypothesis of H2 cannot be rejected. The corresponding graph can be seen in Fig. 5.

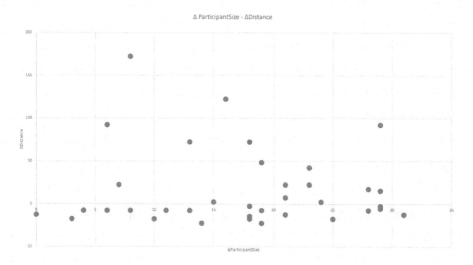

Fig. 5. ΔDistance and ΔParticipantSize, r $= -0.039$, p $= 0.816$

Estimation of the Height of the Telepresence Robot

The null hypothesis of H3 states, that the difference in height between a telepresence robot and its user does not affect the users estimation of the height of the telepresence robot. To prove this, there cannot be a statistical significant correlation between ΔParticipantSize and ΔTeleRobotHeight.

The participants average guess of the height of the telepresence robot was -3.7 cm under the measured distance ($\sigma = 24$ cm) with ΔTeleRobotHeight ranging from -57 cm to $+43$ cm.

A Pearson correlation was performed to test whether there was a relationship between ΔTeleRobotHeight and ΔParticipantSize. The results of the Pearson correlation showed that there was a significant positive relationship between

ΔTeleRobotHeight and ΔParticipantSize, r = 0.408, $p \leq 0.01$. Therefore, the null hypothesis of H3 is rejected.

Figure 6 shows the data in addition to a regression line. This regression line intercepts the x-axis at x = 20, meaning that participants who are 20 cm taller than the telepresence robot, are on average more likely to guess the right telepresence robot height.

6   Threats to Validity

As the experiment was conducted with only one fixed height of the telepresence robot, the results are limited to this specific height. Repeating the experiment with a different height could lead to different results. Due to technical limitations, the video quality was substandard. This could have influenced participants' estimations. Also, the dimensions to be estimated could be known independently from the experiment, as participants could be familiar with the Pepper robot and the person in the video. Additionally, participants could be familiar with the location the video was shot, allowing them to estimate the driven distance not only by means of the video. All participants were larger or the same height than the used telepresence robot. Also, conducting the experiment with humans smaller than the used telepresence robot could lead to different results. The participants' age was mainly between 20 and 30 years. Having the participants more distributed between all age groups could have lead to different results.

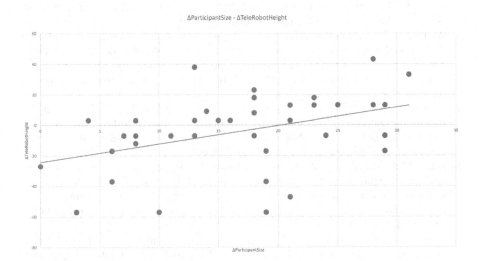

Fig. 6. ΔTeleRobotHeight and ΔParticipantSize with regression line, r = 0.408, p = 0.01

7   Conclusion and Outlook

The results of this study show, that the difference in size between a telepresence robot and its user does have an effect on parts of the users' spatial awareness. It seems to only affect the perceived height of the telepresence robot, but not external factors like object sizes and distances. This means, that in situations, where the users' perception of external sizes is key, the robots height is not a concern and can be adjusted to fit other needs, such as an increased movement speed at smaller heights. On the other hand, in situations, where the users' perceived height is more of a concern, the telepresence robots height should be adjusted accordingly to the users' size to have the spatial awareness least affected. The tests concluded, that this height might be 20 cm below the participants' size, but as discussed in Sect. 6, this might be only true for the in the experiment used height. This is why this topic needs more research regarding spatial awareness at different robot heights. If those confirm our findings and create a conclusive result, it could create an incentive to telepresence robot manufacturers to empathize on the height of their product, either by asking users their size beforehand and adjust, or by simply mentioning the effects of the height difference to its users.

References

1. Perez, S.: Videoconferencing apps saw a record 62 m downloads during one week in march (2020). https://techcrunch.com/2020/03/30/video-conferencing-apps-saw-a-record-62m-downloads-during-one-week-in-march
2. Weibel, M., et al.: Back to school with telepresence robot technology: a qualitative pilot study about how telepresence robots help school-aged children and adolescents with cancer to remain socially and academically connected with their school classes during treatment. Nurs. Open **7**(4), 988–997 (2020). https://doi.org/10.1002/nop2.471
3. Edwards, A., Edwards, C., Spence, P.R., Harris, C., Gambino, A.: Robots in the classroom: Differences in students' perceptions of credibility and learning between "teacher as robot" and "robot as teacher." Comput. Hum. Behav. **65**, 627–634 (2016). https://doi.org/10.1016/j.chb.2016.06.005
4. Scott, M.J., Parker, A., McDonald, B., Lewis, G., Powley, E.J.: Nurturing collaboration in an undergraduate computing course with robot-themed team training and team building. In: Proceedings of the 3rd Conference on Computing Education Practice - CEP 2019, pp. 1–4. ACM Press (2019). https://doi.org/10.1145/3294016.3294019
5. Keller, L., John, I.: How can computer science faculties increase the proportion of women in computer science by using robots? In: 2019 IEEE Global Engineering Education Conference (EDUCON), pp. 206–210 (April 2019). https://doi.org/10.1109/EDUCON.2019.8725212
6. Keller, L., John, I.: Motivating female students for computer science by means of robot workshops. Int. J. Eng. Pedagogy (iJEP) **10**(1), 94–108 (2020). https://doi.org/10.3991/ijep.v10i1.11661

7. Ortiz, O.O., Franco, J.P., Garau, P.M.A., Martín, R.H.: Innovative mobile robot method: improving the learning of programming languages in engineering degrees. IEEE Trans. Educ. **60**(2), 143–148 (2017). https://doi.org/10.1109/TE.2016. 2608779

8. Keller, L., Gawron, O., Rahi, T., Ulsamer, P., Müller, N.H.: Driving success: virtual team building through telepresence robots. In: Zaphiris, P., Ioannou, A. (eds.) Learning and Collaboration Technologies. Human and Technology Ecosystems - 8th International Conference, LCT 2021, Held as Part of the 23nd HCI International Conference, HCII 2021, Washington DC, USA, 24–29 July 2021. Lecture Notes in Computer Science, Springer (2021, accepted)

9. Winterstein, K., Keller, L., Huffstadt, K., Müller, N.H.: Acceptance of social and telepresence robot assistance in German households. In: Zaphiris, P., Ioannou, A. (eds.) Learning and Collaboration Technologies. Human and Technology Ecosystems - 8th International Conference, LCT 2021, Held as Part of the 23nd HCI International Conference, HCII 2021, Washington DC, USA, 24–29 July 2021. Lecture Notes in Computer Science, Springer (2021, accepted))

10. Bae, I., Han, J.: Does height affect the strictness of robot assisted teacher? In: Proceedings of the Companion of the 2017 ACM/IEEE International Conference on Human-Robot Interaction, pp. 73–74. HRI 2017. Association for Computing Machinery, New York (2017). https://doi.org/10.1145/3029798.3038401

11. Rae, I., Takayama, L., Mutlu, B.: The influence of height in robot-mediated communication. In: 2013 8th ACM/IEEE International Conference on Human-Robot Interaction (HRI), pp. 1–8 (2013). https://doi.org/10.1109/HRI.2013.6483495

12. Eliot, J., Czarnolewski, M.Y.: Development of an everyday spatial behavioral questionnaire. J. Gener. Psychol. **134**(3), 361–381 (2007). https://doi.org/10.3200/ GENP.134.3.361-381. pMID: 17824404

13. Mensink, G., Schienkiewitz, A., Haftenberger, M., Lampert, T., Ziese, T., Scheidt-Nave, C.: Übergewicht und adipositas in deutschland. In: Bundesgesundheits-blatt - Gesundheitsforschung - Gesundheitsschutz, vol. 56. Robert Koch-Institut, Epidemiologie und Gesundheitsberichterstattung (2013). https://doi.org/10.1007/ s00103-012-1656-3

Driving Success: Virtual Team Building Through Telepresence Robots

Lisa Keller[✉][iD], Oliver Gawron[iD], Tamin Rahi, Philipp Ulsamer,
and Nicholas H. Müller

University of Applied Sciences Würzburg-Schweinfurt, Sanderheinrichsleitenweg 20,
97074 Würzburg, Germany
lisa.keller.it@gmx.de

Abstract. Since the corona pandemic, the demand of remote communication solutions has increased significantly. A more uncommon platform to communicating remotely is given through telepresence robots. Telepresence robots are used by schools and universities for giving lectures or for students attending classes. In human-robot teams or at university, robots are also used for teamwork. However, the use of telepresence robots in virtual team building exercises has not been investigated immensely. Therefore, this work examines if telepresence robots are suitable for virtual team building exercises. Moreover, it is investigated whether an overall team building effect can be achieved. Thereby, subjects are divided in smaller telepresence robot groups (communicating via video conferencing). In turn the smaller telepresence robot groups communicate with the overall group through their telepresence robot. As team building exercises Pictionary as well as a QR code scavenger hunt were performed. The study took place as part of the virtual freshmen week at the faculty of computer science and business information systems. Team building was measured through a quantitative questionnaire. The results show that an overall team building effect could be achieved and that telepresence robots can be used successfully for virtual team building. However, the team building effect was significantly higher in the small telepresence robot groups than in the overall group.

Keywords: Telepresence robots · Virtual team building · Remote communication

1 Introduction and Background

Since the ongoing COVID-19 pandemic, the need of remote communication solutions has increased immensely. Moreover, since teamwork and collaboration are facing challenges as nearly every activity takes place digitally, universities mostly use Zoom or other video conferencing platforms for lectures and other activities. These platforms offer a great opportunity for discussing and conducting activities virtually. However, the part of motion we usually have in activities such as moving freely in the lecture room or the building is missing. Building connections

© Springer Nature Switzerland AG 2021
P. Zaphiris and A. Ioannou (Eds.): HCII 2021, LNCS 12785, pp. 278–291, 2021.
https://doi.org/10.1007/978-3-030-77943-6_18

with fellow students in virtual classes is harder compared to face-to-face classes as there is less opportunity to talk and most students leave the virtual room straight after the lecture ends. This is especially hard for freshmen as they are not familiar with the university system and they do not know any of their fellow students. Also, getting to know fellow students is aggravated. In order to enable freshmen to get to know each other, we designed, conducted, and evaluated a virtual team building event by means of telepresence robots. We used telepresence robots as a novel approach for team building, as online games might be too ubiquitous these days. As telepresence robots have not been used frequently for team building, related work could not give insight whether they are suitable for team building in bigger groups or not. Therefore, we examined if telepresence robots are suitable, and if an overall team building effect can be achieved. Thereby, in each iteration around 20 participants (overall group) where divided into four smaller groups (called robot group in this work). Within the smaller groups the participants communicated with each other through video conferencing, while the smaller groups communicated through telepresence robots with the other smaller groups (refer to Sect. 2). All in all, 184 subjects participated. In the following we will discuss related work regarding telepresence robots, virtual teams, and robots in team building.

Telepresence Robots

Apart from more common remote communication platforms such as Zoom, also robots can be used in communicating remotely. Telepresence robots are mobile robots which are especially designed for communicating remotely. They are equipped with cameras, microphones, a screen as well as motion control. Thereby, telepresence robots enable their operators to feel more present at the remote location. Moreover, operators can move freely and are not dependent on another person to turn camera view.

This element of moving freely was also positively stated by subjects participating in a study which examined the influence of using telepresence robots in long distance relationships [1]. Also, in what way telepresence robots impact human perception as well as conversations, was examined. In a study by Tsui et al., subjects visited an art gallery at first through a telepresence robot and afterwards in person. Conversations with a person in the gallery as well as the gallery itself were perceived fairly akin [2]. The work of Keller et al., systematically investigated this aspect further with respect to human affinity. The results of the study show, that there is no significant difference regarding perceived human affinity towards a person, whether a guided tour in a university is undertaken in person or through a telepresence robot [3]. This pleads for further successful usage of telepresence robots in social interactions. Moreover, Keller et al. also measured human affinity towards a humanoid robot interlocutor. The results indicate that there is no significant difference regarding human affinity, whether it is interacted with a humanoid robot in person or through a telepresence robot [4]. This suggest that telepresence robots cannot only be applied successfully in human-human interactions but also in human-robot interactions. Moreover, that there seems to be no difference in perceived human affinity in both cases, also benefits the use of telepresence robots in collaboration and virtual team building. Furthermore, the results of a study investigating the potential use of telepresence robots in German homes, indicate that people could imagine to have one at home [5].

Furthermore, multiple studies have examined the use of telepresence robots in a learning environment. They concluded, that telepresence robots can be effectively deployed for students, that are medically not able to visit a classroom [6]. In addition, a study showed, that this form of distant learning is more effective as more common screen-based video-conferencing solutions [7]. Mobility was also a highly valued feature for students attending classes through telepresence robots [8]. Also, having teachers using this displacing technology indicated to create positive learning attitudes [9]. Moreover, it has been shown, that the usage of telepresence robots is not affected by the users' size regarding spacial awareness at the distant location [10]. This allows school children and graduate students alike to use the same robots.

Virtual Teams

As other challenges occur in virtual teams compared to face-to-face teams, the literature review of Morrison-Smith and Ruiz deals with these challenges of collaboration. Moreover, they developed remedial strategies to illuminate and categorize these challenges [11]. Since collaboration tools are used in the sense of communication, studies also examined on which communication level information is ultimately processed in virtual teams and compared with face-to-face teams. For this purpose, a subdivision of the meaning was created on three levels [12]. In addition, researchers also dealt with the design and construction of team-building games in virtual worlds. The development of these games are based on principles from social psychology such as in Ellis et al.'s work [13]. This helps team members to develop better communication and cooperation skills [14]. Moreover, the study of Lin et al. has shown that factors of social dimensions need to be taken into account at an early stage in the formation of virtual teams. A research design within this study has been developed that includes the factors that affect the effectiveness of virtual teams [15]. Moreover, they developed a questionnaire to measure the effectiveness of virtual teams on multiple dimensions such as relationship building and cohesion. They designed their questionnaire based on a conducted literature review. We developed our questionnaire to measure the effectiveness of telepresence robots in virtual team building based on Lin et al.'s questionnaire.

Robots in Team Building

In order to examine human-robot collaboration, a study conducted a trial to investigate the effect of team building activities on humans when team building took place between humans and robots. It was found that human perception of robots improved after the team building activities were carried out [16]. Furthermore, the performance of a human-robot team has been investigated and it has been found that when a robot takes over the coordination tasks, the performance is improved [17]. Using robots in education, students were also brought closer to the topic of teamwork and were made aware of coordination mechanisms that should help to clarify and manage conflicts [18]. Furthermore, studies have shown that the usage of robots impacts students' motivation positively [19–21].

Also, telepresence robots were applied in teamwork activities. In the study of Tsui et al., they investigated the use of a telepresence robot in teamwork when one team member of the company is based at another location. The results show that some robot drivers felt more engaged with their team compared to regular video calls [22].

2   Research Questions and Hypothesis

As outlined in Sect. 1, research on virtual teams has been widely undertaken, mostly from a company working situation. Also, games have been proofed for successful team building. Likewise, robots involved in teamwork showed positive effects. Nevertheless, only little research has been undertaken regarding telepresence robots in virtual team building. Mostly interactions between humans and how they are influenced by the use of a telepresence robot were investigated. However, whether multiple telepresence robots can be used successfully in team building especially involving a bigger group had not been investigated immensely. Therefore, this work investigates the following questions:

RQ1: Are telepresence robots suitable for virtual team building exercises?
RQ2: Can a team building effect be achieved in the robot groups?
RQ3: Can an overall team building effect be achieved with subjects divided in smaller groups that communicate with each other by means of telepresence robots?

Thereby, it is assumed that a higher team building effect is present within the robot groups (which communicate via video conferencing) compared to the overall group (communicating through telepresence robots with other telepresence robot groups). This might be the case as communication in the robot groups themselves is simpler and less influenced by possible technical issues. Therefore, the following hypothesis will be examined:

H1: If subjects are divided in smaller groups that communicate with each other through telepresence robots, then a greater team building effect is present within the small groups as in the overall group.

3   Approach

In the study were five Double 3 robots (seen in Fig. 2) from the company Double Robotics used [23]. Four of them were in use with an additional robot as a backup in case of technical difficulties. Double 3 robot is a telepresence robot consisting of a head and a base part. The base consist of two electric engines allowing the robot to move freely around and self balances the rest of the robot. In the head are two 13MP Cameras integrated, allowing the user to access the robot's view with different zoom levels. In order to see the operator's face on the robot it also has a 9.7" LED-backlit Multi-Touch LCD screen. The robot can either be controlled by using arrow keys, WASD keys, or by clicking on the desired spot to which the robot automatically navigates with the help of multiple sensors.

The participants ($N = 184$) of this study were all freshmen participating in the university's orientation week of the computer science and business information systems department. One day before, they met in person during the orientation week. The group consisted of 20 participants maximum plus 4 guides. All participants were constructed to meet up in a Zoom video conference meeting [24] at a set time. After a brief explanation from one of the guides about the following steps, all participants were randomly divided into four smaller groups consisting of 5 participants maximum and one guide. These smaller groups communicated in so-called breakout sessions, small video conference meetings with the ability to share your screen with others present in the meeting. After all participants joined these, the guide of each group explained how to use a previously generated link to connect to the telepresence robot. Limitations to do so, like the necessity to use the Google Chrome Browser and the inability to control the robot with a mobile phone were communicated the day before, so participants had enough time to setup the needed software and hardware. Since each group only got to control one robot each, the driver of the telepresence robot had to share his or her screen, so the other participants could also hear and see the robot's actions. To allow every participant to control the robot at least once, multiple tasks were given between which the participants exchanged the driver.

(a) One of the guides   (b) Zoom call

Fig. 1. Guide and Zoom call

The first task, which allowed the participants to get used to the interface and the controls, was to drive from a starting point along a hallway to the cafeteria. This environment was familiar to the participants, since they were there shortly the day before. On their way they met the guides, they were communicating with, as they were onsite with the telepresence robots. Since all groups had the same tasks, all telepresence robots would meet each other there, allowing the robot drivers to talk to each other. At the same time, the rest of the groups could follow the action through the shared screen of the driver while talking to him or her and with each other.

Double 3 telepresence robots have the ability, besides displaying the operator's face, also to show a given website on its screen. The current robot driver was now asked to let the robot show an instance of the aggie.io website [25]. Aggie.io is a collaborative drawing space, allowing multiple users to draw together on the same canvas. The whole robot group was now asked to also open said website and draw a given object. Each team had a different object to draw. The possible objects were: forklift truck, dwarf, a native American, and a kangaroo. Since all robots were now showing different paintings of the different groups, the drivers task was to position each other in a way that allows the robots to see each other so that the groups could play a game of Pictionary though the telepresence robots.

The next task was to find and scan four hidden QR codes in the previously mentioned hallway. Since the robot itself has no build in QR code scanner, the participants used their mobile phones to scan these codes. The difficulty in this task was the QR code being captured by the robots camera, streamed to the controller's device and again streamed to the other participants in the group through the screen share, which deteriorated the image quality in every step, making the code hard to scan. To overcome this obstacle, the driver had to drive as close and straight on to the codes as possible, to allow his or her teammates an easy scan. The codes itself contained a letter each. With the letters being B, I, T and S the participants had to assemble them into the right code word BITS.

(a) Pictionary   (b) QR code scanning

Fig. 2. Tasks

The experiment always lasted an hour maximum, though some groups finished earlier than others. In the end, all participants were asked to fill in a questionnaire (refer to Sect. 4).

4 Methods

In order to examine the research questions (refer to Sect. 2), a quantitative questionnaire was designed which participants filled in at the end of the experiment. Additionally, the participants had the opportunity to give qualitative feedback by evaluating the freshmen orientation week.

Questionnaire

The designed questionnaire (listed below) consists of five categories: relationship building, cohesion, communication, coordination, and satisfaction. Each category consists of four quantitative questions. Therein, two questions relate to the subjects' robot group (question 1 and 3) and the other two questions to the whole group (question 2 and 4). Moreover, a 7-point Likert scale is applied where 1 means "not at all" and 7 "very". The questionnaire is based on the work *A model to develop effective virtual teams* by Lin et al. [15]. Therein, also a 7-point Likert scale and the five categories are applied. As the sixth category "performance" did not suit entirely to our experiment, this category was not applied. Moreover, two questions per category of Lin et al.'s work were chosen and adjusted towards the study settings and the use of telepresence robots.

Relationship Building

1. I had the feeling that my robot group had a common goal.
2. I had the feeling that the whole group (all robot groups together) had a common goal.
3. I have the feeling that I have established a connection to my robot group.
4. I have the feeling that I have established a connection with the whole group.

Cohesion

1. I had the feeling that my robot group was working together.
2. I had the feeling that the whole group was working together.
3. I had the feeling of being integrated in my robot group.
4. I had the feeling of being integrated in the whole group.

Communication

1. I had the feeling that we communicated effectively in my robot group.
2. I had the feeling that we communicated effectively throughout the group.
3. I had the feeling that my robot group was listening to me.
4. I had the feeling that the whole group was listening to me.

Coordination

1. I had the feeling that the coordination within my robot group worked well.
2. I had the feeling that the coordination within the whole group worked well.
3. I knew what I had to do within my robot group.
4. I knew what I had to do within the whole group.

Satisfaction

1. I was satisfied with the commitment of my team members in my robot group.
2. I was satisfied with the commitment of my team members throughout the whole group.
3. I felt comfortable in my robot group.
4. I felt comfortable in the whole group.

Qualitative Feedback

During the whole experiment, participants gave feedback about the experiment itself. Also, qualitative feedback was collected through the freshmen orientation week evaluation by means of a questionnaire about the complete orientation week. Therein, participants had the opportunity to write about what they especially liked and disliked about the week. Thereby, only feedback that could be specifically linked to the experiment was used in the virtual team building's evaluation.

5   Results and Analysis

For analysing data, IBM's SPSS was used. As the samples are from the same population and conducted Kolmogorov-Smirnov tests showed that the data is not normally distributed, Wilcoxon signed-rank tests were applied for each category. Thereby, the applied tests were two-tailed at the significance level of $p \leq 0.05$.

Demographics

Participants ($N = 184$) were aged 17 to 36. Moreover, 134 (72.8%) were male, 37 (20.1%) female, and 13 (7.1%) did not specify their sex. 74 (40.2%) subjects started studying e-commerce, 55 (29.9%) computer science, and 55 (29.9%) business information systems. The average participant was male, 20.85 years old ($\sigma = 2.82$), and started studying e-commerce.

Team Building

In each category of the applied questionnaire, question 1 and 3 refer to the small robot groups whereas question 2 and 4 refer to the whole group. The results of the robot group as well as of the whole group in each category are computed by adding both selected values of the 7-point Likert scale. So, a minimum of 2 and a maximum of 14 points can be achieved. Thereby, we define that if an average of 7 points is achieved, then we consider the category of virtual team building by means of telepresence robots as successful.

Relationship building was rated as $M = 9.95$ ($\sigma = 2.53$) in the robot group and $M = 7.76$ ($\sigma = 3.06$) in the whole group. The conducted test shows that there is a significant difference between relationship building between the whole group and the robot group ($Z = -9.55$, $p < 0.001$). The distribution of the ratings can be seen in Fig. 3.

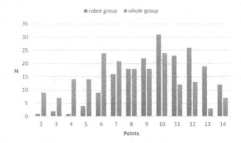

Fig. 3. Relationship building

Likewise, cohesion was rated as $M = 10.84$ ($\sigma = 2.56$) in the robot group and $M = 8.52$ ($\sigma = 3.30$) in the whole group. Moreover, a significant difference between both groups could be detected ($Z = -9.41$, $p < 0.001$). Figure 4 shows the distribution of the rated cohesion.

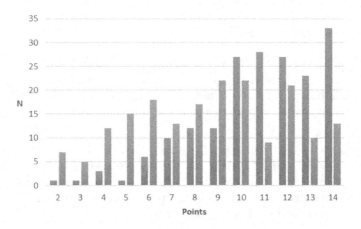

Fig. 4. Cohesion

Communication was perceived as $M = 11.01$ ($\sigma = 2.50$) in the robot group and $M = 8.02$ ($\sigma = 3.41$) in the whole group. Furthermore, a significant difference between both groups could be observed ($Z = -9.58$, $p < 0.001$). The distribution of the communication rating is illustrated in Fig. 5.

Coordination was perceived as $M = 11.31$ ($\sigma = 2.63$) in the robot group and $M = 9.66$ ($\sigma = 3.20$) in the whole group. Moreover, a significant difference

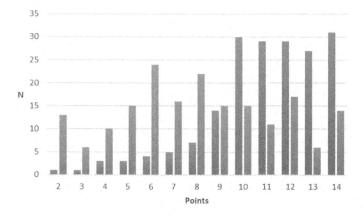

Fig. 5. Communication

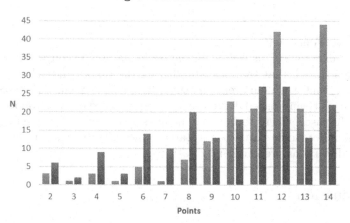

Fig. 6. Coordination

between both groups could be identified ($Z = -7.97$, $p < 0.001$). Figure 6 shows the distribution of the coordination rating.

Satisfaction was rated as $M = 11.73$ ($\sigma = 2.38$) in the robot group and $M = 10.67$ ($\sigma = 2.67$) in the whole group. Also, a significant difference between both groups could be identified ($Z = -6.78$, $p < 0.001$). Moreover, the distribution of the satisfaction rating is shown in Fig. 7.

Considering the distributions of the robot groups and the whole group, it can be seen that a higher team building effect (point score) could be achieved in the robots group regarding all categories. Also, the applied statistical tests support this significant difference as all $p < 0.001$. Therefore, evidence supporting H1 is found.

Nevertheless, an overall team building effect could be achieved as the means of the whole group in each category are above the average of 7 points. Therefore, telepresence robots can be successfully applied for virtual team building, especially in the robot groups.

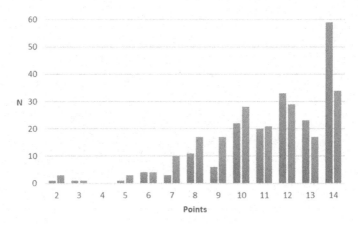

Fig. 7. Satisfaction

Qualitative Feedback

During the experiment, as well as in the freshmen orientation week evaluation, participants stated, that they had fun driving the robots and solving the challenges. Also, that it was an event and something new to them was stated. Moreover, some of them wished for more time to spend with the robots and the exercises. In cases, where technical difficulties (see Sect. 6) hindered the operation of the robot, some participants stated to not like the experiment. Still, the overall feedback was predominantly positive.

6   Discussion

The results of the study show that telepresence robots can be used successfully in virtual team building (RQ1). Moreover, a team building effect could be achieved in the robot groups (RQ2) as well as an overall team building effect (RQ3). Thereby, all research questions (see Sect. 2) could be answered. Furthermore, evidence supporting H1, that the team building effect in the robots groups is higher compared to the overall group, is given.

Furthermore, the quantitative feedback was mostly positive. Some participants stated that it was special and totally new to them. Moreover, they enjoyed controlling the robot and taking part in the exercises. However, some subjects stated that they did not like the experiment as technical difficulties hindered controlling the robot.

Moreover, other factors which might have influenced participants' rating and may limit the study's results occurred. Due to technical difficulties such as disturbed audio transmission, communication between the robot groups was affected. Therefore, instructors helped coordinating occasionally. Moreover, some subjects faced difficulties controlling the telepresence robot due to software or hardware issues. Therefore, less time for team building exercises was available in some groups, as those issues needed to be fixed in order to continue. All in all, this might have influenced participants' ratings.

Finally, not only online games [13,14], robots on-site [18–21], or robots as team colleagues [16,17] but also telepresence robots can be applied successfully in team building exercises as this work indicates. Moreover, the results of this study go hand in hand with findings of other studies which showed that telepresence robots can be successful used in education and company teamwork [6–9,22]. Nevertheless, future work has to evaluate telepresence robots in virtual team building in more depth. Also, measures increasing the overall team building effect need to be researched further. Moreover, it would be good to enhance audio transmission between the robot groups.

References

1. Yang, L., Neustaedter, C., Schiphorst, T.: Communicating through a telepresence robot: a study of long distance relationships. In: Proceedings of the 2017 CHI Conference Extended Abstracts on Human Factors in Computing Systems, pp. 3027–3033 (2017). https://doi.org/10.1515/pjbr-2015-0001
2. Tsui, K., et al.: Accessible human-robot interaction for telepresence robots: a case study. Paladyn J. Behav. Robot. 6 (2015). https://doi.org/10.1515/pjbr-2015-0001
3. Keller, L., Pfeffel, K., Huffstadt, K., Müller, N.H.: Telepresence robots and their impact on human-human interaction. In: Zaphiris, P., Ioannou, A. (eds.) HCII 2020. LNCS, vol. 12206, pp. 448–463. Springer, Cham (2020). https://doi.org/10.1007/978-3-030-50506-6_31
4. Keller, L., Ulsamer, P., Müller, N.H.: Double pepper: mediated-human-robot interaction and its influence on human perception. Int. J. Soc. Robot. (in Review)
5. Winterstein, K., Keller, L., Huffstadt, K., Müller, N.H.: Acceptance of social and telepresence robot assistance in German households". In: Zaphiris, P., Ioannou, A. (eds.) Learning and Collaboration Technologies. Human and Technology Ecosystems - 8th International Conference, LCT 2021, Held as Part of the 23nd HCI International Conference, HCII 2021. LNCS, Washington DC, USA, 24–29 July 2021. Springer (2021, accepted)
6. Weibel, M., et al.: Back to school with telepresence robot technology: a qualitative pilot study about how telepresence robots help school-aged children and adolescents with cancer to remain socially and academically connected with their school classes during treatment. Nursing Open 7(4), 988–997 (2020). https://doi.org/10.1002/nop2.471
7. Shin, K.W.C., Han, J.: Children's perceptions of and interactions with a telepresence robot. In: 2016 11th ACM/IEEE International Conference on Human-Robot Interaction (HRI), pp. 521–522, March 2016. https://doi.org/10.1109/HRI.2016.7451836
8. Khojasteh, N., Liu, C., Fussell, S.R.: Understanding undergraduate students' experiences of telepresence robots on campus. In: Conference Companion Publication of the 2019 on Computer Supported Cooperative Work and Social Computing, pp. 241–246. ACM, November 2019. https://doi.org/10.1145/3311957.3359450
9. Edwards, A., Edwards, C., Spence, P.R., Harris, C., Gambino, A.: Robots in the classroom: differences in students' perceptions of credibility and learning between "teacher as robot" and "robot as teacher". Comput. Hum. Behav. 65, 627–634 (2016). https://doi.org/10.1016/j.chb.2016.06.005

10. Gawron, O., Keller, L., Huffstadt, K., Müller, N.H.: Effect of height in telepresence robots on the users' spatial awareness. In: Zaphiris, P., Ioannou, A. (eds.) Learning and Collaboration Technologies. Human and Technology Ecosystems - 8th International Conference, LCT 2021, Held as Part of the 23nd HCI International Conference, HCII 2021. LNCS, Washington DC, USA, 24–29 July 2021. Springer (2021, accepted)

11. Morrison-Smith, S., Ruiz, J.: Challenges and barriers in virtual teams: a literature review. SN Appl. Sci. 2(6), 1–33 (2020). https://doi.org/10.1007/s42452-020-2801-5

12. Bjørn, P., Ngwenyama, O.: Virtual team collaboration: building shared meaning, resolving breakdowns and creating translucence. Inf. Syst. J. 19(3), 227–253 (2009). https://doi.org/10.1111/j.1365-2575.2007.00281.x

13. Ellis, J.B., Luther, K., Bessiere, K., Kellogg, W.A.: Games for virtual team building. In: Proceedings of the 7th ACM Conference on Designing Interactive Systems, pp. 295–304. DIS 2008. Association for Computing Machinery, February 2008. https://doi.org/10.1145/1394445.1394477

14. Kutlu, B., Bozanta, A., Nowlan, N.: Multi-user virtual environments and serious games for team building in organizations. In: Proceedings of the Sixth International Conference on E-Learning in the Workplace (ICELW 2013), July 2013

15. Lin, C., Standing, C., Liu, Y.C.: A model to develop effective virtual teams. Decis. Support Syst. 45(4), 1031–1045 (2008). https://doi.org/10.1016/j.dss.2008.04.002

16. Carlson, Z., Sweet, T., Rhizor, J., Poston, J., Lucas, H., Feil-Seifer, D.: Team-building activities for heterogeneous groups of humans and robots. ICSR 2015. LNCS (LNAI), vol. 9388, pp. 113–123. Springer, Cham (2015). https://doi.org/10.1007/978-3-319-25554-5_12

17. Shah, J., Wiken, J., Williams, B., Breazeal, C.: Improved human-robot team performance using chaski, a human-inspired plan execution system. In: Proceedings of the 6th International Conference on Human-Robot Interaction - HRI 2011, p. 29. ACM Press (2011). https://doi.org/10.1145/1957656.1957668

18. Scott, M.J., Parker, A., McDonald, B., Lewis, G., Powley, E.J.: Nurturing collaboration in an undergraduate computing course with robot-themed team training and team building. In: Proceedings of the 3rd Conference on Computing Education Practice - CEP 2019, pp. 1–4. ACM Press (2019). https://doi.org/10.1145/3294016.3294019

19. Keller, L., John, I.: How can computer science faculties increase the proportion of women in computer science by using robots? In: 2019 IEEE Global Engineering Education Conference (EDUCON), pp. 206–210, April 2019. https://doi.org/10.1109/EDUCON.2019.8725212

20. Keller, L., John, I.: Motivating female students for computer science by means of robot workshops. Int. J. Eng. Pedagogy (iJEP) 10(1), 94–108 (2020). https://doi.org/10.3991/ijep.v10i1.11661

21. Ortiz, O.O., Franco, J.P., Garau, P.M.A., Martín, R.H.: Innovative mobile robot method: improving the learning of programming languages in engineering degrees. IEEE Trans. Educ. 60(2), 143–148 (2017). https://doi.org/10.1109/TE.2016.2608779

22. Tsui, K.M., Desai, M., Yanco, H.A., Uhlik, C.: Exploring use cases for telepresence robots. In: 2011 6th ACM/IEEE International Conference on Human-Robot Interaction (HRI), pp. 11–18, March 2011. https://doi.org/10.1145/1957656.1957664

23. Double Robotics: Double 3 - overview. https://www.doublerobotics.com/double3.html. last visited 26 Oct 2020

24. Zoom Video Communications: Zoom. https://zoom.us/. last visited 29 Oct 2020
25. Code Charm Inc.: Aggie.io - a collaborative painting application. https://aggie.io/. last visited 29 Oct 2020

Design of Children's Entertainment and Education Products Based on AR Technology

Yi Lu[1], Tao Huang[1], Jian Liu[1(✉)], and Jiangtao Gong[2]

[1] Beijing University of Technology, Beijing 100124, China
{huangtao,ljym}@bjut.edu.cn
[2] Lenovo Group Co., LTD., Beijing 100085, China

Abstract. In the *Plan for New-generation Artificial Intelligence Development* promulgated by the state in recent years, the introduction of artificial intelligence and immersive teaching into smart education has been put forward, aiming to construct the online education model with an XR integration and to build interactive learning environment through the energizing of 5G. This project discusses about how to design education products integrating virtual and real factors so as to effectively improve the situationality and experience of children in the learning of music theory, mobilize children to learn through visual sense, kinesthesis, hearing and other senses with the help of AR recognition technology, thus presenting abstract concepts and theories to the children in a more intuitive way, thus improving their learning efficiency. Finally, the researchers designed and developed a set of game products for music learning combining software and hardware, and a usability test of the prototype was conducted so as to carry out the iterated design. The design in this project addresses the problems of boredom and passive learning seen in children learning music theory in the traditional way, combines obscure knowledge of music theory with interactive games, thus promoting children learners' understanding of music theory. The way of immersive learning with an integration of virtual and real factors, interactive means and perception methods have improved the learning efficiency and creativity of the learners, optimized the design and realization process of the interaction and feedback mechanism, and brought about game-changing changes to educational ideas and teaching approaches.

Keywords: Interactive design · Children's products · AR recognition · Online courses

1 Background

In the era of rapid development of the information society, artificial intelligence technology has been popularized in all aspects of our lives. Studies have shown that highly-immersive learning experience, which can make children more focused, engaged and creative during the learning process, provides better learning outcomes than lowly-immersive experience [2]. AR, namely Augmented Reality technology, can integrate

© Springer Nature Switzerland AG 2021
P. Zaphiris and A. Ioannou (Eds.): HCII 2021, LNCS 12785, pp. 292–301, 2021.
https://doi.org/10.1007/978-3-030-77943-6_19

the environment of the real world with the virtual world, thus bringing the reality into the virtual world, and integrating the virtual world into real conditions [1]. The project focuses on children's immersive smart music education, and the research is completed in cooperation with the smart education team of an enterprise. Through the analysis of preschool children's cognitive characteristics and needs for music education, in combination with the research of AR technology in children products, this project extracts the design points based on preschool children's needs for music learning, develops the prototype product in the process of iterative experiment and design, and further optimizes the design through usability testing.

2 Current Situation of Currently Available Children's Educational Products and Trends

The authors conducted a lot of research on smart products for children's education at home and abroad, and found that most of the currently available products focus on developing children's ability in specific subjects such as mathematics, Chinese and English. For example, in foreign market, there are such products as "AR Math Game", which cultivates children's math ability [1]; and "SpeechBlocks", which helps children with English learning [11]; in Chinese market, there are "Read Boy", a brand of early education tablets and "Marvellous Circuit" [4], a brand of circuit education aid used in the teaching of physics, etc. The authors have found that there are few educational products based on music learning, especially on the learning of music theory. At present, there are mainly "Drums", which helps practice rhythm and reaction speed, and "Children's Music Cognition", which helps children play a few simple nursery rhymes. Both of them have a common problem: they are limited to music playing, but do not cover the most fundamental knowledge of music in their functions. By means of literature review, the authors conducted research and analysis on the content of music theory courses and children's music courses, and found that in children's music learning courses, obscure and complex knowledge of music theory (chords, sums, etc.) is more difficult to teach, and introductory courses usually teach relatively simple things like notes and beats. This study will further conduct the innovative design of the immersive introduction learning of music theory for preschool children.

3 User Study

The target population of this study is children aged between 4–7 years, who have short attention span, poor ability of autonomous learning. They are at the initial stage of concrete thinking ability and have no patience to accept complex and boring content. Through the analysis of the training target in the Guide to the Learning and Development of Children, we have learned that the abilities that preschool children need to develop include artistic perception (musical sense, aesthetic sense), understanding of appearance description (color, size, shape), basic mathematical ability, basic expression and social contact, and perception of basic physical attributes (quality, volume) [5]. Through a close observation of children in this age group for a period of time, the authors have found

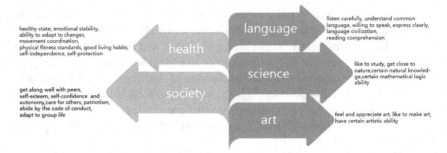

Fig. 1. Cultivation targets of children aged 3–6 years (from the authors)

that preschool children are more sensitive to musical sense -- they can swing to rhythms and can feel different emotions transmitted in music (Fig. 1).

Through an interview survey of 30 families with children, the authors studied the learning status of preschool children, and analyzed the common problems of preschool children in learning: a. Too many tutoring classes have deprived the happiness of learning and made children tired of learning before they go to school; b. Preschool education is turned into "primary school education" too early; c. Direct instillation of knowledge is not conducive to children's all-round development; d. In traditional classrooms, children do not have enough concentration; e. Parents attach great importance to education, but they do not have enough time and energy to teach their children, and their professional knowledge is not complete enough to enable them to do so.

4   Game Design

This study designs and develops an AR recognition-based game to help preschool children aged between 4–7 years to learn music theory, and designs the supporting hardware and software. In the game, when children take out an object and put it in the recognition area, the system will recognize it and then gives feedback (music feedback and feedback of whether the operation is right or wrong). The learning of music theory mentioned in this paper is discussed with the knowledge of chord as an example. Children can first learn music theory step by step, and then play the music piece and the chord. The music theory game involves various types of interaction and feedback mechanisms.

4.1   Tangible Interaction

In the interaction of game levels such as level 1, children need to take out the blocks according to the voice instructions of the game, assemble them through self deliberation according to the prompts and then put the them in the recognition area, where the system will then recognize the blocks. After correct recognition, the children put aside the blocks that have been assembled, and then carry out the subsequent chord assembling. The assembling of different blocks represent different chord tones in the game. After all the chords in a music piece (the number of chords selected is 3–5) are assembled, the entire accompaniment of the music will be carried out. The theme of the music does not change and is continuously played. The sound of chords will be inserted in the music only when the correct chords are taken out in time. When a chord is missed or the wrong blocks are picked during the period, the chord sound will not be played in the music.

4.2 Touchscreen Interaction

The game interface is designed for touchscreen interaction based on mobile terminals. The steps designed in the game are: "starting the game - playing the background story - selecting levels - playing the chord course - tangible assembling -AR recognition". To enter the game, click the "Play" button; When playing the background story, click anywhere on the screen to skip the video, and click anywhere on the screen at the end to switch to the level selection page; Click the level menu to enter the game; After entering the level, the game plays a video explaining the concept of a chord, and then two buttons will appear on the screen: "Try again" or "Continue the game", and again, click anywhere on the screen to continue at the end of each level.

4.3 Feedback Mechanism

When the building block corresponding to the first note is successfully recognized, the mobile terminal will play the sound of that note, thus enhancing children's sense of learning experience and sense of achievement, and stimulating their learning interest and curiosity. When a whole set of blocks are assembled, the sound of corresponding chord will be played after successful recognition. Finally, the sound of completion rewards will be played when the game is successfully completed, which will visually enrich the game and produce some changes. When the whole piece is accompanied in a big level, the keynote is played constantly. In terms of chord accompaniment, the sound of chord will be played when the chord corresponding to the paragraph of a single unit is recognized. Otherwise, the sound of chord will not be played. Successfully played chords will get points, while wrong or vacant chords won't get any point. At the end of the level, there will be statistics of score and ranking, thus stimulating children's initiative.

5   The Key to Design Implementation

5.1   Principle Experiment of the Recognition Technology

The immersive music education product based on AR recognition relies on the camera recognition of mobile terminals. In order to verify the feasibility of the recognition technology, two recognition schemes were prepared: ① The rear camera of iPhone11 can recognize static objects placed on the desktop in a space. ② Other front or rear cameras recognize plane graphs (if building blocks need to be recognized, stickers must be designed to assist the recognition). Based on the two recognition experiments, the authors have conducted two related experiments of the cameras, turning once and twice respectively, as shown below:

Experiment 1. Rear camera of iPhone 11 with two turnings. The iPhone 11 was chosen as the game device, and the lens steering device was designed using the principle of light reflection on plane mirrors. For ease of use, the desktop area in front of the phone need to be reflected into the lens. Therefore, two mirrors are needed to realize the transverse change of the optical path. If the vertical angle remains unchanged, the path of the reflected light will be wider when the included angle of the mirrors is obtuse. The mirror facing the camera needs to have an angle greater than or equal to 45° with the cross section formed on the back of the phone (as shown in Fig. 2). Under the condition that the angle between two mirrors remains fixed, the authors changed the angle of the whole device in the vertical direction, and carried out the simulation diagram drawing of several reflection structures. The proposal shown in the figure below is the optimal one (as shown in Fig. 3).

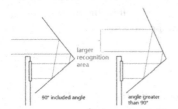

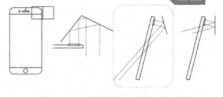

Fig. 2. Comparison of the light path width (from the authors)

Fig. 3. The optimal proposal (from the authors)

Experiment Conclusion. The authors modeled the draft model from the Angle shown in Fig. 3. As shown in Fig. 4, the two surfaces in the upper right corner we pasted with glass for verification, and it was found that due to the auto focus function of iPhone, the problem of focus instability occurred when facing the two mirrors. The focusing states of the picture changed too frequently, making it impossible to recognize the picture successfully. So the second recognition experiment was designed.

Fig. 4. Modeling of the draft model (from the authors)

Experiment 2. Recognition of plane graphs with the cameras of other devices. The authors conducted the design for the second recognition method. The second method uses the front-facing camera for recognition. Considering the ease of operation for children, a recognition area was set on the product. The front camera can recognize blocks that children place in the area. A mirror was installed to reflect the image in the gray recognition area of the desktop to the front-facing camera.

Experiment Conclusion. In the experiment, it's found that the image formation in single reflection is stable and the focus is not changed randomly. There is no problem in the recognizing effect of the stickers.

5.2 Design of the Supporting Product

After the test of the recognition technology, the authors began to design the supporting product for the mobile terminal. In the front of the supporting product, an AR recognition area and a block assembling panel were designed to facilitate various ways of game playing. The built-in drawers on both sides of the product can store teaching aids. The detail of the drawer buckles makes it not easy to be detached. At the same time, division of the recognition area solves the problem of children's poor spatial response and reduces their cognition burden when using the device. The way of mirror reflection makes the recognition more cost-effective. The supporting product can also be used as an iPad or phone stand, thus realizing higher rate of repeating utilization. Figure 5 shows the processing effect of the physical model.

Fig. 5. Renders and physical models of the final proposal (from the authors)

The authors also designed the APP interface and recognition stickers, from the story background, detailed content of knowledge for explanation, specific ways of gameplay, and changes of difficulties (as shown in Fig. 6). ① Explaining the story background: this can attract children's attention and interest to play, the content of the story also has a certain degree of motivational effect. ② Inviting the user to participate in the chord part of the game: it shows that the chord is not the theme of the song, but bears the role of icing on the cake instead. The authors chose the knowledge of chord, which has not appeared in children's music education, and then simplified the obscure knowledge. In order to do this, the authors have done a lot of learning, understanding and research, summed up the connotation of chord, and simplified it. ③ In level 1, single chords are taught, which then leads to the entire chord. The design of the stickers has a corresponding relationship with the notes, and there are certain rules, explaining and guiding the children to do things step by step. The blank space in the design encourages children to think by themselves. It allows children to constantly deliberate while playing the game, thus developing their ability of logical thinking. ④ Level 2 and Level 3 follow the same way as Level 1. ⑤ In the big level, children play along with the music, and the system simulates the real effect of playing. ⑥ Considering that the piano can help beginners consolidate their basic skills and make it easier to understand [9], the authors referred to the seven keys of the piano when designing game stickers, which correspond to CDEFGAB respectively. There is a gray scale below, with falling notes on the left and rising notes on the right, thus reaching the range of 49 keys of the piano. This leaves room for the design of more difficult games later. ⑦ The game cultivates such skills as autonomous thinking, memorizing, comprehension, strategy and musical sense.

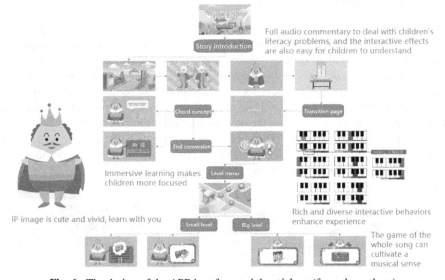

Fig. 6. The design of the APP interface and the stickers (from the authors)

5.3 Operation Process of the Game

The specific operation process of the game is as shown in Fig. 7. When children see the game instructions on the iPad or mobile interface, they will put corresponding blocks or the combinations of blocks in the recognition area, so as to have learning interaction and pass levels according to the feedback shown on the interface. In addition, spare blocks that have been assembled can be arranged on the gray assembling panel for easy access.

5.4 Usability Testing

In the stage of lab usability test, the authors verified whether the design can help children better understand and learn the knowledge of music theory by observing and recording

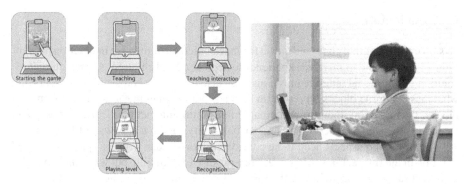

Fig. 7. Demonstration of game operation (from the authors)

the behavior performance of a 5-year-old boy with no knowledge of music and a 7-year-old girl with some foundation of music theory and playing skills during the music game of the product (as shown in Fig. 8) and analyzing the problems during the use. The task flow in the test is: first, we told the story behind the music theory game to stimulate their interests in the game; Then we played the video of chord story for input learning, so as to help them understand the basic concept of chords; Finally, we guided the children to play the primary level 1 and the advanced level 4, observed their behavior during the game and the problems they had, and assisted them with explanation and provided guidance when necessary. In the test, both children were interested in the assembling of Lego bricks, and both of them liked the music game. But the test also revealed some problems of the design: ① Children often get Lego blocks in order to build the shapes they want, and will sometimes easily ignore the rules of the game; ② The AR recognition area and the feedback mechanism need to be improved, children are impatient when playing interactive games. ③ Children without knowledge of music are more likely to understand the concept of chords in the game, while children with a foundation of music theory may find it more difficult to understand (due to the influence of the instrument knowledge they have learned) ④ The rhythm of the advanced level is fast, and children cannot quickly understand the appearance of each chord; ⑤ The basic points of knowledge in the game content are not easy to understand, such as the concept of "stave", etc., requiring further optimization of the content.

Fig. 8. Usability testing of the prototype product (from the authors)

6 Conclusion

To sum up, the tangible game and music feedback based on immersive interaction brought more excitation and immersive experience to beginner-level children. As an "Internet +" solution of traditional tangible music instruments, this design helps children understand what these tangible blocks represent and guides them to play music with the assembled blocks, thus enabling them to participate more in the interaction of music theory and promoting their physical coordination, spatial ability, etc. in a new way of learning.

The following aspects need to be considered more in our work of optimization and iteration in the future. First, AR games are a novelty for children, but when the feeling of novelty disappears, they will lose their interest in the games [6], we need to further study how to design games to not only increase children's learning experience, but also improve the difficulty of the games and enrich the interactive content, so as to keep children fresh and motivated to learn more; second, in addition to the most basic knowledge of music theory, such as chords, we also need to focus on the games of other knowledge points (the playing method of higher-order games with a wider range), the design of dynamic effect and voice interaction, and the collection of big data for children's individual learning. In future research, we will focus on these fields and design gameplay, interaction and feedback mechanisms in detail so as to effectively provide children with immersive and stimulating learning experience.

References

1. Hu-Au, E., Lee, J.J.: Virtual reality in education: a tool for learning in the experience age. J. Innov. Educ. 4(4), 215–226 (2017)
2. Xubing, Z., Kechen, Q.: On the promoting effect of immersive virtual reality teaching on learning effect (2019)
3. Wei, G., Yulin, W., Jin, G.: The hot spot of foreign virtual reality and augmented reality technology education research and China's enlightenment. J. Beijing Radio TV Univ. 2 (2020)
4. Mou, Q.C.: Making children's education products of "TuTuLe" based on AR technology. Comput. Inf. Technol. 4 (2017)
5. Mengning, L.: On the application of augmented reality technology in children's educational products. Nanjing University of the Arts (2018)
6. Ming, L.: Application and challenge of immersive virtual reality technology in education. J. Educ. Modernization 5(51), 208–209 (2018)
7. Zelei, P., Qiuqin, F., Yanqun, W.: On the design of children's educational products based on sensory integration theory. J. Aesthetics Times. 1(5) (2019)
8. Li, J., van der Spek, E., Hu, J., Feijs, L.: Exploring tangible interaction and diegetic feedback in an AR math game for children. In: Proceedings of the 18th ACM International Conference on Interaction Design and Children, pp. 580–585 (2019)
9. Changxue, P., Xingyu, W., Weiru, Z.: Research on immersive interactive design of medical anatomy teaching based on virtual reality technology. J. Decoration. 3, 66–69 (2020)
10. Ministry of Education. Guide for the learning and development of children aged 3–6 (2012)
11. Berlyne, D.E.: Curiosity and learning. Motiv. Emot. 2(2), 97–175 (1978). https://doi.org/10.1007/BF00993037
12. Micheloni, E., Tramarin, M., Rodà, A., Chiaravalli, F.: Playing to play: a piano-based user interface for music education video-games. Multimedia Tools Appl. 78(10), 13713–13730 (2018). https://doi.org/10.1007/s11042-018-6917-1

13. Nadolny, L., Valai, A., Cherrez, N.J., Elrick, D., Lovett, A., Nowatzke, M.: Examining the characteristics of game-based learning: A content analysis and design framework. Comput. Educ. **156**, 103936 (2020)
14. SpeechBlocks. https://www.media.mit.edu/projects/speech-blocks/overview/.
15. Santos, M.E.C., et al.: Augmented reality as multimedia: the case for situated vocabulary learning. Res. Pract. Technol. Enhanced Learn. **11**(1), 1–23 (2016)
16. Alhalabi, W.: Virtual reality systems enhance students' achievements in engineering education. Behav. Inf. Technol. **35**(11), 919–925 (2016)
17. Lindgren, R., Tscholl, M., Wang, S., Johnson, E.: Enhancing learning and engagement through embodied interaction within a mixed reality simulation. Comput. Educ. **95**, 174–187 (2016)
18. Krokos, E., Plaisant, C., Varshney, A.: Virtual memory palaces: immersion aids recall. Virtual Reality **23**(1), 1–15 (2018). https://doi.org/10.1007/s10055-018-0346-3

Heritage Augmented Reality Applications for Enhanced User Experience

A Case Study of AR Videogames for Children at Archeological Site of Empuries, Spain

Isidro Navarro[1]([⊠]) [iD], Albert Sánchez[1] [iD], Lluís Gimenez[1] [iD], Miguel Ángel Pérez[2] [iD], Teresa Vidal Peig[1] [iD], Alia Besné[3] [iD], and Ernest Redondo[1] [iD]

[1] Universitat Politècnica de Catalunya-BarcelonaTech, 08028 Barcelona, Spain
{isidro.navarro,albert.sanchez.riera,lluis.gimenez,
ernesto.redondo}@upc.edu
[2] Universidad Autónoma Metropolitana, Unidad Azcapotzalco,
02200 Ciudad de México, Mexico
maps@azc.uam.mx
[3] Arquitectura La Salle, Universitat Ramón Llull, 08022 Barcelona, Spain
alia.besne@salle.url.edu

Abstract. This paper presents the continuous research in enhanced learning in heritage with user experience evaluation. The objective is to evaluate learning methodologies with students of architectural degree with visualization technologies applied in projects for the understanding of heritage. The projects are developed with the aim of enriching how we experience our patrimony using Augmented Reality techniques. The main contribution of this research is the design of experiences that embrace new technologies and tourism, to offer innovative projects for the enhancement of cultural and natural heritage. The present research shows the results of the last workshop. The purpose was to develop an AR video game applied to Architectural Heritage for children. The analysis of user experience is based in quantitative and qualitative surveys. Results extracted from the evaluation reveals that 'motivation' category was the best valued by the students. The main conclusions are that AR technology applied in applications for visitors of heritage sites improves the user experience, PBL methodology enhances learning with the use of new technologies and evaluation methods demonstrates the adoption of AR is acceptable by students in development of innovative projects.

Keywords: Augmented reality · Heritage · Enhanced learning · User experience

1 Introduction

AR for the visualization of architectural heritage is demonstrated as a useful technique for the reconstruction and analysis of ancient urban settlements and for the understanding of valuable culture of ancient civilizations [1]. The significance of reconstruction of digital culture heritage are to preserve, protect and interpret of our cultural and history [2]. Other factors must be considering for the mass public adoption and acceptance of

© Springer Nature Switzerland AG 2021
P. Zaphiris and A. Ioannou (Eds.): HCII 2021, LNCS 12785, pp. 302–312, 2021.
https://doi.org/10.1007/978-3-030-77943-6_20

the use of new technologies [3]. The results show that both perceived usefulness and perceived enjoyment has a direct impact on the intention to use mobile AR applications.

Videogames combined with new visualization technologies provides strategies focused on user's engagement of technology [4]. The implementation of mobile AR applications for cultural heritage improves visitors' understanding of the site and its history via an engaging and playful games that connects the site with museums where the objects that have been excavated from the site are exhibited [5].

Enhanced Learning in education with technology is a consummate factor, and the implementation of AR needs to be evaluated with a proper methodology. Previous studies in educational programs have been conducted in architecture representation [6] and its adequation to AEC industry transformation [7].

Education programs are considering to include new visualization technologies for the enhanced learning in architecture representation [8]. It is validated as a potential resource in students' achievement of their learning specific competences in architecture degree. This validation process uses mixed methods that verifies motivation, satisfaction and performance of students [9–12].

In May 2014, the AM "International Augmented Med" workshop was held in Empuries, promoted by organizations that exchange experiences and technical assistance in the promotion of innovative services within the tourism sector. The Barcelona School of Architecture from the Polytechnic University of Catalonia (UPC) participated in partnership with i2CAT Foundation, in the European International Augmented MED project (IAM), developing new augmented reality techniques applied to ancient Greek and roman buildings in the Empuries archaeological site.

As a result of the transversal learning between architects, archaeologists and computer scientists, and the good results obtained, a framework agreement was signed between the Museum of Archeology of Catalonia and the UPC to establish a collaboration in training-oriented programs and projects. academic, research, dissemination and management in the fields of archeology and architectural heritage. Within this framework, from May 2014 to 2019, four workshops were held to study methodologies for disseminating the heritage of Empuries through new technologies.

The workshop allows participants to learn different disciplines in order to visually communicate architectural or spatial content in the best possible way. The contents of the workshop are based on new technologies, the generation and representation of videogames for mobile devices while enhancing learning in AR.

2 Method

2.1 Workshop

The methodology was a project-based learning (PBL) structured in four phases for the design of a human computer interaction system with videogames and evaluation of user experience. The First phase was the introduction by experts and collection of data form the archeological site with techniques of photogrammetry using cameras and drones, the second phase consisted in the digital 3D reconstruction of the site and the modeling of the ancient buildings, the third phase was the design and development of the videogame that includes the 3D content, the fourth phase was the presentation and user experience evaluation with quantitative and qualitative surveys.

Phase 1. The experts in archeology and heritage from the Museum contributed to define accurate 3D models and achieve the maximum realism possible to reconstruct the resulting spaces (Fig. 1). Students used real-time rendering software and video game engines. Several techniques and software will be tested during the process of development. Geometry data was collected on site, after groups used software for digital reconstruction. Since the workshop took place on the museum's premises, it allowed the results to be verified upon completion.

Fig. 1. Phase 1. Archeologist and museum experts introducing content to students

Phase 2. Proposals were developed by groups with students of architecture, video games, programmers and experts). The projects included the digital 3D reconstruction of the site and the modeling of the ancient buildings with software for 3D modeling, aerial photogrammetry with drones, AR and VR (Fig. 2).

Fig. 2. Phase 2. Photogrammetry and Virtual Reality reconstruction techniques

Phase 3. Students created mobile AR applications including the digital reconstruction of the settlement. The proposal was oriented for a possible real use in the Museum of Empuries, for that reason, the target users will be children that visit the museum, the projects should be videogames designed as an adventure at the same time as a lesson (Fig. 3). The applications were videogames adapted to devices such as tablets, mobile phones or AR glasses.

Fig. 3. Phase 3. Augmented Reality application developed by students during the workshop

Phase 4. The proposals were presented to the experts and archeologists from the museum to evaluate the adequation to the requirements and accurate approach to the historical content (Fig. 4).

Fig. 4. Phase 4. Presentation of the project to museum experts and archeologists

The analysis of user experience was based in Likert grading format for quantitative surveys. It was in the second part of the survey, the Technological Acceptance Model (TAM). For qualitative evaluation it was used a Bipolar Laddering Assessment (BLA). There was a population of 25 participants, of whom 68% were men and 32% women, with varied ages ranging from 20 to 72 years. It was also a heterogeneous group in terms of nationalities, with Spain with the highest participation with 14, followed by Mexico and the United States, Cuba, Norway, Ukraine and Israel.

2.2 User Experience Evaluation

System Used for Data Collection: Anonymous paper questionnaire, distribution and recovery during the workshop.

Description of the Questionnaire Used: The questionnaire consists of 2 blocks, the first of which includes 20 multiple-choice closed questions. At the end of this section, 4 dichotomous or excluding questions are included, with the aim of inducing the second section on augmented reality. This second block consists of 20 statements, where the participants rated the Likert scale of 7 categories, the degree of agreement with the proposed statements, being 1 "totally disagree" and 7 "totally agree". In addition, this section contains an open-ended question, in which the participant can contain the comments they consider appropriate on the relationship of the workshop.

Construction of Indicators: Once the responses were grouped by topic and based on their arithmetic means, four quality indicators were constructed, which are: understanding, motivation, utility and ease of use. These indicators give an idea of the degree of satisfaction achieved by the group in a global way.

Finally, in order to delve into the degree of motivation of each participant in relation to the rest, a specific indicator was constructed for this area through Principal Component Analysis (PCA). In it, 72.84% of the variance of the responses was explained with only three components. And once these components and their contribution rates were estimated, each of the participants was rated according to the index derived from a general expression that weights the scores achieved for each main component, by the square root of its variance [13] (Fig. 5).

$$I_{mj} = \frac{\sum_{i=1}^{r} Z_{rj} \cdot \sqrt{\lambda_r}}{\sum_{i=1}^{r} \sqrt{\lambda_r}}$$

Fig. 5. Formula used for the construction of the motivation indicator of the participants.

3   Results

Population

A convenience sample was used, being this one, students from different universities of architecture and videogame development and design.

- There was a population of 25 participants, of whom 68% were men and 32% women, with varied ages ranging from 20 to 72 years. It was also a heterogeneous group in terms of nationalities, with Spain with the highest participation with 14, followed by Mexico and the United States (2 each) in addition, one from Cuba, Norway, Ukraine and Israel. Of the 25 participants, 3 did not specify nationality.
- 68% of the respondents indicated that it is the first time that they participated in a Workshop of this type.

Questionnaire - First Section

The first section of the survey sought to find out how much the population is used to using ICTs on a regular basis. What you want to understand are the preferences of the students regarding the technological and digital tools, to understand the use they make of them in their daily life. One of the tools where this survey was emphasized is in augmented reality.

- The survey showed that the most used devices by the participants are the mobile or smart phone (100% use it), followed by the laptop (92%), where 19 operate Windows and 4 Mac. The fixed computer is used by 72%. Some devices, such as video game consoles, tablets, and digital cameras, are also popular devices (Fig. 6).

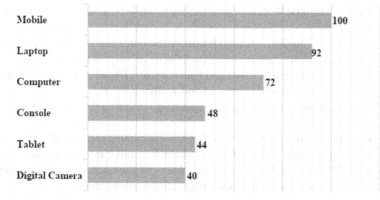

Fig. 6. Devices. The graph shows the students' responses to the question: which device from the following list do you usually use?

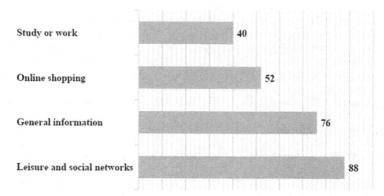

Fig. 7. The graph shows the students' responses to the following statement: use the mobile phone to:

- 88% of the participants indicated that they use the computer to study, 80% for leisure, 76% said that they obtain general information and 68% use it to work professionally, buy online or on social media (Fig. 7).
- Mobile is commonly used for leisure and social media (88%), general information (76%), internet shopping (52%) and only 40% of icon use for study or professional work.
- The devices with which the participants connect to the Internet are mobile phones, where 100% connect with their smartphone, while 88% use their laptop and 60% with their fixed equipment. Only 44% generally connect to the network with a tablet.
- All participants indicated to connect to the network from their home, 76% also connect from the university, 60% said they use mobile data, 52% mentioned connecting from work and only 20% usually use a public WIFI network.
- 100% of respondents use email and search engine services. 88% usually make downloads on the web. 80% use social networks for work, study, leisure or friendship. 72% see general news and 60% architecture websites, while 52% use internet services to chat or play.
- The social networks most frequented by the participants are WhatsApp first, where 100% of the respondents indicate that they have an account in this application. They are followed by Instagram with 80% and Facebook and Dropbox with 72%. The least used applications were Spotify, Pinterest and Twitter (Fig. 8).
- Most of the participants had the Android operating system on their smartphone (60%) while iOS was used by 40%.
- All the participants indicated that they know it is augmented reality and virtual reality. Even 84% said they had used it before, of which 60% did it through a smartphone or tablet game, 42% at an exhibition, while less than 33% used it at home, in an organized event, a professional project or an attraction in a shopping center.
- Regarding the mixed reality, only 36% of the respondents indicated knowing it, while 56% said they did not know what it was about. It should be noted that two of the participants omitted their response.

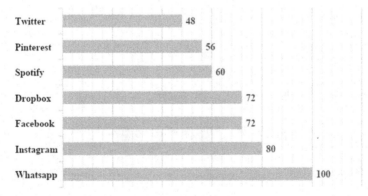

Fig. 8. The graph shows the students' answers to the question: in which applications or social networks do you have open accounts?

Questionnaire – Second Section

The second section of the survey sought to recover the opinions and experiences of the population on the use of RA during the workshop. The objective is to observe your preferences in the use of this tool as a means of learning. This second part consists of 20 items with the option of forced response (only one possible), to obtain the evaluation of the following categories: understanding, motivation, utility and ease of use. These indicators were constructed as explained in method. Students chose from from the following options: strongly agree, strongly agree, agree, neutral, disagree, strongly disagree, strongly disagree. A score based on the Likert scoring method is assigned to each answer. Next, the data with the mean scores for each of the categories are presented, specifically, the frequencies in percentage are presented (Fig. 9).

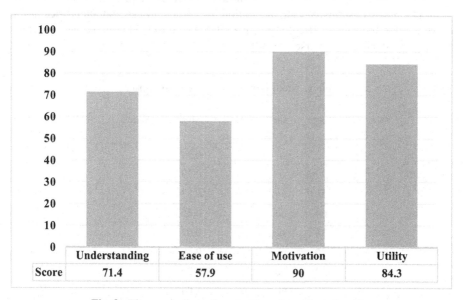

Fig. 9. The graph shows the valuation of augmented reality.

The previous graphic shows that the **motivation** category was the best valuated by the students, obtaining a total score of 90 and this means 6.3 out of 7. This indicates that there was a very favorable attitude towards augmented reality. It was also concluded that the participants consider that AR had a positive impact on their understanding, that's why they gave the **utility** a value of 84.3 and the mean of 5.9 out of 7. Regarding **understanding** with the use of the system, the survey yielded a favorable result where the participants claimed to have had a clear and understandable interaction of the AR, the value given was 71.4 and the mean of 5 out of 7. Finally, the least valued concept was **ease of use**, with a score of 57.9 and the mean of 4.05, where many, not being so familiar with this system, consider that it was still somewhat complex to use and to use in their usual practice (Fig. 10).

The constructed motivation indicator shows the following results in relation to age and the fact of having attended the course for the first time (Table 1).

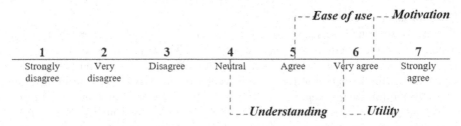

Fig. 10. The image shows the mean valuation of augmented reality

The highest score was obtained by a 39-year-old woman (above the average) who had never attended a course of this type followed by two participants aged 37 and 41. In a correlation analysis between the motivation indicator, and age and attendance at the course for the first time, a slightly positive relationship (0, 27) with age and negative with having attended the course (−0, 44).

Table 1. Motivation index for each participant

ID	Age	First time in a workshop	Motivation index
1	22	si	0,39
2	23	si	0,79
3	32	no	0,83
4	64	no	0,65
5	34	si	0,67
6	26	no	0,69
7	32	no	0,99
8	39	no	**1,00**
9	23	no	0,70
10	30	no	0,87
11	72	si	0,54
12	25	si	0,90
13	22	si	0,71
14	21	si	0,23
15	20	si	0,73
16	37	no	**0,99**
17	41	si	**0,99**
18	20	si	0,67

(continued)

Table 1. (*continued*)

ID	Age	First time in a workshop	Motivation index
19	27	si	0,75
20	21	si	0,50
21	33	si	0,59
22	20	si	0,15
23	21	si	0,00
24	21	si	0,28
25	34	si	0,97

4 Discussion

Results extracted from the evaluation reveals that 'motivation' category was the best valued by the students, obtaining a total score of 90 and the mean of 6.3 out of 7 (Likert scale). This indicates that there was a very favorable attitude towards augmented reality. It may also mean that motivation is one of the most important factors for their learning. It was also concluded that the participants consider that AR had a positive impact on their understanding, that is why they gave 'utility' a value of 84.3 and the mean of 5.9 out of 7. Regarding 'understanding' with the use of the system, the survey yielded a favorable result where the participants claimed to have had a clear and understandable interaction of the AR, the value given was 71.4 and the mean of 5 out of 7. Finally, the least valued concept was 'ease of use', with a score of 57.9 and the mean of 4.05, where many, not being so familiar with this system, consider that it is still somewhat complex to use and to use in their usual practice.

Motivation also seems to be correlated with age and with being the first time attending the course. Thus, older people, above the average, showed higher levels of motivation, especially those who attended the course for the first time. It may be because young people are more used to experimenting with technology for learning.

5 Conclusion

The main conclusions are that AR technology applied in applications for visitors of heritage sites improves the user experience, PBL methodology enhances learning with the use of new technologies and evaluation methods demonstrates the adoption of AR is acceptable by students in development of innovative projects. Motivation is the most important factor in AR technology learning. This factor generally increases with the age of the participants and the fact of using it for the first time.

References

1. Delgado, I.N., de Reina, O.: Realidad virtual y localización interior de contenidos para gafas inteligentes. Casos de estudio en el patrimonio de la UNESCO. Comunicación y pedagogía: Nuevas tecnologías y recursos didácticos **287**, 71–75 (2015)
2. Noh Z., Sunar M.S., Pan Z.: A review on augmented reality for virtual heritage system. In: Chang M., Kuo R., Kinshuk, Chen G.D., Hirose M. (eds.) Learning by Playing. Game-based Education System Design and Development. Edutainment 2009. Lecture Notes in Computer Science, vol. 5670, pp. 50–61. Springer, Heidelberg (2009). https://doi.org/10.1007/978-3-642-03364-3_7
3. Haugstvedt, A., Krogstie, J.: Mobile augmented reality for cultural heritage: a technology acceptance study. In: 2012 IEEE International Symposium on Mixed and Augmented Reality (ISMAR), pp. 247-255 (2012). https://doi.org/10.1109/ISMAR.2012.6402563
4. Redondo, E., Zapata, H., Navarro, I., Fonseca, D., Gimenez, L., Pérez, M.Á., Sánchez-Sepúlveda, M.: GAME4CITY. Gamification for citizens through the use of virtual reality made available to the masses. Viability study in two public events. In: Zaphiris, P., Ioannou, A. (eds.) Learning and Collaboration Technologies. Human and Technology Ecosystems. LNCS, vol. 12206, pp. 315–332. Springer, Cham (2020). https://doi.org/10.1007/978-3-030-50506-6_23
5. Angelopoulou, A., Economou, D., Bouki, V., Psarrou, A., Jin, L., Pritchard, C., Kolyda, F.: Mobile augmented reality for cultural heritage. In: Venkatasubramanian, N., Getov, V., Steglich, S. (eds.) mobile wireless middleware, operating systems, and applications. LNIC-SSITE, vol. 93, pp. 15–22. Springer, Heidelberg (2012). https://doi.org/10.1007/978-3-642-30607-5_2
6. Navarro, I., Redondo, E., Sánchez, A., Fonseca, D., Martí, N., Simón, D.: Teaching evaluation using Augmented Reality in architecture: Methodological proposal. In: 7th Iberian Conference on Information Systems and Technologies (CISTI 2012), Madrid, pp. 1–6 (2012)
7. Becerik-Gerber, B., Gerber, D.J., Ku, K.: The pace of technological innovation in architecture, engineering, and construction education: integrating recent trends into the curricula (2011)
8. Navarro Delgado, I., Fonseca Escudero, D.: Nuevas tecnologías de visualización para mejorar la representación de arquitectura en la educación. ACE Archit. City Environ. **12**(34), 219–238 (2017). https://doi.org/10.5821/ace.12.34.5290
9. Fonseca, D., Redondo, E., Villagrasa, S.: Mixed-methods research: a new approach to evaluating the motivation and satisfaction of university students using advanced visual technologies. Univ. Access Inf. Soc. **14**(3), 311–332 (2014). https://doi.org/10.1007/s10209-014-0361-4
10. Fonseca, D., Navarro, I., de Renteria, I., Moreira, F., Ferrer, Á., de Reina, O.: Assessment of wearable virtual reality technology for visiting World Heritage buildings: an educational approach. J. Educ. Comput. Res. **56**(6), 940–973 (2018)
11. Navarro, I., Redondo, E., Sanchez Riera, A., Fonseca, D., Martí, N., Simón, D.: Evaluación docente en el uso de la realidad aumentada en arquitectura. Propuesta metodológica. Sistemas y tecnologías de información. In: actas de la 7ª Conferencia Ibérica de Sistemas y Tecnologías de Información, Madrid, España, 20 al 23 de junio de 2012, pp. 685–690 (2012)
12. Fonseca, D., et al.: Student motivation assessment using and learning virtual and gamified urban environments. In: Proceedings of the 5th International Conference on Technological Ecosystems for Enhancing Multiculturality, pp. 1–7 (2017
13. Peters, W.S., Butler, J.Q.: The construction of regional economic indicators by principal components. Ann. Reg. Sci. **4**, 1–14 (1970). https://doi.org/10.1007/BF01287726

Evaluation Design for Learning with Mixed Reality in Mining Education Based on a Literature Review

Stefan Thurner[1], Lea Daling[2], Markus Ebner[1], Martin Ebner[1]([⊠]), and Sandra Schön[1]

[1] Educational Technology, Graz University of Technology, Graz, Austria
martin.ebner@tugraz.at

[2] Institute of Information Management in Mechanical Engineering, RWTH Aachen University, Aachen, Germany

Abstract. Mixed Reality technologies are on the rise in the educational sector. However, research shows that there is still a lack in knowledge concerning the evaluation of these technologies. In this paper we present a research on current practices in evaluation for Mixed Reality. For this purpose, we selected 94 publications from between 2015 and 2021 and reduced them to 45 which included formal evaluation processes. We then adapted a classification scheme by Duenser et al. [5] and categorized these papers according to their evaluation methods. We present our overall findings and explain some examples more detailed. The results are then compared to previous work outside and within the MiReBooks project and applied on the didactical framework. This allows us to illustrate the development of this sector over the last years and it helps us to enhance our own evaluation approaches. First results also show that there is a rise in evaluation approaches recently and that the overall goals for these processes did not change much from 2008.

Keywords: Mixed Reality · Evaluation for Mixed Reality · User evaluation · Evaluation methods

1 Introduction

Virtual Reality (VR) devices and other Mixed Reality (MR) technologies were not just invented in the last years. They have been a topic for scholars for over 50 years by now. The possibilities of these tools lead to a tremendous potential as a learning platform. A variety of studies explain some of the many ways to integrate these technologies into the classroom [1]. Especially in the mining engineering sector and its education system, the industry had to face massive changes over the past few years. In many countries mining operations became unprofitable, got closed or did get privatized [2]. This development does not make it easier for students to experience mining operation in practice and on site. In order to face these challenges, the project MiReBooks focuses on the development of a Mixed Reality framework supporting professors and students of mining education. This framework offers tools, methods, examples, and technologies that bring Mixed

P. Zaphiris and A. Ioannou (Eds.): HCII 2021, LNCS 12785, pp. 313–325, 2021.
https://doi.org/10.1007/978-3-030-77943-6_21

Reality into mining education [2]. Research shows, despite already finding use in today's classrooms, MR has still not found its way into the tertiary education sector fully [1]. In addition to that, formal evaluations of MR applications have only been a topic for researchers for a few years by now [5].

Beginning with a short description of MiReBooks itself, we give some insight into the key data of the project. In the main chapter of this paper, we examine the current state of evaluation that was done in the recent years within the field of MR. The authors will give an overview of these studies, which will also be classified according to their evaluation type. The goal of this step is also to get a first impression of how the sector has developed over the last years. The results will then be discussed in view of our own research process and how the gathered data can help improving this task. We will also give an outlook on upcoming evaluation research within the MiReBooks project. Finally, the authors will present the didactic concepts behind the project and apply the results of our study on them.

2 The MiReBooks Development and Research Project

2.1 Mixed Reality in Education

Mixed Reality (MR) describes a continuum between reality and virtuality. It includes Virtual Reality (VR), Augmented Reality (AR) and different stages between [10]. Within the last years, techniques are finding their way into the educational sector more and more [11]. However, MR is still not widely acknowledged by teachers in the tertiary educational sector [1].

As already mentioned in the introduction chapter, MR is a potent technology for enhancing learning processes in different ways. Especially the interactive and immersive nature of virtual environments brings potentials not only for serious games and three-dimensional worlds: Granic [7] mentions that entertainment is not the primary purpose of MR technologies, but to increase the motivation of learners and involvement into learning activities. In addition, virtual learning environments (VLEs) should also be beneficial in terms of learning outcomes [7]. Dawley and Dede [12] state that MR experiences enable situated learning. This concept is widely acknowledged as a powerful didactic concept. Schiffeler et al. [13] also mention that collaborative forms of MR can promote communicative skills and problem-solving by interaction with other students.

Overall, lecturers confirmed positive effects of MR in education [14]. However, there is still not a lot of empirical evidence within the field to confirm such expectations in general [8,9]. Using MR in mining courses is a particularly challenging task and there is still little knowledge of their efficient usage in mining engineering education [15].

2.2 The MiReBooks Project

We already introduced shortly into the difficult situation of the mining industry and its educational sector. This situation has led to a decline of social acceptance and damages the public image of the raw materials industry [2]. Following the sector becomes less and less attractive for students, while the demand in the sand, gravel and quarry industry is rising [18].

To counteract this, the European Institute of Innovation & Technology (EIT) Raw Materials launched the project MiReBooks (Mixed Reality Books) in 2018 [15]. 14 Pan-European partners work on different methods, technologies, and tools to address the current problems in the field of mining education. The purpose of the project is to increase the attractiveness of mining engineering for students [3]. The researchers work on possibilities to transfer theoretical knowledge into practical work [14]. This is one of the major challenges within the mining sector [19] since blasting, loading of rubble onto trucks or visiting a mine in general lead to safety risks, logistical challenges, and further problems [14].

Kazanin and Drebenstedt [19] compared the educational sector for leading countries in the mining industry like USA, Russia, and Germany. This research showed that education programs must meet "changing demands of national and global mining industry" and that it should incorporate "active involvement of the professional community in the process of training" [19]. Knowing these constraints, we can state that highly practice-oriented teaching in the field of mining engineering education is difficult to implement [14].

A possibility to ensure a more practical way of teaching is the use of MR. These technologies can be a helping tool when trying to overcome such constraints. Lee [20] and Winn [21] state that AR and VR enable more natural processes for interaction with virtual objects. According to Radu [22] such interaction increases the quality of the learning outcomes. Santos et al. [23] could also measure a positive effect on the performance of students using AR compared to traditional methods in their meta-analysis.

The MiReBooks project uses these findings and creates a framework for assisting teachers and students in mining engineering education. It is "a new digital learning experience that explores the way mining is taught, applied and changed in the future" [14]. We use AR and VR technologies to enhance traditional learning material. These learning experiences allow lecturers to provide situations similar to hard-to-get real-life experiences. The didactical concept behind the project will be discussed after explaining the literature study and explaining our results.

3   Evaluation of MR Tools in Education

As described in the previous chapters, Mixed Reality is still a rather little researched topic when used as a teaching method. Especially in the domain of mining engineering education, the use of MR in the classroom is a relatively new approach [15]. To enhance these new tools, it is mandatory to evaluate the learning outcomes and technologies themselves. However, as Swan et al. [16] could show, evaluation processes are not conducted as often as expected. In 2004 they produced a study that reviewed over 1,100 articles from multiple sources connected to Augmented Reality. From these publications, only 21 described some form of formal user evaluation [16]. Santos et al. [23] conducted a meta-analysis in 2014, where they analyzed 87 research articles on augmented reality learning experiences. 43 of these papers included formal user studies which measured factors like ease of use, satisfaction, immersion, student motivation or performance [23]. This shows that there has been an increase of evaluation processes in MR over the last years. However, there is still limited knowledge about MR as an educational tool and there is even less information about fitting evaluation methods for these technologies.

Duenser et al. [5] put up the theory that the main reasons for this lack of user evaluations in AR could be "a lack of education on how to evaluate AR experiences, how to properly design experiments, choose the appropriate methods, apply empirical methods, and analyze the results." These aspects can be found within the six stages of evaluation design, presented by Oliver [17]. Therefore, evaluation design consists of "identification of stakeholders, selection and refinement of evaluation question(s), based on the stakeholder analysis, selection of an evaluation methodology, selection of data capture techniques, selection of data analysis techniques, and choice of presentation format". It is also mandatory to understand, that evaluation processes should be designed in an iterative or cyclic way to maximize benefits.

3.1 Research Design

After showing the difficulties and challenges connected with the evaluation process of MR tools in education, it is now mandatory to explain the research method. We started by defining the search queries. These were the terms "Virtual Reality", "Augmented Reality" and "Mixed Reality" connected with strings like "evaluation", "study", "education" or "classroom". The research was conducted on the academic databases ERIC Database, Researchgate, IEEE Xplore and LearnTechLib. We also performed a search on Google Scholar. Additional constraints were the date of publication and availability of each paper. The authors focused their research on works, which were published between 2015 and 2021 and are freely available online.

The authors then selected 94 papers for a first examination where they were checked for relevance. After this selection process 59 publications remained in our selection from which further 15 were dropped. These papers were excluded because they either only suggested an evaluation, the actual evaluation was explained in a different paper or the study did not evaluate an MR technique or tool itself. We then began with the formal analysis of the remaining 45 papers by classifying their aspects according to a predefined grid. Our main interest was the evaluation techniques used in each study. For this purpose, we adapted the approach by Duenser et al. [5] and created a grid to classify each paper into five types:

1. Objective Measurements
2. Subjective measurements
3. Qualitative analysis
4. Usability evaluation techniques
5. Informal evaluations

As our research goal was getting insight into current state-of-the-art practice in MR evaluation, we decided to allow assignment of one paper to multiple categories. We wanted to generate an overview of all used techniques and put them in perspective. This differs from the original approach by Duenser et al. [5], as they only classified each paper according to its main evaluation approach. However, the analysis of multiple papers showed, that a clear assignment to only one method would have been problematic. Several researchers conducted multilayered studies with multiple measurement goals which complicate the assignment to only one category. Another deviation of the original concept was made when the authors decided to check each paper for explanations of an iterative development process. Beside these formal aspects, which were registered into an Excel sheet while reading each paper, the authors also took notes about factors like evaluation types, research outcomes or study participants. The results of this analysis will be discussed in the following chapter. The authors will also talk about some examples in more detail.

3.2 Results

Examination of the 94 initial papers led to 59 publications, which met our general selection criteria. From these, 15 were dropped due to different reasons. Lee et al. [28] and Merengo et al. [30] did both not conduct a study within their papers, but rather used feedback from studies that have been explained in different publications. Takala et al. [29] developed and evaluated a course on creating VR experiences, which did not match our research question. Thanyadit et al. [31] created a promising AR tool which allowed the lecturer to supervise a group, using VR, but did not conduct an evaluation. Despite their scientific value, these publications were discarded, because they did not contain any information on practical evaluation techniques.

The remaining papers presented different studies which were categorized according to the evaluation techniques used, mentioned in the former chapter. The most common participants in these evaluations were students. 31 publications presented a study, where this group of test subjects were represented and 22 of them were carried out in the area of higher education. Aside from educational settings, other studies were carried out in the context of professional work or medicine, therefore another common group of participants were patients or representatives from the specific domain. One example of a study with patients was explained by Summers et al. [32], where the researchers used a variety of methods to evaluate their application, like observations or a questionnaire. Only two papers contained experts as the test subjects and there were four publications, which did not describe the test subjects in detail aside from sex or age. The number of evaluators varied between five and 829. The last number stems from Scullion et al. [9], where the researchers first let 720 participants answer a questionnaire about subjective experiences and later conducted another survey with 102 students on three different universities.

As mentioned in the research design chapter, the authors also took notes on explanations of iterative evaluation processes. It turned out, that many studies were conducted within such a procedure. However, only nine publications described such iterative evaluation processes more detailed. Examples for this can be found in Pombo et al. [33] and Shahriari-Rad et al. [34]. A detailed description of a multilayered evaluation design is presented in Lozada-Yánez et al. [35]. The researchers of this paper explained five stages of testing, which started with a first review of their test environment in the construction phase. The original items were then validated according to their relevance and clarity. After this stage, the test was further adjusted, and a pilot study was conducted. As a final step, the researchers performed a reliability analysis of the obtained data.

Overall, we found 21 methods about objective measurement and 29 about subjective measurement. 16 publications contained a qualitative analysis and five used usability

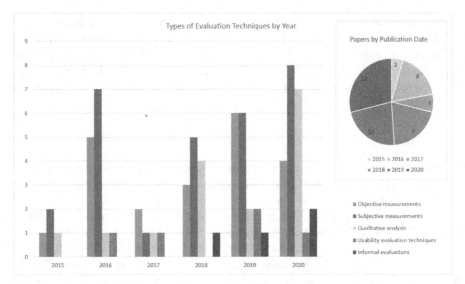

Fig. 1. Types of evaluation techniques by year and publication date.

evaluation techniques. Another five described informal evaluation approaches. The distribution of all analyzed papers and the types of evaluation techniques they presented is shown in Fig. 1.

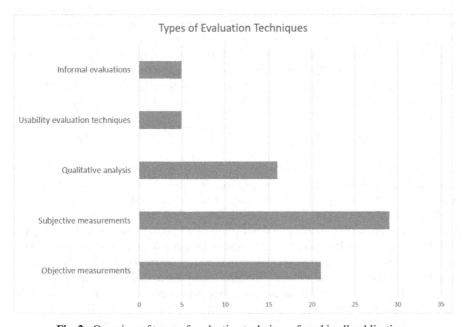

Fig. 2. Overview of types of evaluation techniques found in all publications.

Objective Measurements

This category includes studies, which conducted objective measurements. Aspects, which are measured in this category are consumed time, error rate, accuracy, scores, number of actions or other objective factors. As seen in Fig. 2, we found 21 papers, which conducted such objective methods in their evaluation. This marks the second most common category in our research. An example for this is Caputo et al. [36], where participants had to solve tasks in MR with different types of object manipulation. Researchers measured aspects like execution time or actions per task and additionally measured subjective factors with a post-test questionnaire.

Subjective Measurements

In this section, the authors selected papers that measured subjective experiences of the participants. Common techniques are questionnaires, subjective ratings, or judgements. As depicted in Fig. 2, subjective measurements were the most common type of evaluation techniques among all publications with 29 studies. Papers categorized under this term often measured aspects like immersion, authenticity, preferences, motivation, mental effort, or attitude towards the application. An example for such techniques can be looked up in Lemheney et al. [37].

Qualitative Analysis

In this category the authors collected studies with formal user observations, formal or semi-structured interviews or classification of behavior. 16 papers were classified in this category. Summers et al. [32] is one example for such methods, as the researchers observed the behavior of patients during VR sessions and compared it with a control group.

Usability Evaluation Techniques

This category compiles studies with evaluation techniques that measure interface usability like heuristic evaluation, expert based evaluation or think aloud method. However, it is still possible to measure factors of system usability with other techniques. This category strictly consists of papers which used the aforementioned methods. With 5 studies, that could be attributed to this section, it was the least common category together with informal evaluations. Examples for papers with this evaluation type are Chujitarom et al. [38] and Nuanmeesri et al. [39] as they both conducted expert based evaluation.

Informal Evaluations

These are papers which included informal user evaluations like observations, informal collection, or user feedback. It must be stated that an attribution to this category was a bit problematic since it was not always possible to clearly detect such kind of evaluation. Therefore, only papers that unambiguously described an informal evaluation were selected. This led to 5 papers collected under the term informal evaluations. As shown in Fig. 2 this category is the least common one together with usability evaluation techniques.

4 Discussion

After gathering data about evaluation techniques used in MR over the last five years, we can now compare these findings with each other, with older data and with our own previous research within the MiREBooks project.

As depicted in Fig. 2, subjective methods were the most common type of evaluation methods used. These findings affirm the assumption, that researchers are still actively trying to maximize user experience in terms of immersion or motivation and it also aligns with our own motivations within the MiReBooks Project. We can propose the theory, that objective factors like error rate or consumed time are not seen as important as these subjective aspects. However, objective factors are still considered to be very important to a large number of researchers, as the difference between the number of objective and subjective evaluation methods is rather small.

There is also another explanation to this observation. In most studies subjective measurements act as a kind of addition to the main research topic. Many authors focused on other aspects and only conducted a subjective questionnaire after the main evaluation process. This could also explain the difference between our study and the study conducted by Duenser et al. [5] from 2008. While we allowed attribution of one paper to multiple categories, Duenser et al. only categorized them according to their main focus. In their publication, the authors presented objective measurements as the most common type of evaluation between 1995 and 2007, while subjective methods were only second or third in most years. However, both studies show, that the overall number of conducted studies about evaluation in MR is steadily rising.

In 2004, Swan et al. [16] only identified 21 from 266 AR-related papers, that contained information about formal user evaluation processes, which are about 8%. Four years later, in 2008, Duenser et al. [5] conducted a similar study and identified 161 (~29%) of 557 papers, that included evaluation. Santos [23] also found 43 (~49%) formal evaluation approaches within their 87 research articles on Augmented Reality in 2012. In our own research we selected 94 papers and identified 59 (~63%) publications connected with evaluation processes and 45 (~48%) explaining an informal evaluation of MR. These numbers clearly show a positive trend in the amount of evaluation within Mixed Reality. However, this conclusion is limited, as our own study differs in some aspects from the other three and shares similar limitations.

Another observation that coincides with the work by Duenser et al. [5] is the low number of usability testing. In their findings, this category was only identified in studies between 2003 and 2007 and it was the least common type in every year, just like in our own study. This suggests that usability is not seen as important to MR applications as factors like immersion, motivation, or performance data.

We can also compare the findings of our research with our own previous evaluation approaches within the MiReBooks project. The most common evaluation methods attribute to the category about subjective measurements. The researchers within the MiReBooks project explained their findings of subjective measuring methods within three publications. There were multiple methods to measure subjective aspects like questionnaires or interviews [3,14]. In addition to that, another study conducted an evaluation of the usefulness of 360° videos in VR [4]. Feedback forms were used to capture the individual perception of each participant. Another important area was usability of different tools [14]. These findings can now be used within the didactical framework of MiReBooks.

5   Applying the Results on the Didactical Framework of MiReBooks

Based on the current findings and basic didactic principles, the didactic concept of the MiReBooks project is presented below. The concept includes current research findings and aims to take into account the interdisciplinary expertise of the project consortium on technical and didactic requirements in the best possible way. Overall, the didactic concept addresses four phases of integrating MR technologies into teaching. The planning phase (I), content production (II), the implementation phase (III) and evaluation and reflection (IV). The whole procedure is visualized in Fig. 3.

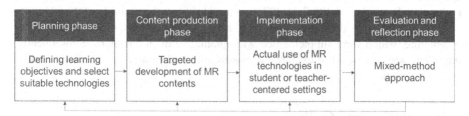

Fig. 3.   Four phases of integrating MR technologies into teaching.

The planning phase (I) mainly includes reflection on the learning objectives to be achieved. Based on WHAT is to be taught, suitable media and technologies are selected, taking into account the organizational framework conditions as well as individual skills and prior knowledge [14]. Teachers are supported in this process by a decision matrix and a planning table [14]. Here, the basic concept of Bloom's educational objective taxonomy is taken into account [24]. The application of this taxonomy supports teachers in better structuring their individual teaching units or even entire curricula.

The content production phase (II) differs for each medium. For example, Khodaei et al. [25] discuss the specific requirements and different steps in the production of 360° videos. The individual skills and prerequisites of the teacher must obviously be taken into account here as well. Within the framework of the guideline developed in the project, it is pointed out that the targeted development of own MR contents definitely requires the support of technically experienced staff, which was confirmed by various teachers using MR technologies [3]. The MiReBooks project also aims to provide teachers with an authoring tool to share content, adapt it and make it usable for themselves.

The implementation phase (III) refers to the actual use of MR technologies in teaching. Within the MiReBooks project, four different test lectures (open pit bench blasting, hard rock underground drift development, hauling in mining, and continuous surface mining) were developed and conducted at several European universities. The integration of MR technologies is preceded in the project by an examination of the learning objectives, organizational prerequisites (such as size of the classroom or number of participants) and individual skills and competencies of the teachers. This provides opportunities to use the technologies in large groups (teacher-centered learning) as well as in small groups (student-centered learning). Especially in student-centered settings, the approach of integrating MR technologies follows Kolb's concept of experiential learning, which is based on active experiencing the learning content [26].

Within the aforementioned lectures, different sets of MR hardware components were included. During the test lectures, classical teaching materials, such as PPT, Whiteboards, Blackboard were used and combined with small breakout sessions providing MR based experiences. In total, there were 12 test lectures (four on open pit bench blasting, three on hard rock underground drift development, two on hauling in mining, and another three on continuous surface mining). Previously, all lecturers were asked to fill a storybook on their lectures containing the aim and use of the respective media for a certain learning objective.

In the last phase of evaluation and reflection (IV), a mixed-method approach is applied to evaluate the use of MR technologies. Thus, questionnaires with vali-dated scales, e.g., System Usability Scale [27]) are used to assess the usability of the technologies. In addition, questionnaires are used to assess the experience of MR technologies in teaching, which were supplemented with qualitative open questions. Subsequently, interviews are conducted to explore the possibilities and limitations of MR in mining engineering education.

6 Conclusion and Outlook

We began our paper with the statement that evaluation processes in MR are still a very little researched scientific field. To support this statement we presented multiple works, which already conducted analysis of this topic and practical examples. After explaining the key data of the MiReBooks project, we dealt with evaluation methods and techniques. In the main chapter of this publication, the researchers presented a literature research of 45 MR related papers, which conducted formal evaluation. We categorized these works by adapting an approach by Duenser et al. [5] and compared the findings to their data and to further research that has been done within the MiReBooks project.

This research showed that the amount of evaluation in MR is steadily increasing. Where Swan et al. [16] only identified about 8% of all selected papers to be focused on evaluation in 2004, we could measure about 48%. This is another increase from the 29%, Duenser et al. [5] found in 2008. However, there are some clear limitations within our approach. First, we included all MR-related papers, while Duenser et al. and Swan et al. only researched on AR-related publications. Therefore, the comparability of them is limited. Second, our literature research was far smaller, as we only selected 94 papers, while Duenser et al. found over 6000 initial papers which were then reduced to 557, which were related to AR. Third, the main source for our research were ERIC Database and Researchgate supplemented by IEEE Xplore, LearnTechLib and Google Scholar. To overcome these limitations, a future research could extend the time delimitation to ten or 15 years. In addition to that, the number of analyzed papers should also be increased. These measures could help, confirming our findings concerning developments of evaluation in MR and a comparison to older works would not be as necessary as in this paper.

Overall, the research approaches to date show, that MiReBooks mainly focused on subjective measurements. This is also consistent with the results from our literature research and show again, that perception and attitude of participants are very important to the developers of VR tools. Researchers also conducted face-to-face interviews, which belong to the category of qualitative analysis. Methods that are attributed to objective measurement have not been used within these papers and therefore mark a possible gap for future research.

Concerning the MiReBooks project, we could confirm, that the evaluation approaches to date were consent to the current standard. By mainly focusing on subjective measurements, which were supplemented by qualitative methods, the researchers adhered to common practice in Mixed Reality. However, objective evaluation methods or usability evaluation techniques were absent from previous publications. Therefore, a future research could focus on testing the developed tools in terms of error rate, time consumption or accuracy or utilizing usability testing. This could not only lead to new insights withing the development of the MiReBooks tools, but in evaluation of Mixed Reality as a general. As the MiReBooks project is still ongoing, there will be further evaluation approaches in the future. One topic, which is currently undergoing a planning phase is about remote evaluation concepts.

References

1. Kommetter, C., Ebner, M.: A pedagogical framework for mixed reality in classrooms based on a literature review. In: Bastiaens, J.T. (ed.) Proceedings of EdMedia + Innovate Learning, pp. 901–911. Association for the Advancement of Computing in Education (AACE), Amsterdam, Netherlands (2019)
2. Wagner, H.: How to address the crisis of mining engineering education in the western world? Min. Res. Eng. 8(04), 471–481 (1999)
3. Daling, L., Eck, C., Abdelrazeq, A., Hees, F.: Potentials and challenges of using mixed reality in mining education. A Europe-wide interview study. In: Augmented Reality in Education, A New Technology for Teaching and Learning, pp. 185–195, Aachen, Germany (2020)
4. Kalkofen, D., Mori, S., Ladinig, T., Daling, L.: Tools for teaching mining student in virtual reality based on 360° video experiences. In: IEEE VR Fifth Workshop on K-12+ Embodied Learning through Virtual & Augmented Reality, Atlanta, USA (2020)
5. Duenser, A., Billinghurst, M., Grasset, R.: A Survey of Evaluation Techniques Used in Augmented Reality Studies. University of Canterbury, Human Interface Technology Laboratory New Zealand (2008)
6. Tang, Y.M., et al.: Evaluating the effectiveness of learning design with mixed reality (MR) in higher education. Virtual Reality 24, 797–807 (2020)
7. Granic, A., Nakic, J., Marangunic, N.: Scenario-based group usability testing as a mixed methods approach to the evaluation of three-dimensional virtual-learning environments. J. Educ. Comput. Res. 58(3), 616–639 (2020)
8. Calvo-Ferrer, J.: Educational games as stand-alone learning tools and their motivational effect on L2 vocabulary acquisition and perceived learning gains. Br. J. Edu. Technol. 48(2), 264–278 (2017)
9. Scullion, J., Baxter, G., Stansfield, M.: UNITE: enhancing student's elf-efficacy through the use of a 3D virtual world. J. Univ. Comput. Sci. 21(12), 1635–1653 (2015)
10. Milgram, P., Kishino, F.: A taxonomy of mixed reality visual displays. IEICE Trans. Inf. Syst. 77(12), 1321–1329 (1994)

11. Dede, C., Jacobson, J., Richards, J.: Introduction: virtual augmented and mixed realities in education. In: Liu, D., Dede, C., Huang, R., Richards, J.: Virtual, Augmented, and Mixed Realities in Education. Singapore: Springer, pp. 1–19 (2017). https://doi.org/10.1007/978-981-10-5490-7.pdf

12. Dawley, L., Dede, C.: Situated learning in virtual worlds and immersive simulations. In: Handbook of Research on Educational Communications and Technology. New York: Springer (2014). https://doi.org/10.1007/978-1-4614-3185-5_58

13. Schiffeler, N., Stehling, V., Haberstroh, M., Isenhardt, I.: Collaborative augmented reality in engineering education. In: Auer, M.E., Ram B.K. (eds.) REV2019 2019. LNNS, vol. 80, pp. 719–732. Springer, Cham (2020). https://doi.org/10.1007/978-3-030-23162-0_65

14. Daling, L., Kommetter, C., Abdelrazeq, A., Ebner, M., Ebner, M.: Mixed reality books: applying augmented and virtual reality in mining engineering education. In: Geroimenko, V. (ed.) Augmented Reality in Education. SSCC, pp. 185–195. Springer, Cham (2020). https://doi.org/10.1007/978-3-030-42156-4_10

15. Bertignoll, H., Ortega, M.L., Feiel, S.: MiReBooks – mixed reality Lehrbücher für das Bergbau-Studium (MiReBooks – mixed reality handbooks for mining education. Berg Huettenmaenn Monatsh. **164**, 178–182 (2019)

16. Swan, J., Gabbard, J.: Survey of user-based experimentation in augmented reality. In: 1st International Conference on Virtual Reality, Las Vegas, Nevada (2005)

17. Oliver, M.: An introduction to the evaluation of learning technology. international forum of educational technology and society. J. Educ. Technol. Soc. **3**(4), 20–30 (2000)

18. Galvin, J., Roxborough, F.: Mining Engineering Education in the 21st Century – Will Universities Still Be Relevant? The AusIMM Annual Conference Ballarat (1997)

19. Kazanin, O., Drebenstedt, C.: Mining education in the 21st century: global challenges and prospects. Mining education: traditions and perspectives in the 21st Century. J. Mining Institute **225**, 369–375 (2017)

20. Lee, K.: Augmented reality in education and training. TechTrends **56**(2), 13–21 (2012)

21. Winn, W.: A conceptual basis for educational applications of virtual reality. human interface technology laboratory. University of Washington. http://www.hitl.washington.edu/research/learning_center/winn/winn-paper.html. Accessed 08 Jan 2021 (1993)

22. Radu, I.: Augmented reality in education: a meta-review and cross-media analysis. Pers. Ubiquit. Comput. **18**(6), 1533–1543 (2014)

23. Santos, M., Chen, A., Taketomi, T., Yamamoto, G., Miyazaki, J., Kato, H.: Augmented reality learning experiences: survey of prototype design and evaluation. IEEE Trans. Learn. Technol. **7**(1), 38–56 (2014)

24. Bloom, B.S., Engelhart, M.D., Furst, E.J., Hill, W.H., Krathwohl, D.R.: Taxonomy of Educational Objectives: the Classification of Educational Goals, Handbook I: Cognitive Domain. David McKay, New York (1956)

25. Khodaei, S., Sieger, J, Abdelrazeq, A., Isenhardt, I.: Learning goals in 360° virtual excursion - media creation guideline for mixed-reality-based classes. In: ICERI 2020 Proceedings, pp. 2552–2561

26. Kolb, D.A., Boyatzis, R.E., Mainemelis, C.: Experiential learning theory: previous research and new directions. In: Perspectives on Thinking, Learning and Cognitive Styles, NJ: Lawrence Erlbaum, pp. 227–247 (2001)

27. Brooke, J: SUS: A Quick and Dirty Usability Scale. In: Usability Evaluation in Industry. Taylor and Francis, London, pp. 107–114 (1996)

28. Lee, P.Y., Lau, K.W.; Kann, C.W.: Doing textiles experiments in game-based virtual reality. A design of the stereoscopic chemical laboratory (SCL) for textiles education. Int. J. Inf. Learn. Technol. **34**(3), 242–258 (2017)

29. Takala, T.M., Malmi, L., Pugliese, R., Takala, T.: Empowering students to create better virtual reality applications: a longitudinal study of a VR capstone course. Inf. Educ. **15**(2), 287–317 (2016)
30. Marengo, A., Pagano, A., Ladisa, L.: Towards a mobile augmented reality prototype for corporate training: a new perspective. In: 14th International Conference Mobile Learning, pp. 129–135 (2018)
31. Thanyadit, S., Punpongsanon, P., Pong, T.: Investigating visualization techniques for observing a group of virtual reality users using augmented reality. In: 2019 IEEE Conference on Virtual Reality and 3D User Interfaces. Osaka, Japan, pp. 1189–1190 (2019)
32. Summers, B.J., Schwartzberg, A.C., Wilhelm, S.: A virtual reality study of cognitive biases in body dysmorphic disorder. J. Abnorm. Psychol. **130**(1), 26–33 (2021). https://doi.org/10.1037/abn0000563
33. Pombo, L, Marques, M.: The EduPark mobile augmented reality game: learning value and usability. In: 14th Conference Mobile Learning, pp. 23–30 (2018)
34. Shahriari-Rad, A., Cox, M., Woolford, M.: Clinical skills acquisition: rethinking assessment using a virtual haptic simulator. Technol. Knowl. Learn. **22**(2), 185–197 (2017). https://doi.org/10.1007/s10758-017-9308-1
35. Lozada-Yánez, R., La-Serna-Palomino, N., Molina-Granja, F.: Augmented reality and MS-kinect in the learning of basic mathematics: KARMLS case. Int. Educ. Stud. **12**(9), 54–69 (2019)
36. Caputo, F., Mendes, D., Bonetti, A., Saletti, G., Andrea, G.: Smart choices for deviceless and device-based manipulation in immersive virtual reality. In: 2018 IEEE Conference on Virtual Reality and 3D User Interfaces. Reutlingen, Germany, pp. 519–520 (2018)
37. Lemheney, A., Bond, W., Padon, J., LeClair, M., Miller, J., Susko, M.: Developing virtual reality simulations for office-based medical emergencies. J. Virtual Worlds Res. **9**(1), 1–18 (2016)
38. Cujitarom, W., Piriyasurawong, P.: Animation augmented reality book model (AAR book model) to enhance teamwork. Int. Educ. Stud. **10**(7), 59–64 (2017)
39. Nuanmeesri, S., Kadmateekarun, P., Poomhiran, L.: Augmented reality to teach human heart anatomy and blood flow. TOJET: Turkish Online J. Educ. Technol. **18**(1), 15–24 (2019)

Acceptance of Social and Telepresence Robot Assistance in German Households

Karin Winterstein[✉], Lisa Keller[iD], Karsten Huffstadt, and Nicholas H. Müller

University of Applied Sciences Würzburg-Schweinfurt, Sanderheinrichsleitenweg 20, 97074 Würzburg, Germany

Abstract. This work takes a look at different aspects of technical assistance systems acceptance (smart home, cleaning robots, telepresence and humanoid robots) in daily life in German homes. The use of smart home technologies is increasing as well as the development of social and telepresence robots to improve the life and care for people in need and the elderly. Research to develop a robot assisting in daily life by living in an average German household is less focused. This paper describes an approach to find out what Germans actually would like to have as technical support in their homes. Qualitative interviews to find important aspects of the use, the way such a robot should look like and work were conducted. Some interview partners already use smart home equipment. A quantitative questionnaire was used to reach a higher number of participants in order to get an overview about the distribution of the different opinions found in the interviews. The results indicate that Germans are not highly interested in having a robot in their own homes. Using telepresence robots seems to be even less interesting than a humanoid robot in their home. Otherwise, there was a wish for systems supporting the participants' health, for example by monitoring health data. Support to communicate with others was not wanted by many participants, nor that the robot should meet social needs. The main reasons against any robots were data security concerns and the question how a robot could enhance the participants' daily life.

Keywords: Social robots · Telepresence robots · German smart homes

1 Introduction

The use of smart home technologies has consistently increased in the past five years [1]. Studies showed that Germans would like to have smart home technologies not only to save energy, but also for safety reasons and to live a more comfortable life.

Manifold studies researched the development of robots which allow elderly, sick or disabled people to live independently longer in their own homes [2]. In addition to support for daily life activities, such as staying mobile, taking

© Springer Nature Switzerland AG 2021
P. Zaphiris and A. Ioannou (Eds.): HCII 2021, LNCS 12785, pp. 326–339, 2021.
https://doi.org/10.1007/978-3-030-77943-6_22

medications, and preparing food, those studies also focused on the social aspects of the use of these technologies.

Social robots were developed to motivate people by presenting instructions for mental or physical exercises, talk with them or only to be a companion reacting to the owners' attention by moving. A social robot to support the life of everybody by living in an average household was less focused on in recent research. Currently, only two German universities are developing such a system independently. One is the Center for Cognitive Interaction Technology (CITEC) at the University of Bielefeld and the other one is the University of Siegen.

A telepresence robot is a way to communicate remotely, for example to stay in contact with family or friends. Such robots are equipped with communication technologies to allow an interaction similar to a video call. One advantage over using a tablet or computer for a call is that the person controlling the robot can move the camera during the video call independently. Also, human affinity towards a person seems to be similar meeting through a telepresence robot like their affinity meeting physically [3].

Looking at the age of smart home users in Germany, 15.2% of the users were between 18 and 24 years old and more than 50% between 25 and 44 years (26.8% 25–34; 26.6% 35–44) in the year 2020 [1]. Only slightly over 30% were aged over 44 years (18.2% 45–54; 13.2% 55–64). This indicates that there is a relevant interest in technical support in average German households not only in elderly care facilities or retirement homes.

However, what Germans actually would like to have as technical support in their homes has not been investigated immensely. Therefore, this work takes a look on different aspects of the acceptance of technical assistance of the daily life in German homes.

Thereby, the main question is: At which aspects of their private life would Germans like to have technical support? (RQ1) The research focuses on participants' definition of daily life aspects, as well as on the concrete definition how that support should be. Other key elements were the attitude towards telepresence robots and social robots in general and how they should look. The question if smart home concepts should be extended with social robots or be kept functionally and technically only, was also a point of interest.

2 Related Work

Smart home technology is the connection of devices with each other and the possibility to control them online. This programming or use of the devices usually can be done using a smartphone, a tablet, a language assistant, or a remote control unit. The global market and consumer research company Statista distinguishes six categories of smart home technology (see Table 1) [4]. The revenue of each of those six categories has increased constantly in the last four years and the research institute Statista predicts further growth over the next five years. The biggest growth can be seen in smart household appliances. Also the number of smart homes in Germany in total as well as in each category increased while the revenue per smart home decreased.

In 2017, 986 Germans were asked why they use smart home devices and why they do not [5]. The participants were between 18 and 59 years old and already had smart home technology or planned to buy smart devices within the next 12 months. Those already living in a smart home mentioned the most important factor to establish a smart home was their fun with the technology and getting modern devices. The group only planning the use focused on saving energy, increasing their security and simplifying their daily life. Both groups also identified increased comfort as an important factor. The top reason not to buy smart devices was the expense in accquisition and upkeep. Other reasons included concerns about data security, the technical complexity, no need for smart technology, and the lack of compatibility with existing devices and software.

Table 1. Categories of smart home technology [4]

Category	Description
Control and connectivity	Intelligent home network (smart speakers, central control units, programmable control buttons, smart plugs)
Smart appliances	Household appliances (e.g. fridge, coffee machine, robotic vacuum cleaner)
Security	Surveillance products (e.g. security cameras), programmable and remote control door locks, risk monitoring (e.g. smoke detectors)
Home entertainment	Multi-room entertainment, connected remote controls, streaming devices
Comfort and lighting	Improvement of the living atmosphere (sensors, actuators), connected and remote controllable light sources
Energy management	Control and reduction of energy consumption (automated heating control, timers, sensors)

A **robot** in general is a machine doing something due to the program running inside it [6]. They can be attached to a wall or floor or be mobile, be designed to work without others around them or together with or around humans or animals. Those machines are used in factories to do repeating or heavy work or in research and military to perform tasks in dangerous environments. They are also used to do things humans are not able to, like moving very precisely in robot assisted surgery. Another branch of robots are robots as toys or service robots to do housework.

Robots assisting humans in their daily life can be divided whether they have social aspects or not [7]. The group with social aspects contains service robots which physically do something for their user and companion robots whose main purpose is to be there for their user and support social interaction. It is also possible that a **social robot** has both of those aspects.

An important dimension of robots living with humans is the communication. Next to screens or remote controls, communication is oftentimes possible with voice. Robots can process human speech and talk to them. **Language assistants** are voice-controlled robots. They can be used to answer the users' questions from the internet, modify texts saved on the cloud or as control for smart home equipment.

In 1994 the three year *Ontario Telepresence Project*, as part of the *International Telepresence Project*, ended [8]. In the report of the findings of the collaboration between the University of Toronto, Carleton University and industry partners, **telepresence** is defined as "the art of enabling social proximity despite geographical or temporal distances through the integration of computer, audio-visual, and telecommunications technologies." [8]. The ability to feel present in a distant environment is another part of telepresence. To enhance that feeling, **telepresence robots** allow not only to see, hear and speak through the technology, they also enable the user to move around and decide where he or she wants to go and what he or she wants to see without being dependent on the help of somebody who is at that distant environment.

Moreover, telepresence robots can be used for communication in private or business settings as well as in education.

There is current research on the effect of telepresence robots on human-human interaction as well as on human-robot interaction [3,9,10]. A case study gave couples living in a long distance relationship the possibility to use a telepresence robot and found out, that this added a new dimension of closeness to the relationship. In contrast to video calls it was now possible to have a look to the partners back or communicate by moving towards or away from the partner [11]. Another study examined the influence of telepresence robots on the success of team building exercises [12].

Other studies investigated the perception of the distant environment depending on the robots physical properties. One focused on the influence of the height of the camera of the telepresence robot on the spatial awareness of the user [13].

Another field of usage of telepresence robots is the contact to caregivers as part of telemedicine, which can be extended by telemonitoring systems [14]. Such a system provides access to measured health data like temperature or heartrate which can support the caregivers decisions about needed treatment [15]. Such systems can enhance the quality of life and the ability to live longer independently in one's home. The development of smart assisted living has the goal to allow sick or elderly people to live as long as possible in their own homes. To reach this goal different technologies like sensors, smart home devices or robots can be used [16].

3   Methods

First of all research in literature was done to get an overview about existing smart home concepts and the development of robots as well as the attitude of Germans to smart home, robots and social robots.

Interview

The second part was a qualitative study using a semi-structured interview with four interview partners. The structure ensured the same sequence of topics in each interview. For each topic were only the key points defined, which should be mentioned, but not the explicit questions and their order. That allowed the interview leader to react to the answer the interview partner gave to open questions.

For the development of the catalogue of questions, different theoretical aspects were evaluated. First of all, Maslow's hierarchy of needs and Alderfer's alternative ERG (short for the three aspects Existence needs, Relatedness needs, Growth needs) were used [17,18]. While Maslow categorized human needs and motivations into the five levels *Basic needs*, *Safety needs*, *Social belonging*, *Self-esteem* and *Self-actualization*, Alderfer simplified the system into three categories of subjective perception of wishes and satisfaction. Those categories are *Existence Needs*, *Relatedness Needs* and *Growth Needs*. Thereby, existence needs include Maslows first two levels, the relatedness needs the third and the external part of the fourth. The growth needs summarize the remaining parts of Maslow's hierarchy.

Based on these theories, the three clusters **physiological need**, **social need**, and **security** were defined for this work. The aspects *situation and interaction with robots* and *social influence of robots* of the NARS were part of the cluster social [19]. The NARS is the *negative attitudes towards robots scale*, which was developed to measure the attitudes of humans toward communication robots in their daily life [20].

Other studies found that an important aspect of acceptance of robots is the **perception**, which was added as a fourth cluster [21,22]. This includes the perceived security and intelligence of the robot as well as its appearance in contrast to its role.

The aspects of the Almere model, which was created to test the acceptance of robots assisting in private households, could also be mapped to those four clusters [7]. For each of the three main aspects (smart home/household robot, social robot, telepresence robot) of the study, questions to all clusters were formulated.

To get different opinions two groups of interview partners were found. One who uses smart home technologies and the other one who does not. In both groups were singles and people living in a long term relationship or with their family. Some interview partners lived in an apartment for rent and others in their own house. All in all, four persons were interviewed. After each interview a transcript was created. Those transcripts were compared and evaluated after all interviews took part.

Questionnaire

Since there were so manifold answers given in the interviews, a questionnaire was used to get an idea about the percentage of Germans agreeing to each given opinion. The quantitative online questionnaire was created from the interview questions with respect to the interview partners' answers.

Table 2. Questionnaire

---

1. How do you use the following in your household?

2. /4a./6a./8a. I use technical devices/cleaning robots/language assistants/smart home equipment in my household, because...

3. /5a./7a./9a. Do you have security concerns using technical devices/cleaning robots/language assistants/smart home equipment?

4b./6b./8b. Why do you not use cleaning robots/language assistants/smart home equipment?

10. Regardless of the mentioned concerns – for which activities would you like support?

11. How would you like to use the following in your household?

12. Please rank the following options to get support in your household

13. Why have you chosen that ranking?

14. /26. Can you generally imagine living with a robot in your household/imagine using a telepresence robot?

15. Can you imagine getting assistance from a robot to live longer independently?

16. I would get a robot, by the time

17. Do you know the concept of a social robot?

18. /27. A robot/telepresence robot in my household should ... do

19. /28. What do you want to use the robot/telepresence robot for?

20. /29. How can you imagine such a robot/telepresence robot to look?

21. How do you want to control the robot?

22. How important are the following properties of the robot?

23. When I get visitors,

24. /30. What concerns do you have if a robot is at your home/using a telepresence robot?

25. Which of the following aspects did you know talking about telepresence?

For the translated questions refer to Table 2. Depending on previous answers either the questions version *a* or *b* was shown to the participant. Answer options were presented to the participants from which they could choose, except for question 13. Those options were answers the interview partners had given. Only the questions 12, 14, 17, and 26 did not allow the participant to add more answer options. The questions 1 and 11 used a scale to map the kind of usage consisting of the options *manually, remote or via app, automated, other/no matter how, not at all*. Question 19 used the scale *if I tell him, if it is necessary, automated, not at all*. Likert scales were used for the questions 21 and 22 containing the options *absolutely, willingly, unwillingly, not at all*, respectively *very important, important, not very important, not important, not at all*. The answer options for question 12 were a ranking from *first choice, second choice, third choice*, and *fourth choice*. Additionally, the option *not at all* was given, which was the only one who could be chosen more than once.

All in all, 45 people filled in the questionnaire. That allowed a first look on the distribution of the given answers.

4   Results

The top reasons why Germans use smart home technologies are security, the possibility to save energy and the increase of their comfort. The main reasons not to use smart home technologies are ethical and economical concerns, psychological and social aspects, as well as technical and legal uncertainty.

Especially for elderly people it can be interesting to use social robots to get encouraged and activated by them. They can also allow them to train their social skills without the pressure to have to fulfill the expectations of their human interaction partners. Thereby, they help their users to satisfy emotional as well as communication needs. The German Ethics Council warns about the risk to lose even more contact and social interaction to humans when living with a social robot [23].

Telepresence robots include systems to monitor vital signs and access that data remotely. That way a health caregiver or physician can supervise them and ensure that the monitored person is getting help if needed. The second advantage is the possibility to stay in contact with relatives and friends over large distances using a video call functionality [24].

The robots are usually equipped with a camera and a monitor so the two interaction partners can see and hear each other. The difference to a phone call is that the caregiver does not only see what the user of the telepresence robot wants him to see and has more possibilities to get an impression of the health and living conditions of his communication partner.

Interview

All four interview partners used household supplies like a stove top or a washing machine. Two of them also owned a robotic vacuum cleaner. Even though all interview partners knew what smart home technologies were, only one used it. Most reasons mentioned why not more technical support was used in the household were, that they do not need or want support in those fields, or it is easier to perform those tasks manually. One interview partner mentioned that he is faster vacuuming himself then preparing the room to allow the robotic vacuum cleaner to work, since he would have to move furniture and carpets.

All interview partners stated that they do not need a robot to live with them because there is so much other technology. Even though the impression was that there are no activities for a robot left to do, all said they would live with a robot when they need support in old age. While two of the interview partners want the robot not until they really need it, the other two would like to test its functionality as long as they are still mentally and physically unimpaired. But also one of the last group confessed that he would probably not meet his own intent to get the robot early. The desired functions of such a robot were to bring things or to remind the user of important things. Social aspects – like holding conversation – were no functions of interest for the interview partners.

While three interview partners described the look of a robot in their home as humanoid, kind and harmless, the other one does not care, as long as the look fits into his home. More important than the look was the functionality and safety of the robot. The contact of the robot with visitors seemed totally normal for two of the interview partners. The other two would not want the robot to get in contact with their visitors. They mentioned that they would prefer to ask the visitors to do the tasks the robot does if they are on their own.

The opinion towards telepresence robots was the same by all interview partners. They were not feeling like it would be necessary or improve their life very much. But the reasons for this opinion were different. The interview partner who already used smart home technologies mentioned that he already has access to cameras, different sensors and geolocation data, as well as a system that recognizes if he falls down and sends an alarm to his contacts. He also could not imagine using a telepresence robot to visit somebody or an interesting site. He already can do video calls and watch online videos of sites he is interested in. If he wants to explore something like an exhibition, he prefers to go there physically. The other interview partners mentioned, that systems detecting if they fall down or a way to easily make a call in an emergency situation seems to be useful especially in higher age. But they still do not want to be monitored (especially not via video) all day. They also pointed out, that nowadays different systems are on the market that allow to answer calls even if you are not very mobile anymore. One interview partner also explained that video contact to medical staff is not reasonable today, since the German health care system requires personal contact in the end. In his opinion there is no big enough difference to have a video call now or not if you have to see the health care provider in two hours in person anyway.

The reasons against smart home technology as well as a robot in his or her own home were manifold but similar for each technical manifestation. All devices with contact to the internet had the risk of data collection, storage, use (legal and illegal), unwanted remote control, and would be a potential access point for hackers. Additionally, one interview partner had concerns what happens if he spills water over the devices or if a robot would accidentally harm him. All devices listening and especially those using video cameras have the risk of violating the privacy of the user or other persons being in the monitored area.

Questionnaire

In the following, the results of the online questionnaire will be discussed. From the 45 participants only 35 answered questions about their age and sex. Those participants were between 18 and 60 years old. The average age was 35.6 years ($\sigma = 13.6$). 19 participants stated they were male, 14 female, and 2 did not specify.

Figure 1a shows that male participants want more technical support in their daily life than female participants. No women mentioned that they would like to have support in communication.

Generally, there was a wish to increase technical support. Figure 1b shows that the wish of that support still focuses on single devices to be controlled manually (first choice of 61%). The second choice was to use single devices remote controlled (56%). Far after the option of a smart home concept some participants could also imagine getting that support from a robot (25% as sum of first to third choice, 47% fourth choice) but also 28% can not imagine getting supported by a robot at all.

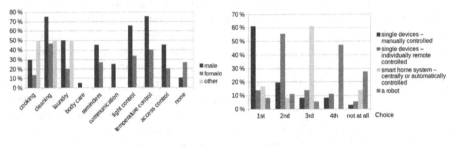

(a) Wish for support by gender   (b) Ranking: kind of support

Fig. 1. Support

Regarding how a robot should look like at home, 48% pointed out that they could imagine the robot to look like a human. Only 14% thought about a robot looking like an animal and 34% wanted something looking like an object. The most given answer to the question of how the look of the robot should be, was that it should fit into the look of the home itself (52%).

Many participants (87%) can imagine living with a robot, but 64% of those people have no idea what advantage the use of a robot would have for their life at the moment. Of those, 84% mentioned that they would use a robot to stay longer at home if they are elderly. 91% would like to get the robot as long as they are mentally and physically unimpaired to test how to control the robot.

Asking what that robot should do, no one wanted only social aspects. 30% would like a combination of social and technical aspects, 70% prefer a robot to only doing its functional job. Figure 2a shows that over 70% want the robot to do housework as well as bring them things. A remember function is also wanted by 38% if they tell him, but also if it is needed (34%) or automated (28%). Caregiving activities (45% if they tell him; 42% if needed) and the support of movement (59% if they tell him; 31% if needed) are wanted if the robot is told to or if it is needed. The only aspect more participants want automated than any other option, was the motivation to move (38% automated; 34% if I tell him). 31% of the participants did not want the functionality that the robot holds conversation with them or their visitors and supporting social contacts. Also, 17% pointed out, that the robot should not motivate them to think or move.

Overall, 22% said, that they can not imagine using a telepresence robot. 72% could imagine the use, but had no idea for what. Only 8% claimed that they would use a telepresence robot. All those participants were male. Thereof, 15% of the male participants could not imagine using a telepresence robot and 85% could imagine it (15% yes and 70% yes, but at the moment I don't know for what). Female participants answered with 36% no and the remaining 64% with yes, but at the moment I don't know for what.

Of those participants who could imagine using a telepresence robot, 70% would like to use it to guarantee their health care. Also, 59% liked the idea that somebody notices if something happens to them. Only 33% could imagine using the telepresence robot to maintain their social contacts. Less than a third said that they would like a telepresence robot to make it easier for them to contact somebody (26%) or to get contacted by somebody (18%).

Asking what a telepresence robot shall do, 54% of the participants wanted a supervision of their health data as well as support if they get elderly (ref. Fig. 2b). 43% of the participants wanted the robot to be used to communicate. But only 14% of the female participants chose that answer. While 37% would like a telepresence robot also to do housework, only 14% - only males - wanted also social needs to be met by the robot.

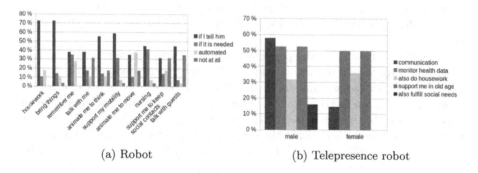

(a) Robot   (b) Telepresence robot

Fig. 2. Duties

Similar to the imagination of robots in the own home, 37% answered with similar to a human, matching to my home as well as don't care and 26% would want something looking like an object. Also here, 44% could imagine the telepresence robot to look like a human or similar to a human, but only 11% could imagine it to look like an animal.

The reasons why the participants would not use cleaning robots, were mainly the expenses in acquisition (32%) as well as concerns about data security and the opinion that the use has no benefit for them (19% each). Data security concerns were also the most often given answer to the question, why no language assistant was used (51%). Oftentimes, this was mentioned in combination with the continuous connection to the internet, which the user cannot control (39%) as well as an access point for hackers (27%). Other reasons were that the participants simply do not want a language assistant (37%), they do not see a benefit in using one (34%), or they do not need it (27%) and are able to perform the tasks that it would support on their own (20%).

Reasons for the participants not to use smart home technology also were concerns about data security and the permanent communication with the internet (37% each). Followed by providing an access point to hackers (32%). Next to the expenses in acquisition (24%). The advantage of using smart home technologies was not seen by 27% of the participants. The answers I do not want a smart home, I do not need one, I can perform the supported tasks on my own were mentioned by 20% of the participants respectively. Only 15% were concerned about malfunctions. The reason that it is not possible due to the current living conditions applied only to 12% of the participants.

Thinking about a robot living in their own household, 84% of the participants who could imagine getting a robot were concerned about the data security and the legal monitoring by relatives or the company the robot sells. Next to the concern not to be able to control the robot (60%), 57% also worried about the robot being an access point for hackers which could gain control over it. 27% were concerned about technical issues as well as household security – for example causing a fire – or that the robot starts to take on a life of its own. Only 22% were concerned about getting physically harmed. The low percentage of participants worrying about emotional violation (5%) was probably caused by the fact that most of them already mentioned that the robot should not satisfy their social needs.

The main concerns for the participants about telepresence robots were data security (76%), legal monitoring, and a violation of their privacy (73% each) as well as giving an access point to hackers (65%). 46% worried not to be able to control the telepresence robot or that the health care system is not ready yet to provide reasonable help remotely (27%). Concerns about technical malfunctions were expressed by 24% and that the telepresence robot takes on a life of its own by 22% of the participants. 14% found a robot for their use case overdesigned.

5   Conclusion and Outlook

To know the impact of different aspects on the acceptance of social as well as telepresence robots in Germany, allows researchers to create highly accepted and functional products. The advantage of such products is, on the one hand, the economical benefit. On the other hand, they make good support in daily life available to a wide range of people.

The aspects of their private life were Germans would like to have technical support (RQ1) are mainly cooking, cleaning, laundry, reminders as well as light, temperature, and access control as illustrated in Fig. 1a. Men in general wish more support than women and some men also want support in communication.

The results of the questionnaire suggest that Germans mostly would prefer single devices or smart home concepts before the use of a robot to support their daily life. That in combination to the high percentage not wanting social aspects with the robot, lead to the question, if the development of robots for everyone is an important field of research today.

A robot looking like a human or thing, would be more accepted than one looking like an animal. But the most important factor regarding the look of the robot, would be if its design matches to the design of the users' home.

The attitude towards telepresence robots is similar to the one towards social robots. Here, also most of the ones who could imagine using one, were not sure what they should do with it. The fields of usage are seen mostly in increasing the users' safety by having an eye on its health data and the possibility that someone notices when something happens. The idea to communicate through the telepresence robot was more acceptable for the participants than to communicate with the robot itself. Like with the social robot most participants can imagine the telepresence robot to look like a human or fitting into their home. The look of an animal seems not to be so pleasing.

Further research is needed to answer the question if the findings are similar with a larger group of participants or in other countries. Also, the question of the desired appearance will be subject to further research. Regarding to the results of this work, an interesting aspect is the uncanny valley problem, which makes non-human characters perceived stranger the more indistinguishable they are from humans [25].

References

1. Statista: Smart home deutschland (Oct 2020). https://de.statista.com/outlook/279/137/smart-home/deutschland
2. Remmers, H.: Pflegeroboter: Analyse und Bewertung aus Sicht pflegerischen Handelns und ethischer Anforderungen. In: Bendel, O. (ed.) Pflegeroboter, pp. 161–179. Springer, Wiesbaden (2018). https://doi.org/10.1007/978-3-658-22698-5_9
3. Keller, L., Pfeffel, K., Huffstadt, K., Müller, N.H.: Telepresence robots and their impact on human-human interaction. In: Zaphiris, P., Ioannou, A. (eds.) HCII 2020, Part II. LNCS, vol. 12206, pp. 448–463. Springer, Cham (2020). https://doi.org/10.1007/978-3-030-50506-6_31
4. Statista: Smart home report 2020. Digital Market Outlook (Nov 2020)
5. Statista: Smart home 2017 (Sept 2017). https://de.statista.com/statistik/studie/id/48055/dokument/smart-home/
6. Siciliano, B., Khatib, O. (eds.): Springer Handbook of Robotics. Springer, Berlin (2008). https://doi.org/10.1007/978-3-540-30301-5
7. Heerink, M., Kröse, B., Evers, V., Wielinga, B.: Assessing acceptance of assistive social agent technology by older adults the Almere model. Int. J. Soc. Robot. 2, 361–375 (2010). https://doi.org/10.1007/s12369-010-0068-5
8. Karam, G.M.: Telepresence - current and future technologies for collaboration. In: Final Report of the Ontario Telepresence Project, pp. 35–58. John Chattoe and Peter Leach and Ron Riesenbach (Mar 1995)
9. Keller, L., Ulsamer, P., Müller, N.H.: Double pepper: mediated-human-robot interaction and its influence on human perception. Int. J. Soc. Robot. (2021) (in Review)
10. Tsui, K.M., et al.: Accessible human-robot interaction for telepresence robots: a case study. Paladyn J. Behav. Robot. 6, 1–29 (2015). The Gruyter

11. Yang, L., Schiphorst, T., Neustaedter, C.: Communicating through a telepresence robot: a study of long distance relationships. In: Late-Breaking Work (May 2017)
12. Keller, L., Gawron, O., Rahi, T., Ulsamer, P., Müller, N.H.: Driving success: virtual team building through telepresence robots. In: Zaphiris, P., Ioannou, A. (eds.) Learning and Collaboration Technologies. Human and Technology Ecosystems - 8th International Conference, LCT 2021, Held as Part of the 23nd HCI International Conference, HCII 2021, Washington DC, USA, July 24–29, 2021. Lecture Notes in Computer Science, Springer (2021, accepted)
13. Gawron, O., Keller, L., Huffstadt, K., Müller, N.H.: Effect of height in telepresence robots on the users' spatial awareness. In: Zaphiris, P., Ioannou, A. (eds.) Learning and Collaboration Technologies. Human and Technology Ecosystems - 8th International Conference, LCT 2021, Held as Part of the 23nd HCI International Conference, HCII 2021, Washington DC, USA, July 24–29, 2021. Lecture Notes in Computer Science, Springer (2021, accepted)
14. Häcker, J., Reichwein, B., Turad, N.: Telemedizin: Markt, Strategien, 1st edn. Unternehmensbewertung. De Gruyter, Oldenbourg (2008)
15. Wahl, M., Schönijahn, L., Jankowski, N.: Telemonitoring in der Pflege - Chancen für eine bedarfsgerechte Versorgung. In: Digitale Transformation von Dienstleistungen im Gesundheitswesen IV - Impulse für die Pflegeorganisation, pp. 103–111. Mario A. Pfannstiel and Sandra Krammer and Walter Swoboda (2018). https://doi.org/10.1007/978-3-658-13644-4
16. Chen, F., García-Betances, R.I., Chen, L., Cabrera-Umpiérrez, M.F., Nugent, C. (eds.): Smart Assisted Living. CCN, Springer, Cham (2020). https://doi.org/10.1007/978-3-030-25590-9
17. Maslow, A.H.: A theory of human motivation. Psychol. Rev. **50**(4), 370–396 (1943)
18. Alderfer, C.P.: An empirical test of a new theory of human needs. Organ. Behav. Hum. Perform. **4**(2), 142–175 (1969). https://doi.org/10.1016/0030-5073(69)90004-X. Elsevier
19. Syrdal, D.S., Dautenhahn, K., Koay, K.L., Walters, M.L.: The negative attitudes towards robots scale and reactions to robot behaviour in a live human-robot interaction study. In: Proceedings of the AISB, Symposium on New Frontiers in Human-Robot Interaction (Jan 2009)
20. Nomura, T., Kanda, T., Suzuki, T., Kato, K.: Psychology in human-robot communication: an attempt through investigation of negative attitudes and anxiety toward robots. In: Proceedings of 2004 IEEE International Workshop on Robot and Human Interactive Interactive Communication, pp. 35–40. IEEE (Sept 2004). https://doi.org/10.1109/ROMAN.2004.1374726
21. Bartneck, C., Kulić, D., Croft, E., Zoghbi, S.: Measurement instruments for the anthropomorphism, animacy, likeability, perceived intelligence, and perceived safety of robots. Int. J. Soc. Robot. **1**, 71–81 (2009). https://doi.org/10.1007/s12369-008-0001-3. Springer
22. Williams, T., Briggs, P., Pelz, N., Scheutz, M.: Is robot telepathy acceptable? investigating effects of nonverbal robot-robot communication on human-robot interaction. In: The 23rd IEEE International Symposium on Robot and Human Interactive Communication, pp. 886–891. IEEE (Aug 2014). https://doi.org/10.1109/ROMAN.2014.6926365
23. Ethikrat, D. (ed.): Stellungnahme: Robotik für gute Pflege. Deutscher Ethikrat (2020)

24. Ziegler, S., Dammert, M., Bleses, H.M.: Telepräsenzroboter in der Häuslichkeit von Personen mit Demenz im ländlichen Raum. In: Zukunft der Pflege. Tagungsband der 1. Clusterkonferenz 2018. Oldenburg, pp. 168–173. Susanne Boll et al. (2018)

25. MacDorman, K.F., Ishiguro, H.: The uncanny advantage of using androids in cognitive and social science research. Interact. Stud. **7**, 297–337 (2006). https://doi.org/10.1075/is.7.3.03mac. John Benjamins Publishing Company

Correction to: Mobile Game-Based Learning in Distance Education: A Mixed Analysis of Learners' Emotions and Gaming Features

Katerina Tzafilkou ⓘ and Anastasios A. Economides ⓘ

Correction to:
Chapter "Mobile Game-Based Learning in Distance Education: A Mixed Analysis of Learners' Emotions and Gaming Features" in: P. Zaphiris and A. Ioannou (Eds.): *Learning and Collaboration Technologies*, **LNCS 12785,** **https://doi.org/10.1007/978-3-030-77943-6_8**

The original version of chapter 8 was revised. The acknowledgements section was missing and has been added.

The updated version of this chapter can be found at
https://doi.org/10.1007/978-3-030-77943-6_8

Author Index

Printed in the United States
by Baker & Taylor Publisher Services